THE LIMITS OF CONVERGENCE

THE LIMITS
OF CONVERGENCE

GLOBALIZATION AND ORGANIZATIONAL

CHANGE IN ARGENTINA,

SOUTH KOREA, AND SPAIN

Mauro F. Guillén

PRINCETON UNIVERSITY PRESS

PRINCETON AND OXFORD

SECOND PRINTING, AND FIRST PAPERBACK PRINTING, 2003
PAPERBACK ISBN 0-691-11633-4

THE LIBRARY OF CONGRESS HAS CATALOGED THE CLOTH EDITION
OF THIS BOOK AS FOLLOWS

GUILLÉN, MAURO F.
THE LIMITS OF CONVERGENCE : GLOBALIZATION AND ORGANIZATIONAL
CHANGE IN ARGENTINA, SOUTH KOREA, AND SPAIN / MAURO F. GUILLÉN.
P. CM.
INCLUDES BIBLIOGRAPHICAL REFERENCES (P.) AND INDEX.
ISBN 0-691-05705-2 (ALK. PAPER)
1. INDUSTRIAL ORGANIZATION—ARGENTINA. 2. ORGANIZATIONAL
CHANGE—ARGENTINA. 3. INDUSTRIAL ORGANIZATION—KOREA (SOUTH).
4. ORGANIZATIONAL CHANGE—KOREA (SOUTH). 5. INDUSTRIAL
ORGANIZATION—SPAIN. 6. ORGANIZATIONAL CHANGE—SPAIN.
7. INTERNATIONAL ECONOMIC INTEGRATION. I. TITLE.
HD70.A65 G84 2001
658.4′06—DC21   00-041659

BRITISH LIBRARY CATALOGING-IN-PUBLICATION DATA IS AVAILABLE

THIS BOOK HAS BEEN COMPOSED IN ELECTRA TYPEFACE

PRINTED ON ACID-FREE PAPER. ∞

WWW.PUPRESS.PRINCETON.EDU

PRINTED IN THE UNITED STATES OF AMERICA

3   5   7   9   10   8   6   4   2

To Sandra and Daniela

CONTENTS

ILLUSTRATIONS

TABLES

PREFACE

THIS BOOK'S GOAL is to shatter the notion that globalization encourages convergence toward a single organizational pattern. I begin by casting the debate about globalization in terms of the key conceptual categories of the fields of organizational theory and the sociology of development. I then systematically compare the development experiences of Argentina, South Korea, and Spain since 1950 to illustrate that countries and firms take different paths to development in the global economy. I shift back and forth across levels of analysis—from the country to the industry and the firm—and engage in a number of cross-national and within-national comparisons in order to demonstrate that organizational outcomes in the global economy are contingent on country-specific trajectories. I further argue and document that country differences enable firms to play different roles in the global economy, with no one of them being superior to all others under all circumstances.

The most enjoyable aspect of writing this book has been to do field work in Argentina, South Korea, and Spain, although I often found myself in awkward situations. During a dinner with the head of a Korean *chaebol* I was talked into a competitive liquor-drinking race that ended inauspiciously for me. An Argentine executive attempted to bribe me into testifying in favor of his company at an international arbitration hearing. And a Spanish Communist labor leader received me at his home in his underwear. The global economy, however, is not only about hangovers, bribery, and exposés of Communism. It is indeed about surprise, idiosyncratic behavior, and diversity, a far cry from the conformity and convergence that so many people take for granted. My only frustration about doing comparative research on these three countries is the classic one observed by Clifford Geertz, namely, that one always seems to arrive too late and leave too early.

The research leading to this book has been supported by several institutions over the last six years. Data collection in Spain was funded by the Carnegie Bosch Institute for Applied Studies in International Management, in Argentina by the Joint Massachusetts Institute of Technology–Province of Mendoza Research Program, and in South Korea by the International Centre for Research on East Asian Development, Kitakyushu, Japan. The Edward Pennell Brooks Assistant Professorship at the Sloan School of Management, the Reginald H. Jones Center and the International Research Fund at the Wharton School, and the University of Pennsylvania's Research Foundation provided additional resources. I must confess to having spent in excess of a quarter million dollars gathering and analyzing empirical data for this project.

The manuscript was completed at the Institute for Advanced Study in Princeton during the 1998–99 academic year sponsored by a generous membership in the School of Social Science and a John Simon Guggenheim Memorial Foundation fellowship. I am grateful to Clifford Geertz, Albert Hirschman, Joan Scott, and Michael Walzer for the superb intellectual environment that they have managed to create at the Institute, and to the other annual members, from whom I learned a great deal about social science and comparative research. Deborah Koehler and Linda Garat made my stay easier and more enjoyable.

My greatest debt goes to my colleagues and Ph.D. students at MIT, Harvard, and the University of Pennsylvania, who provided me with numerous comments and suggestions. At MIT Don Lessard, Paul Osterman, and Eleanor Westney read several of the chapters and encouraged me to persevere during the early, uncertain stages of the project. Bruce Kogut and Marshall Meyer of Wharton, Randall Collins of Penn, Frank Dobbin of Princeton, John Meyer of Stanford, and Clifford Geertz of the Institute for Advanced Study read preliminary versions of one or more chapters and gave me superb advice. Mark Suchman of Wisconsin helped me clarify some aspects of the key argument. My joint research with Nicole Biggart of the University of California at Davis, José Manuel Campa of New York University, Omar Toulan of McGill, and Adrian Tschoegl of Wharton helped me refine some of the ideas presented in the book. As always, Paul DiMaggio, Juan Linz, and Charles Perrow went beyond the call of duty, providing detailed comments and writing letters of recommendation to obtain funding. In Spain, Álvaro Cuervo of the Complutense University of Madrid, Jesús de Miguel of the University of Barcelona, and Diego del Alcázar of the Instituto de Empresa facilitated access to several resources and people. In Korea, Dr. Kwon Yong-Won of the Ministry of Trade, Industry and Energy facilitated access to data and government officials. Hai-Kyung Jun provided invaluable research assistance for over six years on both South Korea and Argentina, and Laura Chaqués, Ignacio Madrid, and Carlos Pereira assisted me with half of the interviews conducted in Spain. An army of Federal Work-Study Program undergraduates at Penn did most of the tedious tasks involving data manipulation and bibliographic searches. Finally, I am enormously grateful to Peter Dougherty for his editorial guidance and commitment.

Parts of chapters 3 and 5 were previously published in the *Academy of Management Journal* (Guillén 2000a) and in the *Industrial and Labor Relations Review* (Guillén 2000c), respectively. Chapters 1 and 6 contain some material previously published in the *American Sociological Review* (Biggart and Guillén 1999).

The book is dedicated to my wife Sandra—who gave me comments on several chapters and offered an unlimited supply of understanding—and to my daughter Daniela Emma, who was born just one month before I completed the first draft of the manuscript, and thus helped me put things in yet another kind of a comparative perspective.

Guaynabo, Puerto Rico, January 2000

A NOTE ON SOURCES

WHENEVER POSSIBLE, references to newspapers, magazines, reports, documents, and archival materials include the relevant page numbers. However, worldwide web editions of such material do not normally include a page number. Therefore, the absence of page numbers in material referenced in the text or the notes indicates that the source was consulted over the worldwide web. In particular, the web editions of the following newspapers and magazines are often referred to in the text:

El País (Madrid): www.elpais.es
Korea Herald (Seoul): www.koreaherald.co.kr
Korea Times (Seoul): www.korealink.co.kr
La Nación (Buenos Aires): www.lanacion.com.ar
Mercado (Buenos Aires): www.mercado.com.ar

THE LIMITS OF CONVERGENCE

ONE

ORGANIZATIONS, GLOBALIZATION, AND DEVELOPMENT

*Material progress [is not simply] a matter of settled determination,
reliable numbers, and proper theory.*
(Geertz 1995, 139)

CONVENTIONAL wisdom has it that the world is undergoing rapid globalization and that this process compels countries, industries, and firms to converge toward a homogeneous organizational pattern of "best practice" or "optimal efficiency"—those who fail to conform are doomed to fail in the global economy. I argue against this modernist, flat-earth view of globalization. Countries and organizations do not gravitate toward a supposedly universal model of economic success and organizational form as they attempt to cope with globalization. Rather, the mutual awareness that globalization entails invites them to be different, namely, to use their unique economic, political, and social advantages as leverage in the global marketplace. This is the central argument of this book on organizational change in the newly industrialized countries.

Observers and theorists of globalization have variously argued that the rapid increase in cross-border economic, social, technological, and cultural exchange is civilizing, destructive, or feeble, to borrow Albert Hirschman's (1982) celebrated metaphors. Many management scholars and gurus promise a world of boundless prosperity and consumer joy as a result of globalization, that is, the global as civilizing (Levitt 1983; Ohmae 1990; Naisbitt and Aburdene 1990). Other scholars see danger and uncertainty in globalization because we lack structures to deal with post-cold-war politics or with free international economic and financial flows (Kennedy 1993; Rodrik 1997; Mander and Goldsmith 1996; Mittelman 1999). As in the civilizing thesis, the destructive interpretation regards globalization as leading to convergence, albeit predicting harmful rather than beneficial consequences. A few skeptics propose yet a third perspective, arguing that globalization is a feeble process that has failed to advance enough to challenge the nation-state and other basic features of the modern world (Hirst and Thompson 1996; Wade 1996).[1]

---

[1] See Berger 1996 and Guillén 2001 for a more detailed account of the arguments and the evidence in favor of each of the three metaphors.

In this book I cast doubt on the civilizing and destructive metaphors of globalization by documenting that this process actually encourages diversity in economic action and organizational form rather than convergence. I also refute the argument of feebleness on the grounds that globalization is in fact redefining the modern world as we knew it. My conceptual and empirical analysis rests on the assumption that the study of globalization needs to be firmly rooted in the debate about economic development. Globalization and economic development are intimately related to each other (Giddens 1990, 63–65; Kobrin 1998; Sklair 1991; Waters 1995). In fact, globalization is simply impossible without development. In turn, globalization is not only the result of an intensification of long-standing trends—such as increasing cross-border flows of goods, money, and people, and a growing mutual awareness and inter-dependence among social, economic, and political units in the world—but also the very context in which development has taken place during the post–World War II period. Economic development is about finding politically feasi-ble, ideologically tolerable, and economically workable combinations of do-mestic and foreign resources to promote growth. Obsessed with the obstacles to economic growth, previous theories of development and globalization ne-glected evidence showing that countries and organizations look for ways to be different. The comparative institutional perspective on globalization and development advanced in this book emphasizes that countries and firms seek to find a unique place for themselves under the sun of the global economy.

While most previous theories of development have seen global forces as tending either toward convergence and homogeneity or toward duality and oppression, there is ample evidence suggesting that governments and coun-tries can and do exercise policy choice in the global economy. In making decisions, governments follow their political and ideological instincts and preferences, and they try to strike a balance among competing claims and pressures (Boix 1998; Campbell 1998a; Garrett 1998; Gilpin 1987; Haggard 1990). Like governments, organizational actors such as labor unions and firms also respond in a variety of ways to globalization, adopting different approaches and organizational forms. Following economic sociologists (Smelser and Swedberg 1994), I take actors and their preferences as problem-atic, and assume that they may shift over time as they learn how to cope with globalization.

This book documents and makes sense out of the diversity in organizational form induced by processes of economic development and globalization. An appreciation of diversity, however, should not lead to an "atheoretical, 'every case is different' indeterminateness. . . . Not everything is possible" (Geertz 1963, 146). Following the anthropologist, I look for "intensive comparative investigations," searching for "regularities," for "middle-range" sociological theories of economic and organizational change (Geertz 1963, 147). I adopt a variation-finding comparative approach that seeks to establish "a principle of variation in the character or intensity of a phenomenon having more than one form by examining systematic differences among instances" (Tilly 1984, 116; Skocpol 1984, 368–74).

The analysis focuses on three newly industrialized countries—Argentina, South Korea, and Spain—which initially differed relatively little in terms of government policy and dominant organizational forms. Back in the late 1940s and 1950s the three countries attempted to develop their manufacturing industries by protecting domestic producers from foreign trade and investment. Business groups and state-owned enterprises reigned supreme, while foreign multinationals were kept at bay and small firms remained largely oriented toward the domestic market. Over time, however, the patterns of organizational change diverged, largely as the result of shifting interactions between sociopolitical institutions and government policies in a context of increasing globalization. I document that Argentine firms remained largely oriented to the domestic market as policies toward foreign investors and traders oscillated between relative openness and closeness. By contrast, South Korean firms pursued export-oriented growth under restrictive policies toward foreign investors and traders. Finally, Spanish firms also became more export oriented but, unlike Korean companies, under conditions of free foreign investment and trade. While Korean business groups have grown rapidly at the expense of small firms and foreign multinationals, it is the latter that have thrived in Spain. In Argentina, business groups and foreign multinationals have ended up becoming the dominant organizational actors. This diversity in organizational form has enabled each country to pursue certain activities more successfully than others in the global economy. It is the diversity in organizational form and its consequences that I seek to document and explain in subsequent chapters.

The Controversy over Globalization

Globalization is among the most contested topics in the social sciences. Its nature, causes, timing, and effects are hotly debated issues, including whether globalization induces convergence in economic and organizational patterns across countries or not (for a review of the globalization literature, see Guillén 2001). Intuitively, globalization is associated with increasing cross-border flows of goods, services, money, people, information, and culture, although most scholars are not sure whether it is a cause or an effect of such exchanges. Globalization and the spread of economic development across the world appear to be related to a disjunction of space and time (Giddens 1990, 64; 1991, 21), a shrinking of the world (Harvey 1989; Mittelman 1996). The global economy—driven by increasing technological scale, connections between firms, and information flows (Kobrin 1997, 147–48)—is one "with the capacity to work as a unit in real time on a planetary scale" (Castells 1996, 92). It is also one in which national economies become more interdependent in terms of trade, finance, and macroeconomic policy (Gilpin 1987, 389). What is perhaps most distinctive about globalization is that it *intensifies our consciousness of the world as a whole, making us more aware of each other, and perhaps more prone to be influenced by one another without necessarily making us more like each other* (Robertson 1992, 8; Albrow 1997, 88; Waters 1995, 63). It is in this reflexive sense that globalization is defined for the purposes of this book.

The effects of globalization are perhaps the most hotly debated issue. While some sociologists have observed greater similarity among countries in terms of such rationalized features as bureaucratic administration, formal education, civil and citizenship rights protection, and organized science (Meyer and Hannan 1979, 3, 13–15; Meyer et al. 1997, 145, 148, 152–54, 161), convergence in the organizational forms adopted by labor unions or firms across countries has generally not been found. In fact, many sociologists have documented the opposite: the resilience of indigenous organizational patterns in the face of economic development and globalization (Dobbin 1994; Guillén 1994; Orrù, Biggart, and Hamilton 1997; Biggart and Guillén 1999; Whitley 1992). Comparative studies of corporate governance have also found that countries differ in the extent to which families, banks, the state, multinationals, and other actors play a role as owners and controllers of incorporated firms. No convergence is observed as to who owns and controls the corporation around the world (Guillén 2000b; La Porta et al. 1998; La Porta, Lopez-de-Silanes, and Shleifer 1999; Roe 1993; see also chaps. 3 and 4). *It is precisely because globalization enhances mutual awareness in the world that diversity in organizational form is expected* as countries and firms seek to differentiate themselves in the global economy.

Examining the impact of globalization on organizational patterns at the country, industry, and firm levels requires careful analysis because scholars do not agree as to when globalization started and to what extent it has made inroads (Guillén 2001). While some date the beginning of globalization with the first circumnavigation of the earth or the rise of the European-centered world-economy in the early sixteenth century, others would rather wait until the turn of the twentieth century, World War II, the oil crises of the 1970s, the rise of Thatcher and Reagan, or even the collapse of the Soviet Union in 1989. For most analytical purposes—including the study of cross-national organizational patterns—it is preferable to date the beginning of globalization with the post–World War II period, that is, with the emancipation of colonies, the efforts to accelerate growth and development, and the renewed expansion of foreign trade and investment (Gilpin 1987, 341–44; Kennedy 1993, 47, 50; McMichael 1996; Guillén 2001).

A sound analysis of the impact of globalization on a certain organizational variable should avoid assuming that globalization is a uniform and inexorable trend. Rather, globalization is a fragmented, incomplete, discontinuous, contingent, and in many ways contradictory or incongruous process. Sociologist Anthony Giddens (1990, 64, 175) observes that globalization "is a process of uneven development that fragments as it coordinates. . . . The outcome is not necessarily, or even usually, a generalized set of changes acting in a uniform direction, but consists in mutually opposed tendencies." Anthropologist Jonathan Friedman (1994, 210–11) further notes that globalization is the product of cultural fragmentation as much as it is the result of modernist homogeneity, and that "what appears as disorganization and often real disorder is not any the less systemic and systematic." These perspectives are consistent with the *reflexive* definition of globalization proposed above, which emphasizes that it creates mutual awareness as opposed to mindless conformity.

Main Approaches to Globalization and Development

Despite the intensity of current controversies, the social sciences' interest in economic development and globalization is not new. Right from their beginning as scholarly disciplines, sociology and economics concerned themselves with industrialization and socioeconomic change (Giddens 1990; Robertson 1992; Smelser 1976; Smelser and Swedberg 1994). Such pivotal social scientists as Comte, Saint-Simon, Spencer, Marx, Durkheim, Weber, and Parsons formulated theories to understand the social and economic change induced by industrialization, and could be considered as pioneering theorists of globalization as well (Albrow 1997; Robertson 1992; Waters 1995). However, the systematic study of the causes of economic development and underdevelopment, and the formulation of specific prescriptions as to how to generate economic growth in an interdependent world, did not start until the end of World War II. The time was then ripe for development studies to flourish: economies had to be reconstructed, colonies were emancipating themselves, and the two superpowers competed with each other to extend their influence throughout the developing world (Bell 1987; Gereffi 1994b; McMichael 1996; Portes 1997). Not surprisingly, the first students of economic growth adopted a "developmentalist" approach, first formulated in terms of modernization and later of dependency.

The publication of Walt W. Rostow's *Stages of Economic Growth* in 1960 marked the heyday of modernization theory. In his view, countries evolve from "undeveloped" to "developed" via five stages as long as the right value incentives are in place: traditional society, preconditions for takeoff, takeoff, maturity, and high mass-consumption. Each stage is a prerequisite for the next because new political, economic, and social institutions make possible ever more economically advanced and differentiated activities over time, a point also underscored by Kerr, Dunlop, Harbison, and Myers in their land-mark book, *Industrialism and Industrial Man* ([1960] 1964). Political scientists (e.g., Apter 1965) refined the argument when asserting that the primary engine of change was a piecemeal shift from traditional to modern values, that is, a transformation of authority structures, a perspective also embraced by many sociologists (see the review by Smelser 1976, 144–63). As reflected in table 1.1, the modernization approach to economic development regards globalization as a civilizing force.[2] In addition, modernization theorists think of economic development as contributing to a "shrinking" of the world, a convergence of economies and societies, a trend toward homogeneity, or at least toward a restricted set of alternatives (Kerr et al. [1960] 1964; see also Robertson 1992, 91; Waters 1995, 13–19). In their eyes, traditionalism stands in the way as the main impediment to economic growth, and development can occur only if modernizing elites—social, political, economic, financial— act as the agent of change (Kerr et al. [1960] 1964; Rostow [1960] 1990, 4– 12, 26, 31). Modernization scholars are adamant that "technology and specialization . . . are necessarily and distinctively associated with large-scale organizations." Economic activity is "carried on by large-scale enterprises which require extensive coordination of managers and the managed" (Kerr et al. [1960] 1964, 21; see also Rostow [1960] 1990, 9–11, 40). Family firms and cooperatives are predicted to disappear as traditional patterns of behavior are replaced by modern ones (Kerr [1960] 1964, 67, 227).

Modernization theory's tenets were challenged by a second strand of developmentalist thinking. During the 1950s and 1960s dependency scholars noted that developing countries were dependent on more advanced ones, often former colonizers, for capital, technology, and access to markets. Dependency theorists observed that the terms of trade between advanced (core) countries and developing (peripheral) countries tended to evolve against the latter, who would become more impoverished as they engaged in international trade (Prebisch 1950; Frank 1967; Furtado 1970; Bruton 1998). Thus, the tendency of capitalist development was to create exploitative relationships between developed and underdeveloped countries as first-world multinational corporations sought to exploit their oligopolistic advantages in developing countries (Haggard 1990, 16–21).

According to dependency theorists, only an autonomous state bureaucracy capable of imposing a logic of import-substitution industrialization can offer

---

[2] The original thesis about how economic development affects democratization was formulated by Lipset in the 1950s (Lipset 1981, chap. 2). However, political scientists have always been reluctant to argue that economic growth necessarily results in democracy (Lipset 1981, 53–54, 469–76; O'Donnell 1979).

TABLE 1.1
A Comparison of Theories of Development and Globalization

	Modernization	Dependency	World-System	Late Industrialization	Neoclassical	Comparative Institutional
View of globalization	Civilizing, convergent, homogenizing	Oppressive, dualizing.	Oppressive, dualizing, teleological	Process of catching up, convergent	Civilizing, convergent, homogenizing	Promoting diversity and renewal.
Obstacle to development	Traditionalism	Neocolonialism	Peripheral status	Right prices, meager investment	Wrong prices, state intervention	Institutional disregard
Solution	Staged institution building and gradual change of values	Import substitution of not only consumer goods but also intermediate and capital goods	Radical social and political change at the world-system level	Price distortions to stimulate economic activity, especially exports	Swift move toward free markets, protection of property rights	Match of logics of social organization with opportunities in the global economy
Agents or actors	Modernizing elites who foster gradual change in stages	Autonomous state that imposes its logic on actors	Internal contradictions that trigger change	Developmental state that imposes its logic on large industrial enterprises	Autonomous technocracy that imposes its logic on actors.	Different actors and relationships allowed and enabled
Expected organizational forms	Large-scale, bureaucratized enterprises; family firms, worker cooperatives, and other traditional enterprises not viable	Large, rent-seeking business groups with ties to multinationals and the state, state-owned enterprises, and subsidiaries of multinational enterprises (the "triple alliance")		Business groups guided by state subsidies and tied to multinationals through arm's-length contracts	Business groups while market failure persists; otherwise, efficient scale enterprises, "serviced" by smaller firms	Social organization and government policy, which shape relative role and proportions of business groups, small firms, and multinationals
Representative scholars	Rostow 1960, Kerr et al. 1960, Apter 1965	Prebisch 1950, Frank 1967, Furtado 1970, Cardoso and Faletto 1973, Evans 1979	Wallerstein 1974, Evans 1979	Gerschenkron 1962, Johnson 1982, Amsden 1989, Wade 1990	Leff 1978, 1979, Balassa et al. 1986, Caves 1989, Sachs 1993	Bendix 1956, Geertz 1963, Dore 1973, Orrù et al. 1997

Source: Adapted and expanded from Biggart and Guillén 1999.

a feasible solution to dependency in the long run (Bruton 1998). Thus, policies were consciously designed to discourage imports (especially of consumer goods) and promote local production. The emphasis was placed on escalating import-substitution quickly to include not only consumer goods but also intermediate inputs and capital goods (Frank 1967, 205–7; Cardoso and Faletto [1973] 1979, 5, 128–30; see table 1.1). Dependency theorists were, of course, aware of the "inefficiencies" of import-substitution due to lack of experience in applying new technology, limited competition, insufficient scale of production, and diversion of resources away from agriculture and export-oriented activities. Still, they argued that its countercyclical and developmental effects would outweigh its pitfalls, and that it was one feasible way for peripheral countries to catch up with the technologically advanced core (Prebisch 1950, 6–7, 44–46, 53–54; Furtado 1970, 59). Other leading theorists such as Hirschman (1958, 1968) endorsed import-substitution industrialization as one way of turning "unbalanced growth," shortages, and bottlenecks into sustainable economic development, a position that stood in sharp contrast to the staged model of modernization theorists. In practice, import-substitution resulted in the gradual displacement of the small-scale local bourgeoisie not connected to foreign and state capital, with the "triple alliance" of state-owned enterprises, subsidiaries of foreign multinationals, and local business groups gaining in importance (Evans 1979; see also Frank 1967; Cardoso and Faletto [1973] 1979, 163, 174, 213).

Immanuel Wallerstein (1974) proposed another influential theory of development that emphasized systemic patterns of dependence in the world economy. Wallerstein saw underdevelopment as the result of a country's integration into the modern "world-system" created by the capitalist development of western Europe since the sixteenth century. Thus, the longer a country remains outside the world-system, the more easily it will develop (Ragin and Chirot 1984, 292–94). In this view, global capitalist forces have not only generated oppression and duality between the "core," on the one hand, and the undeveloped "periphery" and developing "semiperiphery," on the other, but also a momentum of their own as the capitalist world-system inexorably experiences a series of recurrent crises that result from its inherent contradictions. Unlike dependency theorists, however, states (and not social classes) are central to world-system analysis because they manage the social problems generated by the expansion of world capitalism and thus contribute to the stabilization of the world-system (Waters 1995, 22–26).

Dependency theory and world-system analysis lost clout during the 1980s and 1990s. Two other approaches—late industrialization and neoclassical economics—have come to dominate debates about policymaking over the last 15 years. The origin of the late-industrialization thesis dates back to the pioneering work of Gerschenkron (1962), who argued that economic laggards must engage in certain price distortion and protectionist policies so as to foster local manufacturing activities. More recently, Johnson (1982), Amsden (1989), and Wade (1990) have refined this model and provided extensive empirical evidence on the Japanese, South Korean, and Taiwanese cases, respectively. Amsden (1989, 1994) has contributed the most elaborate account of the theory. Globalization and development are seen as processes of "catching up" that exhibit certain patterns of convergence, including the growth of large enterprises in industries similar to those found in the advanced countries. A "developmental state" is proposed as the key actor, whose role it is to distort prices using subsidies and protectionism so as to encourage local firms to increase investment, production, and exports. Like dependency theory, the late-industrialization approach expects (and prescribes) large business groups with arm's-length relationships with foreign multinationals. The emphasis on export-led growth, however, clearly sets late-industrialization theory apart from the dependency approach.

By contrast to the dependency and late development perspectives, recent neoclassical theory and practice of development and reform argue that "market-driven" policies and "getting the prices right" are the only sustainable way of achieving high growth. Opening to foreign trade and direct investment, deregulation, fiscal discipline, privatization, and capital market liberalization are proposed as prerequisites of sustained development (Balassa et al. 1986). Neoclassical economists take globalization as a given, arguing that countries cannot possibly ignore or resist its convergent and homogenizing effects without paying a dire price. Like modernization theorists, market-driven economic reformers see the global economy as a civilizing force. Unlike in modernization theory, however, gradualism is frequently abandoned in favor of swift deregulation or transition to the free market, a strategy commonly known as "shock therapy" (Sachs 1993). Although countries are asked to dismantle most of the state regulatory apparatus, careful attention is given to the role of an autonomous technocracy that is supposed to impose a logic of market-driven reform on actors and to protect property rights. Countries are advised to emulate a laissez-faire model, to expose their economies to the winds of global investment and trade. The emphasis on comparative advantage, specialization, and free exchange within and across borders leads neoclassical economists to criticize both "industrial gigantism" and worker ownership, and favor instead efficient scale firms and plants. They see an important role for small enterprises to play, albeit merely "servicing" larger firms (Sachs 1993, 18–20, 82–83). However, as market failure is rampant in newly industrialized countries, economists expect the rise of business groups that internalize inefficient markets for managerial talent, worker skills, capital, and intermediate goods until adequate markets are developed (Caves 1989; Leff 1978, 1979).

The Curse of Modernity in Development Studies and a
Comparative Institutional Alternative

Modernization, dependency, world-system, late-industrialization, and neo-classical theories have shared the stage of development studies and policymaking over the last half-century. This book's contention is that previous theories of development and globalization suffer from an infatuation with what Jürgen Habermas has called "the project of modernity," or the revolt "against the normalizing functions of tradition" (Habermas 1983, 5, 8; Guillén 1997a). Modernity is "the imposition of practical rationality upon the rest of the world through the agency of the state and the mechanism of the market, [and] the generation of universal ideas to encompass the diversity of the world" (Albrow 1997, 33; see also Robertson 1992, 97–105). Modernism—the cultural glorification of things modern—developed a fascination with the "regularity, continuity, and speed of technology and mass production" and a taste for the "one best way" to fix social and economic problems (Guillén 1997a, 697).

Common to the main five theories of development are three quintessentially modernist features. First, *development is about overcoming obstacles* rather than building on strengths (other than those captured by the rather narrow concept of comparative advantage, in the case of neoclassical theories). Tradition, dependency, peripheral status, right prices or wrong prices—depending on the theory—are constructed as stumbling blocks standing in the way of development. Thus, countries must eliminate, surmount, or circumvent such obstacles so as to develop economically (Bell 1987; Biggart and Guillén 1999; Evans and Stephens 1988; Portes 1997; Portes and Kincaid 1989).

Previous theories of development assume not only that there are discernible, self-evident obstacles to development but also that the *policy prescriptions proposed to overcome obstacles apply to most, if not the whole range, of developing countries.* Thus, little, if any, serious attention is paid to historical particularity or institutional variation when it comes to extrapolating specific success stories into general policy recipes. As Haggard (1990, 9) has put it, development theories are intrinsically voluntaristic in their view of how to overcome obstacles. For them, "policy is simply a matter of making the right choices; 'incorrect' policy reflects misguided ideas or lack of political 'will,' " and "economic successes can be broadly replicated if only 'correct' policy choices are made" (Haggard 1990, 21). This universality of application and replication represents a second modernist feature of previous theories.

The third modernist feature is the *intimate linkage that previous theories establish between economic development and the modern nation-state, both as a geographic entity and as an agent of change* (Block 1994; Evans and Stephens 1988; McMichael 1996; Pieterse 1996). Development policies—as proposed and interpreted by modernizing elites, state bureaucrats, or a cadre of neoclassical economic experts—are instruments designed to accelerate the growth of the national economy.[3]

In contrast to the main theories of the last 50 years—modernist each in its own way—this book approaches economic development as a process by which countries and firms seek to find a unique place in the global economy that allows them to build on their preexisting economic, social, and political advantages, and to learn selectively from the patterns of behavior of other countries and actors. A comparative institutional perspective on development sees *globalization as promoting diversity and renewal* (see table 1.1). The reason lies in that globalization increases mutual awareness, and mutual awareness is at least as likely to produce differentiation as it is to cause convergence (Robertson 1992, 8; Albrow 1997, 88; Waters 1995, 63). Although globalization has some of its roots in the tremendous expansion of trade, investment, communication, and consumption across the borders of nation-states over the post–World War II period (Louch, Hargittai, and Centeno 1998; Sklair 1991), it is not necessarily the continuation of the homogenizing consequences of modernity or modernization, as such social theorists as Anthony Giddens (1990, 64; 1991, 22) have argued. However, one does not need to go as far as Martin Albrow (1997, 100, 101) and declare that globalization is the "transition to a new era rather than the apogee of the old." From a comparative institutional perspective, it suffices to be noted that "globality restores the boundlessness of culture and promotes the endless renewability and diversification of cultural expression rather than homogenization or hybridization" (Albrow 1997, 144; see also Mittelman 1996).

Unlike previous theories, a comparative institutional approach to development sees the *social organization unique to a country not as an obstacle to economic action but as a resource for action* (Biggart and Guillén 1999; Portes 1997; Stinchcombe 1983). Thus, countries and firms do not fall behind in the global economy because they fail to adopt the best policy available or to conform to best practice but because their indigenous sources of strength are not taken into account when policies are designed and implemented. Thus, preexisting institutional arrangements are regarded in this book as the path-dependent context of action, as guiding and enabling socially embedded action (Douglas 1986; Geertz 1973, 220; Granovetter 1985; Swidler 1986). Following a comparative institutional perspective, Biggart and Guillén (1999, 725) have argued that "organizing logics vary substantially in different social milieus. For example, in some settings it is 'normal' to raise business capital through family ties; in others, this is an 'inappropriate' imposition and fostering ties to banks or to foreign investors might be a more successful or legitimate fund-raising strategy. Logics are the product of historical development,

---

[3] Perhaps world-system theory is to be exempted from this criticism, for it sees little possibility of national development without change at the world-system level.

are deeply rooted in collective understandings and cultural practice, and resilient in the face of changing circumstance. Culture and social organization provide not only ideas and values, but also strategies of action."

Social-organizational logics enable different types of actors to engage in different activities. They are sense-making frames that provide understandings of what is legitimate, reasonable, and effective in a given context (Barley and Tolbert 1997; Clegg and Hardy 1996; Nord and Fox 1996; Powell and DiMaggio 1991; Scott 1995; Smelser and Swedberg 1994). Only practices or organizational forms that "make sense" to preexisting actors are adopted. The comparative institutional literature has long documented that foreign models seen as a threat to preexisting roles and arrangements tend to be rejected (Arias and Guillén 1998; Cole 1989; Djelic 1998; Dobbin 1994; Guillén 1994, 1998a; Kenney and Florida 1993; Orrù, Biggart, and Hamilton 1997; Westney 1987).

If local patterns of social organization are resources for action, then successful economic development involves *matching logics of social organization with the opportunities offered by the global economy*. A corollary of this proposition is that there are multiple institutional configurations or paths to development, that is, several ways of becoming part of the global economy. A comparative institutional approach warns that it is futile to attempt to identify the best practice or model in the abstract (Guillén 1998a, 1998b; Lazonick and O'Sullivan 1996; Whitley 1992). Rather, countries and their firms are socially and institutionally equipped to do different things in the global economy. Thus, German, French, Japanese, and American firms are justly famous for their competitive edge, albeit in different industries and market segments (Cantwell 1989). Germany's educational and industrial institutions—dual apprenticeship system, management-union cooperation, and tradition of "hands-on" engineering or *Technik*—enable companies to excel at high-quality, engineering-intensive industries such as advanced machine tools, luxury automobiles, and specialty chemicals (Hollingsworth et al. 1994; Murmann 1998; Soskice 1999; Streeck 1991, 1995). The French model of elite engineering education has enabled firms to excel at large-scale technical undertakings such as high-speed trains, satellite-launching rockets, or nuclear power (Storper and Salais 1997, 131–48; Ziegler 1995, 1997). The Japanese institutional ability to borrow, improve, and integrate ideas and technologies from various sources allows its companies to master most categories of assembled goods, namely, household appliances, consumer electronics, and automobiles (Cusumano 1985; Dore 1973; Gerlach 1992; Westney 1987). And the American cultural emphasis on individualism, entrepreneurship, and customer satisfaction enables its firms to become world-class competitors producing goods or services that are intensive in people skills, knowledge, or venture capital, such as software, financial services, or biotechnology (Porter 1990; Storper and Salais 1997, 174–88). Trade economists have demonstrated that countries' exports differ in the degrees of product variety and quality depending on their social organizational features (Feenstra, Yang, and Hamilton 1999). The empirical chapters in this book further demonstrate that newly industrialized countries and their firms—based on their social organization—also excel at different activities in the global economy.

The argument about the diversity in institutional configurations, however, should not be used to deny the importance of theory and generalization. A balance between theoretical generalization and historical particularity needs to be struck, using "general principles, economic or sociological, not as axioms from which policies are to be logically deduced but as guides to the interpretation of particular cases upon which policies are to be based" (Geertz 1963, 157). Even the most modernist development scholars and policymakers must take into account that "material progress [is not simply] a matter of settled determination, reliable numbers, and proper theory" (Geertz 1995, 139). A comparative institutional approach to development is a "critique of conceptions which reduce matters to uniformity, to homogeneity, to like-mindedness—to consensus," preferring instead to open things up "to divergence and multiplicity, to the non-coincidence of kinds and categories" (Geertz 1998, 107).

A comparative institutional approach also differs from previous theories of development in that it allows for *different actors and relationships*, and in that it expects to find *different proportions of business groups, small firms, and foreign multinationals* across countries and over time (table 1.1). While previous approaches to development and globalization predict the proliferation of the same organizational form in countries undergoing development—large-scale, bureaucratized firms and/or business groups—the comparative institutional perspective does not expect the dominance of any particular organizational form under all circumstances. Rather, it makes arguments about how the interaction between sociopolitical patterns and state development policy affects dynamics among business groups, small firms, foreign multinationals, and other organizational forms.

Elements of a Comparative Institutional Approach

A comparative institutional approach to development and globalization argues that there are multiple viable paths to development and insertion in the global economy. Countries embark on different trajectories depending on a complex set of variables that is very difficult to reduce to simple principles. Some of these variables lie beyond the control of the country, for example, its natural endowments, including factor endowments and geographical location. Others have to do with international constraints and opportunities that countries can shape at least in part. Finally, a third group of variables has to do with such sociopolitical aspects as ideologies, traditions, cultural norms, domestic politics, and state structures. These variables make certain development policies and paths more feasible than others. The dynamic unfolding of development policies over time interacts with natural endowments, international constraints and opportunities, and sociopolitical patterns to produce different combinations of organizational forms. The core argument of the comparative institutional approach is that the emergence of a specific combination of organizational forms in a given country enables it to be successful in the global economy at certain activities but not others. Thus, development and incorporation into the global economy are processes that require a careful understanding of the diverse combinations of actors and relationships that emerge in different countries.

Actors and Relationships

As a society-centered approach to development, the comparative institutional perspective advanced in this book focuses on the categories of *actors* and the types of *relationships* among them that social organization enables and sustains over time (Biggart and Guillén 1999; Hollingsworth, Schmitter, and Streeck 1994; Portes 1997; Smelser and Swedberg 1994; Stark and Bruszt 1998; Storper and Salais 1997). The availability and legitimacy of different categories of actors—individuals, families, large companies, business groups, small and medium firms, state-owned enterprises, banks, worker-owned cooperatives, foreign multinationals, and, of course, the state itself—are invoked to explain how countries develop and firms make a dent in international competition. Ideologies, taken-for-granted assumptions, politics, and geopolitical conditions will be used to understand which categories of actors are legitimate in a particular country and hence available to pursue development and integration with the global economy (Haggard 1990; McGuire 1994).

The second element—relationships between actors—points to a major departure from previous theories of development. The post–World War II period's modernist obsession with the territorial nation-state as the target of development elevated location as the key variable in development studies. An actor's location in geographic space—defined as a system of generally nonoverlapping nation-states—became a key determinant of its possible role in the global economy, basically because of the factor-endowment issues so intimately related to geography. Development scholars studied nation-states as having various degrees of control over relatively immobile factor endowments and actors located within their territorial boundaries. Actors were literally trapped in their local environments, and it was the duty of the state to mobilize them in the pursuit of economic growth (McMichael 1996; see also Kogut 1991).

A world tending toward globalization requires a reexamination of the impact of location on development possibilities (Kobrin 1998; Porter 1998).

Globalization makes actors more mutually aware of each other and lowers the barriers and costs of cross-border activity. Accordingly, a comparative institutional theory of development downplays actors' geographical location in favor of actors' ability to network across national boundaries.[4] Moreover, globalization reduces the chances for a relationship across borders to be mediated by the state, the professions, and other influential organizations that the sociological literature has usually identified as cross-border brokers (Arias and Guillén 1997; Guillén 1994). As globalization enables actors to look for opportunities, resources, and potential relationships by themselves, without paying tribute to intermediaries, it encourages diversity rather than homogeneity, an outcome supported by the empirical evidence presented in subsequent chapters.

Location, of course, still matters in a global world because it shapes the very ability, propensity and desire of actors to network. Thus, social, cultural, political, and even geopolitical conditions facilitate or privilege different types of relationships, for example, vertical, horizontal, cooperative, competitive, domestic, or cross-border. In a context of globalization, Gereffi (1994a, 1994b) has proposed a particularly useful distinction between "producer-driven," or push linkages to the global economy, and "buyer-driven," or pull linkages, both of which emerge from the increasing international division of labor produced by globalization (Giddens 1990, 75–76; Kogut 1985). A vertical pattern of social organization (e.g., Korea's patrimonialism) facilitates producer-driven linkages fostering large-scale, capital-intensive activities by local firms, while a horizontal pattern (Taiwan's family business networks) enable buyer-driven linkages leading to flexible, knowledge-intensive activities (Biggart and Guillén 1999; Orrù, Biggart, and Hamilton 1997). In addition to push and pull linkages, countries may also relate to the global economy by means of direct ownership ties. In certain societies, for example, prevailing social organizational patterns or ideologies have fostered relationships between certain categories of domestic and foreign actors, or simply allowed foreign actors unrestricted access to the country. This pattern of linkage to the global economy has proved essential to the development of countries such as Ireland, Singapore, Puerto Rico, or Spain (Dietz 1986; Huff 1994; Shirlow 1995; Suárez 1998; see also chap. 5). These three types of relationships—push, pull, and direct—will serve as the basis for making arguments in subsequent chapters about diversity and renewal in the global economy.

---

[4] This line of thought is indebted to Merton's (1968) classic distinction between cosmopolitans and locals, suggesting that the role of an actor in a social setting follows from its ability, propensity, or desire to engage in different types of relationships. Thus firms and, by implication, countries will play different roles in the global economy depending on their relationships to other actors (Biggart and Guillén 1999; Castells 1996, 66–150; Kanter 1995; Orrù, Biggart, and Hamilton 1997; Reich 1991).

In many ways, a comparative institutional approach to development in an era of globalization shares much intellectual ground with the "cultural turn" in sociology (Robertson 1992, 32–48). In particular, a comparative institutional theory of development and globalization centered on actors and relationships highlights *reflexivity* as the process through which actors acquire the ability to participate in social and economic life in relation to others (Mead 1934). Modernist theories of economic development neglected the reflexive aspect of actors' behavior as socially constructed behavior, as action rooted in patterns of social organization, thus making it very difficult to make sense of their resilient desire to be different. If globalization is seen as a process tending toward enhanced mutual awareness in the world, then the reflexive character of action becomes a central concept for understanding how countries and organizations find a place for themselves in the global economy.

The Role of the State

Except for world-system and neoclassical theories, existing approaches to development give the state an important, even leading, role to play in development efforts (Kerr et al. [1960] 1964, 22–24; Rostow [1960] 1990, 7, 30–31; Cardoso and Faletto [1973] 1979, 127–48, 154, 205–6; Evans 1979; Amsden 1989). As explained above, the comparative institutional perspective is a society-centered one. Globalization may be regarded as a challenge to the modern nation-state, but not because the state will lose relevance as an institution or will not have a role to play as an actor—as Evans (1997a) has feared. Rather, *globalization undermines certain modernist assumptions but not the existence of the state as an actor.* It is important for a comparative institutional theory of development not to reify the state but rather to deal with it as yet another institutionalized actor with its own set of relationships to other actors. Thus, in a context of globalization the state ceases to be the center of attention but retains all of its characteristics as a social actor as well as an institution inducing patterns of political culture, group formation, political activity, and issue orientation (Skocpol 1985; see also Sassen 1996, 25–30).

It is also important to clarify that in a global world the state may have a role to play that goes well beyond the economists' (and conservatives') minimalist functions of enforcing property rights and providing for a few other public goods. The state also needs to foster the development of governance structures and rules of exchange among economic actors, both domestic and foreign (Campbell and Lindberg 1990; Fligstein 1996; Lindberg, Campbell, and Hollingsworth 1991). In particular, countries need the state to articulate and encourage the kinds of relationships actors may have with the global economy, as enabled by social organization and prevailing ideologies (see chap. 2). It is also important that the state puts in place mechanisms to protect the country from global shocks, including policymaking institutions and, especially, social and welfare programs (Boix 1998; Esping-Andersen 1985; Katzenstein 1985). These roles of the state are key to understanding development efforts and the categories of actors that will thrive as countries relate to the global economy (see chap. 3).

Thus, a comparative institutional perspective on development goes several steps further than recent studies emphasizing the nature of state-society relations. For example, in his landmark book *Embedded Autonomy*, Evans (1995) argues that successful development obtains only when an autonomous and capable state can establish a collaborative relationship with business actors in the society (see also Evans 1997b). This approach is an important step in the right direction because it places state-business relations at the core of the explanation (see also Block 1994). However, it does so at the cost of assuming that business actors are a given, an objection raised by several institutional researchers (Biggart and Guillén 1999; Campbell 1998b; Stark and László 1998, 124–29). By contrast, a comparative institutional approach does not take for granted that actors exist or that, if they do, they are equally capable, legitimate, or embedded in networks of relationships among themselves. A comparative institutional perspective on development makes actors as well as action problematic.

Some 70 years ago, the philosopher José Ortega y Gasset (1986, 149) warned against nation-states choking the spontaneity of society, a theme subsequently revisited by influential writers of various political persuasions (e.g., Hayek 1944; Putnam 1993; Schumacher 1975). As Albrow (1997, 164, 168) cogently argues, globalization "has revivified the social" and reminded us that "the modern nation-state is not . . . the crowning political achievement in human history." Globalization has made it apparent that "the nation-state has failed to confine sociality within its boundaries, both territorial and categorical. The sheer increase in cross-national ties, the diversification of modes of personal relationships and the multiplication of forms of social organization demonstrate the autogenic nature of the social and reveal the nation-state as just another timebound form" (Albrow 1997, 164).

Thus, globalization offers a unique opportunity to reassess the role of the state (Mazlish 1993), and to bring society—actors and networks of relationships—back into the study of economic development and organizational change. The challenge of a "critical globalism" is, as Pieterse (1996, 554, 560) argues, to theorize about each and every one of the realms impinging on development: the state, the market, the civil society, and international forces. From this critical globalist perspective, states, firms, labor unions, community groups, and other associations are neither asked to resist globalization nor to celebrate it, but rather to *engage* it, to make choices, to be selective, to assess and reassess how they relate to the global economy (Geertz 1998).

Intellectual Lineages of the Comparative
Institutional Approach

The comparative institutional perspective on development advanced in this book has its intellectual roots in three classic comparative analyses of industrialization: *Work and Authority in Industry* (Bendix [1956] 1974), *Peddlers and Princes* (Geertz 1963), and *British Factory—Japanese Factory* (Dore [1973] 1990). These books underscore that economic and organizational arrangements spring from social and institutional structures. In this book, I take institutional logics as repositories of distinctive capabilities that allow organizational actors and countries to pursue certain activities in the global economy more successfully than others, thus echoing the so-called resource-based view of the firm (Barney 1986; Nelson 1995; Nelson and Winter 1982; Peteraf 1993). I also build on Schumpeter's (1934) society-centered theory of development, which highlights the role of the innovative entrepreneur as a key actor in development. Finally, my approach is indebted to the "varieties of capitalism" research tradition, as initially outlined by Polanyi (1944), and subsequently developed by several political economists and political scientists (Boyer 1996; Hollingsworth, Schmitter, and Streeck 1994; Katzenstein 1985; Lindberg, Campbell, and Hollingsworth 1991; Piore and Sabel 1984; Sabel 1982; Soskice 1999; Storper and Salais 1997; Streeck 1991, 1995). All of these scholars argue one way or another that there are multiple solutions to the problem of economic performance, and that development (and hence globalization) induces a diversity of economic action and organizational forms.

It is important to note that a sociological concept of institutions as constituting actors stands in contrast with the economic view of institutions as mechanisms to overcome anomalies, for example, market failure due to the costliness of measurement and enforcement (North 1990, 1997; Williamson 1985). Institutions do much more than fill in the gaps of the market. They enable actors to engage in socially meaningful action. Business groups, small and medium-sized firms, and multinationals, among other forms, are not equally legitimate as actors across countries, a variable that affects development outcomes (see chaps. 3–7). Institutions also shape actors' preferences. Thus, the comparative institutional approach adopted in this book differs from economic institutionalism in that neither actors nor preferences are taken for granted.

The comparative institutional perspective on development also represents a radical departure from economic theories of comparative advantage. First, it considers social and political endowments in addition to economic ones (Biggart and Orrù 1997). And second, it takes economic, social, and political resources as malleable, socially constructed, and subject to change. A country's institutional resources and logics, though resilient, are not to be seen as

entirely fixed.[5] Rather, they are subject to social construction and transformation over time through the agency of the various economic and political
actors, including entrepreneurs, labor, organizations, and the state (Biggart
and Guillén 1999; Storper and Salais 1997; see chaps. 2 and 5).

A Comparative Study of Globalization and Organizational Change

This book's empirical chapters seek, first, to establish a principle of variation
in organizational forms as countries develop and become integrated with the
global economy (chaps. 2–5) and, second, to examine the performance outcomes of such variations (chaps. 6–8). The analysis is based on a considerable
amount of multifaceted evidence collected since I started work on this book
back in 1994. First, my research assistants and I have conducted some 120
semistructured interviews with key informants (see the appendix for a complete list). My interviewees included top managers of companies and banks,
secretaries-general of labor unions, government officials, and cabinet ministers. Second, I have visited the manufacturing plants of some 25 companies.
Third, I have conducted several large sample surveys with closed question-
naires: a survey of 163 firms in the Argentine province of Mendoza; surveys
of 120 large firms and of 1,150 exporting firms in Spain; and a survey of
attitudes toward economic policymaking in Spain among 1,200 respondents
representing the country's adult population. I have also analyzed in depth the
census of 3,971 foreign direct investments by Korean companies undertaken
between 1960 and 1995 as compiled by the Bank of Korea. Fourth, I have
collected data on the ownership of the largest 100 firms in each country in
terms of total sales, exports, and foreign investment. Fifth, I have analyzed
confidential data on companies collected by government agencies, central
banks, industry associations, consulting firms, and research institutions. And
sixth, I have consulted archival and documentary material on companies
and labor unions referring to the period between 1950 and 1999 (see the
appendix).

This first chapter having established the reciprocal relationship between
globalization and development, formulated the fundamentals of a comparative institutional approach, and outlined the main message of the book—that
is, countries and firms seek to become different rather than to converge on
a universal pattern—the second chapter characterizes the different paths to
development implied by the various development theories, and justifies the
choice of Argentina, South Korea, and Spain for intensive comparative study.

[5] I thank Clifford Geertz, Mark Granovetter, and John Meyer for encouraging me to clarify
this important point.

The central goal of this chapter is to document each country's development path and to provide an understanding of the complex reasons why each country shifted development policy over time.

The next three chapters (3–5) examine the effects of each country's development path on various types of enterprises, namely, business groups, small and medium enterprises, and foreign multinationals. The third chapter analyzes the political-economic conditions under which entrepreneurs prefer to diversify and create business groups straddling multiple industries as opposed to remain product-focused with a tightly integrated firm. I argue that it is primarily when a country maintains asymmetric international economic relationships with the global economy that entrepreneurs find it most attractive to create business groups. Using data on the largest 100 companies each in Argentina, South Korea, and Spain over a 20-year period, I find that cross-national contrasts in the presence of business groups persist when controlling for the obvious differences in industry composition across countries, and that this organizational form is associated with the asymmetric international economic relationships so typical of Argentina and South Korea. It is precisely because Spain has followed a more symmetric development path that business groups have lost ground. In this chapter I also elaborate on how business groups have engaged in political action so as to preserve their privileges. I conclude that business groups grow at the expense of both small and medium enterprises and foreign multinationals.

The fourth chapter deals with how small and medium enterprises (SMEs) have adapted to the processes of economic development and globalization. I begin by noting that modernist approaches to economic development have frequently privileged large firms at the expense of SMEs. I argue that SMEs are neither good nor bad. The point is to understand under what circumstances they become successful exporters, foreign investors, and technological innovators. The chapter compares the fortunes of SMEs in Argentina, South Korea, and Spain, drawing from statistical surveys and case studies of firms in the railway equipment, alcoholic beverages, and publishing industries. Spanish SMEs are found to outperform larger firms in terms of technological innovation, exports, and foreign investment, while Argentine SMEs excel only at foreign investment, not exports. Korean SMEs have been hurt by the rise of the big business groups.

The fifth chapter addresses the interaction between foreign multinationals and labor unions in newly industrialized countries. Drawing on interviews, archival materials, and union publications, I assess organized labor's ideologies toward foreign investment and their effects on the development paths pursued by each country. In particular, I document how Spanish labor unions evolved from a negative view of multinationals in the 1960s to a full acceptance of their presence in the country as "partners" during the 1980s and 1990s. By contrast, South Korean labor unions have come to tolerate multinationals only as "arm's-length collaborators" of locally owned firms, whom they provide with technology and marketing skill. Finally, the Argentine labor unions have regarded multinationals as "villains" trying to plunder the country's riches, with only a few spells of grudging acceptance of their presence as "necessary evils" in order to surmount acute financial and economic difficulties. I conclude with a reflection on how the sequence of political and economic change affects development paths, arguing that political authoritarianism and exclusionary labor regimes are not conducive to ideal outcomes of economic reform.

After reviewing the roles business groups, SMEs, foreign multinationals, and labor unions have played under different development circumstances, chapters 6 and 7 analyze two industries in depth—automobiles and banking—so as to assess the performance consequences of different development paths and organizational forms. In chapter 6 I review the rise of the automobile assembly and components industries in the three countries to illustrate that organizational logics specific to each country have mediated in the relationship between state policies and development outcomes, producing a wide range of unintended consequences. I chose the automobile industry because it is a key sector that most developing countries wish to participate in. I compare two cases in which high-volume, export-oriented auto assembly has taken hold—Spain and South Korea—with one in which the industry remains backward, Argentina. I document that a competitive auto components industry developed in Spain but not in Korea, where the state and the big business groups choked the activities of small and medium firms. Lastly, the Argentine state misread the capabilities of local auto components firms, failing to encourage backward supply linkages between assemblers and domestic firms. Spanish firms, however, gradually fell into foreign control, whereas in Korea the automobile industry remains domestically owned. I conclude that a comparative institutional view taking into account not only resource endowments and degrees of state autonomy and capacity but also logics of social organization offers the best perspective to study development outcomes at the industry level in an era of globalization.

In chapter 7 I apply a similar logic of analysis to the banking sector both as a service industry and as a critical activity in any development effort. A comparative study of banking is useful for two reasons. First, banks play a key role in any industrialization effort. Second, banking is one of the most misunderstood sectors of the economy because most scholars fail to see in it more than a support activity of manufacturing. While Korea nationalized its banks in the 1960s and Argentina allowed them to fall into foreign hands, Spain has a thriving, domestically owned banking sector ranking among the most competitive and profitable in the world. Based on interviews with over 30 bank regulators and executives, I review the evolution of banking in each country and compare the contributions of this industry to the economic development of the manufacturing sector. Issues of ideology and happenstance figure prominently as part of the analysis in this chapter.

Finally, chapter 8 assesses development outcomes at the country level and presents the conclusions. I first summarize the major findings of the empirical chapters, showing that the Argentine, South Korean, and Spanish paths to development entail a mixture of strengths and weaknesses, and of successes and failures. The book ends on a positive note as to the effects of globalization. Evidence is presented to demonstrate that it is possible—though not easy—for countries to break through the glass ceiling separating the poor countries from the rich, that globalization encourages diversity in economic action and organizational form, and that democracy is the best form of government to deal with the contingencies of globalization.

PART ONE

DEVELOPMENT AND ORGANIZATIONAL CHANGE

TWO

THREE PATHS TO DEVELOPMENT,
THREE RESPONSES TO GLOBALIZATION

Those who know only one country, know no country.
(*Lipset 1996, 17*)

ECONOMIC development engenders a massive amount of organizational change, but different kinds of it take place under different development circumstances. This chapter characterizes three ideal-typical paths to development and three corresponding responses to globalization. It thus prepares the ground for subsequent chapters to analyze from a comparative institutional perspective the extent to which business groups, small and medium enterprises, foreign multinationals, labor unions, and specific sectors of economic activity have changed and succeeded in the global economy. The economic histories of Argentina, South Korea, and Spain since 1950 provide archetypical illustrations of each of the three paths to development and of the circumstances leading to them.

Globalization and Paths to Economic Development

Over the last half-century countries have variously adhered to the policies proposed by modernization, dependency, world-system, late-industrialization, and neoclassical theories of development. Policy choices have been shaped by a complex combination of causes or constraints, including natural endowments, international pressures and opportunities, and domestic sociopolitical patterns (Haggard 1990). Before venturing into the vexing question of why Argentina, South Korea, and Spain made specific policy choices, however, it is useful to establish the fundamental ways in which the policies themselves vary from one another.

The literature on political economy has typically characterized different approaches and paths to development by means of pairs of opposed policies, such as export-led growth versus import-substitution, modernizing versus populist, nationalist versus pragmatic, or protectionist versus liberal (Maravall 1993; Haggard 1990; Gereffi 1990a; Gilpin 1987). While the specific features of the theoretical models and typologies in the literature differ from one another, they all underline the importance of understanding the extent to which policies create linkages or relationships to the global economy in terms of foreign trade, investment, aid, and debt (Gereffi 1989).

Development Paths in a Context of Globalization

This book's analysis of organizational change in newly industrialized countries follows an ideal-typical characterization of paths to economic development based on the economic relationships between each country and the global economy. In particular, *foreign trade* and *foreign direct investment* tend to have a momentous impact on organizational change and on the types of organizations that predominate over time in a country undergoing development and integration with the global economy. While foreign aid and debt are also important in many historical instances (Gereffi 1989), they can be seen as substitutes for foreign direct investment.

Previous research on the political economy of development suggests that it is crucial to distinguish between *outward* and *inward* foreign trade and investment flows because they need not be correlated with each other (Haggard 1990). In fact, one of the prerogatives of the modern state—that institution so intimately linked to development efforts—is precisely to establish the extent to which the domestic economy is exposed to imports and inward foreign investment, and the degree to which exports and outward investment are important to its economic development effort. Decisions about levels of foreign trade and investment are directly related to the "rules of the game" that states are supposed to establish as they implement their development strategy: definitions of property rights, governance structures, and rules of exchange among economic actors, both domestic and foreign (Fligstein 1996). Modernization, dependency, world-system, late-industrialization, and neoclassical theories of development propose policies that result in different configurations of inward and outward flows of foreign trade and investment.

For a given country, outward flows—exports and investment by nationals in foreign countries—will remain at a low level if the emphasis is placed on inward-looking development and on devoting all resources to local investment. The political economy literature has referred to policies that keep outward flows at low levels as the "populist" solution to development, one promoting short-term compromise and income redistribution among interest groups. By contrast, outward flows will reach higher levels when policies encourage firms to sell and, eventually, invest abroad. Such policies may be labeled as "modernizing" (Bresser Pereira 1993; Dornbusch and Edwards 1991; Kaufman and Stallings 1991; Mouzelis 1988).

A similar logic can be applied to inward flows. Imports and investment by foreigners in the country will remain at a low level if there is protectionism and subsidization of domestic firms (trade) or if there is a preference for national private and state ownership of the productive assets in the country (foreign investment). It should be noted that imports and inward foreign investment can be restricted to low levels while firms in the country obtain capital and technology at arm's length via foreign debt (or aid) and licensing, respectively (Gereffi 1989). Inward flows will reach higher levels as imports and investment by foreign firms are allowed into the country. The political economy literature has referred to policies restricting inward relationships to low levels as "nationalist," and those allowing for high levels as "pragmatic" or "liberal" (Gilpin 1987, 31–34, 180–83, 274–90; Maravall 1993).

Inward and outward flows appear cross-classified in table 2.1. The low-low configuration follows from a "nationalist-populist" approach. This is a situation in which most developing countries found themselves at midcentury (Haggard 1990; MacIntyre 1994; Maravall 1993). Only extremely autarkical versions of dependency theory and world-system analysis would recommend that countries indefinitely pursue this approach (see Ragin and Chirot 1984, 292–94). Economists and social scientists making very different theoretical assumptions remind us that acute balance-of-payments crises and rampant inflation are likely to occur repeatedly when countries persevere in their efforts to maintain low levels of both inward and outward flows (Bruton 1998; Diaz-Alejandro 1965; Dornbusch and Edwards 1991; Kaufman and Stallings 1991; Haggard 1990; Maravall 1993).

One frequent option to surmount such crises is to allow imports and inward investment to increase, that is, to relax nationalist policies without abandoning populism. The shift toward the "pragmatic-populist," or high-low, configuration can help stabilize the economy and promote growth by attracting foreign investment and imports of essential capital goods until the economy is ready to fully substitute local production for imports. These changes, however, frequently produce economic and political problems if the domestic interests affected by the opening of inward flows mobilize against it, or if multinationals fail to contribute to local development in terms of technology transfers and profit reinvestment. Thus, it is common to observe populist countries oscillating between cells 1 and 2 of table 2.1 as they apply the policy prescriptions of dependency theory. Argentina, Venezuela, Brazil, and India provide examples of this "erratic" populist path to development (Encarnation 1989; Evans 1979; Haggard 1990; Mouzelis 1988; Tulchin 1993).

The "nationalist-modernizing," or low-high, configuration in table 2.1 represents the policy prescriptions of late-industrialization theory. It is exemplified in the political economy literature by the so-called developmental or mercantilist states of East Asia (Amsden 1989; Haggard 1990; Johnson 1982; Wade 1990). The state protects domestic firms with policies restricting imports and inward investment, lends money at subsidized rates, and allocates licenses to import technology, machinery, and components to entrepreneurs who commit to increase exports and outward investment in support of such exports. In line with dependency theory, barriers to imports are established to discourage the consumption of consumer goods manufactured abroad. But late-industrialization scholars emphasize the importance of forcing local firms

TABLE 2.1
Ideal-Typical Foreign Trade and Investment Configurations

Inward Flows	Outward Flows	
	High (modernizing)	Low (populist)
High (pragmatic)	Pragmatic-Modernizing: HIGH: Allow Imports and Inward investment HIGH: Export-led growth and Outward investment Underlying development theories: Modernization, Neoclassical 4	Pragmatic-Populist: HIGH: Allow Imports and Inward investment LOW: Import substitution and Local investment Underlying development theories: Dependency 1
Low (nationalist)	3 Nationalist-Modernizing: LOW: Protectionism and Local ownership HIGH: Export-led growth and Outward investment Underlying development theories: Late-industrialization	2 Nationalist-Populist: LOW: Protectionism and Local ownership LOW: Import substitution and Local investment Underlying development theories: Autarkical versions of dependency and world-system analysis.

to deliver export growth in return for protection (Amsden 1989). Also at variance with dependency theory, the nationalist-modernizing approach rests on a " 'decoupling' of foreign capital and foreign technology from foreign direct investment." The necessary foreign capital and technology are obtained in the forms of loans and licenses, respectively, as opposed to direct investment (Mardon 1990, 119–20). Nationalist-modernizing development may also be denominated "mercantilist export-led" growth.

Finally, the "pragmatic-modernizing" configuration in table 2.1 implies high levels of both imports and exports and of inward and outward investment, and has been recently adopted by emerging economies adjacent to developed areas—Mexico, Ireland, Puerto Rico, or the southern European countries—

as well as by the commercial enclaves of Singapore and Hong Kong (Haggard 1990; Maravall 1993). Both modernization and neoclassical theories of development propose pragmatic-modernizing policies that are conducive to high inward and outward flows of foreign trade and investment. In modernization theory, increasing exports are thought to facilitate economic takeoff because trade widens the market and allows for more specialization. Foreign investment, while neither a necessary nor a sufficient precondition for takeoff, is deemed to facilitate development (Kerr et al. [1960] 1964, 92–94; Rostow [1960] 1990, 39, 49). Modernization scholars even argue that "external intrusion by more advanced societies" in the form of imports and foreign investment exposes traditional patterns of behavior and encourages modernization (Rostow [1960] 1990, 6, 31–32). Similarly, neoclassical theories of economic development and reform invariably propose open or liberal foreign trade and investment policies (Balassa et al. 1986; Sachs 1993). Pragmatic-modernizing development can also be labeled "liberal export-led" growth.

Why Argentina, South Korea, and Spain?

This book focuses on the cases of Argentina, South Korea, and Spain because these countries illustrate the three paths to development that can be inferred from the four ideal types in table 2.1. Back in the late 1940s and 1950s, the three countries were pursuing relatively similar import-substitution policies in order to improve their lot as relatively backward developing countries. They became members of the International Monetary Fund during the late 1950s. Their development paths, however, diverged considerably over the following 40 years. Argentina has oscillated between the nationalist-populist and pragmatic-populist orientations, that is, followed an "erratic populist" path. Korea, by contrast, shifted from nationalist-populist to nationalist-modernizing, becoming an export and foreign investment power but without allowing imports or inward investment. Finally, Spain shifted from nationalist-populist to nationalist-modernizing and pragmatic-modernizing.

Figure 2.1 presents evidence corroborating these assertions. In the upper panel the levels of imports and exports as a percentage of GDP are plotted for each country and shown for every five years between 1970 and 1995. In the lower panel inflows and outflows of foreign investment are shown. While Argentina has oscillated vertically (i.e., remained fairly populist in orientation), Korea and Spain shifted toward higher levels of exports and outward foreign investment over time. Unlike Korea, Spain has also allowed imports and inward foreign investment to increase rapidly. Thus, the strategy of case selection for intensive comparative study follows the "variation-finding" approach (Skocpol 1984, 368–74; Tilly 1984, 116–24). The three cases will be systematically compared in subsequent chapters to arrive at a "principle of variation" linking development paths to organizational forms.

(a) Foreign Trade (% of GDP)

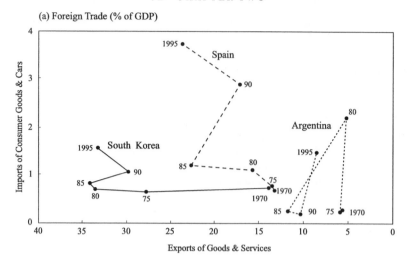

(b) Foreign Direct Investment (% of GDP)

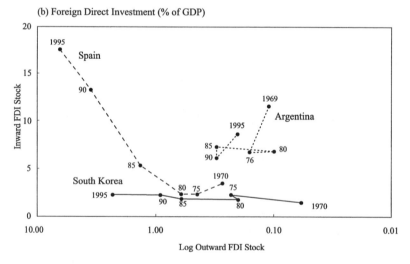

Figure 2.1. Outward and Inward Foreign Trade and Investment for
South Korea, Spain, and Argentina. (*International Trade Statistics Yearbook;
World Investment Report; World Investment Directory.* Dorfman 1983, 426; Katz
and Kosacoff 1983, 140).

South Korea and Spain have seen their per capita incomes rise very quickly
over the last 40 years, suggesting perhaps that nationalist and pragmatic approaches to development work reasonably well as long as they are combined
with outward-oriented growth. Argentina's erratic populism, by contrast, produced no growth between the mid-1970s and the early 1990s. However, Argentina and its firms are not to be seen as a general failure, for they have
succeeded in several respects. The argument in this book is not that some

development models work better than others—which is a risky proposition given the continuing turmoil in the global economy—but rather to show that development and globalization produce diversity in economic action and organizational form. Moreover, each approach to globalization and development results in different combinations of strengths and weaknesses, and of successes and failures (see chap. 8).

Before describing in detail why each of the three countries followed a different development path, it is important to highlight the key advantages in comparing Argentina, South Korea, and Spain over the 1950–99 period. First, these are three countries of roughly similar size. A country's size, especially in terms of population, has a major impact on the export-orientation of its firms, the possibilities for import-substitution, and the behavior of foreign multinational enterprises (Haggard 1990, 26). Second, while these three countries' development paths have diverged considerably over time, they all started in the nationalist-populist configuration back in the 1950s (Amsden 1989; Lewis 1992; Sachs 1993, 22–26). Third, in spite of the obvious differences in natural endowments, the importance of agriculture in each country has dropped considerably over the last four decades (table 2.2, panel A). Fourth, in addition to their increasingly different degrees of incorporation into the global economy (table 2.2, panel B), these three countries barely engage in foreign trade among themselves or invest in each other.[1] The lack of significant interconnections between these economies over the last 50 years makes it safe to assume that developments in one country are not affecting those in the other two. Fifth, the distribution of manufacturing activities by industry four decades ago was very similar across the three countries (see table 2.3). Sixth, policymaking in each country was long shaped by authoritarian regimes (like in most other newly industrialized countries), making this book a tale of three generals—Perón, Park, and Franco.[2] And perhaps most importantly, previous development approaches have identified these three countries as paradigmatic illustrations of each path. Neoclassical theorists extol the Spanish model (Sachs 1993, 22–26), while late-industrialization proponents sing the praises of South Korean policymaking (Amsden 1989), and Argentine development until the 1990s is presented as a textbook case of populism (Cardoso and Faletto [1973] 1979, 133–38; Mouzelis 1988). It should be carefully noted, however, that during the 1990s Argentina has perhaps applied neoclassical policies most extensively, while the South Korean and Spanish states

---

[1] It is true, however, that Spanish foreign investment in Argentina increased steeply during the 1990s. But it has been concentrated in telecommunications, utilities, oil, and airlines, and trade between the two countries is still almost negligible.

[2] "Authoritarian regimes are political systems with limited, not responsible, political pluralism: without elaborate and guiding ideology (but with distinctive mentalities); without intensive nor extensive political mobilization (except at some points in their development); and in which a leader (or occasionally a small group) exercises power within formally ill-defined limits but actually quite predictable ones" (Linz 1964, 297).

TABLE 2.2

Agriculture and Incorporation into the World Economy: Spain, Argentina, and South Korea, 1960 and 1990s

	Spain	Argentina	Korea	Spain	Argentina	Korea
	A. Importance of Agriculture					
	1960			1990		
Agriculture and fishing						
% of GDP	23.7	16.6	39.9	4.9	6.7	8.3
% of employment	41.6	15.2	75.6	12.0	12.0	18.0
% of exports	39.6	66.3	30.5	8.5	27.3	2.6
	B. Degree of Incorporation into the World Economy					
	1960			1992		
As % of GDP						
Exports	10.5	10.2	3.4	21.3	10.0	37.6
Imports	7.5	11.3	12.7	27.5	13.7	41.5
Exports plus imports	18.0	21.5	16.1	48.8	23.7	79.1

Sources: World Tables; Yearbook of International Trade Statistics; Banco de Bilbao; Estadísticas de Argentina, 1913–1990; Korea Statistical Yearbook.

continued to intervene massively in the economy through industrial and welfare policies, respectively.

For these seven reasons, comparing the impact of the Argentine, South Korean, and Spanish development paths on organizational change is not only intellectually exciting but also appropriate and instructive. After 50 years of development efforts, the three economies contain different types of organizational forms, with distinctively different consequences for the role their firms play in the global economy. In the next sections I set the stage for the analysis of organizational change and economic performance contained in subsequent chapters by reviewing the economic development trajectories of each of the three countries. I systematically compare how natural endowments, international context and policies, and sociopolitical patterns affected development policy choices (see table 2.4).

Argentina: The Paradigm of Erratic Populism

One of the mysteries of the second half of the twentieth century is how Argentina, so rich in so many ways, has had such difficulty fulfilling its great potential.

(De la Balze 1995, 1)

TABLE 2.3

Manufacturing Structures of Spain, Argentina, and South Korea in 1964
(in percentages)

Industry (SIC codes)	Employment			Output		
	Spain	Argentina	Korea	Spain	Argentina	Korea
Food, beverages, and tobacco (20, 21)	15.8	20.6	13.8	26.9	29.6	17.6
Textiles, apparel, and leather (22, 23, 31)	20.0	17.3	31.5	20.1	16.1	25.0
Lumber and furniture (24, 25)	8.7	5.7	4.6	3.9	2.2	4.2
Chemicals, paper, and rubber (26, 28, 30)	10.4	8.3	14.3	10.2	11.7	18.2
Printing and publishing (27)	3.4	3.2	4.7	2.2	2.0	4.3
Oil and gas (29)	0.6[a]	0.9	3.7[a]	4.6[a]	6.3	6.3[a]
Stone, clay, and glass (32)	8.8	5.9	6.0	4.6	3.1	5.4
Metals (33, 34)	⎫	11.3	7.4	13.5	9.5	9.5
Nonelectrical machinery (35)	24.1 ⎬	5.6	4.2	1.8	4.7	2.6
Electrical machinery (36)	⎭	3.6	2.8	2.5	3.1	3.2
Transportation equipment (37)	5.9	15.1	4.3	7.9	10.1	2.1
Other manufacturing	2.3	2.5	2.7	1.9	1.7	1.6
Total	100.0	100.0	100.0	100.0	100.0	100.0

Source: *Anuario Estadístico de España, 1966; Censo Nacional Económico, 1964; Korea Statistical Yearbook, 1966.*

[a] Includes coal as well as oil and gas.

Argentina—like Venezuela, Brazil, or India—is a case study of erratic populism, that is, an economy that has remained relatively inward looking since the end of World War II, but with policies toward imports and inward foreign investment oscillating between openness and hostility in short cycles of five to eight years.[3] Argentina's economic and political instability is legendary: 19 presidents (nine generals among them) and 47 economy ministers from 1943 to 1999. Even in the late 1990s, after the introduction of some of the world's most liberal economic and financial policies, the Argentine economy, especially the manufacturing sector, remains relatively inward oriented, with exports and outward foreign investment growth lagging behind imports and inward investment (Toulan and Guillén 1997).

[3] On Venezuela, see Tulchin 1993; on Brazil, Haggard 1990, chap. 7; and on India, Encarnation 1989.

TABLE 2.4
Conditions for Development in Argentina, South Korea, and Spain since 1950

Variable	Argentina	South Korea	Spain
Natural endowments	Rich in natural resources. Remote location.	Poor in natural resources. Distant from major markets except Japan.	Poor in natural resources, with some exceptions. Superb location.
International context and policies	Hostile though not powerful neighbors (Brazil, Chile). Alternating isolationist and integrationist foreign policies	Large, powerful, and expansionist neighbors (China, Japan, Russia). Nationalist foreign policy	Rich and friendly neighbors (western Europe). At first, isolationist foreign policy, later integrationist (EU, NATO)
Sociopolitical patterns			
Culture, traditions, and ideologies	Populism and nationalism; corporatist social structure	Patrimonialism cements hierarchical relationships; Confucian emphasis on hierarchy and on education; nationalism	Nationalism and inner-looking attitudes give way to pragmatism; corporatist social structure
Domestic politics	Alternating authoritarian, semiauthoritarian, and democratic regimes. Strong personalities, weak parties. Strong labor unions increasingly marginalized.	Long period of authoritarian rule (1961–87); incomplete transition to democracy. Weak parties. Strong labor unions repressed by both authoritarian and democratic presidents	Long period of authoritarian rule (1938–75); complete transition to democracy. Gradually stronger parties. Strong labor unions incorporated into the political and economic decision-making process
State structures	Weak federal state with relatively strong provincial governments; lack of a capable state bureaucracy.	Strong, centralized state structure since Japanese colonization; capable and relatively autonomous state bureaucracy	Centralized state challenged by centrifugal nationalisms; capable but not autonomous state bureaucracy

The Origins of Nationalist-Populism: Natural Wealth,
Isolationism, Political Personalism

At the turn of the century Argentina was fully integrated into a global economy ruled by Britain. Argentina was the tenth largest trading country in the world, and ranked sixth in terms of per capita income. This relatively high level of prosperity was maintained up until the 1930s. Argentina's economic growth after 1870 was supported by the twin pillars of a vast supply of treeless land (the *pampas*), and a steady inflow of immigrants from Europe. Between 1880 and 1912 the economy grew at an average annual rate of over 6 percent, thanks to staggering exports of wool, leather, and grains. Improvements in transportation and refrigeration technology helped the country become a leading exporter of perishable foodstuffs to the Northern Hemisphere. British capital financed an extensive railway network, and both domestic and foreign investments completed the infrastructure with ports and roads. Export-led growth allowed for the accumulation of private capital then invested in beverages and food processing, textiles, oil, and the construction business (De la Balze 1995, 24–27; Bethel 1993, 47–77). On the eve of the Great Depression, Argentina was the world's largest exporter of chilled beef, maize, linseed, and oats, and the third largest of wheat and flour. European markets accounted for the bulk of shipments.

Argentina's pattern of integration into the global economy, however, contained what many began to regard as an intrinsic weakness: dependence on foreign markets for the sale of goods intensive in natural resources, and on foreign producers for machinery and many manufactured goods. Ships returned from Europe or the United States replete with consumer goods, luxury items, automobiles, and, most importantly, industrial equipment. The economic downturns of 1880, 1910, and 1921 as well as wars and trade tensions in the Northern Hemisphere provoked sharp fluctuations in Argentine export shipments. Conflicts between those situated upstream at the relatively less profitable stages of the value-added chain and those closer to the market (e.g., cattle ranchers versus meat-packers or crude oil producers versus refiners and distributors) became quite virulent during the 1920s and 1930s, especially because the former tended to be Argentines and the latter foreigners (Smith 1969; Solberg 1979).

Limited manufacturing activities started thanks to both domestic and foreign capital. Light manufacturing of consumer products concentrated in the greater Buenos Aires area, where an industrial proletariat began to emerge. During the 1920s American foreign investment transformed the manufacturing economy. Total inward investment in 1920–39 averaged a fairly high annual rate of 3.7 percent of GDP. Domestic and foreign capital contributed to the inception of new industries: oil exploration and refining, chemicals, cement, metals, food processing, electrical machinery, and rubber (Bethel 1993, 139–63).

Of critical future importance were developments in the oil industry. Foreign and domestic capital flocked to the Patagonian oil fields after their discovery in 1907. In 1922 the state reorganized its oil interests, accounting for one-third of total production, through the creation of the Yacimientos Petrolíferos Fiscales (YPF) agency, which made history as the world's very first state-owned oil company. In 1925 YPF built a large refinery at La Plata, south of Buenos Aires. In 1927, the rows between state and private interests were manipulated for political reasons, with the government riding a wave of nationalist fervor that prompted it to promise the expropriation of foreign interests in the industry. After U.S. president Calvin Coolidge, yielding to the pressures of the domestic farm lobby, imposed an unfair ban on imports of Argentine dressed beef, Standard Oil's operations in Argentina were nationalized. This action set a precedent and signaled the presence of a solid anti-American sentiment among the landed and exporting interests in Argentina that was picked up by public opinion and exploited by politicians of all inclinations (Bethel 1993, 163–68). Against the backdrop of contentious politics and a global economic depression, a military coup d'état in 1930 interrupted the democratic tradition initiated with independence in 1810.

The Great Depression in Argentina was shallower than in the industrialized nations, but nonetheless painful due to the sharp drop in agricultural exports. Recovery was swift after 1934. By the end of the 1930s two-thirds of manufacturing were concentrated in food processing, beverages, and textiles. These years marked a second important phenomenon in addition to the rising anti-Americanism. Locally owned, quasi-monopolistic firms consolidated their position in key industries, and even started to engage in foreign direct investment in Uruguay, Brazil, and Chile: Siam DiTella in metals and appliances; Bunge & Born in cereals, foodstuffs, textiles, and petrochemicals; Miguel Miranda in canned foodstuffs; and the textile and footwear firm Alpargatas, which in 1890 became the first company based in a developing country to set up a foreign manufacturing affiliate, in Uruguay, followed by a second one in Brazil. These firms would benefit from close ties with the state, which in some instances was an important customer. The import-substitution policies implemented in response to the Great Depression proved a windfall for Argentine businesses. Their manager-owners were to occupy key political and economic positions in the government at various points during the next decades (Bethel 1993, 196; Katz and Kosacoff 1983; Peralta Ramos 1992).

Besides anti-Americanism and the rise of the business groups, a third consequential trend was the growth in the size and militancy of the labor movement during the 1930s and early 1940s, comprising anarchist, socialist, and communist factions. The concentration of the proletariat in such large cities as Buenos Aires and Córdoba made it easier for unions to be formed and grow in membership (Waisman 1987; Bethel 1993, 173–241; see also chap. 5).

General Perón and the Institutionalization of Nationalist-Populism

In 1943 these changes—anti-Americanism, industrial concentration, labor militancy—converged on a pivotal event of Argentine history: the coup by army colonels of fascist inclinations. The parallels with developments in Spain at roughly the same time are stunning (Guillén 1994, 175–83; Linz 1964, 1970, 1981). The United States imposed a diplomatic quarantine that, as in many other cases of American foreign policy, exacerbated the problem. Then colonel Juan Domingo Perón was put in charge of the Labor Department. After winning the 1946 presidential election, he introduced corporatist and paternalistic labor reforms in order to secure his power base. In 1947 a Peronist Party consecrated political personalism. As Perón's wife accurately observed, "the people surrender themselves more easily to a man than to an idea" (Lewis 1992, 218). The antipluralist, authoritarian political movement of *justicialismo* consolidated and occupied most of the political, economic, and social spheres of influence. Perón's endorsement of the social doctrine of the Catholic Church gained him an important ally. His populist doctrine was enshrined in a comprehensive corporatist system of interest representation, monopolistic in nature, with the state acting as arbiter of disputes.[4] Membership in the official and exclusive labor and business organizations soared. The judiciary, the universities, and the labor movement were purged.

The timid import-substitution policies of the 1930s were broadened, solidifying the position of the diversified business groups, often by granting them lucrative contracts with the state or by protecting the domestic market. The telephone system, gas utilities, railroads, airlines, merchant marine, and financial system were nationalized. Social programs were expanded. A crucial development was the decision not to sign the General Agreement on Tariffs and Trade or to participate in any of the Bretton Woods institutions in 1947, thus marginalizing Argentina and preventing it from taking part in the big world trade boom of the 1950s (De la Balze 1995, 37–41). After a few years of strong economic expansion, the economy stalled as a consequence of yawning fiscal and trade deficits and mounting inflation. Trade and foreign investment plummeted. The country that had once been deeply embedded in the

---

[4] Corporatism is "a system of interest representation in which the constituent units are organized into a limited number of singular, compulsory, noncompetitive, hierarchically ordered and functionally differentiated categories, recognized or licensed (if not created) by the state and granted a deliberate representational monopoly within their respective categories in exchange for observing certain controls on their selection of leaders and articulation of demands and supports" (Schmitter 1974, 93–94).

global economy was well on its way toward becoming the vanguard of economic populism and the pariah of post–World War II capitalism. The acute economic problems brought about by staunchly nationalist-populist policies forced Perón to "retreat" from economic nationalism in the early 1950s by stabilizing the economy, seeking foreign investment, and allowing the business groups to conduct some of the activities previously allotted to the state or the state-owned enterprises (Lewis 1992, 195–210, 349–59). A 1955 army coup ousted Perón as the church turned against his anticlerical educational reforms, and the military feared the appearance of a worker militia (Bethel 1993, 243–363).

Argentine politics never recovered from Peronist populism. Semidemocratic governments alternated with army-led, authoritarian ones until 1976, when the military initiated a brutal "dirty war" against insurgent leftist groups. More so than in other Latin American countries, the alternation of import-substitution policies and protectionism with brief periods of the most brutal economic liberalism created instability, capital flight, and rampant corruption. The periods of economic boom following episodes of fiscal expansion or sharp economic opening typically lasted too briefly to raise living standards over the long run (Lewis 1990). Foreign investors came to Argentina in the 1960s to manufacture price-inflated goods for the protected domestic market, but almost no new investment came in during the 1970s. Still, multinationals operating in Argentina were profitable (Lewis 1992, 310–13). In this once leading exporting country, the ratio of exports to GDP decreased to less than 15 percent. The infamous "costo argentino" undermined international competitiveness of both agricultural and manufactured goods.

The final blows to the Argentine economy were assessed by Perón's return to the presidency in 1973–74, the gross macroeconomic mismanagement of the military juntas during the 1976–83 period, the ill-fated war with Britain over the Malvinas Islands (Falklands) in 1982, and the pusillanimity of the first democratically elected government in 1983–89, during which the unions staged as many as 13 general strikes. A pattern of erratic populism had become established over time as foreign trade and investment policy shifted abruptly from friendly to hostile and vice versa in 1946, 1953, 1962, 1966, 1970, 1976, 1981, and 1986 (Lewis 1990; Waisman 1987). These swings translated into rapidly changing patterns of imports and inward foreign investment, with outward flows remaining relatively low (see fig. 2.1). Unlike in other Latin American countries or in Spain, the relative size of the Argentine underground economy actually increased between 1950 and 1990 (Castells and Portes 1989, table 1.1; De la Balze 1995, 108; Toharia Cortés 1994, 1370–94). Meanwhile, the state's presence in the economy also grew. The saying, "Todo lo que se mueve se promueve" (everything in motion is by promotion), captured very well the reality of a superlative state whose spending had reached 60 percent of GNP by the 1980s, with 40 percent of it devoted to subsidizing the losses of the state-owned enterprises (Lewis 1992, 250, 488). In May 1989 food riots took place in this agriculturally resourceful country. The following March hyperinflation exceeded an annualized rate of 20,000 percent.

The Resilience of Populism in the Face of "Successful" Reforms: Import-Substitution in the Mercosur

The virtual meltdown of the Argentine economy in the late 1980s was a direct consequence of erratic populist policymaking. After decades of emergency economic programs, visionary currency stabilization plans, and economic and social hardship, in 1989 Argentine voters elected another Peronist, Carlos Menem, as their president. Menem ran for office on an intriguingly ambiguous platform. Upon assuming office several months ahead of schedule given the gravity of the situation, he surprised virtually everyone by appointing to his cabinet and staff several liberal economists from one of the leading business groups in the country, the mythical Bunge & Born, and some noted anti-Peronists. The failure of the Austral Plan of 1985 to reduce inflation still fresh, Menem perceived the need to force changes onto state finances and labor negotiations as well as to fix the perennial problem of currency instability. He succeeded rather quickly at reducing government expenditures with a bold program to privatize state-owned companies (Lewis 1992, 488). His early reforms also allowed him to split the labor union leadership and to impose sector-by-sector wage deals (Adelman 1994). His first few months in office, however, finished disastrously at the end of 1989 with the failure of the "Bunge & Born Plan" to arrest hyperinflation. Success in fighting price increases proved elusive during 1990 in spite of the harsh therapy of the bank deposit-bond conversion (Bonex) plan (Beckerman 1995). It was not until the implementation of Domingo Cavallo's dollar-peso convertibility plan of February 1991 that inflation finally subsided. During the early 1990s, Menem's reforms affected virtually every aspect of the economy, including money and banking, the state budget, state-owned enterprises, trade, and regulation (Toulan and Guillén 1997).

According to free-market enthusiasts, Menem's U-turn yielded results of magical proportions: inflation below 5 percent within two years of convertibility and close to zero thereafter, annual GDP growth rates ranging between 5 and 10 percent, and rising inward foreign investment signaling a renewed confidence in the Argentine economy. In spite of the severe impact of the Mexican crisis of 1994–95 and the Brazilian flu of 1998–99, Argentina seems to have successfully navigated the treacherous waters of the global economy of the 1990s. It has maintained the currency convertibility scheme in place, reduced public spending, and even attained some modest budget surpluses, completed a far-reaching program of privatization of over 60 state-owned firms totaling U.S.$60 billion worth of assets (including such flagships as oil firm YPF, telephone company ENTel, the flag carrier Aerolíneas),[5] introduced labor market and social security reforms, implemented trade liberalization measures, and integrated the economy into the Mercosur customs union with Brazil, Paraguay, and Uruguay (De la Balze 1995, 88–99, 115–22; Ganboa 1995; República Argentina 1993). Although privatizations and the surge in inward foreign investment have increased the capitalization of the stock market ninefold since 1991, the size of financial and capital markets barely reaches 15 percent of GDP, compared to over 50 percent in the most advanced countries (De la Balze 1995, 78–79).

However, students of the Argentine economy agree that most Argentine firms—whether domestic or foreign owned—have not made inroads in terms of their outward orientation toward the global economy (Chudnovsky, López, and Porta 1997; Toulan and Guillén 1997; Guillén and Toulan 1997). Argentine exports are increasingly tilted toward commodity products or semi-processed industrial goods, while branded goods are primarily sold in the domestic market. Manufactured goods are sold in markets that are not the toughest in the world, thus creating limited competitive effects. Although Mercosur has persuaded many Argentine firms to think in terms of a market larger than the domestic one, it is a protectionist and defensive trade bloc that has allowed inefficient capital-intensive manufacturers to survive. Scholars and policy analysts concur in that the Mercosur represents *not an abandonment of import-substitution policies but a continuation of them* (Yeats 1998; Chudnovsky, López, and Porta 1997; López and Porta 1995; Toulan and Guillén 1997). Argentine exports amounted to a meager 7.5 percent of GDP in 1995, with a larger share than ever going to Mercosur partner Brazil—26.2 percent, up from 11.5 percent in 1990. Exports of automobiles, chemicals, petrochemicals, and steel to Brazil have increased because of bilateral administered or balanced-trade arrangements, and not because Argentine firms excel at producing such goods (see chap. 6). It should also be remembered that the trend toward increased trade with Brazil in autos, chemicals, petrochemicals, and steel as well as in energy and agricultural commodities started not with President Menem in the 1990s but back in 1986 with President Alfonsín, who signed the Program of Integration and Economic Cooperation with Brazil, a system of bilateral trade preferences. Thus, it is difficult indeed to argue that

[5] Approximately 57 percent of the value of privatizations may be attributed to foreign investors: 15 percent from the United States and Canada, 13.5 percent from Spain, 8.3 percent from Italy, 6.4 percent from France, and 5.6 percent from Chile. Argentine private business groups have been the most active domestic acquirers of privatized companies: Pérez-Companc/Banco Río (13.9 percent), Techint (7), Astra (5.2), Sideco (2.6), and Comercial del Plata (2).

Argentine policymaking has wholeheartedly shifted toward an export-led model of growth under free-market assumptions. The domestic market has been opened to imports, although local manufacturers can still lobby the government for temporary protection, as in the trade wars with Brazil in 1999 following the devaluation of the real. Argentine firms have not yet been successful at reversing 50 years of inward orientation.

A similar picture emerges when it comes to foreign direct investment (see fig. 2.1). Argentine companies are not investing abroad in pursuit of markets or production opportunities to nearly the same extent as their Spanish or Korean counterparts. Firms in other Latin American countries—Chile, Brazil, Mexico—are also investing abroad more than Argentine ones. Outward foreign direct investment stock represents only 2.4 percent of GDP in 1997—compared to 3.4 for South Korea and 9.0 for Spain—while inward stock is 12.3 percent of GDP. Only a handful of business groups and small, family-owned firms have multinational operations (Bisang, Fuchs, and Kosacoff 1995; Kosacoff 1999; see also chaps. 3 and 4). Taken together, the acute imbalances between exports and imports, and outward and inward foreign investment point to a country that is still engaged with the global economy in a very asymmetric way.

Table 2.4 summarizes the reasons why Argentina embarked on an erratic populist development path. Its vast natural wealth has made it possible for governments to pursue import-substitution policies within Argentina or in the Mercosur for a longer time than would have otherwise been possible (Haggard 1990, 35). Zigzagging and disastrous foreign policies have made it hard for the country to achieve its due stature in the international system of states. Economic and political agreements with Brazil are inherently volatile and subject to constant renegotiation during economic downturns. At the same time, the culture of populism and nationalism seems to have shifted slowly since it became institutionalized under Perón. In addition, political parties remain less important than political personalities, making it hard for policies to have continuity over time. Meanwhile, labor unions remain outside the political mainstream and lack an institutionalized voice in economic policymaking (see chap. 5). Still, Argentina has achieved a measure of economic and financial stability that has eluded many of its regional neighbors.

After 50 years of a love-hate affair with the global economy, Argentina is still a captive of the pattern of erratic populism that it has only recently attempted to abandon. As chapters 3 and 4 will establish, this development path has fostered relatively large business groups but worked against small and medium enterprises. Although the South Korean government also embraced import-substitution during the 1950s, it abandoned it in a radical way during the 1960s by developing a more outwardly oriented relationship to the global economy.

South Korea: A Nationalist-Modernizing Path

> . . . this "miracle on the Han." There you have it: no capitalists,
> no Protestants, no merchants, no money, no market, no re-
> sources, no get-up-and-go, let alone no discernible history of
> commerce, foreign trade, or industrial development, so on
> and so forth—and yet there it is.
> (*Cumings 1997, 300*)

South Korea is a perfect case to illustrate an export-oriented growth strategy accompanied by restrictions on imports and inward foreign investment. Within one generation, this once backward country of 45 million people inhabiting the southern tip of an arid peninsula devoid of any significant natural resources other than cheap labor has become the world's largest shipbuilder, the sixth steelmaker, the fifth automobile manufacturer, and the second assembler of consumer electronics and semiconductors.[6] The bulk of Korean manufacturing is conducted by a handful of family-controlled, diversified enterprise groups, known as *chaebol*.[7] Hyundai, LG, Samsung, and Daewoo, among others, have become household names around the world. These groups make textiles, household appliances, consumer electronics products, chips, cars, trucks, machine tools, heavy industrial equipment, even ships. In the mid-1990s Korea boasted 14 firms on the Fortune Global 500 list of the world's largest companies, many more than any other newly industrialized country or even some of the developed countries (e.g., Canada, Italy, the Netherlands, Switzerland). Neither Argentina nor Spain has been able to produce such an armada of large manufacturing firms. As figure 2.1 testifies, South Korea has become an export power following a modernizing economic model, but without allowing imports or foreign direct investment, that is, retaining a nationalist approach toward foreigners.

Korea—long known to the world as the "Hermit Kingdom"—was ruled for half a millennium by the Yi dynasty (1392–1910). The country actually operated as a vassal state of China and enjoyed a good measure of autonomy as long as its domestic and foreign policies did not conflict with Chinese interests. When Chinese decline accelerated after the Opium War of 1839–42, Korea suffered a string of foreign interventions by Britain, France, Russia, Germany, and the United States. Foreign powers forced the Koreans to open up their sources of raw materials and their markets for manufactured goods.

---

[6] North Korea does harbor significant mineral deposits and hydroelectric potential.

[7] The Korean term *chaebol* is the transliteration of the Japanese *zaibatsu*. Both are written with the same two Chinese characters and mean "wealth clique." Only four of the giant Korean chaebol have their origins in the colonial period (Kang 1996b, 11, 86–90; Kim 1997; Woo 1991, 13, 35, 66).

The handicrafts never evolved into a real manufacturing sector, and they were severely damaged by the arrival of Western traders. After centuries of isolation under Chinese tutelage, foreign powers fought several wars to settle, among other things, who would be Korea's master: the Sino-Japanese War of 1894, the Russo-Japanese War of 1905, the Pacific War of 1941–45, and the Korean War of 1950–53 (Cumings 1997).

The Japanese occupation of Korea after 1910 resulted in rigid economic dependence and backwardness at first, and in rapid industrial growth through foreign direct investment during the 1930s as the peninsula became a stepping stone in Japan's imperial dreams in Northeast Asia. Over 90 percent of all industrial capital and facilities were owned by the various Japanese *zaibatsu*. Heavy industries were located in the northern part of the peninsula, while light industries such as food processing, machine tools, and consumer goods clustered in the southern area (Woo 1991, 19–42). The Republic of Korea was founded in 1948 to the south of the armistice line. The United States initiated in 1945 a vast economic and military assistance program, expanded during the Korean War of 1950–53, that was to last until the 1960s. Originally, U.S. generosity came with one string attached: the funds had to be used to purchase goods from Japan. The nationalistic response of the Republic of Korea's first president, Rhee Syngman (1948–60), was to initiate an import-substitution policy of industrialization while he reinforced the state's administrative, repressive, and military apparatuses. His policies were fully supported by the United States. The success of his economic policy in achieving industrial growth during the 1950s relied heavily on international aid and foreign investment (Stallings 1990; Cheng 1990; Woo 1991, 43–72). Rhee's regime, however, indulged in corruption and giveaways to the emerging, rent-seeking chaebol (Amsden 1989, 39–40), a form of enterprise rooted in Korea's traditional patrimonial concept of authority—members of the firm owe obedience and personal loyalty to the patrimonial figurehead, the president or *hoejang* (Biggart 1990; Fields 1995, 38–44; Woo 1991, 67–68). Fiscal deficits forced the government to introduce a classic stabilization program in 1957 (similar to Perón's in the early 1950s). It failed miserably to stimulate private investment. The ensuing economic recession and unemployment took their toll, and the Rhee regime collapsed in 1960 under the pressure of student protests.

The Shift toward Export-Led Growth

The key to understanding Korea's export-led growth during the 1960s and the "Big Push" of the 1970s lies in the role played by an autonomous state since the army-led coup d'état of 1961. The emerging authoritarian regime of General Park Chung Hee (1961–79) was eager to find an alternative to the disastrous import-substitution policies of his predecessor. At roughly the same time, Walter Rostow, the leading modernization theorist who had just published *The*

Stages of Economic Growth ([1960] 1990), became national security adviser to President Kennedy and suggested a shift in South Korea's economic strategy. Rostow identified South Korea's large and cheap labor pool as a key resource for development and asked the U.S. and South Korean governments to promote export-led growth in light manufacturing. He was able to follow up on this recommendation during his years as head of the State Department's Policy Planning Staff. General Park, however, was thinking about drawing not only from modernization theory and American policy recommendations but also from Japanese industrial planning, which he had observed at close range during his years in Manchuria. Thus, Park's basic economic model included both the prescriptions of modernization theory and of Japanese mercantilism; it was simultaneously modernizing and nationalist. "Steel equals National Power" *(Ch'ol un kunggyok)*, Park was fond of saying (Cumings 1997, 299, 310–14; Woo 1991, 71–79, 120). As a government official explained years later, policies were consciously designed to keep foreigners out. "Loans have always been preferred over direct investment because more benefits stay in Korea" (Mardon 1990, 120). A last element of Park's approach was his quintessentially technocratic set of priorities: "In human life, economics precedes politics or culture" (Park 1962, 224).

General Park's development genius lay in finding a way to strike a delicate balance between, on the one hand, policies protecting and subsidizing private enterprises, and, on the other, tight controls on the performance and competitiveness of the favored firms. He astutely charged the chaebol with profiteering during the Rhee years, forcing them to submit to his authority. Park, however, was also adamant about the importance of building a strong Korean economy based not on state-owned enterprises but on large, powerful private firms whose activities would be orchestrated by the state. "One of the essential characteristics of a modern economy is its strong tendency towards centralization. Mammoth enterprise—considered indispensable, at the moment, to our country—plays not only a decisive role in the economic development and elevation of living standards, but further, brings about changes in the structure of society and the economy. . . . Therefore, the key problems facing a free economic policy are coordination and supervisory guidance, by the state, of mammoth economic strength" (Park 1962, 228–29).

Following Park's designs, the state imposed on businesses a panoply of restrictions, including export targets, price controls, restraints on capacity expansion, limits on market entry, and prohibitions on capital flight. In addition, the government nationalized the private banking system so as to be able to allocate credit at will (Woo 1991, 81–84; Amsden 1989, 146–47; Fields 1995; Song 1990; Sakong 1984). Normalization of relations with Japan in 1965 allowed for technological transfer as well as huge reparations payments, used to set up a steel mill, while the Vietnam War effort created myriad trade and procurement opportunities for Korean firms (Woo 1991, 85–100, 124, 134–35; Cumings 1997, 321–22).[8]

The most dynamic and proportionally important sector during the 1960s—textiles, apparel, and leather (see table 2.3)—was negatively affected in the early 1970s by President Nixon's political liabilities to southern cotton growers and textile mills. A quota-based protectionist regime (the Multifiber Arrangement or MFA) was imposed by the United States and Europe on the low-wage East Asian textile manufacturers (Woo 1991, 125–26). The exhaustion of growth opportunities in light manufacturing led Park to initiate a "Big Push" into heavy industrialization during the 1970s: steel, chemicals, machinery, shipbuilding, and so on. Subsidized credit and administrative allocation of licenses and permissions were the instruments used to channel private initiatives into the targeted industries. The government also rescheduled the debt of the nearly bankrupt big business sector at the expense of small savers in 1972 (Fields 1995, 53–58). When the 1973 oil crisis struck, the government boldly devalued the currency. Meanwhile, the chaebol absorbed the sharply higher costs of raw materials and fuels by increasing the reliance on the then abundant foreign sources of lending. The bargain paid off by 1976 as the Korean product quality-cost mix allowed its firms to expand market shares across the world while manufacturing firms in Western Europe and North America went bust.

The oil shock of 1979–80 created excess capacities worldwide just as the new Korean plants were ready for large-scale production. The government of President Chun Doo Hwan (1979–87)—who seized power after Park's assassination—orchestrated a vast and heavily subsidized program of "industrial reorganization" or consolidation of producers (affecting 78 firms in heavy industries), and implemented liberal macroeconomic adjustments to curb a widening trade deficit and rising inflation (nearly 30 percent in 1980). He froze wages, cut subsidies, tightened credit, privatized the banks that Park had nationalized, and, under U.S. pressure, timidly liberalized foreign trade and investment regulations (Haggard and Kaufman 1995, 83–91; Woo 1991, 148–59, 177–79). Chun succeeded at arresting inflation and accelerating economic growth. His successors—now elected democratically through universal suffrage—reacted similarly to the cycle of boom and bust. Korean business under Roh Tae Woo (1987–92) benefited from low oil prices and interest rates as well as from the yen's appreciation. The slowdown of 1990–91, however, forced him to devalue the currency and expand credit. Kim Young Sam (1993–98) presided over a long global economic boom, but

---

[8] South Korea was hardly a free-rider on the Vietnam spending spree. It had contributed over 300,000 ground troops by the time the war was over, a per capita contribution larger than that of the United States (Woo 1991, 93).

Kim Dae Jung (1999–) had to deal with the country's worst financial and economic crisis ever (see chap. 7; Fields 1995; Moon 1994; E. M. Kim 1997, 178–200).

Despite the frequent short-term crises and adjustments, the Korean economy has expanded vigorously over the long run following a nationalist-modernizing strategy with increasing exports and outward foreign investment but restricted imports and inward investment. The results of the export drive of the 1960s, the Big Push of the 1970s, and the policy adjustments of the early 1980s and 1990s were rapid economic growth, averaging about 8 percent annually, and the rise of large business groups. Korea avoided significant inflows of direct foreign investment but at the cost of accumulating a mountain of foreign debt. Continued increases in exports thus became essential to service debt payments, which amounted to between 20 and 30 percent of export earnings from the 1960s to the 1980s (Amsden 1989, 95).

Korean businesses have expanded abroad not only as exporters but also as foreign direct investors (see fig. 2.1). During the 1960s, Korean firms made small international investments to distribute their Korean-made exports. In the 1970s a new kind of foreign expansion emerged when they invested in manufacturing and procurement of raw materials (Kumar and Kim 1984). At the same time, the general trading companies associated with the chaebol started to grow quickly, aided in part by a new government subsidy program introduced in 1975 (Cho and Heo 1989; Fields 1995, 183–208; Woo 1991, 164–65). By the mid-1980s the trading companies were handling half of all Korean exports (Cho 1987, 55; Fields 1995, 193–94). Since the early 1980s Korean manufacturing firms have gone abroad in order to distribute exports, access protected markets, and, to a much lesser extent, guarantee sources of raw materials (Euh and Min 1989).

But the biggest increase in foreign investment by Korean companies came with labor unrest in 1987 and is primarily taking place at low-cost locations in the People's Republic of China and elsewhere in Southeast Asia (Guillén 1999; Tcha 1998; Van Hoesel 1999). Between July and September 1987—two years after the first democratic, if rigged, election to the National Assembly—more labor conflicts occurred than during the entire 25 years of the Park and Chun regimes. Most significantly, conflict shifted from small and medium establishments in light manufacturing to the large chaebol in heavy industries (Koo 1993b, 149, 156). The upward pressure on wages was exacerbated by increasing remittances by Korean guest workers abroad, particularly those staffing the vast construction projects undertaken by the chaebol in the Middle East. Rising labor costs in Korea and protectionism in the United States and Europe encouraged Korean firms to look for foreign production opportunities. Presently, Korea's stock of outward direct investment stands at 3.8 percent of GDP.

Domestic Politics and State Structures

There appear to be two key differences separating Argentina from Korea. First, the corporatist regime of labor relations (see chap. 5), and second, the lack of effective mechanisms to discipline the private sector. Free from interest groups—after the Americans enforced land reform in the late 1940s—General Park was able to use the state budget deficit to finance industrial investments while the large private business groups dealt with their workers' welfare by investing in everything from company housing to primary schools. The contrast with the huge social security and welfare programs organized and funded by the state in Argentina (and Spain) could not be sharper. The Korean state did invest in education at all levels. But, unlike in Argentina and Spain, the big firms played a key role in the creation of firm-specific skills through in-house technical education and training programs (Amsden 1989, 208–9).

The second crucial difference between Korea and Argentina has to do with the ability of the state to discipline private business groups in order to check rent-seeking behaviors in a protected domestic market (Amsden 1989; Koo 1993b). Business groups had to deliver export growth. Otherwise, they would not be granted permits to expand capacity, enter new industries, diversify product lines, reduce their taxable income, and access cheap credit (Woo 1991; Amsden 1989; Eckert 1993, 102–3; Fields 1995). Poor performance, or political deviance,[9] was ultimately punished by outright dismemberment, as happened to several chaebol during the 1970s and 1980s, including Kukje, the country's sixth largest, Korea Shipbuilding and Engineering, and Yulsan (Amsden 1989, 15; Fields 1995, 127–32; E. M. Kim 1997, 200–203; Woo 1991, 170–71). Two circumstances allowed President Park to pursue his policies single-mindedly: the creation of a relatively strong, autonomous, and self-regulating state in the 1960s and 1970s, and the nationalization of the private banking sector (Woo 1991, 159–69; see chap. 7). As the chaebol grew in size, however, the relationship has become much more "symbiotic," with the state and business depending on each other (E. M. Kim 1997; Lew 1999).

The contrast between Korean and Argentine state structures is worth recounting (see table 2.4). A modern state bureaucracy first emerged in Korea during the Japanese occupation (Kohli 1994) and was subsequently reinforced in both South and North Korea as a consequence of war or the threat of war, in agreement with the general path observed by Mann (1988) and Tilly (1990) for state-building in Europe. Unlike Japanese rule in Korea and Taiwan, the Iberian tradition of decentralized rule in Latin America failed to produce

---

[9] Unofficial taxes to fund political, social, and cultural causes were imposed by the government on the big chaebol. In 1986 such taxes amounted to more than 1 percent of the firms' sales and about 7 percent of the labor costs (Eckert 1993, 109). Based on stock market data, Woo (1991, 9) estimates those contributions at 22 percent of net profit.

the foundations for the rise of a modern state bureaucracy (McGuire 1994). Moreover, the absence of wars during the nineteenth and early twentieth centuries meant that Latin American countries did not face the need of creating strong state structures (Centeno 1997).

The South Korean state is certainly a strong one, as late-industrialization theorists point out (Amsden 1989). But it has been a powerful state not only with the ability to intervene in the economy so as to accelerate growth but also with a formidable coercive capacity (Cumings 1989). In fact, the capacities to direct economic growth and to coerce are but two sides of the same coin. Korean industrialization and the growth of the chaebol have been as dependent on the exploitation of labor as on subsidized credit, in a pattern similar to other East Asian economic "miracles" (Deyo 1989). Korean workers, particularly women in the clothing and simple assembly industries, have labored under appalling conditions. For example, as many as four or five lives were claimed *daily* by work accidents during 1986 in Korean manufacturing. Rather than decreasing, the figure kept on growing to reach six daily deaths during 1991. No comprehensive minimum wage law was introduced until 1988 (Bedeski 1994, 115–16). During 1985 Korean male employees worked an average of 2,833 hours, compared to 2,180 in Japan and 1,934 in the United States They took just 4.5 vacation days per year, compared to 9.6 in Japan and 19.5 in the United States (Koo 1994, table 9.7).

Many chaebol owners and managers have landed or slave-owning family backgrounds. Not surprisingly, paternalism and disdain for workers have been the typical approach to labor relations; employees have never been considered equals or partners in the industrial enterprise. "[S]triking or otherwise disgruntled workers are often depicted [in official company histories] as simple, naive, and easily led astray by subversive leftist forces" (Eckert 1993, 114). Based on the traditional Confucian view of capitalism as a means toward independence from the West and toward national aggrandizement—in contrast to the rational, predestination-driven, individualistic conception of Protestantism— Korean entrepreneurs and employers have historically emphasized their unselfish contributions to national progress (Eckert 1993, 117–20). Characteristically, employers have downplayed labor's contribution and been unwilling to accept workers' legitimate right to voice their demands and to fight for them collectively, as a group or class. The occupying powers or the state have provided the means to repress labor until the mid-1980s. Overall, Korean employers have been slow to recognize the epochal change in labor relations taking place since the onset of democratization. In 1989 the six largest chaebol belatedly created a National Federation of Business Organizations to take a common stand against rising labor contestation of managerial prerogatives and make up for the government's diminishing willingness and ability to repress labor (Eckert 1993, 112; Koo 1993b, 158). Thus, when the crisis of 1997 struck Korea, employers and managers found themselves still wrestling with how to deal with workers and their unions (see chap. 5).

Korea's nationalist-modernizing path to development illustrates a second ideal-typical pattern of integration in the global economy. After the failure of import-substitution in the 1950s, South Korea embarked on export-led growth on the basis of its only natural "endowment," that is, cheap labor. Nationalism, previous colonial history, and the cold-war context, however, led to a combination of modernizing policies and nationalist mercantilist practices. This mix was consistent with a patrimonial cultural tradition favoring large business groups, with the widespread fear of foreign economic intervention, and with the availability of a strong state apparatus that could engage in economic planning and labor repression (see table 2.4).

As we shall see next, there is an alternative, less nationalist and more pragmatic, pattern of global integration, one that balances high exports and inward foreign investment with high imports and outward investment. Like the Argentine and Korean paths, Spain's pragmatic-modernizing approach also has its strengths and weaknesses.

Spain: From Nationalism to Pragmatism

> That they invent things? Let them invent! The electric bulb illumi-
> nates here as much as where it was invented.
> (*Miguel de Unamuno in Robles, ed. 1987, 42*)

Spain's relationship to the global economy has gone through nationalist-populist, nationalist-modernizing, and pragmatic-modernizing phases (see fig. 2.1). Unlike in postwar Korea, inward foreign direct investment has always played a pivotal role in Spain. Multinationals found in Spain first a large domestic market, and then an export platform. While the government has generally failed at creating technological assets, it succeeded at promoting general education, infrastructures, and the country's integration in Europe. This mixture of institutional factors has facilitated the arrival of foreign investment and the survival of pockets of previously state-owned or regulated companies as well as family-controlled or worker-owned firms with strong export and foreign investment potential.

The Long Road to Pragmatic-Modernizing Development

Spain is a case combining an early start of industrialization in the 1840s with a late completion of the process in the 1960s and 1970s after a long, agonizing trek stretching over more than a century and punctuated by sharp ups and downs (Nadal 1975; Martín Aceña and Comín 1991; Tortella 1994). The country is substantially better endowed with natural resources than Korea but not nearly so well as Argentina. As a result, primary or extractive activities attracted foreign investment a long time ago but are no longer enough to sustain a pragmatic-modernizing development path. By contrast with Korea, the state neither introduced systematic incentives for export performance to discipline firms nor nationalized the private banks. In fact, private banks have dominated finance since the 1920s.

The state followed a strategy of tariff-based infant-industry protectionism from the turn of the century to the 1930s, shifting to more active import-substitution policies during the 1940s and 1950s, similar to the ones then being pursued by Argentina and Korea. Large state-owned enterprises and foreign multinationals have dominated heavy industry. Simultaneously, a fairly comprehensive corporatist system of interest representation and coordination inherited from the policies of the 1920s and 1940s has consolidated as the various interest groups created or displaced by industrialization found a mutual accommodation. Smaller firms under family control and worker-owned cooperatives did relatively well because of their ability to shield themselves from the pressures of corporatism and the demands of the banking cartel.

At the middle of the century Spain still was a predominantly agricultural country (table 2.2). After the Civil War of 1936–39, the authoritarian regime of General Francisco Franco was composed of an uneasy mix of populist and staunchly nationalist policymakers (De Miguel 1974). They implemented a series of foreign exchange controls and protectionist measures, nationalized foreign investments in utilities and public services, expanded the corporatist framework of industrial relations, and made large-scale, import-substitution investments in industry. Meanwhile, the Allied powers imposed a trade embargo that remained fully in place until the late 1940s. Capital flight and almost zero inward foreign direct investment were the natural results of a nationalist backlash against foreign investors, the overvaluation of the currency, the intricate system of multiple exchange rates, and mounting inflation. Slow growth for almost two decades and recurrent balance-of-payments crises testified to the limitations of this inward-oriented, nationalist-populist model of growth (Tortella 1994, 255–306; Guillén 1994, 175–203; Martín Aceña and Comín 1991; Linz 1964, 1981).

The incorporation of the country and its firms into the global economy has proceeded gradually since 1953, when Spain signed a military and economic treaty with the United States, and especially since 1959, when liberal economic reforms substituted steep tariff barriers for nontariff barriers to trade. Drawing from French "indicative planning" techniques, the government created incentives for firms to become more export oriented. Meanwhile, policies remained somewhat nationalist in terms of trade protection and inward foreign investment throughout the 1960s and 1970s, resulting in a pattern of nationalist-modernizing development (see fig. 2.1). In spite of the restrictions, foreign multinationals in both consumer and capital goods set up plants in the country so as to overcome punitive tariffs on imports (Muñoz, Roldán, and Serrano 1978, 34 n. 43; Hawkesworth 1981; Campa and Guillén 1996a). Foreign enterprises were, of course, better equipped than domestic firms to react promptly to the incentives toward internationalization. While annual inward foreign investment flows ranged between 0.15 and 0.59 percent of GDP during the 1960s and 1970s, outward FDI stayed under 0.10 percent. By the mid-1970s and despite the reduction in new foreign activity in Spain, inward investment was still about four times higher than outward investment. Only a few Spanish manufacturing firms ventured abroad during the 1960s: Tudor (batteries), Sarrió (paper), Hispanoil (oil), Pescanova (frozen fish), Laboratorios Ferrer (pharmaceuticals), and ENASA (light trucks, currently Iveco-Pegaso), among others, mostly to exploit their incipient technological assets or to source some critical inputs. Meanwhile, foreign firms created new industries and markets, modernized existing ones, and even started to turn their Spanish operations into an export platform. The state-owned enterprise sector grew in size as existing firms leveraged their monopoly rents, new enterprises were set up in activities ranging from food processing to transportation to hotels, and bankrupt private companies in mining, steel, and other activities were taken over by the state (Martín Aceña and Comín 1991).

While foreign multinationals, state-owned companies, and the industrial groups associated with the large private banks grew in prominence—albeit to a lesser extent than in Argentina or Korea—smaller firms were starved of funds. The government's French-style indicative planning practices of the 1960s required the introduction of "privileged financial circuits" to channel cheap credit to targeted industries and to exporters (Tamames 1977). Unlike in Korea, however, no performance standards were imposed on the favored firms. In addition, the state assumed all of the financial risk either directly or indirectly through special rediscount lines and the creation of state-owned industrial credit institutions (which were not allowed to compete with the private banks for funds). This arrangement consolidated a cartel of seven large private banks accounting for over two-thirds of total deposits. As political scientist Sofía Pérez (1997) has shown, no matter whether financial regulation or deregulation was the issue, the banking cartel always found ways to maximize oligopolistic advantage at the expense of the state and industrial firms. Unlike in manufacturing, foreign investors were prevented from entering the banking sector. Thus, the big private banks amassed huge profits as lenders to industry in a virtually risk-free environment and without competing for deposits on the basis of price (see chap. 7).

The Spanish economy rode the wave of world economic and trade prosperity—growing almost as fast as Japan—until the implicit contradictions of nationalist-modernizing development began to emerge in the midst of the staggering international financial and economic turbulence of the late 1960s and 1970s. Cheap credit without full trade liberalization or export targets fueled inflation and ultimately, an erosion of comparative productivity levels. Wages grew in excess of productivity. Heavy and light manufacturing industries declined. Higher international interest rates and easier mobility of funds across borders increased net capital outflows sharply. In response, interest rates were allowed to rise steadily until the late 1980s, forcing Spanish firms into an unmanageable position: the lowest self-financing ratios among OECD countries, very limited opportunities to raise money in a backward and tiny stock market, and, as a result, dependence on bank loans. Further oligopolistic practices by the private banks, branch saturation in particular, forced them to translate higher operating costs into high lending rates and commercial fees (Pérez 1997).

The consequences of the government's economic and financial policies for industrial companies are fairly well known. With the exception of a couple of years, between the late 1970s and the early 1990s Spanish nonfinancial firms suffered from financial costs averaging more than their returns on investment (Maroto Acín 1990). Spain's financial system is dominated by universal banks, as in Germany, Switzerland, and Austria (Steinherr and Huveneers 1994). But Spanish banks do not play the role of the long-term, informed shareholder; rather, they behave as the moneylenders and commercial partners of industrial firms. Nonfinancial firms "with a bank among their top three shareholders are less profitable and more leveraged" (Cuervo-Cazurra 1995, 7). This situation is taking place in a country in which more than 80 percent of nonfinancial firms are under majority control by their top five shareholders (Galve Górriz and Salas Fumás 1992). Under these circumstances, only family, worker, state, or foreign-owned firms could thrive in the long run (see chaps. 3 and 4).

Domestic Politics and State Structures

Within a forest of differences, one crucial similarity between Spain and Argentina stands out thus far: the pervasive influence of corporatist interests, that is, business, labor, the professions, and the banks (Guillén 1989; Linz 1981). The Argentine and Spanish states, unlike the Korean, fell hostage to numerous pressure groups. Governments and dictators in both countries had to allocate ministerial positions among representatives of the various interest groups in such a way that their own chances of survival would be maximized (De la Balze 1995, 47; De Miguel 1974). In both countries "entrepreneurs" found it easier to obtain quasi rents from the state than to come up with process or product innovations. And the emerging state-owned enterprises were plagued by overemployment, huge operational costs, misallocation of resources, and conflicting goals (De la Balze 1995, 57–58; Martín Aceña and Comín 1991).

Furthermore, the state bailed out or nationalized bankrupt private companies both in Argentina (e.g., Giol, Austral, Siam DiTella) and in Spain (in sectors such as coal, steel, shipbuilding, heavy engineering, banking).

Yet, unlike Argentina, Spain has always had a relatively meritocratic and self-regulating civil service (Beltrán 1977; Guillén 1989, 157–60), which started to reassert itself in the 1960s—especially at the Bank of Spain and the Treasury/Economy Ministry. These enclaves of excellence later became the champions of economic reform. In Argentina, by contrast, one still finds today a "patrimonial state" (Weber 1978, 2:1028–31; Silberman 1993) fully at the mercy of interest groups, and an officialdom lacking competitive examinations for entry, rational specialization, or enclaves of excellence (De la Balze 1995, 44–47).

There is another significant difference between Spain and Argentina that merits discussion. It has to do with the underlying causes of political confrontations in the country, a contrast with direct implications for this comparative study. In Spain, political conflict has frequently had to do more with ideology and centrifugal nationalist movements than with economic interests. In Argentina, in addition to the much exaggerated threat of leftist insurgency, the cleavage between the export-oriented, agriculturally based sector, and the import-competing, domestically oriented one has generated much conflict (Peralta Ramos 1992; Waisman 1987). Not that Spain lacks that type of an economic conflict, but during the twentieth century it was overshadowed by ideological and ethnic-nationalist tensions. Since the 1940s, Argentine governments have stepped in vigorously to mediate in the dispute between the two economic sectors, taking sides with one or the other depending on their ideological preferences and bases of support. As a result, Argentina oscillated between nationalist and pragmatic populism, while Spain shifted toward nationalist-modernizing and later pragmatic-modernizing policies.

The Embrace of Pragmatism during the 1980s and 1990s

If the 1960s were referred to in Spain as the "prodigious decade," the 1980s and 1990s represent an even more revolutionary period. The Spanish transition to democracy following a model of institutional continuity became a textbook case of negotiated political reform, and one that has enabled the various interest groups—labor included (see chap. 5)—to become full political and economic actors. Economic reform, however, took longer and was much more painful than anticipated. Inflation soared during the 1970s and early 1980s, especially because entrenched interest groups (the professions, protected business interests, banks, labor) organized fairly quickly under the new democratic system so as to advance their price or wage demands (Bermeo 1994a, 1994b; Pérez Díaz 1993). Cost inflation and higher interest rates resulted in lower investment and hence higher unemployment. Demography did not help either. As the baby-boom generation of the early 1960s hit the labor market, unemployment skyrocketed to over 20 percent of the labor force during the early 1980s. Corporatist structures provoked a sharp fragmentation of the labor market along gender, permanent-temporary, and regional dimensions (Toharia Cortés 1994).

The Spanish policymaking establishment during the democratic transition became gradually dominated by a cadre of economists that strongly believed in internationalization and liberalization as the twin solutions to the economic crisis that so severely affected such industries as coal, steel, aluminum, shipbuilding, machinery, electronics, and even banking (Smith 1998; Cuervo 1988). This orientation built on the successes of the export-led growth model of the 1960s and hoped to continue the policy of integration in Europe foreshadowed by the Preferential Trade Agreement signed between Spain and the European Economic Community in 1970. In government circles, the focus was to shift gradually from corporatist institution building toward pragmatic-modernizing policymaking (Boix 1998, 105–29; Campa and Guillén 1996a, 1996b; Guillén 1989, 157–60; Maravall 1993; Pérez 1997; Smith 1998). In parallel, public opinion and even the attitudes of labor and business interest groups converged in their support of the process of integration with Europe. All meaningful political forces—from the moderate Right to the Left, and from business to labor—came to share the longing for integration with Europe. No other European country save for Italy scores higher in terms of public opinion support for European integration and institution building. In spite of the other conflicts still haunting Spanish society, a broad social and political consensus had emerged about the need for the country to join the European mainstream of democratic countries with a "social-market" economy (Álvarez-Miranda 1996; De la Sierra, Caballero, and Pérez Escanilla 1981; De Miguel and Linz 1963; Martinez 1993; see also chap. 5).

A crucial event in the trend toward pragmatic-modernizing policies was the commanding electoral victory of the Socialist Party in 1982 drawing on a broad, moderate, left-of-center coalition of blue- and white-collar voters. Historically proponents of import-substitution, nationalization, and fiscal expansion, the Socialists had shed their Marxist credentials during the late 1970s under the leadership of Felipe González. As head of the government, he appointed technocrats with links to the central bank as members of his economic policymaking team. The British and French debacles with fiscally expansionary policies still fresh in mind, González's team opted for fiscal, price, and wage moderation; for restructuring and privatization of state-owned enterprises; and for supply-side investments in general education, physical infrastructures, and social protection. These policies eventually brought inflation under control and stimulated private investment. Meanwhile, negotiations with the European Community were accelerated, causing a boom in foreign direct investment (Boix 1998, 105–29; Campa and Guillén 1996a, 1996b; Maravall 1993; Pérez 1997; Smith 1998).

Spain joined what is now known as the European Union in 1986. In 1998 — 100 years after the fateful end of the Spanish empire and the breakdown of national self-esteem — it became a founding member of Economic and Monetary Union in compliance with the strict Maastricht convergence criteria. As subsequent chapters will document, the road toward European Union membership had momentous consequences for business groups, small and medium enterprises, the banking sector, and foreign multinationals. As foreign trade and investment barriers fell, Spain embarked upon a development path with high inward and outward foreign trade and investment flows with the global economy (fig. 2.1). Inflation came down, investment and GDP grew vigorously (except during the 1991–92 recession), and unemployment stabilized and began to drop, albeit very slowly. The conservative government voted into office in 1996 has by and large continued, and intensified, the pragmatic-modernizing policies of the Socialists.

The massive arrival of foreign multinationals has been matched in part by Spanish direct investment abroad (see fig. 2.1). With a per capita income not far behind Spain's, the Korean stock of outward foreign direct investment represents only 3.8 percent of GDP compared to Spain's 9.0 percent. Spanish family firms started to invest abroad in distribution channels and production plants during the 1960s, especially in food processing, textiles, clothing, machinery, and auto parts (see chap. 4). In addition to these firms, a few large firms in oligopolistic or highly regulated industries such as telecommunications (Telefónica), utilities (Iberdrola, Endesa, Aguas de Barcelona, Gas Natural), oil (Repsol), construction (FCC, Ferrovial, Dragados), banking (see chap. 7), and transportation (Iberia) have invested heavily, especially in Latin America. Some of these companies have catapulted themselves onto Fortune's Global 500 list (Campa and Guillén 1996a, 1996b; Durán 1996, 1997, 1999; see also chaps. 4 and 7).

Free-market enthusiasts have proposed Spain as a model to emulate (e.g., Sachs 1993, 22–26). This once economically isolated country is now a major export power, not only of traditional products but also of automobiles, fabricated metals, machine tools, and a wide array of services. Both small and large Spanish firms have irrupted into the global economy as multinationals in their own right. The pragmatic-modernizing path, however, does not necessarily produce ideal outcomes along all dimensions. Employment, technology development, and managerial control remain areas of deep concern in Spanish society, and inflation has not been completely brought under control (see chap. 8).

Spain gravitated over time toward the pragmatic-modernizing development path in table 2.1 because of a mix of variables (see table 2.4). Its superb location close to rich and friendly countries combined with long-standing corporatist structures to produce a desire for economic integration with Europe. The ghosts of the past—the sense of inferiority, insolation, and authoritarianism—have given way since the early 1980s to a pragmatic, cosmopolitan set of policies proposed by a rather mainstream social democratic party and implemented by a relatively capable state bureaucracy. This shift took place hand in hand with a transition to democracy that—unlike in Argentina and South Korea—consolidated the role of parties as opposed to personalities, and incorporated organized labor into the political process and, occasionally, policymaking.

This chapter has provided an analysis of why Argentina, South Korea, and Spain followed different development paths. The next chapters focus on the consequences of each development path for organizational change at the firm and industry levels. The goal is to assess exactly what countries and firms can best do in the global economy given their institutional strengths and weaknesses. The analysis will show that specific patterns of success and failure result from different approaches to development and globalization, with no one of them being superior under all circumstances.

THREE

THE RISE AND FALL OF THE BUSINESS GROUPS

*The general orientation of the state toward economic development
and business may shape the structure of business groups.*
(Granovetter 1995, 122)

THE RISE of large, diversified business groups in newly industrialized
countries has captured the imagination of academics, journalists, and
policymakers. In this chapter, I argue that the proliferation of business
groups is best approached from a resource-based perspective, that is, by looking at the distinctive capabilities, strengths, and weaknesses of this form of
organization under different development circumstances. Business groups appear in newly industrialized countries because entrepreneurs and firms learn
the capability to combine the necessary domestic and foreign resources for
repeated industry entry. Combining domestic and foreign resources requires
entrepreneurs to establish networks of relationships with relevant actors. Such
a capability, however, can be developed and maintained as a valuable and
rare skill only under asymmetric foreign trade and investment conditions with
the rest of the world, that is, when the development path is either nationalist- *pp 28-30*
modernizing or pragmatic-populist. Such asymmetries allow diversified business groups to thrive at the expense of foreign multinationals and local small
and medium firms. The quantitative and qualitative historical evidence presented in this chapter comes from a variety of newly industrialized countries
and from the three countries under intensive comparative study—Argentina,
South Korea, and Spain. It shows that the proliferation of business groups
increases with asymmetry in foreign trade and investment.

Business Groups in Newly Industrialized Countries

Institutional theory aspires to understand the existence of various organizational forms in terms of economic, sociological, and political variables (Scott
1992, 150–79). One of the most puzzling questions confronting the field concerns the great diversity of organizations engendered by economic development. The relative proliferation of family firms, business groups, state-owned
enterprises, subsidiaries of foreign multinationals, and worker-owned cooperatives, among other organizational forms, exhibits significant differences across

newly industrialized countries (Orrù, Biggart, and Hamilton 1997; Fields 1995; Gereffi 1990b).

The explanation of business groups presented in this chapter combines insights from the resource-based view in the field of business strategy and from international political economy. As outlined in chapter 1, a comparative institutional theory of development and globalization emphasizes resources and capabilities for action. Thus, it rests in part on the assumption that firms and organizational forms are phenomenological accomplishments that differ from each other because they accumulate distinctive capabilities over time (Biggart and Guillén 1999). The so-called resource-based view of the firm in the field of business strategy provides an understanding of the sources and consequences of such heterogeneity across firms (Barney 1986, 1991; Peteraf 1993). Like development theorists, students of business strategy have long been fascinated by why firms find it attractive to diversify into related and unrelated product lines (Hoskisson and Hitt 1990; Ramanujam and Varadarajan 1989). The large modern corporation in the United States and Western Europe grew within a core technology family and, subsequently, through related diversification (Chandler 1990). By contrast, large business groups operating in a wide range of unrelated manufacturing and service industries are characteristic of many capitalist countries that industrialized after World War II (Amsden and Hikino 1994; Granovetter 1995; Khanna and Palepu 1997). Business groups are more diversified than the Chandlerian modern industrial enterprise, but less coordinated (Amsden 1989, 125).

Theories of Business Groups

A business group is a "collection of firms bound together in some formal and/ or informal ways" (Granovetter 1995, 95). Diversified business groups have three main features: they are active in a wide variety of industries, operate under the general guidance of a single entrepreneur, and fall short of constituting a fully integrated organizational structure. The Korean *chaebol*, the Indian *business houses*, the Pakistani and Turkish family holdings, or the Latin American and Spanish *grupos*, among others, come to mind as examples of such business groups. By contrast, the Japanese *keiretsu* (Gerlach 1992), the Chinese *guanxiqiye* networks in Taiwan and among the overseas Chinese throughout Southeast Asia (Orrù, Biggart, and Hamilton 1997), or the Italian small-firm industrial districts (Piore and Sabel 1984) are mere interorganizational alliances lacking the entrepreneurial coordination proposed in the above definition. Diversified business groups in newly industrialized economies are also different from the conglomerates of the advanced countries in that they grew not in search of financial diversification but as a result of their ability to set up new business ventures across a variety of industries quickly and at low cost.

The existence of diversified business groups in newly industrialized economies long after the conglomerate form fell from grace in the most advanced countries has generated a considerable theoretical and empirical literature (Amsden and Hikino 1994; Caves 1989; Granovetter 1995). This section reviews the assumptions, predictions, and pitfalls of previous theories of development when it comes to understanding the importance of business groups in newly industrialized countries. I then propose an alternative, resource-based approach that draws on the classification of development paths outlined in chapter 2.

Development scholars have proposed three different ways to approach the phenomenon of business groups in newly industrialized economies. They have made different assumptions and formulated different predictions as to the conditions under which business groups become an important actor in the economy. Each of the theories emphasizes a different domestic factor to account for the importance of business groups: market failure, state autonomy, or dependency.

Modernization and neoclassical theories assume that diversified business groups fill "institutional voids," especially because of the absence of well-functioning markets for production inputs. Thus, they regard business groups as functional substitutes for markets that fail (Leff 1978, 1979; Khanna and Palepu 1997, 1999). Entrepreneurs seek to internalize "market failures" as they try to obtain the capital, labor, raw materials, components, and technology they need to undertake production. Business groups step in where the market does not work or is not allowed to work by "information problems," "misguided regulations," or "inefficient judicial systems" (Caves 1989; Khanna and Palepu 1997, 1999). For example, if the capital market is narrow and does not work efficiently, economists predict that the firm will tend to withhold earnings and develop internal capital allocation mechanisms to guide funds to their best economic use within the firm itself, either in an existing business or in a new one. Business groups appear and grow in an economy to the extent that the failure of its capital market invites firms to invest retained earnings in new businesses as the rate of return in existing businesses drops with further additions of capital. Thus, the main prediction of the market failure view is that economies with greater market imperfections will contain more business groups.

Late-industrialization theorists propose to see business group formation and growth as a process driven by the state and/or the banks. Scholars of East Asian development have observed that "autonomous" states with the ability to allocate capital and other resources at will encourage a few entrepreneurs to enter new industries, thus facilitating the proliferation of business groups. Autonomous states are those that are free from socially rooted demands and from struggles among class or group interests when it comes to setting their goals and/or pursuing them (Carruthers 1994). Autonomous policymakers are in a position to formulate their own economic agenda ahead of social demands or even against those demands. Moreover, late-industrialization scholars are adamant that autonomous states prefer to deal with only a few entrepreneurs as their agents in the private sector so that accountability and control can be maximized and the state's freedom of action safeguarded (Amsden 1989). These entrepreneurs will be repeatedly asked by the state to enter new industries as development efforts escalate from light manufacturing to heavy industry and capital goods production. South Korea is presented as a typical illustration of this state-driven pattern of business group growth (Amsden 1989; Fields 1995; E. M. Kim 1997). Therefore, late-industrialization theory predicts that the importance of business groups in newly industrialized economies will be greater in countries in which the state is an autonomous actor.

Dependency theorists argue that even if the state pursues an import-substitution strategy and falls prey to interest groups or lacks control over the financial system, business groups will become important as the "nonautonomous" state uses its budget and activities to secure the political and economic support of entrepreneurs for its strategy of internal development by enabling them to exploit rent-seeking opportunities. The technological and organizational requirements of import-substitution industrialization are predicted to result in a pattern of "dependent development" in which a "triple alliance" among foreign multinationals, the state, and a few large local business groups dominates the economy (Evans 1979, 280–85; see also Frank 1967, 281–318). It should be carefully noted that Evans (1979, 277–79) sees the state as the central actor in the triple alliance. Dependency scholars expect newly industrialized countries with greater levels of state and/or foreign multinational activity to be home to more business groups.

Previous development theories, however, do not consider how entrepreneurs and firms build rare, valuable, inimitable, and excess *capabilities* that enable them to diversify into unrelated product-market areas *in the face of competition from other organizational forms such as nondiversified firms and foreign multinationals.* Existing theories of business groups do not clarify how exactly entrepreneurs manage to acquire distinctive capabilities that enable them to diversify. Market failure theory focuses entirely on factor markets to the exclusion of product markets in which the business group as an organizational form competes against other types of domestic and foreign producers. Like market failure theory, dependency and late-industrialization analyses (e.g., Amsden 1989; Amsden and Hikino 1994; Evans 1979; Frank 1967) fail to explain how an entrepreneur or firm can sustain diversification in the face of competition from other domestic and foreign firms, or how business groups continue to diversify even after the state decides to curtail their activities because their growing power threatens the state's.

The importance of providing an explanation of how business groups can sustain their diversification requires an alternative view based on limits to resource access and capability building. This chapter argues that entrepreneurs and firms in newly industrialized countries create business groups if political-economic conditions allow them to acquire (and maintain over time as valuable and inimitable) a Schumpeterian capability of combining foreign and domestic resources—inputs, processes, and market access—to repeatedly enter new industries (Schumpeter 1934). The logic of diversification of business groups in newly industrialized countries entails repeated access to combinations of domestic and foreign resources rather than scope economies or transaction-cost minimization. Therefore, diversifying entrepreneurs or firms will rarely bother to build integrated organizational structures capable of capturing cross-industry synergies (e.g., Chandler 1982, 1990; Hoskisson 1987; Hill and Hoskisson 1987). The looser business group form will suffice.

The next section specifies the relationship between business groups and the different political-economic conditions or development paths described in chapter 2. The point of departure is Granovetter's (1995, 122) lead: "the general orientation of the state toward economic development and business may shape the structure of business groups." The central argument is that nationalist-modernizing and pragmatic-populist paths lead to the proliferation of business groups, while the pragmatic-modernizing or the nationalist-populist paths privilege other organizational forms.

Resources, Economic Development, and Business Groups

Entrepreneurs and firms need to gain access to three types of resources when entering an industry: inputs (labor, capital, raw materials), technology, and market access in the forms of distribution channels and contracts with foreign and domestic customers or with the state (Markides and Williamson 1996). Entrepreneurs and firms that learn how to combine such resources quickly and effectively will be best able to create a business group by repeatedly entering a variety of industries. This capability for repeated industry entry consists of a bundle of complementary skills that facilitate conducting feasibility studies, obtaining licenses from the state, arranging financial packages, securing technology and know-how, building plants, hiring and training the workforce, and establishing supply and distribution channels. While modernization and neoclassical economists remain silent on the issue of firm-level resources, dependency theorists refer to the skills required for new industry entry as "integrative abilities" (Evans 1979, 281), and late-industrialization scholars call them "project-execution capabilities" (Amsden and Hikino 1994) or "capabilities to diversify" (Amsden 1989, 151, 174). In fact, both dependency and late-industrialization scholars note that business groups emerge at the center of dense networks of contacts with the state and with foreign multinationals (Evans 1979, 154–58, 280–82; Frank 1967, 210–11; Amsden 1989, 139–55, 231–35).

Implicit in dependency and late-industrialization analyses is the fact that the capability to combine resources for industry entry is generic in nature and difficult to trade because it is embodied in the organization's founder, owners, managers, and routines. It is also assumed to be in excess supply immediately after the entrepreneur or firm consummates entry into a new industry. Once the new plant has been set up and is in production, the capability to enter new industries becomes idle. Therefore, it is a capability that, as predicted by the resource-based view (Peteraf 1993), encourages those who possess it to diversify across industries rather than become specialists in one industry or product line.

While dependency and late-industrialization theories identify a generic and nontradable capability as the key to business group formation, they fail to specify the conditions that enable entrepreneurs to maintain that capability as an inimitable and valuable asset against the interests and competition of other organizational forms, including nondiversified firms and foreign multinationals. This theoretical problem is most apparent in Amsden and Hikino's (1994) analysis. A generic and nontradable capability to combine the resources necessary for industry entry is not sufficient for a business group to sustain its advantages in a variety of industries over time. According to the resource-based view, it is imperative that certain limits to competition exist so that the capability can be accumulated through a process of learning by doing, and maintained over time as inimitable and hence valuable (Peteraf 1993; Markides and Williamson 1996). Such limits may result from a variety of "barriers," ranging from causal ambiguity and time lags to size advantages and preferential access to resources. For reasons of superior foresight or even sheer luck, entrepreneurs and firms may be heterogeneous in their ability to enter new industries because access to the required resources is, or has been, unevenly distributed (Barney 1986).

Development Strategies and Limits to Resource Access

Previous development scholarship has not paid enough attention to the fact that access to resources by entrepreneurs and firms in newly industrialized countries is very sensitive to the development path followed by each country. In particular, foreign trade and direct investment patterns tend to have a momentous impact on resource accessibility by entrepreneurs and firms. In newly industrialized countries—unlike in the more advanced ones—some of the resources for new industry entry are domestic (labor, access to home market), while others, at least in part, are situated beyond the country's boundaries (raw materials, capital, technology, know-how, access to foreign markets). If foreign trade and investment policies are such that only local entrepreneurs and firms can combine the required domestic and foreign resources, they may be in a position to accumulate a valuable and inimitable capability that enables them to enter a variety of industries quickly. Business groups will result as entrepreneurs and firms with that capability enter one industry after another.

As explained in chapter 2, research on the political economy of development suggests that it is crucial to distinguish between outward and inward foreign trade and investment flows because they need not be correlated with each other. When flows are asymmetric, they create the potential for heterogeneity in resource access and capability building by entrepreneurs (Guillén 1997b, 2000a). Inward and outward flows appear cross-classified in table 3.1. The impact of different development paths on the proliferation of business groups and other organizational forms can be directly derived from the characteristics of each of the four configurations in the table. Subsidiaries of foreign multinational enterprises (MNEs) are more likely to proliferate in the two upper cells, characterized by permissive policies toward inward investment, while state-owned enterprises should be more likely in the two lower cells, with restricted inward flows resulting from nationalist policies such as protectionism and a preference for domestic ownership.

Predicting which cells are more munificent to business groups (or to firms affiliated to business groups) is a more complicated question that requires additional analysis. The circumstances associated with the two symmetric cells on the diagonal of table 3.1, that is, the high-high/pragmatic-modernizing and the low-low/nationalist-populist, do not produce heterogeneity in resource access across entrepreneurs and firms. By contrast, the other two configurations are asymmetric situations in which only some (local) entrepreneurs and firms have access to domestic and foreign resources simultaneously. Business groups will appear when such asymmetries persist long enough to allow entrepreneurs and firms to develop a combinative capability that encourages them to enter multiple industries. Let us examine each configuration, noting the implications of foreign trade and investment flows for business group formation, and the limitations of previous theories of development in predicting the rise of various organizational forms.

Business Groups under Asymmetric Conditions

The two off-diagonal cells in table 3.1 describe situations with asymmetric foreign trade and investment flows. First, the low-high configuration of nationalist-modernizing countries offers the well-connected entrepreneur or firm the possibility of contributing to export-led development by combining domestic and foreign resources under such restrictive inward policies as protection against imports and limited inward foreign investment. As resource-based researchers have argued (Markides and Williamson 1996; Peteraf 1993), preferential access to resources constitutes a competitive capability only if it enables diversification that is beyond the means of other actors. Under nationalist-modernizing development such inputs as local labor or physical resources

TABLE 3.1
Foreign Trade, Foreign Investment, and Business Groups in Newly
Industrialized Countries

Level of Inward Flows	Level of Outward Flows	
	High (modernizing)	Low (populist)
High (pragmatic)	HIGH: Allow Imports and Inward investment HIGH: Export-led growth and Outward investment Context conducive to: Foreign MNEs & SMEs 4	HIGH: Allow Imports and Inward investment LOW: Import substitution and Local investment Context conducive to: Foreign MNEs & Business groups 1
Low (nationalist)	3 LOW: Protectionism and Local ownership HIGH: Export-led growth and Outward investment Context conducive to: State firms & Business groups	2 LOW: Protectionism and Local ownership LOW: Import substitution and Local investment Context conducive to: State firms & SMEs

Note: MNEs stands for multinational enterprises; SMEs for small and medium enterprises.

will be available only to domestic entrepreneurs and firms and not to foreign MNEs as long as their access is restricted by nationalist policies. In its drive to increase exports, the state is likely to channel preferential investment or export loans to certain entrepreneurs and firms. Process-related knowledge will be available only to the few entrepreneurs who have connections to foreign multinationals or can be trusted by them. Given that the ability to set up and run manufacturing plants or service operations is subject to a steep learning curve, entrepreneurs and firms who manage to repeatedly obtain operating permits from the government and technology licenses from a foreign MNE will be in a position to reduce the cost of entering new industries (Amsden and Hikino 1994; Caves 1996, 168, 171). This experience effect will advantage diversified business groups over nondiversified firms when it comes to enter a new industry. Finally, access to markets can be allocated in discriminating ways by the government (domestic market entry permissions, contracts with the state, certification of general trading companies for export) or by foreign MNEs (original equipment manufacturing contracts for export).

Late-industrialization theorists prescribe policies conducive to nationalist-modernizing development. However, they predict the rise of business groups because the autonomous state prefers to deal with only a few entrepreneurs for control and accountability reasons (Amsden 1989). The continued growth of business groups, however, is likely to undermine the presumed reason for their own existence—state autonomy. The resource-based view adopted here improves late-industrialization analysis because it can account for the continued growth of business groups even when the government starts worrying about their increasing power and leverage. The capability to combine resources for industry entry will remain inimitable as long as low-high foreign trade and investment flows persist, encouraging those who possess it to enter multiple industries so as to fully utilize it. It is important to realize that in restricting imports and inward foreign investment governments make it possible for business groups to grow at the expense of foreign firms and, indirectly, small and medium firms. Thus, business groups are seen here neither as a substitute for poorly developed markets nor as the result of state autonomy but as substitutes for foreign MNEs and small and medium firms.

The second off-diagonal cell in table 3.1 represents the high-low, or pragmatic-populist, strategy. Entrepreneurs and firms who manage to establish ties to the state, foreign MNEs, and moneylenders will benefit in a way that mirrors the low-high configuration. Typical of countries in the pragmatic-populist cell is a relaxation or even liberalization of regulations concerning foreign equity investment, especially when import-substitution efforts escalate from consumer nondurable goods to intermediate, durable, and capital goods (Haggard 1990; Evans 1979). This is an asymmetric development path insofar as exports and outward foreign investment remain low. MNE involvement in an import-substitution environment is more likely if the state introduces incentives and limits entry to only a few, noncompeting players (Evans 1979, 163–64). Moreover, states invoke "nationalistic" ideologies to support policies encouraging foreign multinationals to add value locally (Evans 1979, 49). In the pragmatic-populist environment, foreign MNEs will tend to manufacture or distribute their products in collaboration with local entrepreneurs who know how to navigate the treacherous conditions created by economic and political populism, including powerful labor unions, import-competing interests among the local businesses, idiosyncratic credit allocation practices, and attempts by the state to force MNEs to contribute to "local accumulation" through control sharing (Evans 1979, 44, 163–212). MNEs may also choose to sell manufacturing licenses to local entrepreneurs either because attaining minimally efficient plant scales is difficult inside the country or because access to personnel, natural resources, and distribution channels is important but hard for a foreigner to obtain. A similar argument applies in the case of privatizations of state-owned enterprises, a typical policy initiative in pragmatic-populist countries that tends to attract coalitions of foreign MNEs and local entrepreneurs with complementary skills.

Dependency theorists predict the rise of business groups under pragmatic-populist development as part of the triple alliance among the leading local entrepreneurs, foreign MNEs, and the state. Moreover, they argue that the "vast majority of the local bourgeoisie"—the small and medium-sized firms—will be marginalized (Evans 1979, 282–83). The resource-based view, however, clarifies that state and multinational activity in an economy undergoing import-substitution growth is not enough to sustain the advantages of diversified business groups over time. Trade and foreign investment flows need to be asymmetric for entrepreneurs and firms to be able to enter a variety of new industries, forming a business group in the process. Their cumulative experience in repeated industry entry will advantage them over nondiversified entrepreneurs or firms and MNEs as long as conditions do not shift. Most importantly, the resource-based view presents business groups as brokers between domestic and foreign actors, while dependency theorists argue that the state is the broker (Evans 1979, 277–79). Finally, the resource-based view sees business groups as substitutes for foreign MNEs, while dependency sees them as complementary organizational forms.

The Disadvantages of Business Groups under Symmetric Conditions

Symmetric foreign trade and investment flows reduce or even delete the value of the generic capability to enter a variety of industries. When both inward and outward trade and investment flows are simultaneously at high or at low levels, domestic entrepreneurs have no exclusive claim to resources. Under high-high conditions foreign MNEs, for example, can freely operate inside the country and across its borders in either direction, and they will locate activities in the country that are export competitive. Local knowledge about inputs might still be important, but freedom to operate will facilitate international sourcing and other integration strategies that are likely to lie beyond the reach of local business groups. Knowledge about the domestic market will lose value as the MNE uses its operations in the country to sell in foreign markets where it is already established. Moreover, a local firm not affiliated to a business group will also be at an advantage over those affiliated to one as long as it develops product-focused expertise and avoids the liabilities that membership in a group entails: resource sharing, mutual loan guarantees, cross subsidization, and so on. Hence, one would expect the capability to combine domestic and foreign resources to lose its inimitability, rarity, and value as inward and outward trade and investment become more symmetric.

The market-failure approach to the existence of business groups—espoused by modernization and neoclassical theories of development—cannot explain why it is local business groups and not foreign MNEs that internalize inefficient input market transactions by bringing them within the boundaries of the firm. The resource-based view, by contrast, offers an explanation based on limits to resource access. The capability to enter new industries is only valuable and inimitable when foreign trade and investment flows are asymmetric. When development policies cause inward and outward flows to be simultaneously high—as prescribed by both modernization and neoclassical theories—foreign MNEs can tackle whatever market failures persist much more readily than local business groups. Thus, market failure could be conceptualized as a necessary condition for the appearance business groups, but never as a sufficient condition because, in the absence of asymmetries, foreign MNEs are generally better prepared to fill in for market failures.

The low-low configuration in table 3.1 is not conducive to business groups either, for two reasons. First, import-substitution processes that exclude direct foreign activity typically result in a variety of bottlenecks that slow down the growth of new industries due to the lack of appropriate technology and capital, either in form of loans or direct investment. Opportunities for diversification will be reduced if the requisite technology and capital are not available. Thus, low-low conditions are likely to result in market saturation and sluggish economic growth, problems that tend to inhibit business concentration in the long run, for they make it difficult for firms to obtain the foreign resources necessary to grow and diversify. As Evans (1979, 315) has pointed out, "strategies that put autarky ahead of accumulation are not permitted to countries in which the triple alliance [among business groups, multinationals, and the state] dominates the political and economic scene." The second reason is that maintaining a "low profile" is politically more advantageous in a nationalist-populist context because private businesses, whether domestic or foreign, come under the threat of expropriation (Haggard 1990; Kaufman and Stallings 1991). It should be noted that nationalist-populist conditions usually lead to widespread market failure. Contrary to modernization and neoclassical theories of development, however, the resource-based view (or dependency theory for that matter) does not predict the rise, growth, or proliferation of business groups under such circumstances.

Based on the analysis summarized in table 3.1, business groups are expected to appear and thrive in newly industrialized countries when asymmetric trade and investment conditions enable a few entrepreneurs and firms to develop the capability of combining foreign and domestic resources for repeated industry entry. These entrepreneurs or firms prosper because they are in a position to act as brokers in a political-economic structure of competition characterized by restricted cross-border access to resources. Such asymmetries—akin to what Burt (1992) calls "structural holes"—enable actors who can bridge them to diversify into a variety of industries. The advantages associated with the capability to act as a cross-border resource broker can be sustained only to the extent that asymmetries in foreign trade and investment persist over time.

It is important to note that a comparative institutional theory of business groups anticipates predictions that are roughly consistent with those made by modernization, neoclassical, late-industrialization, and dependency theories of development, although it presents an alternative, competing explanatory process. Thus, the disagreement lies not in the predictions per se (see table 3.1) but in the causal mechanism that enables sustained diversification in the form of a business group. Modernization and neoclassical theories propose a pragmatic-modernizing development strategy and predict no business groups unless there is input market failure. The comparative institutional perspective argues that business groups do not decline when market institutions are fully developed but when the symmetric foreign trade and investment policies prescribed by both modernization and neoclassical theories render the capability of repeated industry entry obsolete. Asymmetries may be seen as a form of market failure, but primarily on the output side as opposed to the input side.

Late-industrialization theory prescribes a nationalist-modernizing strategy and predicts business groups as the result of the policies of an autonomous state that prefers to deal with only a few entrepreneurs. A comparative institutional perspective points out that business groups will continue to grow even after the state's autonomy is threatened by the growth of the business groups if and only if asymmetric foreign trade and investment conditions persist. Dependency theory predicts the rise of business groups in a pragmatic-populist context because domestic accumulation can only be maximized by a triple alliance of state, foreign, and (some) local capital. The comparative institutional perspective notes, however, that business groups exist to the extent that asymmetries in foreign trade and investment enable them to use their industry-entry capability as leverage against other organizational forms—foreign MNEs, state-owned enterprises, and small and medium firms. The key contribution of the comparative institutional perspective is precisely to bring previous theories of business groups under the same conceptual umbrella, thus exposing some of their inconsistencies and clarifying the underlying causal mechanism common to the four development contexts in table 3.1. The next section presents data corroborating the explanatory power of the comparative institutional theory of business groups presented above.

Comparative Evidence: Quantitative Analyses

Comparable data on the fortunes of business groups across newly industrialized countries are surprisingly lacking in the literature (Amsden and Hikino 1994; Granovetter 1995). Three kinds of evidence are presented in this section to demonstrate that asymmetric foreign trade and investment flows lie at the root of the proliferation of business groups, and that shifts toward symmetric flows cause them to decline. First, aggregate statistics for a sample of nine developing countries will be used to show the limitations of alternative explanations and provide cross-sectional support for the proposition that the presence of business groups is associated with asymmetries in foreign trade and investment. Second, longitudinal evidence is given on the presence of business groups among the largest 100 firms in Argentina, South Korea, and Spain between two points in time, 1975 and 1995. And third, qualitative historical evidence documents that the capability to combine domestic and foreign resources is accumulated under asymmetric foreign trade and investment conditions, and remains rare and valuable only as long as those conditions persist.

Business Groups across Newly Industrialized Countries

Table 3.2 presents an indicator of the importance of business groups for a cross-sectional sample of nine newly industrialized countries in South and East Asia, Latin America, and southern Europe. For each country, the total net sales figure for the top ten business groups circa 1995 was divided by Gross Domestic Product (column A). Comparable data do not exist for other newly industrialized countries because many business groups refuse to disclose financial figures aggregated at the group level. This indicator ranges from 4.9 percent in Spain to 48.6 percent in South Korea. Contrary to the market failure thesis, stock market capitalization (column B) is positively correlated with the total sales of the top ten business groups as a percentage of GDP. The positive correlation between business groups and state autonomy (column C) lends credence to late-industrialization theory (Amsden 1989). Dependency theory, by contrast, does not seem to predict well the importance of business groups across this sample of countries because the correlation of column A with the indicators of state (column D) or multinational (column E) activity in each country is negative. Simple correlations, therefore, do not lend support to the "triple alliance" thesis (Evans 1979).

The measures of asymmetries in terms of foreign trade or investment are highly correlated with the sales of the top ten business groups and in the predicted direction. Columns F and G in table 3.2 show, respectively, the index of asymmetry in foreign trade—calculated as the absolute difference between z-scores for imports and z-scores for exports—and the index of asymmetry in foreign investment—the absolute difference between z-scores for inward and outward stocks of foreign direct investment. These two indexes are highly correlated with each other (0.61), indicating that the countries in the sample tend to adopt mutually consistent foreign trade and investment policies. The indexes are highly and positively correlated with business groups (0.74 and 0.50, respectively). Countries characterized by a higher asymmetry

TABLE 3.2
Correlates of the Importance of Business Groups in Newly Industrialized Countries, 1995

	A. Sales of Top 10 Business Groups (% GDP)	B. Total Stock Market Capitalization (% GDP)	C. State Autonomy Index [a]	D. General Government Consumption (% GDP)	E. Inward Foreign Direct Investment (% GDP)	F. Asymmetry in Foreign Trade [b,c]	G. Asymmetry in Foreign Direct Investment [b,d]
Argentina	11.1	17.05	0.46	17.20	8.70	0.58	0.40
Brazil	7.5	21.46	0.19	17.12	17.80	0.21	0.39
Colombia	27.9	23.51	0.55	8.84	12.10	0.26	0.34
India	5.8	38.37	0.44	11.37	1.90	0.53	0.56
Indonesia	24.5	33.62	1.00	8.21	25.20	1.27	2.01
South Korea	48.6	39.95	0.59	10.36	2.30	1.50	1.69
Mexico	10.4	36.27	0.72	10.28	25.60	0.24	1.31
Spain	4.9	35.41	0.21	16.32	17.60	0.43	0.56
Taiwan	18.6	102.63	0.26	15.07	7.30	0.49	2.07
Theory being assessed		Market failure[e]	Late-industrialization	Dependency	Dependency	Comparative institutional (resource-based view)	
Predicted correlation with A		−	+	+	+	+	+
Actual correlation with A		+0.10	+0.43	−0.55	−0.30	+0.74	+0.50

Source: Column A: Argentina: Bisang 1994a, 17 (data are for 1993). Brazil: *Exame*, <www.uol.com.br>. Colombia: *Poder y Dinero*, March 1997, <www.dinero.com>. India: Centre for Monitoring the Indian Economy (data are for 1993). Indonesia: <www.indobiz.com>. South Korea: Asia-Pacific Infoserv 1996. Mexico: *Expansión*, as provided by McKinsey and Co., Mexico Office. Spain: Fomento de la Producción 1996. Taiwan: China Credit Information Service (data are for 1994). Column B: IFC 1998. Column C: based on data from the Polity III database (Gurr 1990). Column D: World Bank. Column E: United Nations. Column F: World bank, United Nations. Column G: World Bank, United Nations.

[a] Inverse of Henisz's (1998) index of political constraints for 1994 based on data from the Polity III database (Gurr 1990).

[b] The correlation between columns F and G is +0.61.

[c] Absolute difference between z-scores for total exports and z-scores for imports of consumer goods and passenger cars, both as a percentage of GDP. Imports of raw materials and capital goods are usually very high in countries attempting to develop. Therefore, imports of consumer goods and passenger cars and not total imports are used so as to capture to what extent the country protects its domestic firms.

[d] Absolute difference between z-scores for the log of outward FDI and z-scores for inward FDI, both expressed as a percentage of GDP.

[e] Includes the predictions of both moderization and neoclassical theories.

in foreign trade or in foreign investment tend to have a greater presence of business groups. A multivariate regression analysis of the data summarized in table 3.2 shows that the index of asymmetry in foreign investment is the only variable that consistently and significantly predicts the importance of the top ten business groups relative to the size of the economy. The index of asymmetry in foreign trade is a significant predictor in some regression specifications but not others (Guillén 2000a). Thus, the cross-sectional evidence strongly suggests that business groups thrive in newly industrialized countries where asymmetric access to domestic and foreign resources is the rule.

Longitudinal Analysis: Business Groups among the Top 100 Firms in 1975 and 1995

The connection between business group formation and asymmetric political-economic conditions can be further examined empirically by a longitudinal analysis of effects of the different development paths followed by Spain, South Korea, and Argentina. Data on the presence of companies affiliated to business groups among the 100 largest nonfinancial firms in each of the three countries at two points in time provide a useful longitudinal indicator of the importance of business groups. The rankings of the top 100 firms in terms of total sales were obtained from a combination of sources for each country and year. Multiple reference sources and field interviews were used to code whether a firm belonged to one of the 30 largest business groups in the country, a foreign MNE, or the state. Firms that could not be assigned to any of these three categories were left in a residual one, including companies affiliated to a group that was not among the top 30, worker-owned cooperatives, and firms with dispersed control.

Table 3.3 displays the cross-classification of the largest 100 firms by country and organizational form in 1975 and 1995. In 1975 Korea, Argentina, and Spain had proportions of firms affiliated to one of the 30 largest business groups of 41, 22, and 21 percent, respectively. By 1995 the proportion had sharply grown to 79 in Korea, increased slightly to 27 in Argentina, and plunged to 11 in Spain. The growth of the top 30 Korean business groups came at the expense of foreign MNEs and other smaller groups, indicating that increasing asymmetries in foreign trade and investment displace from the top 100 list companies that are not affiliated to one of the 30 largest groups. The distribution of the top 100 firms in Argentina experienced an important change between 1975 and 1995: state-owned enterprises have almost disappeared in the wake of privatization, with business groups and MNEs gaining share albeit modestly. In Spain, by contrast, the same 20-year period witnessed a sharp rise in the presence of MNEs among the top 100 firms, primarily at the expense of the business groups.

TABLE 3.3

The Top 100 Nonfinancial Firms in South Korea, Spain, and Argentina in
1975 and 1995, by Organizational Form

Organizational Form	South Korea 1975	South Korea 1995	Spain 1975	Spain 1995	Argentina 1975	Argentina 1995
Firms affiliated with a business group[a]	41	79	22	11	21	27
Subsidiaries of foreign multinationals	7	1	28	44	43	46
State-owned enterprises	4	4	24	24	21	2
Other[b]	48	16	26	21	15	25
Total	100	100	100	100	100	100
Explanatory variables						
Stock market capitalization (% GDP)	6.01[c]	39.95	7.85[c]	35.41	5.02[c]	17.05
State autonomy index	1.00	0.59	0.33	0.21	1.00	0.46
Size of the state (% GDP)	11.14	10.36	10.45	16.32	12.59	17.20
Asymmetry in foreign trade	1.15	1.50	1.01	0.43	0.02	0.58
Asymmetry in foreign investment	1.20[c]	1.69	1.67[c]	0.56	0.45[c]	0.40

Source: South Korea: *1978 Ki Eop Che Yeon Kam* (Yearbook of Korean Company, 1978), by Kyung je Tong Shin Sa; *Han Kook Ki Eop Eui Sung Jang Jeon Ryak Kwa Kyung Young Koo Jo* (Growing strategies and management structures of Korean businesses), by Dai Han Sang Kong Hoi Eui So (1987), 207–9; Korea Investors Service, *Financial Report of Korean Companies*, several years; Jones and Sakong 1980; Asia-Pacific Infoserv 1996. Spain: Fomento de la Producción Roldán, and Serrano 1976, 1996; Muñoz 1978. Argentina: Prensa Económica 1975; Acevedo, Basualdo and Khavisse 1990; <www.mercado.com>. Sources for the explanatory variables are reported in table 3.2.

[a] Includes firms affiliated with one of the 30 largest business groups in the country.

[b] Includes unaffiliated firms, worker-owned cooperatives, and firms with dispersed ownership.

[c] Data for 1980 (not available for 1975).

The lower panel of table 3.3 shows the values of the explanatory variables in 1975 and 1995. Stock market capitalization grew in the three countries between 1975 and 1995, while state autonomy dropped in all three. Thus neither of these two variables accounts for the varying fortunes of business groups across countries. The size of the state remained about the same in

Korea, but grew in both Spain and Argentina. Yet in Spain business groups declined while they became slightly more prominent in Argentina. The rise of business groups in Korea between 1975 and 1995 coincided with a sustained increase in the indexes of foreign trade and investment asymmetry. Similarly, the decline of the groups in Spain went hand in hand with a continuous reduction in the asymmetries. In the case of Argentina, however, the analysis of the coevolution of business groups and political-economic asymmetries based on two points in time does not lend support to the theory. By contrast to Korea and Spain, Argentine foreign trade and investment flows did not evolve monotonically between 1975 and 1995 but erratically (see fig. 2.1), making it more difficult to draw inferences with information at just two points in time. On the whole, the patterns of evolution of company control shown in table 3.3 cannot be explained by previous theories of business groups. Foreign trade and investment asymmetries, by contrast, seem to be intimately associated with the fortunes of business groups.

Results from a log-linear analysis of the 600 firms across the three countries and over time indicate that the differences in organizational form shown in table 3.3 are statistically significant (see Guillén 2000a). Relative to Argentina and to the 1975 baseline, significantly more firms were controlled by a business group in Korea by 1995 ($\chi^2 = 8.80$, $p < 0.01$), and significantly fewer in Spain ($\chi^2 = 16.45$, $p < 0.001$). These findings support the argument that business groups rise (decline) in importance relative to other organizational forms as foreign trade and investment become more asymmetric (symmetric) over time.

Comparative Evidence: Case Studies

The quantitative evidence presented above demonstrates a significant correlation between asymmetric development strategies and the presence of business groups, both cross-sectionally and over time. Proving that asymmetric policies cause business groups to rise, however, necessitates qualitative historical evidence. Field research (see the appendix) and the voluminous literature on the industrialization of South Korea, Argentina, and Spain provide myriad details about the origins and growth of each country's largest business groups that lend unambiguous support for a causal argument. The historical evidence presented below shows that business groups in these countries: (1) rose to prominence thanks to their contacts to the state and to foreign MNEs during periods of asymmetric foreign trade and investment conditions; (2) developed the capability to enter a variety of industries drawing on their access to domestic and foreign resources; and (3) resisted attempts by the state to reduce the asymmetries in foreign trade and investment.

The South Korean Chaebol's Rise to Prominence

The underlying logic of business group formation in an asymmetric nationalist-modernizing context is well illustrated by the case of the Korean chaebol.[1] Previous research has noted that establishing and nurturing ties to the government has been essential to the chaebol's growth (Lim 1985, 113–14; Haggard 1990, 197–203; Fields 1995; Levy 1991; Ungson, Steers, and Park 1997). A few studies have pointed out that ties to foreign MNEs have also been important (Westphal, Rhee, and Pursell 1979; E. M. Kim 1997; Ungson, Steers, and Park 1997, 140–51). The overwhelming presence of the business groups in the Korean economy has its roots in the importance of political connections to obtain such resources as permits to enter new industries, government contracts, subsidized loans, export incentives, import licenses to acquire equipment and raw materials, and permissions to hire workers. The state policymaking apparatus created by General Park in the 1960s preferred to deal with a handful of entrepreneurs, for the obvious control reasons, and persuaded the favored ones to enter risky undertakings by expanding their licenses in already established and profitable industries, protecting them from foreign imports, and lending them money at subsidized rates. In addition to favoring a few entrepreneurs, the Korean state exhibited an early bias against foreign-owned enterprises, making it possible for the privileged domestic entrepreneurs to increase their exports and outward foreign investment without having to face significant imports and inward foreign investment (Kang 1996b, 25–31; Fields 1995; E. M. Kim 1997, 125–32; Lim 1985, 90–93; Jones and Sakong 1980; Westphal, Rhee, and Pursell 1979). Thus, business groups (in manufacturing and trading) and state-owned enterprises—in steel, electricity, gas, railroads, and highways (Amsden 1989, 90–92)—grew in importance, as predicted for the nationalist-modernizing configuration of table 3.1.

The Korean entrepreneurs privileged by the state to enter new industries learned how to produce at low cost massive amounts of different types of goods. They neither designed nor marketed the products because rapid economic development could not wait for research or marketing capabilities to be created from scratch (Amsden 1989). Rather, they focused on manufacturing—oftentimes merely assembling—products to specification for Japanese, American, and European MNEs and retailers. This pattern of "original equipment manufacturing" (OEM) was first used in textiles, shoes, toys, and electrical appliances and later extended to more technologically advanced industries in intermediate, capital, and durable consumer goods. In the typical OEM contract, the foreign MNE provides the technology and markets the product

---

[1] By contrast to their Japanese counterparts, the chaebol do not include a bank, are much more managerially centralized, and rely on subcontracting to a lesser extent (Kang 1996b, 11, 86–90; E. M. Kim 1997; Woo 1991, 13, 35, 66).

while the local firm secures permits from the state, hires and manages the workforce, and undertakes the manufacturing activities. Until the early 1990s, more than 80 percent of Korea's exports were accounted for by OEM contracts (Park 1994). Even Samsung Electronics—Korea's largest exporter—derives about two-thirds of its sales from OEM contracts with such companies as Tandy, Unisys, Hewlett-Packard, Apple, IBM, Dell, and Tektronix. Thus, the chaebol established ties to the state to secure critical resources inside the country (labor, capital, domestic market access) and to foreign MNEs in order to access technology and export markets. Increasingly, the chaebol are manufacturing products with their own brands, but they still rely heavily on foreign technology: around 60 percent of total Korean payments for royalties and fees are accounted for by the seven largest chaebol.

The Korean chaebol developed the capability to access domestic and foreign resources for repeated industry entry by creating group-level staff offices to coordinate not only financial allocation but also planning, technology acquisition, plant construction and equipping, human resource management, and export-import activities (Amsden 1989, 167; Kang 1996a, 154; L. Kim 1997, 54–77; Fields 1995, 183–208; Ungson, Steers, and Park 1997). When a chaebol targeted a new industry for entry—frequently in response to government incentives or guidance—the group-level office would conduct feasibility studies and facilitate access to resources and expertise from group companies, the state, and foreign MNEs. Over time, repeated industry entry following the same blueprint has allowed the chaebol to reduce the costs and time of setting up new ventures (Amsden 1989; Amsden and Hikino 1994). While this internalized capability has allowed the largest groups to grow much faster than smaller groups and nondiversified local firms, it represents an advantage over MNEs only insofar as the state restricts imports and inward foreign investment.

In addition to the effects of asymmetric foreign trade and investment, the Korean case has been presented by economic sociologists as an example of a social order characterized by vertical relationships that foster business group formation. The argument is that the Korean patrimonial concept of authority and the widespread acceptance of inheritance rules favoring the eldest son promote business concentration in the form of a business group. Members of the firm owe obedience and personal loyalty to the patrimonial figurehead or group chairman (*hoejang*). New activities or businesses are integrated into the patrimonial household as subordinate units, and every effort is made not to lose control as the household, bound by Confucian norms and hierarchically structured, turns into a collection of businesses of greater size and complexity. Thus, the family patriarch exercises supervision over an assortment of companies run by brothers, sons, sons-in-law, or other relatives, although family members sometimes fight with each other over money and influence (Biggart 1990; Fields 1995, 38–44; Hamilton and Biggart 1988; *Korea Times*, 8 March

1999; Whitley 1992). Moreover, patrimonial entrepreneurs compete with each other without ever collaborating on projects of mutual interest, unlike in social settings characterized by reciprocal relationships (the Japanese *keiretsu*) or horizontal ones (the Taiwanese *guanxiqiye*).

The chaebol have been very active in politics and policymaking. The "symbiotic" relationship between government and business groups in Korea has deep roots in the country's social and political traditions (Biggart 1990; E. M. Kim 1997). The best survey of Korea's top entrepreneurs and managers to date shows that they share with bureaucratic, political, and military elites a common regional origin and educational background. Tellingly, about 20 percent of the Korean entrepreneurial and managerial elite had previously worked for the government. An additional 6 percent of them served as officers in the army, an institution that provided up to half of President Park's and 20 percent of President Chun's political appointees (Jones and Sakong 1980, 210–47; Chul 1994). About one-third of fathers-in-law of chaebol owners are high-ranking government officials (Cumings 1997, 329). In addition, presidential campaigns have routinely been funded by contributions from the largest chaebol. But the importance of political connections should not obscure the equally critical relevance of ties to foreign providers of capital, process-related knowledge, and access to markets, which all Korean business groups have had to establish and maintain if they were to diversify into a panoply of new industries. Those ties have become a valuable and rare capability only insofar as the state has restricted access by foreigners.

It was not long before the organizational dynamics of Korea's nationalist-modernizing development path acquired a momentum of its own. Since the late 1970s the combined sales of the ten largest business groups in Korea have represented more than 40 percent of GDP. Those proportions, of course, are inflated because of the patterns of intense intragroup shipments. A better indicator is value added. The top six chaebol accounted in 1990 for 15 percent of Korea's value added, easily the world's highest concentration of economic power (B.-K. Lee 1994, exhibits 4 and 8; Amsden 1989, 116; Woo 1991, 171–73). As predicted by economic sociologists emphasizing the patrimonial character of Korea's social structure (Biggart 1990), the chaebol compete among themselves to climb positions in the size rankings calculated by the government itself to assess business concentration. Starting in the mid-1970s, the state began to see its authority, autonomy, and freedom of action erode as a result of growing chaebol power (E. M. Kim 1997). Not surprisingly, every single South Korean president since Rhee Syngman attempted at least once to curb chaebol growth. The most important episodes occurred under General Park in 1974, Chun in 1980, Roh in 1990, Kim Young Sam in 1993, and Kim Dae Jung in 1998. The government attempted to slow down the chaebol and reassert state authority by asking or requiring them to shed subsidiaries, focus on core industries, list companies on the stock market, sell real estate, eliminate cross-company subsidies, and reduce debt-equity ratios (Fields 1995, 53–62; *Korea Times*, 21 September 1998, 18 December 1998; *Korea Herald*, 23 September 1998, 19 December 1998; see also chap. 7). These efforts have generally failed to reign in the chaebol.

Late-industrialization theory's emphasis on state autonomy (Amsden 1989) is inconsistent with the chaebol's continued growth even after the state realized its own autonomy was being compromised and took measures to arrest the trend (see the lower panel of table 3.3 for the decline of the state autonomy index for South Korea between 1975 and 1995). It is simply not possible to observe the chaebol growing vigorously during the 1980s and 1990s (E. M. Kim 1997) and argue that it was because an autonomous state continued to allocate resources at will and to control the privileged entrepreneurs' every move. The answer to this puzzle is provided by the resource-based view: Foreign trade and investment asymmetries persisted during the 1980s and 1990s (see fig. 2.1), thus making it possible for the chaebol to continue expanding. Indeed, the chaebol have opposed attempts by the state to reduce asymmetries in foreign trade and investment, knowing that their pattern of diversification and growth owes much to them. For example, President Chun introduced a series of neoliberal reforms during the early 1980s—monetary stabilization, privatization of banks, partial deregulation of credit, selected trade liberalization, and a somewhat less restrictive policy toward MNEs. The attempt to increase imports and inward foreign investment represented a shift from nationalist to pragmatic policies, and the chaebol responded by mobilizing politically to water down the reforms (Lee 1997, 74–77; Lew 1999; Moon 1994). Contrary to the government's expectation, the biggest chaebol ended up benefiting from the reforms to a greater extent than the smaller groups and the independent firms. They managed to access new sources of relatively cheap credit, acquire stakes in the privatized banks, set up financial management companies, and enter into new joint-venture agreements with MNEs (Bedeski 1994, 88; Eckert 1993, 107; E. M. Kim 1997, 181–200).

The growth and diversification of business groups under the nationalist-modernizing conditions present in South Korea may be illustrated with the case of Hyundai (*hyondae* is Korean for "modern" or "contemporary"). In 1947 entrepreneur Chung Ju Yung founded an engineering and construction company that started to grow quickly after its contacts within the Park regime awarded it three key projects: the first bridge over the Han River, Kimp'o international airport, and the Seoul-Pusan highway. Cash-flows from these domestic construction projects helped the company expand abroad, especially in Southeast Asia and the Middle East. The first unrelated diversifications took place in the mid-1960s when Hyundai entered steel manufacturing and oil refining. Since the late 1960s Hyundai was among the fastest growing chaebol thanks to its prominent place in the government's plans for heavy industrialization. During the 1970s Hyundai's assets grew by a cumulative 38 percent annual rate. The group entered automobiles, aluminum, shipbuilding, and heavy engineering. Hyundai was one of a handful chaebol allowed to create a trading company and a merchant marine in the mid-1970s, a tangible resource that proved key to further diversification into new industries. All of these projects were undertaken with subsidized credit, government protection, and foreign technology. For instance, Hyundai's automobile factory began assembling Ford Escorts on contract. During the 1970s the company obtained technology from Japanese, British, Italian, and American companies (see also chap. 6). In shipbuilding, Hyundai acted as a subcontractor to Kawasaki Shipbuilding and later obtained technology from several European companies as well as Japanese ones. In all of these industries the government not only provided cheap loans and guarantees, but also a protected domestic market and a commitment not to let foreign multinationals operate freely in Korea. Thus, Hyundai could use profits from domestic sales to subsidize an increasingly important export effort while obtaining capital, market access, and technology from foreign sources. A similar blueprint of diversification was followed during the 1980s when entering electronics, elevators, robotics, information services, broadcasting, and publishing (Amsden 1989, 175–79, 269–90; E. M. Kim 1997, 131, 155–56). With the takeover of KIA in the wake of the Asian crisis, Hyundai has consolidated its position as the number one chaebol (see chaps. 6 and 7).

A second example of a South Korean group that thrived on the basis of contacts inside and outside Korea is Samsung ("three stars"). Its origins date back to 1938, when entrepreneur I Pyong Ch'ol founded a trading company. After the Korean War, under the asymmetric populist-modernizing conditions created by President Rhee, the company moved into sugar refining and textiles, and then into insurance and banking. As Korea started to pursue an asymmetric export-led, nationalist-modernizing path to development during the 1960s, Samsung found new opportunities for diversification in industries with a potential for export sales. In 1965 Samsung entered the manufacturing of fertilizers first for the domestic market and later for the international one. Further diversification into electronics, shipbuilding, chemicals, petrochemicals, industrial engineering, construction, and aerospace took place during the 1970s and 1980s as the government emphasized heavy industry. While Samsung grew slower than Hyundai and Daewoo during the 1970s because it did not benefit nearly as much as them from the government's heavy industry drive (E. M. Kim 1997, 157), it did take advantage of the protection of the domestic market. In the mid-1990s, Samsung became the world's largest manufacturer of semiconductors, taking the world by storm with its 4-megabit dynamic random-access memory chip (Clifford 1994, 316–24). In 1997 Samsung Electronics obtained some 1,300 patents in the United States, ranking sixth in the world after IBM, Canon, NEC, Motorola, and Sony (Gomes-Casseres and Lee 1988; L. Kim 1997; Lall 1990; STEPI 1995; *Korea Herald,*

13 January 1999). In spite of the government's efforts to curb the power of the chaebol and overcome chronic overcapacity problems during the 1990s, Samsung managed to obtain permission to enter the auto industry in collaboration with Nissan (see chap. 6).

Samsung's consumer electronics diversification is the most interesting from the point of view of understanding how business groups rise in an asymmetric nationalist-modernizing context. The Samsung Electronics Company was created in the early 1970s to make audio and video equipment, household appliances, and electronics products. It was only as late as 1981 that Samsung and another of the chaebol, Goldstar, licensed the videocassette recorder (VCR) technology and trademark from the Victor Company of Japan, a Matsushita affiliate. Samsung learned the manufacturing technology swiftly and—thanks to subsidized loans—became a low-cost VCR manufacturer, exporting as much as 70 percent of production. In the late 1980s Korean-made VCRs represented one-fifth of the U.S. market (Koo 1994, table 9.8). By 1992, a mere decade after entering the industry, Samsung was the second largest VCR manufacturer in the world, with a worldwide market share of about 10 percent. The company has only recently started to establish its own brand name. It still relies on original equipment manufacturing contracts with foreign MNEs for two-thirds of its sales. In 1999 it signed the largest ever contract to supply displays to Dell. As predicted by the resource-based theory of business groups furthered in this chapter, Samsung leveraged its contacts both with the government and with foreign technology and market providers so as to enter mature industries with the intention of engaging in exports.

In addition to their growing export accomplishments, both Samsung and Hyundai have set up foreign manufacturing plants in a variety of industries. As is true of most chaebol, they have shifted production to multiple wholly owned and joint-venture plants in China and other East and South Asian countries in search of lower costs, and to North America and Europe to surmount protectionist barriers. The top Korean chaebol are among the largest multinationals headquartered in the newly industrialized countries (Guillén 1999; Tcha 1998; UNCTD 1999, 86–87; Ungson, Steers, and Park 1997; Van Hoesel 1999).

Despite the apparent success of a Hyundai or a Samsung, it is not entirely clear that the chaebol is a stable form of organization and that these large conglomerates will survive as such. What is clear, though, is that the organizational and technological capabilities they have been accumulating over the last four decades are likely to remain in Korea.[2] The stories of Hyundai and Samsung also illustrate how important it is for firms to network within and across borders in order to thrive under asymmetric foreign trade and invest-

---

[2] Thanks are due to Alice Amsden of MIT for helping me realize this important point. For a qualification of this view in light of the Asian crisis, see chapter 7.

ment conditions. Thus, the rise of the Korean chaebol confirms the usefulness of an institutional theory of development and globalization emphasizing resources for action.

The Vicissitudes of the Argentine Grupos

The rise of business groups under erratic populist conditions is exemplified by the case of Argentina. With only a couple of exceptions, the growth to prominence of the Argentine *grupos económicos* begins in the early 1950s, that is, toward the end of the populist presidency of General Juan Domingo Perón. Acute economic problems brought about by staunchly nationalist-populist policies forced him to "retreat" from economic nationalism by stabilizing the economy, seeking foreign investment, and allowing the business groups to conduct some of the activities previously allotted to the state. The groups diversified into new industries with the cash flows generated in profitable and protected domestic markets subject to import-substitution conditions. They did so by gaining concessions and permits from the state and borrowing technology from foreign MNEs (Lewis 1992, 195–210, 349–59).

The Argentine groups have always been ideal local partners for many of the manufacturing and service MNEs venturing into the country in spite of the frequent zigzags in policies regarding foreign investment. The government privileged the groups when short-run economic instability or financial crises afflicted the country. As Lewis (1992) documents, macroeconomic, credit, trade, and foreign investment policies oscillated between nationalism and pragmatism several times between the 1950s and the 1990s. Previous research on Argentina supports the prediction that business groups expand more rapidly during periods of asymmetric pragmatic-populism than during periods of symmetric nationalist-populism (Bisang 1994a, 20–24; Acevedo, Basualdo, and Khavisse 1990). For example, the first military junta of 1976–81 pursued a neoliberal line away from the nationalist policies of the 1970–76 period; that is, imports and inward foreign investment were allowed to increase. At the same time, however, firms and state-owned enterprises continued in an import-substitution mode, resulting in acutely asymmetric pragmatic-populist conditions (Lewis 1992, 448–75; Waisman 1987). The dictatorship showered the business groups with contracts to provide public services or improve the performance of state-owned enterprises, created better conditions for export, and gave freer access to domestic and international credit. After the groups' expansive strategies failed in 1982, the state nationalized their accumulated foreign debt (Acevedo, Basualdo, and Khavisse 1990, 147–48). The groups also grew rapidly when the first democratic presidency attempted asymmetric policies of the pragmatic-populist kind in 1985–86. The groups, however, retrenched swiftly as more symmetric nationalist-populist conditions set in during the late 1980s after the failure of pragmatism in foreign trade and investment (Lewis 1992, 478–93).

The first years of the Menem presidency, which began in 1989, entailed a rapid increase in imports and inward foreign investment accompanied by a lagging increase in exports and outward foreign investment; that is, an asymmetric pragmatic-populist strategy was followed (Toulan and Guillén 1997). Under Menem, the business groups have been exposed to increased competition due to tariff cuts. They have benefited, however, from the crackdown on the unions' power, renewed technical, licensing, and marketing ties with foreign multinationals, and Latin America's most ambitious privatization program, affecting over 60 state-owned manufacturing and service firms valued at U.S.$26 billion. Of the 54 companies privatized up to February 1993, one or more of the top ten Argentine business groups participated in 32 of them. In 25 of those 32 instances business groups were joined by at least one foreign MNE, which typically provided capital and technology (Kosacoff and Bezchinsky 1994, 135–39). Successful bidding for privatized public services or state-owned manufacturing enterprises has frequently been based on political connections as well as on the ability to meet requirements as to minimum assets and technological know-how. Accordingly, entrepreneurs and firms with connections to the state and foreign MNEs and lenders have benefited the most from privatization. Thus, entrepreneurs with access to both domestic and foreign resources have thrived when Argentina pursued an asymmetric pragmatic-populist development strategy (Bisang 1994a, 50–53; Kosacoff 1999). In so doing, they created business groups across a wide variety of manufacturing and service industries.

While the Argentine *grupos* have not accumulated group-level capabilities to the same extent as the Korean chaebol, they too developed the ability to set up new ventures or to take over privatized companies quickly and in a cost-effective manner. The groups' central offices provide functions such as human resource management, planning, legal advice, cash flow coordination, and targeting of new business opportunities (Bisang 1994a, 32). As in Korea, the business groups have loomed large in Argentine politics and economic policymaking. Cabinet ministers and other top political appointees have frequently been recruited among the managerial ranks of the largest groups, especially when an asymmetric pragmatic-populist strategy, as opposed to a symmetric one, was to be pursued (Lewis 1992). The Argentine business groups, though, have not always succeeded at influencing policymaking in their favor.

The evolution of Argentina's second largest business group, Pérez Companc, illustrates that business groups thrive under the asymmetric conditions of pragmatic-populist development, but suffer under nationalist-populist conditions. Pérez Companc is currently controlled by the second family generation. Its history demonstrates that business groups rise to prominence by leveraging contacts inside and outside the country. Pérez Companc was founded as a shipping company in 1946, the same year Perón won his first presidential election. The company grew slowly during the 1950s and 1960s both in the shipping business and as a subcontractor to the state-owned oil and coal companies (YPF and YCF) and several foreign MNEs.

A period of much faster diversification and growth started under the military juntas in the mid-1970s, which the Fundación Pérez Companc assisted financially. The government pursued policies that resulted in an asymmetric situation of high imports and inward investment but low exports and outward investment. In 1973 Pérez Companc controlled only 10 firms, but by 1983 it included 53 firms in such an assortment of industries as mining, oil, petrochemicals, fertilizers, electrical appliances, machinery, nuclear engineering, agribusiness, food processing, fishing, cement, metals, construction, tourism, and financial services. The group was bailed out in 1982, together with other business groups, when the military junta nationalized its massive external debt.

Pérez Companc's pattern of disorderly and opportunistic diversification, however, resumed during the transition to democracy in the mid-1980s under continuing asymmetric pragmatic-populist conditions. By 1987 Pérez Companc controlled 84 companies, with new entries into fields in which it had little or no expertise: electronics, data processing, and retailing (Acevedo, Basualdo, and Khavisse 1990, 78–81). The group kept on growing domestically, with a very limited participation in the country's exports and foreign investment. Most of the new ventures eventually failed. Pérez Companc was basically diversifying its activities inside a market that, with the exception of the late 1970s, had always been very highly protected. No attempts were made to culminate the timid attempts at vertical integration, technological development, or strategic planning; and no group-level organizational mechanisms were ever put in place to help member firms learn from each other's operational experiences. The hyperinflation of the late 1980s and the economic reforms of the early 1990s signaled that the group's traditional posture had to change. Pérez Companc has since divested from many companies and manufacturing industries, but at the same time entered new ones, especially in services, so as to take advantage of the privatizations.

In most of its new businesses Pérez Companc relies on the state for concessions and other privileges and on foreign MNEs for technology. Interviews suggest that throughout the 1990s, the group's central office has been in charge of identifying opportunities, preparing new venture plans, bidding for privatized companies, and leveraging exclusive contacts inside and outside the country, but without ever engaging in operational coordination or knowledge transfer across subsidiaries. With the help of McKinsey & Company, Pérez Companc has been trying to implement the policies that conventional business wisdom recommends in these cases: focus on areas of competence, create strategic business units, and strengthen the central planning and control office (Prensa Económica 1994). Its pattern of growth, however, is still highly dependent on the domestic market. Exports represent a mere 5 percent of sales (Kosacoff 1999, 103). Group companies account for no more than 2 percent of total Argentine exports, even though its oil operations are the second largest in the country and it has an important presence in Argentina's traditional export star, agribusiness.

In 1995 the group had interests in 69 companies in oil, petrochemicals, agribusiness, food processing, metals, gas transportation and distribution, electrical utilities, telecommunications, railways, banking, and construction. In 1998 Pérez Companc sold off its stakes in gas and construction companies, and in 1999 it acquired the largest Argentine food-processing company, Molinos Río de la Plata, a unit of the Bunge & Born group. This move surprised analysts thinking the group was to focus on oil and utilities and was certainly not the course of action suggested by McKinsey (*La Nación*, 8 January 1999). These events are symptomatic of the evolution of business groups in Argentina. Groups deeply embedded in such an erratic institutional context as the Argentine find it very difficult—and perhaps irrelevant—to focus on a few activities. Instead, they engage in all sorts of opportunistic behaviors.

While Pérez Companc has not developed any proprietary technological or manufacturing capabilities and has largely failed to make a dent in international competition, other Argentine groups have not only diversified into a variety of manufacturing and service activities but also demonstrated that they excel at some activity on a global scale. The two best examples are Industrias Metalúrgicas Pescarmona (IMPSA)—a major player in the world markets for turbines and cranes—and Techint, whose DST firm (Dalmine-Siderca-Tamsa) is the world's largest manufacturer of seamless steel pipe (2.4 million tons), accounting for over 18 percent of total world production and 26 percent of world exports. Over the last 52 years, companies affiliated to Techint have made more than 26,000 miles of pipelines, enough to circle the globe.[3] In 1999, Techint's Tamsa subsidiary tied with Steel Dynamics of the United States and POSCO of South Korea in Morgan Stanley's ranking of the world's most competitive maker of steel products (*Korea Times*, 4 May 1999).

Techint comprises over 100 firms in steel, machinery, engineering, construction, turnkey plant design and construction, oil and gas exploration and production, flat and pressed glass, paper, cement and ceramic tiles, and a bewildering assortment of privatized firms, namely, sanitary services, railways, toll highways, telecommunications, gas transportation and distribution, power generation, and even correctional facilities. Total group sales totaled $5.6 billion in 1997, making it the largest in the country. It exports about 40 percent

---

[3] I have benefited from many conversations with Professor Omar Toulan, a former doctoral student of mine now at McGill University, who has conducted extensive research at Techint (see Toulan 1997).

of its production in Argentina. Sixty percent of its 50,000 employees are located in Latin America, Europe, and Asia, unlike the case of Pérez Companc, which is mostly a domestic group.[4]

The historical origins of Techint go back to fascist Italy. During the Great Depression, bankrupt steel company Dalmine was taken over by the state. Mussolini appointed engineer Agostino Rocca as its chairman. At the end of the war, Rocca exiled himself first in Mexico and then in Argentina, where he opened a branch of Dalmine with capital of Italian and U.S. origin. In 1954 he built the first South American seamless pipe facility some 50 miles outside Buenos Aires. In 1962 he spun off Propulsora Siderúrgica, a firm making flat steel. Rocca organized his businesses under the Techint holding company, which was also the group's engineering and construction arm. He was well connected both internationally and in Argentina. In fact, most of Techint's early contracts came from the state-owned oil, gas, water, and sanitation companies, and the technology from foreign sources. By 1973 Techint included 30 different companies, and 46 by the end of the period of military juntas in 1983, benefiting from asymmetric pragmatic-populist conditions to diversify into textiles, cellulose fibers, paper, nuclear power equipment, insurance, and banking as well as steel, engineering, and construction. Rocca also had interests in the Argentine subsidiary of Italian tire maker Pirelli (Acevedo, Basualdo, and Khavisse 1990, 111–13; Lewis 1992, 266–67, 346–47, 356, 470; Toulan 1997). After the difficult period of decline and hyperinflation during the late 1980s, Techint resumed its growth as a result of liberalization and privatization during the 1990s. By 1997 Techint was the fifth largest business group in Argentina.

Techint's unique strength lies in steel. The group has turned around one of the Argentine state's worst-run companies—flat-steel maker SOMISA, now called Siderar. It also controls steel companies in Bolivia, Brazil, and Venezuela. Most famously, Techint commands the world's largest market share in seamless pipes, used for drilling and transporting oil and gas. Its competitors in international markets include such powerhouses as Sumitomo Heavy Industries, USX, and Mannesmann-Vallourec. In addition to Siderca, whose main plant is located near Buenos Aires, Techint controls two other large pipe manufacturers: Tamsa in Mexico (since 1993), which Agostino Rocca helped found; and Dalmine in Italy, which it acquired in 1996 after the Italian state decided to privatize the company Rocca once managed for Mussolini. These two companies offer Techint a foothold in NAFTA and the European Union, respectively. More recent international ventures include Siderca Romania,

---

[4] Kosacoff 1999, 103; Prensa Económica 1998; *Latin Trade*, 20 April 1998, 20; *Financial Times*, survey, 27 July 1997, 4; *Gazeta Mercantil*, 28 July 1997, A10; *Metal Bulletin Monthly*, April 1996, 17; *Argentina Monthly*, April 1999, internet edition, <www.invertir.com/news/apr99.doc>.

the acquisition of CVG Tubos Industriales & Petroleros and Siderúrgica del Orinoco (Sidor) from the Venezuelan state, and a manufacturing and sales joint venture with NKK of Japan. Techint group companies make flat steel, pipes, rolling mills, heavy steel structures, offshore modules, and electric furnaces.[5] Techint's seamless tubing facilities are considered to be the best in the world. In 1993 they obtained ISO 9001 quality certification for their entire operations (Toulan 1997, 71). As in the cases of Hyundai and Samsung, Pérez Companc and Techint have reacted to their country's asymmetric pattern of insertion in the global economy by establishing ties within and across borders.

The Rise and Fall of the Groups in Spain

A pragmatic-modernizing development strategy is not conducive to business groups, as the case of Spain illustrates. The country initially pursued an asymmetric nationalist-modernizing development strategy until the late 1970s, combining relatively low imports and inward investment with increasing exports. As a result, several diversified business groups formed around banks (Central, Bilbao, Vizcaya, Urquijo, Banesto), large chemical or steel companies (Unión Explosivos Río Tinto, Cros, Altos Hornos de Vizcaya), as well as whenever entrepreneurs diversified out of traditional light industries like food and beverages (Rumasa). With the sole exception of Rumasa—which was more of a freelance player—the other groups grew on the basis of connections to the state and foreign partners, as several meticulously researched case studies of these groups indicate (Muñoz 1969; Muñoz, Roldán, and Serrano 1978; Tamames 1977).

While the industrial crisis of the 1970s hit Spanish industry hard, it was the subsequent process of market liberalization and integration with Europe that caused the definitive decline of many of the groups. Protectionist trade barriers and restrictions against foreign MNEs were lifted during the 1980s. As a result of the reduction in trade and investment asymmetries, some of the business groups collapsed under international competitive pressure, while others succeeded in refocusing on one core activity or were acquired by foreign MNEs. While they had previously developed a capability to take advantage of asymmetric conditions, the sudden and lasting reduction of such imbalances rendered the capability obsolete. By the mid-1990s only the industrial groups organized around such banks as BCH and BBV or large retailers (El Corte Inglés) had survived, while virtually all others disappeared either gradually or as the result of bankruptcy procedures and takeovers (Aguilera 1997; Pérez 1997; Campa and Guillén 1996a). As foreign MNEs found themselves free to operate in the country, business groups built on the assumption of asymmetric

---

[5] *Metal Bulletin*, 5 December 1996, 23–25, 29 June 1998, 21; *AméricaEconomía*, 8 October 1998, 63–66; *Oil and Gas Journal*, 19 January 1998; *La Nación*, 3 November 1999.

foreign trade and investment suffered. Moreover, foreign companies and investors were allowed to take over many privatized public services and state-owned manufacturing companies without the collaboration of a local partner. Although some of the groups and the banks resisted pragmatic-modernizing policies, especially in their core industries, they were unable to derail the considerable political and social momentum created in favor of membership in the European Union, which required the abandonment of nationalist policies toward imports and inward foreign investment.

UERT

Consider the example of Unión Explosivos Río Tinto. UERT was originally founded as a mining company with the participation of British capital. The firm grew via diversification during the 1960s when Spain implemented asymmetric policies similar to those of Korea. Given its contacts with the government, local banks, and foreign MNEs (Rhône-Poulenc, Hoechst, Shell, Toyo, Tioxide International, Gulf, Texaco), UERT diversified into fertilizers, chemicals, oil, plastics, engineering, pharmaceuticals, cosmetics, real estate, and consulting services. By the mid-1970s it was the largest diversified conglomerate in the country, but barely 14 percent of total sales were exports (Muñoz, Roldán, and Serrano 1978, 428–33). The economic crisis of the 1970s forced many of its companies into bankruptcy. Subsequently, Spain's bid to become a member of the European Union meant that trade and investment protectionism had to be abandoned. Like many of the other Spanish groups, UERT collapsed as a business group during the 1980s, with its various companies falling into the hands of several foreign MNEs.

Mondragón

There is a noteworthy case of a business group in Spain that—although originating in the asymmetric conditions of the 1950s and 1960s—has managed not only to survive but to thrive under the less auspicious symmetric circumstances of the 1980s and 1990s. Intriguingly, it is not a family-controlled business group, but the world's most famous system of worker-owned manufacturing and service cooperatives: the Mondragón group. Mondragón represents a fascinating illustration of how being different pays in the global economy, in spite of the predictions of modernization and neoclassical theorists that worker ownership is a "utopia" bound to fail because it creates the wrong kind of incentives (Kerr et al. [1960] 1964, 227; Sachs 1993, 82–83).

Mondragón is the largest cooperative group in the world, with over 25,000 employees, $3.5 billion in revenues, and a surplus of 7 percent of sales, making it one of the ten largest companies in Spain, and among the 500 largest groups in Europe. Unbelievable as it may be, Mondragón has become a multinational enterprise with production and distribution investments in Europe, the Americas, northern Africa, and Asia. Cooperatives belonging to the group are engaged in everything from chips, appliances, auto parts, and furniture to machine tools, robotics, elevators, heavy machinery, and large construction projects. It is the world's largest manufacturer of digital readouts. Mondragón also includes a savings bank (Caja Laboral Popular), and Spain's fifth largest retailer (Eroski). About a dozen books and monographs, as well as myriad articles, published in English or in Spanish testify to the economic and sociological significance of this worker-owned group of cooperatives.

Yet, except for the masterful and balanced study by sociologists William Foote Whyte and Kathleen King Whyte (1991), Mondragón remains a largely misunderstood phenomenon. Depending on the conceptual inclinations and biases of the researcher, the literature on Mondragón has focused too narrowly on either the agency constraints supposedly haunting employee-owned firms, the presumed superiority of worker ownership, or the cultural features of the county of Mondragón and of its charismatic founder. Most prior studies contain little more than half-truths. Perhaps the most serious misconception has to do with the emphasis on trying to understand Mondragón only in the context of the Basque Country's peculiarities without taking into account the shifting *Spanish* institutional environment: nationalist-populist until the mid-1950s, nationalist-modernizing during the 1960s and 1970s, and pragmatic-modernizing during the 1980s and 1990s. The Mondragón cooperatives expanded over the years in response to the reigning conditions inside a country that was attempting to industrialize and, later, to develop a service economy.

Mondragón is a paradox. Although its flexibility and adaptability have allowed it to thrive and grow, it is hardly "unique" in at least three respects. First, once the cooperatives reached a certain size and level of bureaucratization in the 1960s, internal conflicts over production organization and compensation schemes proliferated along lines similar to those experienced by regular capitalist firms (Whyte and Whyte 1991, 91–112; Bendix 1974; Guillén 1994). Therefore, Mondragón has not really contributed a brand-new management and organization model, but rather combined features of capitalist and cooperative enterprises. Second, Mondragón has succeeded not only because it is a cooperative but also because it was smart enough to adapt to the changing institutional environment in Spain and to invest systematically in such intangible assets as technology, brand reputation, worker skills, and organizational capabilities.

Third, as Whyte and Whyte (1991, 272) point out in passing, Mondragón is not the only large and successful cooperative in Spain. Other examples include Agropecuaria de Guissona ($399 million in sales), Cooperativas Orensanas ($298 million), Acor ($292 million), Copaga ($207 million), and Anecoop ($204 million). Spain harbors the world's largest and most successful worker-owned cooperative sector of any capitalist country. The cooperatives are regulated by special corporate law legislation both at the national and regional levels. In 1990 there were almost 18,000 agricultural, industrial, and service cooperatives in Spain,[6] employing 242,000 people, an average of 13 employees per cooperative. The cooperative sector accounts for 2.6 percent of total employment in Spain, 2.7 percent of value added, 3.0 percent of total exports. These figures would be about three times greater if they had been calculated excluding the activities of foreign-owned firms. Two-thirds of the sector's revenues are accounted for by agricultural cooperatives, which represent 28 percent of Spanish agriculture. Cooperatives also play an important role in food processing, beverages, glass, furniture, metals, machinery, electrical appliances, construction, and retailing. Thus, Spain is an excellent illustration of the shortsightedness of modernization and neoclassical theorists who argue that cooperativism is a utopia doomed to fail.

The following discussion will show that Mondragón has tried to combine capitalist managerial techniques in a country undergoing rapid development of the asymmetric kind with the one clear advantage of becoming a worker-owned group of cooperatives in the Spanish context: financial independence over the long run. Later, as Mondragón faced more symmetric conditions during the 1980s, it successfully developed its internal capabilities in specific product areas, invested abroad, and expanded rapidly into services, leveraging ties among cooperatives and to other domestic and foreign companies.

The first cooperative of the Mondragón group was founded in 1956 with the capital raised by five workers under the leadership of a Catholic priest interested in promoting the ideas of self-management, worker ownership, and capital-labor harmony. This northern Basque town, located close to the Franco-Spanish border, was home to the large foundry and metalworking firm of Unión Cerrajera. The area had long been known for its skilled craftsmen and the manufacturing of a variety of high-quality metal products, including swords and firearms. In order to secure the required governmental authorizations to enter new industries, the founders purchased a bankrupt firm that used to make electrical and mechanical household appliances. In subsequent years new cooperatives were created to manufacture machine tools, electro-mechanical components, and metallic products. In 1959 a Workers' Savings Bank was founded to provide funds for social security, cultural and educational activities, and new cooperatives (Whyte and Whyte 1991, 10–11, 25–87). It was during this early stage of small and simple cooperative enterprises that the principles of worker governance and self-management, automatic earnings reinvestment, and flat wage structures (the one-to-three maximum inequality ratio) were successfully implemented. Beginning in the 1970s, however, these principles had to be adapted to the new circumstances or abandoned altogether.

---

[6] The source of data (IEF 1993, 66–69, 106–7) excludes the Basque Country and Navarre because of their special value-added tax regimes. Cooperatives are more important in these two regions than in the rest of Spain.

Dissatisfaction with incentive payment schemes and working conditions on the Taylorized assembly line at one of the electric appliance plants resulted in the epochal strike of 1974. A *strike* at the world's most famous worker-owned cooperative? Not only that: The (self-)management of the cooperative decided to sack the 17 workers it identified as strike instigators as well as 397 others who participated in the stoppage. The management's justification for this unprecedented decision was that the strike represented a naked attack on the entire cooperative project. The dismissed worker-owners were eventually readmitted, but this grave episode exposed a latent conflict between the cooperatives' technocracy and the workers, or, in the latter's own words, between "those on top" and "those on the bottom." In addition, workers complained that the trend toward greater differentiation and technical specialization of roles had exacerbated their feeling of monotony and reduced each worker's understanding of the production process. These problems, of course, will ring a familiar bell among students of bureaucratized capitalist or socialist firms (Bendix 1974). The solutions implemented thereafter would raise eyebrows among believers in worker self-management.

The appointment of a new management team in 1970 empowered the personnel department to conduct surveys, redefine and enrich jobs, shift from assembly-line work to teamwork, introduce quality circles, and expand wage differentials. Managers argued that these initiatives were inspired in the British sociotechnical systems approach and the Swedish work democracy movement; in fact some of them actually come from countries in which "democratic" shopfloor practices are notorious for their absence, that is, the United States and Japan. What is most telling, neither the founder nor the general assembly of cooperative workers took the lead in these initiatives. Rather, they were the result of a reconfiguration of shopfloor roles negotiated between the managers and the workers (Whyte and Whyte 1991, 92–127).

The economic crisis of the mid-1970s and the subsequent pursuit of symmetric pragmatic-modernizing policies by the Spanish government created both the pressure and the opportunity to reorganize the system of diversified independent cooperatives as a multidivisional group, with a strategic-planning department on top staffed by professional managers. The culmination of these efforts was the creation in the early 1990s of Mondragón Corporación Cooperativa, including financial, distribution, and industrial divisions. Simultaneously, the group's multiple brands were consolidated and export growth was emphasized over the domestic market. Between the early 1970s and the early 1990s exports of manufactured goods climbed from 10 to 31 percent of total production, mimicking the transformation of the overall Spanish economy. As the title of an internal report of 1989 suggests unambiguously, Mondragón was making the transition "From Sociological Experiment toward an Entrepreneurial Group" (Whyte and Whyte 1991, 195–211).

Critical to this transformation was the intensification of the firm's traditional commitment to worker training, R&D, and brand advertising (Whyte and Whyte 1991, 63–67, 211–21). Firms based in regional industrial districts have tended to develop extensive apprenticeship programs (Piore and Sabel 1984). A comparison between Mondragón's Fagor cooperative and the German multinational Robert Bosch, famous for its training programs, will help to gain some perspective on this issue. These two enterprises compete with each other in the markets for auto parts, electric appliances, and machine tools. Fagor is just one-twentieth the size of Bosch, which trains 2,800 apprentices in Germany alone, and 6,400 worldwide (3.6 percent of employees). Fagor is making an even greater effort, with approximately 500 apprentices (7.1 percent of employees). Fagor and the Mondragón group as a whole have also introduced technical training programs in the areas of engineering and management with the establishment of several schools offering recognized university degrees at the undergraduate and graduate levels. These schools have a total enrollment of over 1,500 students (some of them employees), who spend substantial periods of time working at the group's cooperatives like Fagor or at the R&D centers helping in the development of new products and processes.[7]

Perhaps one should not find so strange that over the years a large, bureaucratized, worker-owned cooperative should implement scientific management, human relations, and structural reorganization programs and techniques, as well as invest in advertising, R&D, and its workforce. What appears rather unusual for an institution primarily concerned with creating jobs for family members related to the cooperative, and with the well-being of the local community, is that it starts investing and creating jobs in foreign and distant lands. Yet that is precisely what Mondragón and other cooperative groups in Spain have been doing over the last few years, largely in response to the pragmatic-modernizing policies underpinning the country's accession to the European Union. Mondragón cooperatives have a chip facility in Thailand, refrigerator assembly plants in Morocco and Argentina, a bus bodywork joint venture and an acquired refrigerator plant in China, auto parts and electric components plants in Mexico, and several stores of the Eroski supermarket chain in southern France. It has purchased a Dutch electromechanical components firm (Controls International), an elevator manufacturer in the United Kingdom (Cable Lifts & Elevators), two French machine-tool companies (SEI and Cima Robotique), and a Polish household appliances plant. Mondragón is now planning to open an electric appliances assembly line in Egypt, invest in joint-venture auto parts plants in the United Kingdom and the United States, and acquire Ford's and Volkswagen's auto parts subsidiaries in Brazil and Argentina. As of the mid-1990s, the Fagor cooperative had strategic alliances

[7] Robert Bosch GmbH, *Geschäftsbericht über das Jahr 1991*; Whyte and Whyte 1991, 215–21.

with Thomson Electroménager, General Domestic Appliances, and Ocean (household appliances), Societé Européenne de Propulsion (Vulcain engine for the Ariane satellite-launching rocket), and Baumüller (machine tool components) and participated in the European Union's ESPRIT and Eureka high-tech programs.

What is unique about Mondragón is that no other Spanish industrial company unrelated to the state—whether worker owned or not—has ever achieved and sustained Mondragón's size, diversification, and international projection. A key advantage of being a cooperative lies in its financial independence, which allows for a long-term growth strategy. But even this aspect has proved insufficient. In an unprecedented move for a worker-owned cooperative, Mondragón is to be quoted on the stock market through a wholly owned, instrumental subsidiary with the aim of raising about $100 million in fresh capital. And the group has announced plans to hire up to 50 international executives to staff its staggering number of foreign industrial and commercial subsidiaries (*El País Negocios*, 4 June 1995, 8; *Expansión*, 23 June 1995, 2). Ultimately, Mondragón's continued success as a diversified business group under pragmatic-modernizing conditions can only be understood in terms of its ability to reinvent itself, to establish networks of support and exchange among the various industrial, service, and financial cooperatives that belong to the group, and between the group and foreign companies.

Implications and Conclusion

This chapter has approached the rise and fall of business groups in newly industrialized countries from a comparative institutional perspective anchored in the resource-based view of business strategy. Theories emphasizing market imperfections, state autonomy, or the "triple alliance" do not accurately describe the conditions under which business groups accumulate distinctive capabilities that enable them to diversify. Noting that entrepreneurs and firms in newly industrialized countries need to combine domestic and foreign resources in order to enter industries, I proposed that asymmetries in foreign trade and investment facilitate business group formation. Entrepreneurs and firms with the internalized capability to access resources enter one industry after another, creating business groups and not integrated companies because their diversification follows a logic of repeated access to foreign and domestic resources under asymmetric foreign trade and investment rather than one of technological, marketing, or financial strength.

Cross-sectional data on the importance of business groups in nine newly industrialized countries confirmed that previous theories—with the sole exception of late industrialization—fail to account for the wide-ranging differences observed, while asymmetries in foreign trade and investment are highly correlated with them. A longitudinal analysis based on the top 100 nonfinancial firms in South Korea, Spain, and Argentina at two points in time showed that business groups thrive in countries following an asymmetric development path combining high levels of exports and outward investment with low levels of imports and inward investment (e.g., Korea), and they decline in countries following a symmetric development path with high levels of trade and investment in both directions (Spain). Countries on an erratic populist path (Argentina) see their business groups go through cyclical ups and downs following swings in the relative asymmetry of foreign trade and investment levels. Finally, historical evidence on the role of business groups in the industrialization of each country indicated that a few local entrepreneurs and firms benefited from the asymmetries by creating business groups based on the capability to combine foreign and domestic resources for repeated industry entry. No consistent and unambiguous support could be found for the predictions of modernization, neoclassical, and dependency theories as to why business groups become important in a newly industrialized economy. Only the resource-based argument outlined at the beginning of the chapter received consistent support from the cross-sectional, longitudinal, and qualitative evidence presented.

The evidence from both Korea and Argentina strongly suggests that business groups are fully aware of what it means to lose the asymmetric access to resources that allowed them to grow and diversify. This is why they oppose policies that diminish asymmetries in foreign trade and investment. If signs exist that asymmetries are being reduced, the scope and size of the group may become a liability rather than a strength. As foreign trade and investment become more symmetric, competitive pressures from both foreign MNEs and nondiversified local firms will intensify, probably inducing business groups to divest from certain industries and concentrate on those that promise the highest growth and returns.

The interaction between inward and outward trade and investment flows is a key feature affecting organizational dynamics inside newly industrialized countries, and it provides a framework for understanding what organizational forms predominate depending on the conditions of access to foreign and domestic resources. In the next chapter I turn to the predicament of small and medium enterprises in the three countries, comparing their roles under different development circumstances.

FOUR

THE ROLE OF SMALL AND MEDIUM ENTERPRISES

> I was brought up on the theory of the "economies of scale"—
> that with industries and firms, just as with nations, there is an
> irresistible trend, dictated by modern technology, for units to
> become ever bigger.
> (*Schumacher 1975, 64*)

A COMPARATIVE institutional theory of development in a context of globalization certainly argues against the notion that modern technology requires the growth of big organizations. More frequently than not, industries have become dominated by large-scale enterprises due to the monopolistic actions of firms or to state regulation rather than because of inescapable technological requirements. Globalization elevates the role of the ability to network over sheer size. Networks of organizations can certainly undertake large-scale activities without creating large, integrated organizations (Perrow 1992; Powell 1990). Small and medium enterprises (SMEs) have long attracted the attention of scholars. In a famous essay, Alfred Marshall (1919) sang the praises of small firms in "industrial districts" as an alternative to large-scale corporations. Smallness has been described in the literature as beautiful (Schumacher 1975), bountiful (Granovetter 1983), and irresistibly competitive (Naisbitt 1994). Smaller firms are assumed to be more flexible, adaptive, innovative, and perhaps more socially desirable because they spread wealth (Hamilton and Biggart 1988; Perrow 1992; Piore and Sabel 1983; Sabel and Zeitlin 1985; Snodgrass and Biggs 1996, 11–12).

Previous theories of development, however, have a distinctively "modernist" bias in favor of large firms using mass-production technologies (Guillén 1997a). Modernization scholars think it necessary for firms to become large in scale if advanced technology is to be successfully adopted (Kerr et al. [1960] 1964, 21; Rostow [1960] 1990, 9–11, 40). Dependency scholars also believe in the importance of large-scale import-substitution industrialization not only in consumer products but also in heavy capital goods (Prebisch 1950; Frank 1967, 206–8; Cardoso and Faletto [1973] 1979). Late-industrialization theory reads like an ode to economies of scale and scope, although the harmful effects of such policies on SMEs are duly noted and regretted (Amsden 1989, 161–75, 269–318; see also Amsden 1990). Finally, neoclassical theories are not openly biased against SMEs, although they see only a narrow role for them, as suppliers to larger firms. They consider a viable capitalist economy

In the theory of the liberalism or dev, SMEs have been ignored or seen to be mere service providers + TNCs as mere firm

to include "many small and flexible industrial firms servicing the larger enterprises" (Sachs 1993, 18).

More often than not, modernist policymakers have either ignored SMEs altogether or tried to compensate them for the biases that many development efforts have in favor of large firms (Snodgrass and Biggs 1996). For example, Argentina's erratic populist policies inspired by dependency theory frequently sidetracked SMEs, as incentives and emergency programs privileged large firms, whether affiliated with the state, business groups, or foreign multinational enterprises (MNEs). Korea's nationalist-modernizing policymaking only had room for large firms affiliated with the chaebol. Spain's pragmatic-modernizing policies paid considerable attention to attracting large multinationals.

Much of the literature on SMEs is intriguingly one-sided in its approach to the role that this kind of company ought to play in economic development (Ettlinger 1997). An unwarranted assumption runs through many otherwise sound analyses, that is, that all countries should have a "large" small-firm sector regardless of the social structure of the country and the competitiveness of the SMEs in terms of foreign trade and investment. Most accounts of SMEs are insensitive to the different ways in which they seek to play a role in the global economy. A comparative institutional theory of development argues that SMEs are not necessary merely in large numbers but in terms of being innovative and internationally competitive.

Small and Medium Enterprises in Economic Development

Studies of competitive SMEs tend to coincide in identifying the features that make them so different from large companies and business groups such as those discussed in chapter 3 (Simon 1996, 5–12; Snodgrass and Biggs 1996, 11–12; UNCTD 1994a). First, they tend to grow more slowly and organically. Second, they are more labor intensive and hence tend to create a greater number of jobs per unit of output. Third, they are product-focused and tend to compete in supposedly mature and stable markets. Fourth, they pursue international markets early on — if they ever do. Fifth, they prefer to stay "hidden" or relatively unknown. And sixth, they tend to remain family owned or closely held, a feature that modernization scholars wrongly identified as a limitation (Kerr et al. [1960] 1964, 67).

*? L-intensive
? domestically oriented
often family owned*

While SMEs with fewer than 500 employees account for between 40 and 80 percent of total employment and output in the industrialized countries (OECD 1996, 1:17), they represent much lower proportions of exports, foreign direct investment, and technological innovation (Fujita 1997; UNCTD 1994a). In most countries the share of employment and output represented by SMEs tends to decline, in some cases very rapidly, as industry develops. While modernizing, export-led industrialization has been found to be more benign to SMEs than its populist, import-substitution alternative, government intervention in developing countries has generally led to the relative decline of SMEs (Snodgrass and Biggs 1996, 34–37, 51–54). This effect is especially puzzling given the amount of attention and resources devoted in many countries to fostering SMEs (OECD 1997; Snodgrass and Biggs 1996, 81–146).

It should be noted at the outset that the SME sector is an extremely heterogeneous one. Most SMEs are focused solely on the domestic market and tend to stagnate and disappear over time. The relatively few that grow to become midsized companies and engage in R&D, exports, and foreign direct investment tend to do so to a much greater extent than large firms with, say, more than 1,000 employees. Thus, the key question for students of economic development is not how many SMEs exist in an economy relative to large firms—which has occupied most of the previous literature—but rather how many SMEs, and under what specific circumstances, become competitive in R&D, exports, and investment on an international rather than domestic scale.

The predicament of SMEs in Argentina, South Korea, and Spain can be indirectly assessed by comparing the shares of the largest 100 exporting firms in each country's total exports. While the largest 100 exporters in Spain represent only 45 percent of total Spanish exports, the percentages are 73 for Argentina and 83 for Korea. Thus, a larger share of total Spanish exports are accounted for by relatively small exporters, unlike in either Korea or Argentina. It is important to emphasize that in Spain SMEs *and* foreign MNEs do well in terms of exports: the country has both a large proportion of MNEs among its top 100 exporters (56 percent, compared to 39 in Argentina and 6 in Korea) *and* a large share of exports accounted for by relatively small firms. Clearly, the pragmatic-modernizing model of development has allowed both foreign MNEs and SMEs to become major exporters. By contrast, Korean nationalist-modernizing policies have benefited the chaebol at the expense of both SMEs and foreign MNEs, while Argentine erratic populism has privileged both the *grupos económicos* and the foreign MNEs at the expense of the SMEs (see table 4.1).[1]

The SME sectors of South Korea, Argentina and Spain also differ in their propensity to engage in foreign direct investment. Spanish and Argentine SMEs in manufacturing (whether family- or worker-owned) invest abroad disproportionately to their presence in the economy. In Korea, by contrast, it is the chaebol that account for a disproportionate share of foreign investment as well as exports (table 4.1). Why these differences in foreign trade and investment by SMEs? As usual, the answer is complex and directly related to each country's development path. Below I compare the predicament of SMEs in South Korea, Argentina, and Spain. Then I review cases of SMEs in rolling

[1] The differences in organizational form observed across the three countries are independent of the industry distribution of the top 100 exporters (see Guillén 1997b).

TABLE 4.1

The Top 100 Exporters and Top 50 Outward Foreign Investors (OFI) from Spain, Argentina, and South Korea, by Industry and Organizational Form

	Spain		Argentina		Korea	
	Exporters	OFI	Exporters	OFI	Exporters	OFI
By industry (SIC codes)						
Food, beverages, and tobacco (20, 21)	7	28	47	24	1	2
Textiles, apparel, and leather (22, 23, 31)	1	10	20	4	23	14
Chemicals, paper, and rubber (26, 28, 30)	14	0	7	6	11	16
Pharmaceuticals (283)	2	6	0	20	0	0
Oil and gas (29)	4	4	12	8	6	2
Metals (33, 34)	14	4	5	2	13	12
Nonelectrical machinery (35)	5	6	1	16	9	4
Electrical machinery and electronics (36, 357)	19	6	1	4	24	22
Transportation equipment (37)	26	4	5	4	7	4
Other manufacturing[a]	1	8	2	8	2	12
Construction and services[b]	7	24	0	4	5	12
By organizational form						
Firms affiliated with a business group	7	10	15	24	63	60
State-owned firms	16	12	1	2	2	2
Subsidiaries of foreign multinationals (MNEs)	56	—	39	—	6	—
Unaffiliated, family-controlled firms	14	68	30	74	28	36
Worker-owned cooperatives	2	8	3	0	0	0
Other	5	2	12	0	1	2
Total number of firms in sample	100	50	100	50	100	50
Indicators of Concentration						
Top 100 exporters (% of total exports)	45	—	73	—	83	—
Top 50 foreign investors (% of total outward stock of foreign direct investment)	—	80[c]	—	95[c]	—	71

Sources: Spanish Institute of Foreign Trade (ICEX); Prensa Económica 1995, 44–45; Bisang, Fuchs, and Kosacoff 1995, 222–27; Asia-Pacific Infoserv 1995; Bank of Korea.

Note: Data for Spain refer to 1993, while data for Argentina and South Korea refer to 1994.

[a] Printing and publishing (SIC code 27); lumber (24); furniture (25); stone, clay, and glass (32); instruments (38); miscellaneous (39).

[b] Excludes trading and financial services from all calculations.

[c] Estimated.

stock, wines and liquors, and the printed media. I conclude with some observations as to the roles of SMEs in the global economy.

The Hardships of Being Small in South Korea

South Korea stands out as a country where SMEs have a very difficult time. Scholars have thoroughly documented that government policy and the predominant social pattern of patrimonialism militate against smallness (Biggart 1990; Fields 1995, 38–44; Orrù, Biggart, and Hamilton 1997; Ungson, Steers, and Park 1997, 82–109). Amsden (1989, 181) notes that "contrary to . . . Japan, small firms in Korea serve the domestic market, and large firms export." Moreover, during the 1960s and the better part of the 1970s firms with 5 or more employees but fewer than 200 declined relative to larger firms. Employment at such small firms dropped between 1963 and 1976 from 66 to 38 percent of the total, and value added from 53 to 24 percent. The emergency decree that bailed out the large, highly leveraged chaebol in 1972 starved SMEs of funds. The policy of diverting resources toward heavy and chemical industries further debilitated the SME sector (Fields 1995, 53–54; Snodgrass and Biggs 1996, 219–26; E. M. Kim 1997, 149–51). The downward trend of the SME sector was reversed in the late 1970s and throughout the 1980s. By 1995 small firms' shares of employment (then defined by the government as firms with fewer than 300 employees) had gone up to 69 percent of the total and of value added to 47 percent (Ungson, Steers, and Park 1997, 85; Korea Statistical Yearbook, 1997, 182).

The comeback of the SMEs, however, has had little to do with government policies. The single most important factor has been the change in the structure of manufacturing industry with the growth of technologically more complex activities, especially automobiles and electronics, which typically require SMEs to act as suppliers of parts and components. Since the early 1980s, the Korean government eliminated privileges previously given to the chaebol, instituted antitrust policy, and initiated financial and technological programs to help SMEs. Scholars, however, are skeptical as to the effects of these policies, especially given that the chaebol were given new freedoms to operate during the 1980s, including permission to enter financial services and to take minority stakes in banks (E. M. Kim 1997, 179; Lee 1997, 50–53, 71–72; Ungson, Steers, and Park 1997, 98–99).

Korean SME export performance has traditionally lagged behind that of larger firms, a situation sharply different from that in Japan, Korea's economic role model (Amsden 1989, 180–84). Even though SMEs have come to represent larger shares of total Korean employment and value added since the late 1970s, they have failed to increase their share of total exports proportionally to their larger presence in the economy. SMEs were hit quite hard by the wage, interest rate, and real estate price hikes of the late 1980s and early 1990s.

The most forward-looking SMEs have responded to higher costs by shifting production to lower-cost East and South Asian locations, especially China and Indonesia (Guillén 1999). Still, foreign investment by SMEs represents less than 20 percent of Korea's total, although their share in total value added is about 50 percent (Ungson, Steers, and Park 1997, 86–90).

The Asian crisis of 1997–98 has put further pressure on SMEs, with scores of them going under as the government nationalized the debt of several major chaebol deemed too large to fail (see chap. 7). As the surviving chaebol strive to turn their bank debt into equity or bonds, SMEs are being again crowded out of financial markets in spite of the government's attempts to create new financial channels for them (*Korea Times*, 14 September 1998, and 15 November 1998; *Economist*, 14 November 1998, 67–68).

A final problem besetting Korean SMEs is their disadvantage relative to the chaebol in technological development. Fully 83 percent of the patents obtained by Korean firms in the United States belong to one of the ten largest chaebol or to POSCO, the state-owned steel giant, with Samsung owning roughly 50 percent of all patents. Moreover, fewer SMEs are currently engaged in R&D activities compared to the late 1980s (Ungson, Steers, and Park 1997, 95).

Liberalization and the Relative Decline of SMEs in Argentina

SMEs as a group do not seem to have thrived in Argentina regardless of whether the inward economic policies were nationalist or pragmatic. Periods of staunch nationalist-populism asphyxiated SMEs under the pressure of state-owned firms, while pragmatic-populism has generally benefited diversified business groups and foreign multinationals (see chap. 3). In terms of exports, Argentine SMEs declined between the early 1970s and the mid-1990s. Business groups and state-owned enterprises increased their share of total exports from 15 to 25 percent and 2 to 8 percent, respectively, and foreign multinationals with subsidiaries in Argentina neither lost nor gained ground. Meanwhile, firms classified under the "other" category (mostly SMEs) have suffered a decline from 46 to 33 percent of total exports (Bisang and Kosacoff 1995, 93–95). Moreover, there is evidence that—unlike in most other countries—Argentine SMEs that are engaged in exports have lower export-to-sales ratios than larger firms (Gatto 1995, 137; Toulan and Guillén 1997; Guillén and Toulan 1997).

Although the average Argentine SME is not internationally competitive in terms of exports, researchers have identified a handful of successful firms in terms of foreign investment: FV (faucets); Sintyal, Bagó, Roemmers, Beta, Andrómaco, Gador (pharmaceuticals); Carballo (packing machines); Imdec (food-processing equipment); and motorcycle maker Zanella (Bisang, Fuchs, and Kosacoff 1995; Guillén and Toulan 1997). In most cases, these firms invested in other Latin American countries during the 1950s, 1960s, and 1970s in order to jump over protectionist barriers.

The Vibrancy of SMEs in Spain

The reality of a vibrant sector of SMEs in Spain stands in stark contrast with the traditional complaint of economic historians, policymakers, and labor leaders alike that the lack of true entrepreneurs and the small size or *raquitismo* of Spanish firms has retarded the country's development.[2] It is as true in Spain as in Korea and Argentina that SMEs were hurt by the creation of privileged financial circuits during the 1960s. The unusually high borrowing costs of the 1970s also wreaked havoc on the SME sector (see chaps. 2 and 7). During the last two decades, however, SMEs have thrived as state-owned enterprises lost ground and foreign MNEs established export-oriented operations in Spain, using small local firms as suppliers and transferring technology and know-how.

Spanish SMEs are less likely to engage in exports than larger firms, as is true in most countries. Once they do engage in foreign sales, however, their exports as a proportion of total sales are greater than for larger Spanish firms, unlike in Argentina. Surveys of firms show that SMEs with 100–500 employees are not significantly different than larger firms in terms of their orientation to foreign markets (MICYT 1992, 63). Exporting firms with 100–500 employees sell abroad a greater share of their total production than larger firms (Moreno and Rodríguez 1996, 35). In addition, medium-sized manufacturing firms have traditionally invested more in foreign production activities than larger firms, although the reverse is true when it comes to investments in distribution and sales subsidiaries (Alonso and Donoso 1994, 28–41; Campa and Guillén 1996a, 1996b, 1999; MICYT 1992, 115). This is in sharp contrast with Korean SMEs, which trail their larger counterparts in terms of both foreign trade and investment.

Spanish SMEs have also become major contributors to technological development. As with exports, SMEs with 100–500 employees are less likely than large firms to engage in R&D activities. If they do, however, their R&D expenditures as a proportion of sales are larger than those for firms with more than 500 employees (González Cerdeira 1996, 34). Most importantly, the technology areas in which Spanish firms hold a comparative advantage within the OECD—fabricated metals, industrial machinery, and transportation, primarily auto parts and railway equipment—tend to be heavily populated by sophisticated SMEs (Archibugi and Pianta 1992, 69, 76–77). Finally, there are no significant differences in the use of numerically controlled machines and

---

[2] On the economic historians, see Tortella 1994, 179–95; on policymakers see Martín Aceña and Comín 1991, 79–84; on labor leaders see chapter 5.

other advanced manufacturing technologies between firms with 50–500 employees and those with more than 500 (MICYT 1992, 39, 130). Spanish medium-sized firms (300–499 workers) are also more committed to their workers, spending on training about 50 percent more per employee than either smaller or larger firms (Mineco 1994, 269, 290–94).

Some Spanish SMEs have established production plants on three continents or are export powerhouses: Nutrexpa ($208 million in sales and 830 employees), Chupa-Chups ($160 million, 360), Industrias Lácteas Asturianas ($211 million, 420), and Cooperativas Orensanas (Coren, $353 million, 870) in food processing; Freixenet ($271 million, 740) in wines; Azkoyen ($95 million, 665) and Talgo ($83 million, 800) in machinery and equipment; and Hola ($98 million, 96) in printed media; among many others (Campa and Guillén 1996a, 1996b; Durán 1996).

In the following sections I examine the fortunes of SMEs in the rolling stock, wine and liquor, and printed media industries of Argentina, South Korea, and Spain. The case studies illustrate that SMEs thrive in the global economy to the extent that they find a way to be different, although always within the constraints of the development path of their home country.

Railway Rolling Stock

The manufacturing of railway rolling stock and locomotives is generally assumed to be an activity subject to economies of scale in R&D and production, although there is a need to customize products to the diverse technical and design specifications required by different railway companies. In this section I review the rise and fall of SMEs in the rolling stock segment of the railway equipment manufacturing industry. Argentina, South Korea, and Spain all witnessed the rise of SMEs in this activity. Since World War II, however, the nationalization and consolidation of railway companies into state-owned enterprises and the rise of powerful MNEs offering a full-range line of railway equipment products has put pressure on small and medium-sized rolling stock firms.

The Long and Tortuous History of Spanish Rolling Stock Producers

The big Spanish railway boom of the 1850s took place thanks to foreign investment, which typically entailed the import of construction materials, locomotives, and rolling stock. As in other countries, the railway industry was subject to sharp ups and downs, speculation, financial crises and panics, and bankruptcies. More often than not, building the railroad and managing the real estate proved more profitable than transporting passengers and cargo. By the turn of the century, the surviving companies had built a network of railway track that linked the most important population, industrial, and commercial centers in the country. Local manufacturers of railway equipment, however, were seriously lagging behind (Nadal 1975).

The evolution of the rolling stock industry during the twentieth century is illustrative of how Spanish firms have fared under changing political-economic conditions. Although some relatively important companies were founded in the early twentieth century, for example, La Maquinista Terrestre y Marítima and Fábrica de Vagones, the rolling stock industry did not fully develop until the period of import-substitution during the 1940s and 1950s. The 1942 nationalization and merger of the various railway companies into Renfe set the stage for the state's involvement in the industry. Foreign multinationals were persuaded during the 1950s and 1960s to invest in greenfield operations, for example, Babcock & Wilcox Española, or as minority partners in existing firms—La Maquinista Terrestre y Marítima, Ateinsa, Macosa, and Construcción y Auxiliar de Ferrocarril (CAF, the merger of Fábrica de Vagones with several other smaller firms). The acute industrial crisis of the 1970s and the liberalization of foreign trade and investment during the 1980s resulted in a wave of bankruptcies and mergers. The state-owned enterprise holding company (INI) took over La Maquinista in 1971, Ateinsa in 1973, and Babcock & Wilcox in 1980. As part of GEC-Alsthom's successful bid for the high-speed railway link between Madrid and Seville, the INI state-owned holding transferred majority ownership of La Maquinista, Ateinsa, and Meinfesa to the French multinational in 1989, with Macosa being awarded minority stakes in each company (Martín Aceña and Comín 1991, 234, 401, 508–9, 579–82).

Presently, the largest players in the Spanish rolling stock industry are CAF ($270 million in sales, $59 million in exports, and 3,700 employees), now controlled by savings banks based in the Basque Country, and GEC-Alsthom ($336 in sales, $212 in exports, and 2,000 employees). The most interesting player in the industry, however, is neither of these giants, but rather a medium-sized family firm called Talgo.

Patentes Talgo SA, a designer and maintainer of the Talgo natural tilting passenger train, has traditionally been one of the most innovative firms in Spain. Over the years, it has pioneered the application of aeronautical materials and technologies to the design of railway rolling stock, and the development of special automatic mechanisms allowing trains to adapt to different railway widths without stopping, known as wheel bogies.[3] It has annual reve-

---

[3] For geopolitical and technological reasons, several countries have a wider railway track than the international standard, namely, Russia, Portugal, and Spain, among others. Patentes Talgo developed the automatic railway width adaptation technology in the 1960s. In 1993 Talgo licensed Sumitomo of Japan to use this technology. Talgo itself has sold this equipment to the Russian Railways Ministry. See *Kommersant*, 18 January 1995, 9.

nues of $83 million, profits of $6.6 million, and about 800 employees. Two-thirds of its sales come from maintenance work, mostly for the state-owned Renfe railway company and for the German railways system, Deutsche Bundesbahn. Sales of trains represent 25 percent of its total revenues, while sales of maintenance equipment account for the remaining 5 percent. Talgo seems to lack size and financial clout. It is dwarfed by its international competitors, ABB, Alsthom, and FIAT, as well as by the Spanish railway equipment manufacturer CAF. Analysts have repeatedly declared the firm moribund, but Talgo continues to defy the conventional wisdom in an industry that emphasizes size and economies of scale.

Talgo's unusual trajectory began in the late 1920s, when a Basque railway engineer, Alejandro Goicoechea, challenged the traditional way in which railway cars were built with a series of pathbreaking innovations. Instead of making railway cars heavy enough to allow them to make turns at relatively high speeds, Goicoechea sought to minimize the *tara* (equipment's weight) by using materials up to 25 percent lighter and cutting the cars' height by as much as one meter. In this way, the center of gravity could be pushed closer to the ground, and the train would not derail when pulled along curves at high speeds. In addition, the cars would be a mere five meters long and have only one axle with two wheels at the rear end, while the front end would be mounted onto the next car's axle. Unfortunately, the MZA company—one of Spain's main railways at the time—rejected his project in 1939. A couple of years later, however, one of the country's leading financiers and entrepreneurs, José María de Oriol y Urquijo, an industrial engineer by training, liked the idea and provided the startup funds. The first experimental prototype of the Train, Articulated, Light, Goicoechea and Oriol (Talgo) became a reality in 1943, in the midst of one of the darkest periods of Spanish history, with international isolation and famine looming large (*Motor Mundial* 1949).

The Talgo I prototype proved a performance success. World speed records on railway track were broken repeatedly. In 1948 the American Car and Foundry Co. of Hoboken, New Jersey, and Wilmington, Delaware, agreed to manufacture three Talgo II trains. Two of them were shipped back to Spain to enter scheduled commercial service in 1950. The third was tested and used for passenger traffic at the New York Central Railroad until 1958 but without much commercial success. Talgo, however, persevered and pumped more money into R&D, which nowadays represents between 10 and 12 percent of revenues. During the 1950s the newly nationalized Spanish railways, Renfe, turned Talgo into one of its key equipment and maintenance subcontractors. An improved Talgo III design was introduced in 1964 allowing for easy directional reversibility of the train and longer cars. A crucial breakthrough came in 1968 with the Talgo IIIRD, which could travel between Madrid and Paris or between Barcelona and Geneva without having to stop at the border in order to adapt to the different track width. In 1974 the Talgo Camas became the first high-speed sleeper train in the world.

But the most important innovation, the one that sets Talgo apart from its larger foreign competitors, is the 1980 design of the Talgo Pendular, or naturally tilting train. By designing the cars in such a way that the center of gravity lies below the support platform and each wheel has its own axle, the train tilts as it enters a curve, allowing for speeds about 20 percent higher than normal without passenger discomfort. The two other oscillating trains available in the market, FIAT's ETR460 Pendolino and ABB's X2000, require electronic sensors to trigger a complex hydraulic tilting system. The Spanish low-tech design provides risk-free performance levels similar to the high-tech trains of those two powerful multinationals (Strohl 1993, 230–32; *Business Week*, 14 June 1993, 89). The latest Talgo model (TPI 200) has achieved speeds of over 250 km per hour (155 mph) on regular railway tracks during scheduled commercial service, and over 500 km per hour at the Munich, Germany, testing track.

In spite of its unique proprietary technology, Talgo's internationalization has been rather limited. The Renfe state railway monopoly accounts for over 90 percent of revenues, and it is a joint venture between Renfe and a Basque manufacturing firm that actually makes the Talgo trains, not the company itself. In 1993 the firm founded Talgo Deutschland GmbH to maintain the six sleeper trains it sold to the German railways. That same year Patentes Talgo created a joint venture with Deutsche Waggonbau Dessau to make cargo railway cars. In the United States Talgo is trying to become a supplier of low-cost, high-speed, high-comfort trains for commuter service along the Atlantic and Pacific coast's crowded corridors. Renfe and Talgo have created a joint venture (Renfe Talgo of America) to promote and test the train. The Washington-Boston project collapsed in the early 1990s in the face of bureaucratic and financial problems. Talgo trains currently service the Portland-Seattle and Seattle-Vancouver lines. The passenger cars have been assembled by a company located in Washington state from Spanish-made components, and leased by Talgo to Amtrak. Talgo trains will start servicing the Los Angeles–Las Vegas line in late 2000.[4]

In spite of possessing formidable technology, Talgo's problems are legion. Its family-owned character represents an enormous financial constraint in an industry dominated by giant multinational firms, and characterized by excess capacity and the need for huge investments in R&D. Even firms of such stature as ABB and Daimler-Benz have recently agreed to merge their railway

---

[4] *New York Times*, 11 June 1995, sec. 5, p. 3; *Handelsblatt*, 8 July 1995, 17; *Seattle Times*, 24 May 1995; *Contra Costa Times*, 14 May 1996; *Journal of Commerce*, 17 May 1996, 3B, 26 March 1997, 8B; *Travel Agent*, 11 May 1998, 100, and 3 January 2000, 106; *FT Exporter* supplement in *Financial Times*, 11 May 1998, 6.

equipment operations (ADTranz) in an attempt to reach economies of scale and scope. Recently, Talgo has allowed institutional investors to acquire as much as one-fifth of its equity (*Expansión*, 5 June 1998, 8). The Renfe railway monopoly is diversifying its sources of equipment procurement and maintenance and now prefers self-propelled trains, a product absent from Talgo's range because the firm has never been in a position to develop locomotives or self-powered passenger cars.

The case of Talgo illustrates how a technologically successful SME in a capital and R&D-intensive industry can find a place for itself in the global economy. Talgo, however, is somewhat unique not only because of the strong desire of the family not to lose control, but also because of the political-economic conditions in which it grew to prominence. During the 1950s and 1960s Talgo thrived inside a protected domestic market. Even in the 1980s and 1990s, the firm has benefited from continued ties to the state-owned railway company. To its credit, Talgo has managed to realize important foreign opportunities as Spain became more outward oriented. Although such a small firm as Talgo is always under pressure in this industry dominated by large multinationals, the company has already demonstrated that it pays to be different in the global economy.

The Chaebol Take Over Rolling Stock

As in Spain, Korean rolling stock production lagged behind the completion of the basic railway network during the Japanese occupation. Characteristically, the Korean rolling stock industry is dominated by some of the largest chaebol, a consequence not only of government policies favoring large firms but also of the purchasing practices of the Korean National Railways. Hyundai Precision & Industrial, Daewoo Heavy Industries, and Hanjin Heavy Industries—which are diversified machinery and equipment manufacturers—dwarf the other significant rolling stock firm, Soosan Heavy Industries. Only Hyundai and Daewoo are significantly engaged in exports.

Daewoo's involvement in rolling stock production started in the 1970s (the chaebol itself was founded as late as 1967). In 1973 the government nationalized a small manufacturer, Kankook Machine, and merged it first with Bugok Rolling Stocks, and later with Daewoo Machinery, which was renamed Daewoo Heavy Industries in 1976. The company is itself a widely diversified heavy machinery manufacturer: ships, heavy equipment, machines, heavy trucks, and a money-losing minicar division. It barely has any cutting-edge technology of its own, relying on different German and Japanese firms for key components and designs. It makes locomotives and powered passenger cars as well as non-powered rolling stock, and exports to Asia, Europe, and Latin America.

Hyundai Precision & Industry, another diversified heavy machinery firm, was established in 1977 after the chaebol entered the rolling stock business.

Hyundai exports more than half of its railway-related production, competing in Asian, European, and Latin American markets against Daewoo and other companies from newly industrialized countries. Also like Daewoo, it used to spend little on R&D until recently. The third large firm, Hanjin Heavy Industries, is as diversified as Daewoo Heavy Industries. Its origins date back to the 1930s.

The "big deals" rescue program orchestrated by the government after the 1997–98 economic crisis has caused much confusion in the industry. Hyundai, Daewoo, and Hanjin planned to merge their rolling stock businesses into a single company to be jointly managed, an unprecedented move for some of the top Korean chaebol (Biggart 1990). As part of the government's policy of attracting foreign investment, the companies searched for foreign partners—ABB and General Electric seemed to be keen to participate. While Daewoo showed itself to be an active supporter of finding an adequate foreign stockholder and technology provider, Hyundai was rather adamant about taking more control of the joint enterprise into its own hands. However, Daewoo's collapse as a chaebol in the summer of 1999 put the original three-way merger plan on hold.

Smaller rolling stock manufacturers in Korea are also beset by multiple problems. Soosan Heavy Industries (est. 1984, 550 employees), is less diversified than its larger competitors but, like them, has failed to develop its own technology. Besides, rolling stock is somewhat of a peripheral business for the firm, which also makes special vehicles, truck cranes, and various hydraulic parts. Soosan's rolling stock production is almost exclusively sold inside Korea. The company has a small manufacturing plant in China. The Soosan group—of relatively modest size—collapsed in November 1997 after its daring takeover of Korea's sixth largest shipyard and of a shipping, shipbuilding, and construction group went sour (*Korea Economic Daily*, 28 February 1997; *Financial Times*, 29 November 1997; *Korea Times*, 29 November 1997).

The evolution of the Korean rolling stock sector follows the blueprint of other activities believed to be feasible only if undertaken by relatively large firms that are diversified within the heavy machinery industry and beyond. Although the largest firms have engaged in exports and even foreign investment, it is not clear how they fit in a global industry in which technology and design are increasingly more important than cost.

Rolling Stock Manufacturing in Argentina

As in Korea and Spain, the manufacturing of railway equipment in Argentina lagged behind the completion of the basic grid between 1880 and 1900. This state of affairs did not change until General Perón nationalized the mostly British-owned railways in the late 1940s (Lewis 1992, 24–25, 193). Import-substitution policies encouraged the growth of several small, family-owned firms during the 1950s and 1960s. State-owned enterprises also took part in the industry. The market leaders soon became FIAT-Materfer and FIAT-Concord, both founded in 1960. These two companies manufactured locomotives as well as powered and nonpowered passenger cars and freight wagons, with a fraction of production exported to other Latin American countries. In 1983 Materfer became part of the Argentine-owned Intermendoza-Tamales business group, with interests in the areas of turbines, engines, mining, real estate, and banking (Acevedo, Basualdo, and Khavisse 1990, 96). In spite of the group's deep pockets, few resources were devoted to investments in new product and process technology.

The industry languished during the years of hyperinflation until President Menem's privatization program injected new life into the transportation sector. Liberalization of imports, however, prompted the newly privatized railway companies to purchase rolling stock from abroad rather than rely on the backward Argentine manufacturers. The largest firm, Materfer, went bankrupt in the mid-1990s. Nowadays, the bulk of new railway equipment entering service in Argentina comes from the United States, Canada, Spain, and other European countries. Thus, the Argentine railway equipment industry has come full circle between the turn of the century and the 1990s.

Wines and Liquors

The alcoholic beverages industry has rarely been the target of extensive development efforts on the part of the state. The relatively small size of the industry, the importance of traditional production methods, and the small scale of operations have generally rendered it relatively unattractive for modernist policymakers attempting to accelerate economic growth. Even in the liquor industry, where automation and economies of scale are more feasible, states have tended not to intrude. However, to the extent that agricultural interests have political clout, wine and liquor companies have benefited from trade protectionism. The wine and liquor industries are also affected by government policy in indirect ways. First, industrialization and migration to the cities is likely to create labor shortages in the countryside, thus encouraging mechanization of agricultural and wine production. And second, the formation of urban working and middle classes as a result of industrialization tends to increase the demand for wine and other alcoholic beverages. In this section I compare the fortunes of selected Argentine, South Korean, and Spanish wine and liquor producers to illustrate how state policies and institutions affect international competitiveness. Mimicking their intrusive practices in other industries, the Argentine and Korean states also intervened in wine and liquor production, with distinctively harmful consequences. By contrast, the Spanish state stayed away from the industry, while its open policy toward multinationals had beneficial indirect effects on the country's wineries.

Argentine Wine Fordism

The Argentine wine industry began with Spanish colonization around 1560. Wine production remained stagnant until the big immigration wave of the second half of the nineteenth century brought about a steep increase in grapevine plantings. The next period of rapid growth took place during the 1950s and 1960s, as rising incomes in the cities produced by import-substitution industrialization generated strong demand for wine that had to be fulfilled by local wineries. By 1970, Argentina consumed more wine per capita than any other country in the world (over 90 liters annually), and total production was surpassed only by France, Italy, Spain, and Russia. As was typical of other industries in Argentina at this time, virtually all production was consumed domestically, with exports rarely exceeding one percent of total production. Roughly 95 percent of sales were accounted for by low-quality table wine (Tizio 1995).

The collapse of import-substitution industrialization after 1975, and the inability of subsequent neoliberal and left-of-center policymakers to fix the economy, devastated the industry. Per capita consumption and domestic production plummeted to about half of the record 1970 level. Although the share of table wine in total production fell during the 1980s from 95 to 75 percent, exports failed to increase significantly. The economic boom of the 1990s— coupled with an overvalued currency—has again diverted the attention of the industry away from exports and toward an expanding domestic market. Moreover, most exports are still of table wine or semiprocessed grape juice that other countries—especially Spain—use to produce low-quality wine in years of production shortages. While there are 1,500 wineries in Argentina, only 30 are engaged in exports. With a wine industry only one-tenth the size of Argentina's, Chile exports three times as much.[5]

The Argentine wine industry's development is aptly labeled as "Fordist." A standardized, low-quality grape juice is mass-produced in large-scale wineries located on the foothills of the Andes. Part of it is bottled on location, but a significant proportion is transported by railroad to Buenos Aires for bottling and sale. The state-owned company Giol was for many years the world's largest winery. Another Argentine firm, family-controlled Peñaflor, built in 1971 the largest wine mixing tank in the world, a cylinder measuring 36 meters in diameter and ten in height. It is so large that the company rents it for parties and reunions of several hundred people. Let us explain in more detail why

[5] *Vinifera* 1, no. 2 (January 1996): appendix; *El Cronista*, 8 October 1996.

these two firms decided to become Fordist wine producers, a strategy that, while effective for grains and oilseeds, seems implausible for wines.

Giol was originally founded in the 1890s by two Italian immigrants. It grew slowly until 1954 when the government of the Province of Mendoza bought it with the intention of regulating the market and guaranteeing small grape growers a buyer. President Perón's "bread and wine" policies for the working class assured Giol an important role to play, which would persist over time even after the general's fall from power. As a state-owned enterprise, Giol grew rapidly to become the largest winery in the world, with 3,500 employees. It fulfilled its function as a policy instrument. In the typical inward-oriented style of populist policymaking, the firm's role in the wine industry was seen as the provider of jobs in the province, guarantor of minimum prices for growers, and supplier of affordable table wines for the large urban markets of Buenos Aires, Córdoba, and other major cities. Given the inconsistencies inherent to this set of goals, the company suffered from severe financial losses, especially during the 1970s and 1980s, which the official credit institutions were happy to subsidize. Giol was unable to improve quality standards.

Giol also is an important case study because it was one of the first large state-owned enterprises to be privatized in Argentina. In the late 1980s, three years before the currency convertibility plan made headlines around the world, the Peronist, though reform-minded, governor of the Province of Mendoza decided to sell Giol. Fecovita, a federation of wine growing cooperatives, purchased Giol's bottling and distribution facilities in 1990 for 7 million pesos, and some of its grape processing plants in 1997. As a worker- and grower-owned cooperative, Fecovita has focused on providing jobs for the long run. During the 1990s, it turned itself into a successful producer of table and fine wines, with exports representing about one-fifth of total sales, and ranking 159th among Argentina's largest exporters, even though it is only the 203rd largest firm in sales ($100.7 million in 1996). It presently employs about 550 people (Juri and Mercau 1990; *Financial Times*, 13 June 1990, 6; *Los Angeles Times*, 31 July 1990, 4; *Mercado*, rankings, www.mercado.com).

The case of Peñaflor resembles in many respects that of Giol. This third-generation family winery was founded in 1914 by an Italian immigrant in the Province of Mendoza. In 1930 the second generation decided to set up a large distribution facility in Buenos Aires. Betting on the mass production of wines, they began construction of a large winery outside the city of Mendoza in 1948, just two years after General Perón became president. In 1968 it purchased the quality winery Trapiche, then 75 years old. As would be expected from a company obsessed with scale economies, Peñaflor initially attempted to merge its operations with those of Trapiche. This improbable strategy in the wine industry was only recently reversed as the firm realized the importance of having a portfolio of brands and moving toward quality wines. Peñaflor was involved in some early efforts to increase exports. In collaboration with other

Argentine wineries, in the 1970s it set up a Miami distribution office, which was shut down in 1993. A similar experience took place in the United Kingdom. In 1981 it created a grape-processing and bottling facility in Puerto Rico to serve the local market. In spite of these efforts, only 12 percent of Peñaflor's sales were exports as of 1996. Its installed production capacity is a staggering 210 million liters, twice Fecovita's. In 1997 the company's losses amounted to 18 percent of sales (*El Cronista*, 13 January 1998 and 21 August 1998).

Although the Argentine wine industry has produced a number of small high-quality producers, it is still dominated by the likes of Fecovita and Peñaflor. Argentina has traditionally missed the opportunity to export wines, even as other Southern Hemisphere countries like Chile, New Zealand, or South Africa have succeeded. Various government incentives enticed producers to focus on the domestic market and to mass-produce low-quality table wines. Such a strategy discouraged Argentine wineries from improving quality and investing in reputation.

Soju, *State Policy, and the Advantages of Size in the Korean Context*

While grape wine is not big in Korea, *soju* is. This clear, fiery, almost odorless, and economical liquor was introduced from China in the late thirteenth century. Soju is distilled from rice, barley, and sweet potatoes (*so-ju* means "made by burning something"). While other traditional liquors exist in Korea, soju became the most popular alcoholic beverage after the Korean War. The government prohibited the traditional method of distillation for being wasteful of such an important source of nutrition as rice. Instead, it encouraged the method of dilution, which adds water to the distilled rice so as to increase the quantity of resulting liquor at the cost of lowering its alcoholic content and quality. Another interesting feature of this industry is that it is dominated by one firm that accounts for almost half of the market, Jinro, and four other smaller firms that jointly account for another 40 percent. Following the Korean pattern, several of the soju companies diversified into unrelated industries, even though the domestic soju market is quite large: $827 million in annual sales of 2.4 billion bottles, that is, a staggering 54 bottles (some 20 liters) per capita. Although exports of soju started in the 1960s, volumes were very small until the late 1980s. By 1997 Korean soju exports totaled some $55 million, with Japan and the United States as the main markets.[6]

As in Argentina with wines, Korean policymakers could not help but regulate the soju market. In the early 1960s General Park established a policy of

---

[6] Telephone interview, Byeong Joon Hwang, manager, Bohae Brewery, 10 November 1998; *Asia Pulse*, 18 May 1998; *Korea Herald*, 11 August 1998; unpublished data from the Korea Alcohol and Liquor Industry Association.

"one alcoholic beverage company per province." Jinro (est. 1924) was blessed with receiving the Seoul and Kyunggi-Do provinces, which account for about 40 percent of the Korean population. In 1972 the state granted Jinro the right to be the exclusive manufacturer of ginseng liquor, and in 1992 it entered into a joint venture with Coors even though the Korean beer market was shrinking at the time. In 1997 Jinro soju was ranked by *Drinks International* magazine as the world's largest spirits brand, with output of 43.8 million cases (nine liters each). With a large territorial monopoly, Jinro rose to become the largest soju company in Korea, and engaged in unrelated diversification and cross-subsidization—foods, pharmaceuticals, construction, advertising, financial services—eventually becoming the nineteenth largest chaebol. On the eve of the Asian crisis, the Jinro liquors company had a debt-equity ratio of 362 percent, low by Korean standards. The Jinro chaebol as whole, though, had reached a ratio of 3,081 percent. Not surprisingly, Jinro was one of the first highly leveraged chaebol to go bankrupt, five months before the collapse of the Korean currency in November 1997, although it continued operating as a liquors company after shedding real-estate and other businesses. Happily, the crisis reduced the consumption of expensive liquors such as whiskey but increased that of cheap ones such as soju. Exports have also soared, especially to Japan.[7]

The industry's big bang came in March 1993 when the government partly abolished the 30-year-old regional monopolies. Jinro's foray into beer induced the established market leaders to acquire small soju firms so as to compete in Jinro's traditional stronghold. Chosun took over Bobae and Chungbukso, while OB Brewery of the Doosan chaebol acquired Kyungwoul. The most interesting changes, though, came in terms of product innovation. The smaller firms in the industry started to enter regional markets previously forbidden to them with a strategy of new product introduction: Kyungwoul's smoother "green soju" in 1994; Bohae's premium soju (combining rice and honey) in 1996; and Kumbokju's "hangover-free" soju in 1997. In response, Jinro used its market power to introduce its own brands of higher-quality, gentler soju, managing not to lose market share thanks to its larger size and established distribution channels.

The vicissitudes of the smaller firms in the industry illustrate the consequences of an institutional context biased in favor of the large chaebol. Kyungwoul (second largest market share with 17 percent) was an independent company for over 70 years before it became in late 1993 a member of the Doosan chaebol (as of 1998 this company was known as Doosan Joo Ryu, or Doosan Alcoholic Beverages). This new affiliation enabled Kyungwoul to engage in a major export drive, eventually growing in international markets much faster than Jinro. In China, both Jinro and Doosan-Kyungwoul have set up soju

[7] *Asia Pulse*, 13 August 1997; *Far Eastern Economic Review*, 13 January 1994, 68–70.

factories to cater to the large Korean-Chinese population in the northeast part of the country. Bohae was established in 1952 as a family firm and received in the 1960s a monopoly in the relatively small Chonnam region (4 percent of the population). After liberalization, it attained a 9 percent share of the national soju market. Presently, Bohae employs 700 people and remains under family control. Although this was the company that created the premium soju market segment in 1996, it has failed to gain much by way of market share either in Korea—where distribution channels are key—or abroad. Kumbokju, which holds a tiny 5 percent of the domestic market and barely exports, is also encountering difficulties in gaining market share.[8]

The dominance of a financially troubled Jinro and the rise of Kyungwoul after it became a Doosan chaebol affiliate exemplify the overwhelming importance of size and connections in the Korean economy. Small and medium enterprises may come up with innovations, but the larger rivals have the incumbent power and the muscle to mobilize resources so as to neutralize the smaller firms. A look at Spanish sparkling wine producers, by contrast, illustrates that SMEs have a better chance in other contexts not so dominated by big business.

Spanish Sparkling Wines Take Over the World

Unlike Argentina and Korea, Spain has long been an exporter of alcoholic beverages, especially red wines. Spanish sparkling wines, however, did not succeeded in international markets until the 1980s (Mínguez Sanz 1994). French producers traditionally held sway in world markets, especially in the premium segment. Italian and (later) Californian producers could only hope to sell lower-quality sparkling wine enjoying much thinner margins. By the mid-1990s one Spanish firm, Freixenet, had turned the world of sparkling wine upside down, becoming the largest producer with just over 100 million bottles annually. Freixenet also became the leading exporter into the world's largest market, the United States, selling 12.6 million bottles, closely followed by Martini Rossi's 11.2 million and leaving far behind the traditional export leader, Moët Chandon at 8.5 million.

Technically speaking, Freixenet does not make "champagne" but "cava," which is the official denomination for sparkling wines produced in Spain along the Ebro valley and, most importantly, in Penedès County, located to the west of Barcelona, where production first began in 1892. Thus, Spanish firms in the sparkling wine business have always had to surmount the comparative *dis*advantage of not being a producer based in the famous French cham-

---

[8] *Korea Economic Daily*, 13 October 1995, 20 July 1996, and 3 March 1997; *Far Eastern Economic Review*, 13 January 1994, 68–70; *Asia Pulse*, 13 August 1997 and 18 May 1998; *Business Korea* 11, no. 1 (1993): 55–61.

pagne-producing counties, where the *méthode champenoise* was first developed some 300 years ago (Prial 1996). Up to the 1970s, the lower quality and weaker brand reputation of the Spanish producers could only be compensated for by lower labor costs than in France—and by tariff barriers. Spanish cava output was mostly sold in the domestic market. By the early 1990s, however, 40 percent of Spanish production was sold in the United States, Germany, the United Kingdom, the Commonwealth of Independent States, Sweden, Switzerland, Canada, and other countries (Bonet 1993; Mínguez Sanz 1994). Freixenet accounts for 70 percent of total Spanish exports, even though it has traditionally been the second largest Spanish producer. Codorníu, its bigger, neighboring rival, has been much slower than Freixenet at becoming an exporter, investor in distribution channels abroad, and acquirer of vineyards and production facilities in the United States and Latin America. Still, Codorníu is becoming more of an export powerhouse, already ranking among the top six importers in the U.S. market (*Adams/Jobson* 1996, 70).

Freixenet is a family-controlled and family-run company. Its origins date back to 1889. In 1935 it opened a short-lived U.S. sales subsidiary. Beginning in the 1950s it pioneered exports to the United States and Europe, but by the late 1970s export levels were still rather small. The big push came with the creation in 1980 of Freixenet USA and in 1984 of Freixenet Alemania GmbH, located in the two largest export markets for sparkling wines. Freixenet's market entry strategy in the United States was absolutely masterful. First, they studied the different market segments and decided to target the one for champagne bottles priced between four and nine dollars. Below that segment one could find the Californian low-quality competitors. Above it were the Italian and Californian high-quality producers, while the French premium champagnes dominated the uppermost end of the market. Then Freixenet introduced a new brand specifically for that intermediate segment, the Cordón Negro, or "black bottle," which was supposed to appeal to the young professional class. They supported the launch of the new label with a massive advertising campaign, eventually turning the firm into the third largest sparkling wine advertiser in the U.S. market. Freixenet became the U.S. market leader in volume within a short period of time, selling more bottles than all of the French producers combined (*Adams/Jobson* 1996, 71–74). The Cordón Negro was, still, a wine produced and bottled in Spain and exported to the United States and other major markets, thus suffering from a reputation disadvantage relative to the French brands.

In spite of its $33 million annual advertising budget (12.2 percent of sales), however, massive and astute marketing is not enough to account for Freixenet's success. Freixenet was torn between adopting industrialized methods of sparkling wine production using large metallic containers, and emulating the traditional *méthode champenoise*. The former is very efficient, but the quality of the wine suffers greatly. Understanding that its success depended on producing champagne of medium-to-high quality at low cost, Freixenet began spending 1 percent of revenues on R&D, and developed an automated procedure based on *jaulas* or "cagelike" racks for the second fermentation of the wine in the bottle, which produces its characteristic sparkling character. These devices hold a great number of bottles, making it possible to automate the daily operation of turning each bottle so as to shake the sediment of dead yeast cells that accumulate in the neck of the bottle. This operation was traditionally performed by hand. For a high-volume firm producing 100 million bottles annually, automation represented a major advantage, especially at a time when labor costs in Spain were rising quickly. This production innovation has allowed Freixenet to mass-produce sparkling wine of consistent medium-to-high quality at low cost.

After developing its brand image and improving its production methods, Freixenet transformed itself into a full-fledged multinational firm. In 1985 it founded Freixenet Sonoma Caves in California (one million bottles of the Gloria Ferrer label), and acquired the third oldest (1757) French champagne house, Henri Abelé of Reims (400,000 bottles), in a clear attempt to learn about new trends and technologies in the industry. In 1986 it created the Sala Vivé vineyard in Mexico (400,000 bottles). These and other domestic acquisitions allowed Freixenet to almost double its production capacity in a matter of two years and position its new brand offerings in the higher segments of the market.[9] In the late 1980s and early 1990s Freixenet opened marketing and sales subsidiaries in France, Russia, Mexico, Australia, Japan, and China. The U.S. market has lost growth potential as the dollar weakened and antialcohol campaigns reduced overall demand. In addition to its grape and wine-producing facilities in the United States, Mexico, and France, Freixenet is now planning to acquire wineries in Australia, Chile, and Russia. The French and Italian and Californian volume producers can only look enviously at Freixenet's superior price-quality mix while the firm expands into untapped countries and moves up market swiftly during the late 1990s, aided by a weaker peseta.[10]

Freixenet's success is built on a rare combination of capabilities. It certainly has benefited from a judicious application of the concept of economies of scale. However, the firm has refused to grow indiscriminately and to diversify, even into related fields. Moreover, Freixenet remains family controlled and managed. Its drive to be different has allowed it to make a dent in the global economy.

[9] In 1984 Freixenet acquired three domestic producers being privatized by the government after the nationalization of the Rumasa business group: Segura Viudas (11 million bottles), Castellblanch (13 million bottles), and René Barbier (10 million bottles).

[10] *Wall Street Journal*, 29 December 1994, 1, 5; *Dinero*, 21 June 1993, 70–71, 74–76; *Expansión*, 27 August 1993, 3; *El País Negocios*, 4 June 1995, 10; *El País Negocios*, 7 December 1997, 6; *Advertising Age International Supplement*, 29 June 1998, 13.

Policy and Location in the Wine Industry

The export success of Freixenet in an industry traditionally dominated by French and Italian producers demonstrates that firms can adapt to changing circumstances and adverse conditions. Unlike in Argentina and Korea, policymakers in Spain did not intervene heavily in the alcoholic beverage industry. No state-owned company was ever created to regulate the market, even though the Franco regime set up large state-owned enterprises in almost every industry. Moreover, economic policies and conditions during the 1980s and early 1990s tended to hurt the wine producers rather than benefit them: labor costs soared; a strong peseta policy was implemented until 1992 to curb inflation; and trade liberalization eliminated tariffs that had protected the industry for decades. In the midst of adversity, firms like Freixenet and Codorníu successfully pursued international opportunities in the Americas, Europe, and East Asia even though they encountered fierce competition from their better-prepared French and Italian rivals.

Field interviews strongly suggest that the Spanish wineries have had one key advantage when compared to their Argentine counterparts. Spanish firms in the food and beverages industry were long accustomed to competing against foreign multinationals on price, quality, and product differentiation. Spain allowed much more foreign investment in consumer goods during the 1960s and 1970s than Argentina did. Multinationals revolutionized marketing and advertising practices in Spanish consumer markets. Moreover, Spanish wineries—especially those making sparkling wines—are located near the industrial belt surrounding Barcelona, home to many domestic and foreign consumer goods firms. In Argentina, by contrast, most wineries are in the Province of Mendoza, some 600 miles away from Buenos Aires. The transportation and business infrastructure leaves a lot to be desired in Mendoza, but is world-class in and around Barcelona. Machinery, metalworking, and assembly shops are much larger and innovative in the Barcelona area than in Mendoza (Toulan and Guillén 1997; Guillén and Toulan 1997), thus making it easier for wineries to emulate the mechanization and production skills being developed in other industries. Regulation and a bias for size has also hurt Korean liquor manufacturers, which have only recently realized the potential of export markets. The most innovative firms, however, have been swallowed by the chaebol.

Publishing across Borders

Conventional wisdom has it that the media industry is subject to economies of scale and scope. Globalization is not only an economic and political phenomenon. It is most distinctively a cultural one, and the media—from satellite television to the internet—are playing a key role. Books, magazines, newspapers, radio, television, recorded music, movies, and other cultural products and services are increasingly coming under the mantle of large media conglomerates. Globalization, however, also leaves room for small media companies to thrive, as the stories of Spain's Hola and Argentina's Editorial Perfil illustrate. In finding a place for themselves in the global economy, these firms have demonstrated that one can be a leading exporter and even foreign investor without appealing to the concepts of economies of scale and scope.

High-Society Chronicle in Spain

In Spain, the most striking case of an internationally minded company in the printed media business is not the large media groups—Planeta, Prensa Española, Prisa—but a small enterprise called Hola, the leader of the high-society chronicle segment. Its flagship publication, the weekly magazine *¡Hola!* first appeared in Barcelona in 1944. With just over $98 million in annual sales in Spain and the incredibly low payroll of 96 employees, Hola currently reports profits of $8 million. It is only the 28th largest Spanish media company in terms of sales, and the 798th largest in the country. Yet, it ranks among Spain's top 250 exporters (Fomento 1996, 1997), and is one of a handful of publishers in all of Europe to successfully launch a new magazine in a foreign country. *Hello!* is specifically designed, edited, and printed in Madrid for the British market, where chronicles about the royal family, entertainment stars, and the rich and famous are also in high demand. The British edition was first published in 1988 and presently sells close to half a million copies a week, by far the fastest growth pace ever of any British magazine. An additional 130,000 copies of the average 660,000 weekly sales of the Spanish edition are sold in foreign markets, primarily in Latin America and the United States. And in late 1998 a French edition was launched under the title, *Oh La!*[11] What accounts for the success of Hola?

The media business in Spain has always been characterized by stiff competition, low margins, and frequent entries and exits. *¡Hola!* is not the oldest magazine in the segment of weekly color magazines covering the lives of the jet set: *Lecturas* was founded in 1921, two others appeared in the 1950s (*Diez Minutos* and *Garbo*, which went flat in 1987), *Semana* in 1965, and *Pronto* in 1972. Only one of them (*Diez Minutos*) is participated by foreign capital (Hachette). In this context of intense rivalry to cover the lives of the rich and famous, *¡Hola!* has committed to a strategy of product differentiation, offering the best exclusive interviews, the most lavish photographs, and the highest

---

[11] *El País*, 8 September 1994; *¡Hola! 50 Aniversario* (1994), 2:8–17; *Vanity Fair*, March 1994, 74–88.

printing quality. Its cover price is not much higher than its competitors' (about $1.75 in Spain and $4 in the Americas); yet it appeals to middle- and upper-class readers to a greater extent than its rivals. In 1981 ¡Hola! had a readership equal to about 60 percent of Pronto's, the market leader. By the early 1990s, it had narrowed the gap down to a few thousand weekly copies. And that does not take into account Hola's phenomenal growth abroad. As in Freixenet's case, we find in Hola an innovative firm that succeeds internationally but is not the domestic market leader in an industry characterized by intense rivalry (Anuario El País 1998, 178–82).

Will Hola keep on growing as an international leader in the high-society chronicle business? The firm does face two important threats. First, there is the possibility of imitation. The British tabloids and the German and American media conglomerates could conceivably launch a competing magazine. Hola has been considering an American edition in English and a central European edition in German. The reasons they have not yet been launched have to do with the second threat. The firm is owned and operated by the second family generation. Computers are nowhere to be seen in its headquarters: layouts are done manually by the founder's son and his wife, who also manage the firm. The designs for the Spanish, English, and French editions are then rushed to a printing plant in the outskirts of Madrid, and from there distributed throughout Spain, Britain, France, and about 100 other countries. The launching of the American edition has been postponed because of the inevitable loss of control from entering into indispensable distribution agreements with U.S. media groups, and also due to the complexity that North American printing operations would introduce into this quintessentially family business. In the words of the company's boss, America is "the dream," but also a risk, particularly for this kind of a firm. In a statement symptomatic of the limitations of family-run businesses, he confided in an interview that if he were in his forties he would definitely launch the U.S. edition, and that if he were in his sixties he almost certainly would not. He happens to be in his fifties, and his hesitation to take action can only lead to the second outcome.

Hola has certainly found itself a niche in the global economy. It publishes well-known magazines in Spain, Europe, and the Spanish-speaking Americas, and it ranks as one of the most export-oriented firms in its home country. Its strength has always been the vision and hard work of the founding family and a small cadre of close collaborators. Will it survive in an industry already dominated by large multinationals and undergoing rapid concentration? Will its future look like Talgo's or like Freixenet's? The future of a large country like Spain does not hinge on the fate of a tiny firm like Hola. But the country would arguably be much better off if dozens of other SMEs succeeded domestically and internationally to the extent Hola has.

High-Society Chronicle in Argentina

As in Spain, the largest Argentine media groups are not precisely the most successful internationally, even though this is the case in other Latin American countries such as Mexico (e.g., Televisa), Venezuela (Cisneros), or Brazil (Globo, Editora Abril). For example, Grupo Editorial Clarín (which publishes the largest circulation Spanish-language newspaper in the world) stands out for its sheer size and diversification, though not for its international orientation. It is again in the business of high-society chronicle that one finds an Argentine media company with a strong international bent.

The celebrity chronicle segment developed rather late in Argentina, but has helped one company become an international media player in the Mercosur. Editorial Perfil is the publisher of *Caras*, Argentina's best-selling high-society magazine and the second largest magazine in any category after the weekly *Noticias*, also owned by Perfil. The company launched a Brazilian edition in 1994 in collaboration with Editora Abril, becoming the second most popular magazine in Brazil. It is rare for an Argentine company to attain such market shares in foreign markets, let alone in such a difficult industry as the mass media. Perfil publishes 14 magazines on politics, women, sports, and science as well as celebrities, accounting for a combined 45 percent market share in Argentina. In 1996 it ranked as Argentina's 162nd largest company in terms of sales ($126.6 million), employing 401 people.

Editorial Perfil's first magazine, the political weekly *Noticias* (initially *La Semana*), was founded by 21-year-old Jorge Fontevecchia in 1976, the year the military took over Argentine politics and initiated its bloody dirty war against the Left. Fontevecchia himself was detained and tortured for a couple of weeks in 1979. During the 1982 war with Britain the junta accused him of being a spy and forced him into exile for two years. In 1997 one of his photographers, José Luis Cabezas, was murdered under still unexplained circumstances while reporting on police corruption. In 1996 Columbia University awarded Fontevecchia one of its five annual Cabot Prizes for reporting.

Perfil's foray into Brazil catapulted the firm as a major player in the Mercosur. In 1994 it acquired 50 percent of Gráfica Editora Brasil-Argentina, the publisher of six magazines controlled by Editora Abril, and launched the Brazilian edition of *Caras*, also in conjunction with Editora Abril. *Caras* generates sales of $36 million with a circulation of 350,000 in Brazil. As in Argentina, Perfil has followed aggressive price-cutting strategies and very effective marketing campaigns, especially those serializing movie, rock, and classical music collections on videotape or compact disk sold together with its magazines.

Perfil's Brazil adventure emulates Hola's success in Britain. It presently sells 60 percent more copies of *Caras* in Brazil than in Argentina. Unlike Hola, however, Perfil has perhaps overextended itself in pursuing the daily newspaper segment. In May 1998 the long-awaited daily *Perfil* appeared on news-stands throughout Argentina. The incumbent national newspapers—*Clarín* and *La Nación*—had already preempted the launch. Lagging sales and advertising revenue forced a controversial shutdown of the paper by September 1998, resulting in 171 layoffs. As a family-owned and family-run firm, though, Perfil has a long way to go. Fontevecchia is still in his early forties, and he is thinking in terms of "twenty-year projects."[12]

Globalization and Small and Medium Enterprises

The statistical evidence and case studies presented in this chapter strongly suggest that SMEs can and do thrive in a context of globalization if only state policies do not overwhelm them by artificially diverting too many resources to business groups, large firms, and/or state-owned enterprises. As the case of Spain shows, inward foreign direct investment may well be a blessing for SMEs. Foreign multinational subsidiaries create supply links to companies in the host country and bring useful technology and know-how with them. It is important to note, however, that MNEs do not contribute to the development of a vibrant SME sector under all circumstances. The cases of Korea and Argentina illustrate that the presence of MNEs might be harmful to SMEs. In Korea MNEs came to the country in the 1960s and 1970s to assemble foreign-made components using cheap local labor and then re-export the final product. Obviously, local SMEs were not approached as suppliers, nor was much technology or know-how transferred. MNEs were encouraged to come to Argentina during the 1950s and 1960s to substitute imports for local production. Given that production cost was not an issue for the MNEs—protectionism enabled them to charge inflated prices for their products—they typically integrated vertically rather than use local SMEs as suppliers. Moreover, only obsolete technology and products were introduced. By contrast, in Spain MNEs were encouraged to set up export-oriented plants during the 1980s and 1990s, compete against local firms, and source components locally, a policy that enabled local SMEs to link up with the global economy. Thus, MNEs are neither good nor bad for SMEs in the abstract; it depends on the development path, that is, on the way in which MNEs participate in the host country economy.

The case studies presented in this chapter provide four important lessons. First, SMEs can thrive in industries thought to be driven by economies of

---

[12] *Market Latin America*, September 1995, 5; *Latin Trade*, April 1998, 28; *Financial Times*, 6 March 1998, 25; *El Economista*, 12 July 1994, 13; *Gazeta Mercantil*, 18 July 1997, C-1; *Exame*, 14 February 1996, 106; *Mercado*, April 1998; *Advertising Age International Supplement*, 11 May 1998, 3; *El Cronista*, 6 August 1998; *La Nación*, 4 August 1998.

scale. The experiences of Talgo in the rolling stock industry and Hola and Editorial Perfil in the printed media business are cases in point. Second, precisely because of their size disadvantages, SMEs are uniquely positioned to introduce pathbreaking product and process innovations. Left to their own fate, some Spanish SMEs have demonstrated they can outspend and outperform larger firms in exports, foreign investment, technology, innovation, and worker training, even in such mature industries as wines (Freixenet) and rolling stock (Talgo).

The third lesson has to do with the role of family ownership and control in the governance and management of SMEs. Most SMEs are family firms, and certainly all of the specific cases discussed in this chapter are. Family ownership per se does not predict success or failure in the global economy. Talgo, Freixenet, and Hola are successful and family owned; Soosan or Peñaflor are failures and also family owned. Some 40 years ago the authors of *Industrialism and Industrial Man* argued that countries and industrializing elites are "confronted with the prospect of adapting the industrialization process to the existing family system or of altering the family system in the course of industrialization" (Kerr et al. [1960] 1964, 67). The comparative evidence collected and analyzed since the 1960s, however, demonstrates that family ownership is certainly not an impediment to economic growth or business success (Orrù, Biggart, and Hamilton 1997). Contrary to the point of view espoused by Kerr et al., family-owned SMEs happen to promote the accumulation of patient capital and the postponement of immediate gains in favor of long-term prosperity (Church 1993). A combination of relatively small size and family ownership is simply the most common type of enterprise in any country, developed or developing. But depending on the development path taken by the country, family-owned SMEs outperform or lag behind their larger counterparts, as the polar cases of Spain and South Korea illustrate, respectively.

Finally, the fourth lesson suggested by the evidence and analysis presented in this chapter is that the mere numerical presence of SMEs relative to larger firms, business groups, or foreign multinationals is not very relevant in the global economy. What matters is to what extent the SME sector succeeds in exports, foreign investment, and technological development. Spanish SMEs that cross the threshold of internationalization have demonstrated they can be more successful at exporting than larger firms. In many countries—including not only Spain but also Argentina—small firms have been in the avantgarde of foreign investment (Fujita 1996; Jones and Rose 1993; UNTCMD 1993). Spanish medium-sized firms are also more technologically dynamic than their larger counterparts.

A comparative institutional approach to development rejects the modernist fallacy that economic growth requires large-scale organization. SMEs, while not being equally prominent in all countries, cannot only provide jobs but also contribute to the country's exports, foreign investment, and technological growth. Development paths privileging business groups and state-owned enterprises generally hurt the SME sector. Contrary to conventional wisdom, however, policies favoring foreign MNEs may thwart SMEs under import-substitution conditions (e.g., Argentina), but not necessarily when multinationals are encouraged to operate freely in an export-oriented environment (Spain). The possible roles of MNEs in economic development are further examined in the next chapter through a comparison of how a key interest group in society—organized labor—has responded to their presence in each of the three countries.

FIVE

MULTINATIONALS, IDEOLOGY, AND

ORGANIZED LABOR

We the workers will never allow our homeland to be
turned into a colony.
(Argentine labor leader, 1989)

Do foreign investors want our economy to survive? . . .
Once they get profits, they will leave.
(South Korean worker, 1998)

Spain needed the multinationals because of the lack of a
viable domestic bourgeoisie.
(Former secretary-general of the Communist labor union, 1998)

TOGETHER with business groups and small and medium enterprises, foreign multinationals are a key organizational form in newly industrialized countries. Their presence is, however, much more controversial. Critics of the multinational enterprise range from those accusing it of being an "octopus," "agent of imperialism," "dog of capitalism," or "cultural dictator," to those convinced that it is a "dinosaur" on the verge of extinction because of its unwieldy size, bureaucratic inertia, and inability to adapt and innovate. The apologists of the multinational, perhaps fewer in number and less adept at finding colorful metaphors, call it a "dolphin," "leader of modernization," "job creator," or "boon to mankind." The classic economic thinkers already recognized the advantages that capital enjoys from being mobile. Thus, Adam Smith observed in *The Wealth of Nations* that "the proprietor of stock is properly a citizen of the world, and is not necessarily attached to any particular country" (Smith, 1976, 848–49). Karl Marx, for his part, pointed out that capitalists benefit not only from their ability to shift investments from one location to another but also from their expansion into underdeveloped areas: "The rate of profit is higher [in the colonies] due to backward development, and likewise the exploitation of labor" (Marx 1967, 3:238).

Political, industrial, intellectual, and labor elites have historically displayed a propensity to engage in praise or (more often) criticism of the multinationals. Far from being a mere "bread and butter" issue, the presence of foreign multinationals is seen by many as colliding with pride and dignity. Debates over multinationals frequently escalate to tackle questions of economic policy, national sovereignty, property rights, labor exploitation, even cultural identity. Different actors have different views or ideological images of the multinationals. Such ideologies provide ways of constructing reality, identifying problems and opportunities, and guiding proactive or reactive action (Guillén 1994). As cultural systems, ideologies provide blueprints for action and have immediate consequences on the policies and activities of organized actors such as labor unions. "Whatever else ideologies may be—projections of unacknowledged fears, disguises for ulterior motives, phatic expressions of group solidarity— they are, most distinctively, maps of problematic social reality and matrices for the creation of collective conscience" (Geertz 1973, 220).

In this chapter I conceptualize and document the various ways in which organized labor in newly industrialized countries sees the presence of foreign multinationals and develops policies toward them. Labor unions are key actors in development whose attitudes and actions toward the multinationals frequently shape the way in which the country is affected by foreign investment and globalization (Cooke 1997; Cooke and Noble 1998; Haggard 1990). Industrial relations are a key variable in economic development and organizational change. The literature has established that export-oriented growth and import-substitution industrialization are associated with different types of industrial relations systems (Deyo 1989; Frenkel and Peetz 1998; Kuruvilla 1996a, 1996b; Kuruvilla and Venkataratnam 1996) and with different roles played by the multinationals (Haggard 1990). Organized labor's attitudes toward foreign investment, however, have received little systematic attention in the development and globalization literatures.

I begin the analysis by characterizing four ideological images of the multinational firm: *villain, necessary evil, arm's-length collaborator,* and *partner.* I document the adoption of each of these four images since World War II. During the 1940s and 1950s Argentine, South Korean, and Spanish organized labor coincided in their flat opposition to the presence of foreign multinationals. The adoption of the ideological image of multinationals as villains had much to do with the authoritarian and repressive nature of each country's political regime. The initial negative attitude toward the multinationals shifted over time in divergent rather than convergent ways, contrary to what the conventional globalization thesis would predict. In Argentina ideologies toward foreign multinationals oscillated between the villain and necessary-evil images, while in South Korea organized labor has contributed to a restrictive, arm's-length collaborative stand. In Spain, by contrast, labor gradually shifted toward a willing acceptance of multinationals as partners. I find organized labor's images of the multinational enterprise to be the result of a combination of two key factors: democratic versus authoritarian political regimes, and modernizing versus populist labor union mentalities.

The Strife over the Multinationals

Multinationals have long been in the eye of the storm because of their unrivaled ability to develop technology, reap economies of scale, avoid high wages, reduce transaction costs, shift from saturated to emerging markets, exploit tax loopholes, and leverage their power in negotiations with governments, labor unions, local communities, suppliers, and customers. Over 80 million people worldwide are directly employed by the foreign subsidiaries of multinationals, a figure that would be much higher if employment induced by multinational activity were also taken into account. Countries differ substantially in terms of the extent to which multinationals are important job creators (table 5.1). Such differences cannot be explained by looking at each country's level of development. Some advanced countries have allowed (or even encouraged) an extensive presence of foreign multinationals, while others have not. The same is true of newly industrialized countries. Specific policies, based on concrete ideologies, are responsible for the differences.

There is one important contrast between advanced and newly industrialized countries that needs to be borne in mind. The debate over the presence of foreign multinationals tends to be more heated among newly industrialized countries than among advanced ones. There are three main reasons for this. First, newly industrialized countries tend to be rich in natural resources and/ or cheap labor that multinationals find lacking in their home countries. This resource asymmetry typically results in conflicts over how to divide up the pie between the providers of natural resources or labor, on the one hand, and the owners of technology and capital, on the other. Second, during the post– World War II period many newly industrialized countries were ruled by authoritarian regimes. Dictatorships tend to repress labor and mollify its political and economic demands, in part to satisfy local and foreign business interests. There is hard evidence, for example, indicating that multinationals obtain higher rates of return in developing countries ruled by an authoritarian regime (Oneal 1994). In addition, the presence of multinationals frequently boosts the international legitimacy of an unpopular authoritarian regime. Not surprisingly, labor unions in countries ruled by authoritarian regimes often accuse the government of allying itself with the multinationals for mutual gain. The fact that most multinationals tend to be headquartered in democratic countries tends to add insult to injury. And third, newly industrialized countries often perceive multinationals as limiting national sovereignty or being the agents of neocolonialism.

As discussed in chapter 2, the comparative literature on industrialization suggests that the way in which multinationals operate in developing countries differs depending on two factors: first, whether the strategy of development

TABLE 5.1
The Impact of Multinationals in Selected Advanced and Newly
Industrialized Countries

	1995 Per Capita Income [a]	1995 Inward FDI Stock as % GDP	Manufacturing Employment in Multinationals % of total	Year [b]
Advanced Countries				
United States	27,330	7.7	10.8	1991
Singapore	25,500	67.4	58.0	1988
Japan	22,790	0.3	1.0	1990
Norway	22,560	13.4	6.4	1989
Denmark	22,150	13.1	12.4	1986
Austria	21,480	8.0	36.5	1985
France	21,240	9.6	16.4	1990
Germany	20,650	6.9	17.0	1992
Australia	19,890	30.8	23.8	1987
Italy	19,890	5.7	10.7	1991
Netherlands	19,870	28.4	14.0	1987
Great Britain	19,500	28.5	14.9	1990
Sweden	19,270	15.9	11.5	1990
Newly Industrialized Countries				
Ireland	17,490	20.2	42.8	1987
Spain	15,040	17.6	20.9	1990
Portugal	13,220	7.4	12.9	1984
South Korea	12,280	2.3	15.0	1978
Greece	12,060	16.9	21.3	1977
Argentina	9,260	8.7	32.0	1984
Mexico	7,660	25.6	21.0	1988
Colombia	6,700	12.1	16.0	1981
Thailand	6,470	10.3	15.0	1986
Brazil	6,170	17.8	14.0	1977
Turkey	5,660	3.9	3.2	1990
Philippines	3,290	9.2	20.0	1988
Indonesia	3,200	25.2	24.0	1985

Source: UNCTD 1997, 339–52, 1994b, 185, 187; MICYT 1992, 26, appendix table 6; World Bank 1999.

[a] GDP per capita in current U.S.dollars, adjusted for purchasing power.
[b] Latest year available.

seeks to accelerate growth by substituting local production for imports (the import-substitution model) or by increasing exports (the export-oriented model); and second, whether policies toward multinationals are permissive or restrictive (Gereffi, 1989; Haggard 1990; Kuruvilla 1996a). For example, host governments often restrict multinational activity by imposing a certain level of domestic ownership, limiting profit repatriation, demanding minimum local product content and technological transfers, or requiring production to be exported. Table 5.2 lays out the four contexts that result from cross-classifying these two dimensions, each associated with a different ideological image of the multinational firm. Table 5.2 also notes which development theories, kinds of investment strategies, and labor requirements are consistent with each image. Let me analyze each image in sequence.

Import-substitution industrialization can be accompanied by permissive or liberal foreign investment policies (cell 1 in table 5.2). In this situation multinationals gain access to a protected domestic market in exchange for import-substituting investments that create jobs and save hard currency. Dependency theorists justify the arrival of foreign multinationals to invest jointly with local businesses as *necessary evils* because import-substitution in growth or new industries—for example, automobiles or electronics—usually requires technology and capital that the average developing country lacks. The cases of Indonesia, India, Brazil, Argentina, Mexico, and Spain during selected periods illustrate this situation (Gereffi 1989; Haggard 1990). In this context, multinationals expect an industrial relations system that promotes adequate levels of purchasing power inside the protected domestic market, given that exports of local production are not encouraged (Enderwick 1985). The literature, however, has observed that the multinationals attracted to an import-substitution environment rarely make the most innovative products, transfer the most sophisticated technology, or spend large sums on worker training given that trade protection allows them to sell at high prices and thus obtain large profit margins even with mature or plainly obsolete products (Haggard 1990). The multinationals' readiness to enter into coalitions with other inward-looking interest groups to preserve protectionist measures or even to perpetuate friendly governments in power regardless of their legitimacy may also cause tensions with labor unions that feel excluded from the political process (Evans 1979).

Countries pursuing an import-substitution strategy sometimes give way to nationalist sentiment and prevent multinationals from operating in the country, and they justify such policies by reference to autarkical versions of dependency and world-system theories. This is the situation captured by cell 2 of table 5.2. Countries as diverse in their resource endowments as Argentina, Venezuela, Mexico, or India periodically adopted utterly restrictive policies toward the multinationals. In this situation, multinationals are depicted as *villains* that plunder the country's riches, thwarting its economic potential and

TABLE 5.2
Four Images of the Multinational Enterprise (MNE) in Newly Industrialized Countries

Policies toward MNEs	Strategy of Economic Development	
	Export-Oriented	*Import-Substitution*
Permissive	**MNE = Partner** MNEs seen as partners in outward-oriented economic development. *Underlying development theories:* Modernization, Neoclassical. *Possible MNE Investment Strategies:* Acquisitions in mature industries. Wholly-owned in growth industries. *MNE Labor Requirements:* Flexibility, skill formation, stability. 4	**MNE = Necessary Evil** MNEs seen as necessary evils in the effort to sustain and deepen import-substitution. *Underlying development theories:* Dependency. *Possible MNE Investment Strategies:* Joint ventures (JVs) in mature industries. Wholly-owned or JVs in growth industries. *MNE Labor Requirements:* Enhanced purchasing power, stability. 1
Restrictive	3 **MNE = Arm's-Length Collaborator** MNEs seen as arm's-length collaborators to obtain the technology and marketing skill needed to increase exports. *Underlying development theories:* Late-industrialization. *Possible MNE Investment Strategies:* Export Processing Zones (XPZs). Manufacturing contracts (OEM). Minority JVs. *MNE Labor Requirements:* Low wages, docility, union avoidance.	2 **MNE = Villain** MNEs seen as villains to be avoided so as to preserve national sovereignty and independence. *Underlying development theories:* Autarkical versions of Dependency and World-system analysis. *Possible MNE Investment Strategies:* Exodus of MNEs in the face of hostile incentives, expropriations or nationalizations.

limiting its national sovereignty. Typical policy initiatives are expropriations of the subsidiaries of foreign multinationals, especially in such highly visible industries as oil, mining, or public utilities. At least in the short run, workers and their unions have often celebrated the wage increases and enhanced job security afforded by state ownership, especially when compared to the short-sighted attitude of multinationals under import-substitution conditions.

Like import-substitution, the export-oriented strategy can also be accompanied by either permissive or restrictive policies toward the multinationals. Export-led growth with restricted foreign direct investment (cell 3) typically takes the form of export processing zones, original equipment manufacturing (OEM) contracts, and minority joint ventures.[1] These special arrangements allow multinationals to take advantage of the natural resources or cheap labor so plentiful in developing economies but impose on them a number of limitations on the production process and the sale of the output, as proposed by late-industrialization theory. Under such restrictive export-oriented conditions multinationals become *arm's-length collaborators*. Multinationals are attracted to this situation by low wages, labor docility, and the absence of unions (Enderwick 1985; Deyo 1989; Kuruvilla 1996a). The cases of South Korea and Indonesia stand out as instances of this strategy (Haggard 1990). The emphasis on exporting products manufactured with cheap labor often leads to friction between workers and multinationals over wages and working conditions that may escalate into serious political conflict under repressive authoritarian regimes if workers perceive that they cannot improve their economic well-being without eliminating political constraints on their behavior.

An export-led strategy accompanied by permissive policies toward foreign multinationals results in the *partner* image (cell 4). This context is feasible only in countries that are willing to ignore or downplay ownership issues and to pursue full integration with the global economy or trade blocs in exchange for economic growth and job creation, as preached by modernization and neoclassical theories of development. The cases of Singapore, Puerto Rico, Ireland, Spain, and, more recently, Mexico illustrate the image of multinationals as partners (Haggard 1990). Multinationals will stay in an export-oriented country only if they can develop a long-term labor strategy geared toward flexibility, skill formation, and stability, that is, they can invest in a workforce capable of adapting to changes in the global economy (UNCTD 1994b, 168–73, 204–6, 215–36). Tensions may also arise in his context. The government, labor unions, and other interest groups may feel that multina-

---

[1] Foreign firms in export processing zones hire local workers to assemble components of foreign origin for re-export. By contrast, in an original equipment manufacturing (OEM) contract a foreign firm supplies a local company with the technology and most sophisticated components so that it can manufacture goods that the foreign firm will sell under its own brand in international markets.

tionals are not fulfilling their part of the partnership contract if they decide to cut jobs or divest altogether. Another area of friction might be acquisitions of domestic firms by multinationals, which could restrict competition in the host industry.

The ideal-typical scheme of table 5.2 conceptualizes the roles that governments allow multinationals to play in the process of economic development and the possible sources of friction. Such an approach, however, does not take into account whether groups in the society support the government's policy or not. Organized labor is an important group to bear in mind because of its impact on the economy and on foreign investment. In fact, unions frequently, though not always, react to the arrival of multinationals with hostility and attempt to shape policymaking by engaging in industrial action, political protest, or negotiation with the government and other interest groups.

The main argument of this chapter is that organized labor's choice of its preferred ideological image of the multinational enterprise is shaped by a combination of two variables: political regime and economic mentalities (Guillén 2000c). First, a democratic political regime that recognizes extensive labor rights and gives unions a role to play is more likely than an authoritarian regime, especially a repressive one, to generate labor union support for permissive policies toward foreign multinationals (i.e., cells 1 and 4 in table 5.2). The reason is that unions generally feel they have a weaker bargaining position when dealing with multinationals than with local businesses because foreign firms can credibly threaten to "exit," unlike most local businesses. This feeling of powerlessness usually results in apprehension about foreign multinationals. Thus, only a legal and political system with fully recognized labor rights, labor participation in political decisions, well-functioning collective bargaining, and grievance procedures may give the unions enough confidence to agree to (or even promote) the arrival of foreign multinationals. Previous research corroborates this view. Multinationals have been found to be more reluctant than local firms to recognize unions as agents in collective bargaining (Enderwick 1985; UNCTD 1994b, 249–73), and to prefer decentralized and plant-level bargaining (Cooke 1997).

The second variable, the economic mentality prevalent among labor union leaders and members, guides their preference for export-led versus import-substitution industrialization. Mentalities are implicit, nonreflective, and subjective assumptions that predispose members of a group or class to accept one particular ideology over another (Guillén 1994, 25–26). The concept of mentality has its roots in German sociology and French *Annales* history. The distinction between ideology and mentality is analytically important. A mentality is "spiritual disposition," while an ideology is "persuasive content" (Geiger 1932, 77–79). In this chapter I use the distinction between populist and modernizing mentalities (Bresser Pereira 1993; Mouzelis 1988). A *populist* mentality emphasizing short-term compromise and redistribution at the ex-

TABLE 5.3

Organized Labor's Ideological Images of the Multinational Enterprise (MNE)

Political Regime	Economic Mentality of Organized Labor	
	Modernizing	*Populist*
Democratic with full labor rights	**MNE = Partner** Democracy and a modernizing mentality enable unions to play an institutionalized role in the strategy of outward-oriented economic development and to monitor MNE activities in the country. Spain **1980s–1990s.** 4	**MNE = Necessary Evil** Democracy and a populist mentality lead unions to accept the presence of MNEs in key import-substitution industries in exchange for job security and enhanced purchasing power. Argentina **1952–55, 1958–62,** 1986–87, **1990s.** 1
	3	2
Authoritarian and/or repressive	**MNE = Arm's-Length Collaborator** Authoritarianism and a modernizing mentality lead unions to accept the presence of MNEs only as collaborators of local firms on which they can exert a more direct pressure. Korea **1980s–1990s.**	**MNE = Villain** Authoritarianism and a populist mentality lead to a rejection of the presence of MNEs as unions feel powerless. Argentina 1946–52, **1962–86,** 1988–89; Spain 1950s–70s; Korea 1950s, 60s–70s.

Note: Time periods in **bold** indicate overlap between the unions' and the government's positions.

pense of long-term prosperity (for example, wage gains regardless of productivity increases) predisposes unions toward the import-substitution model and toward either the villain or necessary-evil ideological images of the multinational firm, depending on the nature of the political regime. By contrast, a *modernizing* mentality highlighting productivity, flexibility, and competitiveness leads unions to embrace an export-led model, and either the arm's-length collaborator or partner ideological image, depending on the political regime.

The cross-classification of political regime (democratic versus authoritarian) and the mentality of the labor unions (modernizing versus populist) provides a framework for understanding which image of the multinational is more likely to be adopted by labor unions (see table 5.3). Thus, unions subscribing to populism are more likely to adopt the necessary-evil image in a democratic country with full labor rights (cell 1), and to embrace the villain image in an authoritarian one (cell 2). By contrast, unions harboring a modernizing mentality are more likely to accept the arm's-length collaborator image in authoritarian countries (cell 3) and the partner image in democratic ones (cell 4).

It is important to clarify that the argument in this chapter in no way implies that modernization, neoclassical, and dependency theories are associated with democratic regimes, while late-industrialization and world-system theories with authoritarian or repressive ones. Rather, the analytical framework outlined in table 5.3 makes predictions as to the circumstances most likely to lead labor unions to adopt different images of the multinational firm, images that are associated with different development theories. Thus, the argument is that the lack of democracy with full labor rights encourages unions to adopt hostile images of the multinational firm such as those proposed by late-industrialization or world-system theorizing. The next section provides comparative evidence documenting how democratic versus authoritarian regimes and modernizing versus populist union mentalities shaped organized labor's response to the foreign multinationals in the three countries.

Organized Labor and the Multinationals in Argentina, South Korea, and Spain

Back in the 1950s and early 1960s, labor unions in Argentina, South Korea, Spain, and elsewhere in the developing world were equally hostile toward foreign multinationals. They strongly believed that (1) the working class was being exploited in the context of an unequal international division of labor between advanced and developing countries, (2) the presence of foreign multinationals helped authoritarian regimes appear more legitimate, and (3) the country's sovereignty was at risk if the multinationals were allowed to operate freely. They saw multinationals as villains to be avoided at all costs. Like many other developing countries, Argentina, South Korea, and Spain embraced import-substitution policies during the late 1940s and 1950s, when agriculture still accounted for about half of their active populations. During the 1960s and 1970s, however, these economies became fully industrialized.

Industrialization, though, had the unexpected effect of changing organized responses to foreign investors in significant ways that differed by country and did not always follow the government's lead. In Argentina unions oscillated between the villain and necessary-evil images; in Korea they belatedly shifted toward the arm's-length collaborator image; and in Spain they adopted the partner image. This divergence took place even after the labor movement in each country had consolidated its organization into relatively powerful national unions. Moreover, there were no differences in the geographical location of the working class, which was concentrated in a few industrial enclaves: Buenos Aires and Córdoba in Argentina; the Seoul-Inchon and Pusan-Masan corridors in South Korea; and Asturias, the Basque Country, Barcelona, and Madrid in Spain. In the following sections I present evidence from interviews with union leaders and union archives and publications to document how variations in the nature of the political regime and in the unions' economic mentalities produced a divergence across countries in the dominant ideological image toward foreign multinationals.

Argentina: Between Villains and Necessary Evils

Argentina is a textbook case study of import-substitution with alternating restrictive and permissive policies toward foreign investors, as discussed in chapter 2. In the 1940s labor became one of the crucial pillars of the protectionist, import-substituting political coalition of General Perón. Unions adopted a populist credo of immediate economic gain. Foreign investors were accused of plundering Argentina's natural riches and exploiting the working class, especially during the long periods of labor repression. Unions only abandoned this image of multinationals as villains during times of acute economic crisis in favor of a grudging acceptance of their presence as necessary evils, assuming the government did not engage in repression. Partly as a result of labor's attitudes and actions, the presence of foreign multinationals has undergone repeated ups and downs.

Since the 1890s foreign capital contributed to the creation of the transportation infrastructure, utility services, and manufacturing—oil, chemicals, cement, metals, electrical machinery, and rubber (Lewis 1992, 30–51). The Great Depression hurt Argentine exports, and, to make matters worse, a military coup interrupted in 1930 a long democratic tradition initiated with independence. As Britain imposed tough trading conditions in 1933, more and more voices called for a strong role of the state in the economy (Lewis 1992, 86–93). The reaction against British economic imperialism marked the birth of a nationalist conscience among intellectuals, politicians, and labor unionists. Radical intellectuals—mesmerized by the traditional, eternal aspects of Argentine culture—seized the opportunity to denounce that "everything material, venal, transmissible, or reproductive is foreign or is submitted to foreign financial hegemony," and that "FOREIGN TRADE has dominated everything, even our morals. . . . [Argentina] is a COLONY UNDER THE LIBERAL ECONOMY; [the country] can expect from abroad nothing but EXPLOITATION AND SERVITUDE" (Waisman 1987, 49–50; San Martino de Dromi 1992, 149–52; Rock 1993, 21).

The rise of inward-looking attitudes and hatred toward foreign economic powers reached a climax in 1943 with the coup by army officers of fascist inclinations. Juan Domingo Perón, then a colonel, was put in charge of the Labor Department, showering workers with benefits and enhancing their bargaining power. After winning the 1946 presidential election, he expanded populist labor reforms to secure his power base and created a corporatist system of occupational and interest-group representation, monopolistic and compulsory in nature, with the state acting as arbiter of disputes. Perón also deepened import-substitution and created state enterprises. Building on the traditional distrust of foreign investors and on the popular belief that the country was inherently rich, he succeeded in turning fears and prejudice into hostility with his effective populist and nationalist rhetoric. Foreign interests in railroads, telecommunications, utilities, and the merchant marine were nationalized.

The main Argentine peak labor organization, the General Confederation of Labor (CGT), was bureaucratized and domesticated by Perón, who succeeded in turning it into a nationalist and populist union, ridding it of socialist and communist ideals about working-class internationalism. "This movement was not born thanks to a technocrat or an inspired sociologist versed in foreign theories, but out of a long process originating in the words and works of General Perón," reflected a union leader some decades later. A famous union slogan made the same point, only more succinctly: "Neither Yankees nor Marxists; Peronists!" (Bunel 1992, 118; McGuire 1997). The CGT had been against "capitalist imperialists" since its founding in the early 1930s (Reinoso 1987, 99–110). "Ultimately," its secretary-general stated in 1947, "elements of the oligarchy and alien imperialism attempted to deflect the destiny of labor unionism" (San Martino de Dromi 1992, 195 n. 43). Perón also instilled in the unions a populist mentality of short-term economic gain, granting workers average wage increases of 22 percent during the late 1940s while productivity increased by no more than 6 percent (McGuire 1997, 52–53). Absenteeism ran as high as 50 percent (Lewis 1992, 183). Work rules mandating frequent periods of rest during the day and granting workers and their unions discretion as to how to execute tasks proliferated. As Lewis (1992, 183) notes, "trade unions in various branches of industry began declaring their own workless days, 'in celebration of that industry's contribution to the Nation.' Soon it became the practice to declare the day after one of these holidays to be a 'free' day also. . . . By 1951, it was estimated that the ordinary Argentine worker took a day off for every two spent on the job."

The CGT's official discourse on foreign investment only shifted in response to Perón's attempt to overcome a balance-of-payments crisis in the early 1950s by "retreating" from economic nationalism and allowing foreign involvement in automobiles and oil (Lewis 1992, 195–207). Although some individual unions and the rank and file protested, the CGT leadership adopted the necessary-evil image: "Foreign investors are a danger for the country of investment only when those countries lack legislative norms to regulate their activities adequately" (Baily 1967, 141; McGuire 1997, 67–72).[2]

A 1955 army coup ousted Perón after the church turned against his anticlerical educational reforms and the military feared the appearance of a worker militia. But his imprint endured. Semidemocratic governments alternated with authoritarian ones until the military juntas of 1976–83, each trying but failing to put an end to the stalemate between the inward- and outward-oriented interest groups (Adelman 1994; Lewis 1992; Waisman 1987). Multinationals came to Argentina in the late 1950s and early 1960s, but little new investment arrived before the military coup of 1976 pursued a brutal neoliberal economic program. The frequent policy zigzags invited multinationals to focus on short-run gains at the expense of long-term projects, that is, to exploit natural resources recklessly or to manufacture price-inflated goods for a tiny domestic market. In the oil industry, for example, the government canceled in 1955 the contracts that Perón had signed with Standard Oil in 1952. The next president signed new contracts in 1958—resulting in a sharp increase in production—only to see them nullified in 1963 two more presidents down the road. Foreign companies were invited to return in 1966, expelled in 1973, and again encouraged to participate in the industry after 1976 (Lewis 1992, 298–318, 421–22).

With Perón in exile, union attitudes toward foreign investors remained largely intolerant (San Martino de Dromi 1996, 349; Balvé 1990, 56–57; Godio 1991, 144, 147). In 1957 union leaders demanded "the reinforcement of a national popular state aimed at destroying the antinational oligarchy and its foreign allies," and called for the nationalization of foreign trade, meatpacking, and banking (Lewis 1992, 368; Godio 1991, 72, 77; Calello and Parcero 1984, 197, 201). Some unions did acquiesce with the democratic government's policy of attracting foreign investment during the late 1950s and 1960s, but the adherence to the necessary-evil image proved incomplete and shortlived (McGuire 1997, 86–88). The CGT sharply criticized the government's attempts to attract multinationals (Balvé 1990, 57). Thus, the secretary-general of CGT charged that "capital was being imported in exchange for exports of sovereignty." The Struggle Plan of 1964—a thoroughly populist document—called for "building the foundations of a happy people with sufficient welfare so as to enable a decent existence *in a country that is immeasurably rich.*"[3] In the mid-1960s the unions acted on their populist instincts and sought to obtain immediate economic gains with factory occupation campaigns, often of for-

---

[2] The CGT's temporary acceptance of the necessary-evil image had more to do with its dependence on the state for resources than with democratization (McGuire 1997, 57).

[3] Emphasis added. *Boletín Informativo Semanal de las Actividades de la Confederación General del Trabajo* 2 (1963): 4, 7 (1963): 5, 10 (1963): 8, 11 (1963): 2, 44 (1964): 13, 48 (1964): 9; Balvé (1990, 48); *Informes Laborales,* May 1960, 31, June 1961, 26.

eign-owned firms. Labor leaders that obtained the best deals for their members were more likely to make it to the top of the CGT organization (McGuire 1997, 82, 86–88, 94, 114–15, 153–56). The CGT also began to support a leftist guerrilla movement that became especially violent during the early 1970s.

Demands for nationalization mounted during the 1960s, as the unions felt multinationals were taking advantage of labor repression.[4] The unions thought that "the government formed with the support of the armed forces—elected by nobody—lowered import tariffs, the [foreign] monopolists applied the law of the jungle—dumping—, domestic firms went bust. . . . This is the power of the monopolists, which kills domestic private firms with one hand, and with the other threatens state enterprises, where restructuring measures are merely the prologue to a surrender, thus tying the last strings of financial dependence" (Calello and Parcero 1984, 231–32). The 1968 program criticized foreign firms for wanting to circumscribe Argentina's "role to the export of raw materials, precisely when the technological age is dawning" (Godio 1991, 185–86, 191, 195, 215–16). This was a sharp criticism of the government's policy of allowing multinationals under the import-substitution model, though not a rejection of the model itself (see cell 1 of table 5.2).

Labor leaders were quick to point out that the bourgeoisie, state elites, and the military had forged a "conspiracy" with foreign multinationals to plunder the country.[5] The antiforeign rhetoric became particularly virulent when confronting American interests, mostly because of the activities of the American Institute for the Development of Free Labor Unionism, which as part of President Kennedy's Alliance for Progress received funding from U.S. multinationals and was endorsed by the AFL-CIO. "To liberate oneself is to reverse radically and forever that process of [semicolonization of Argentina]: until there are no meat-packers from the Chicago pool, no Shell refineries, no DuPont de Nemours factories, no Morgan or Rockefeller banks."[6]

Antiforeign attitudes were also exacerbated by well-publicized court cases against the abuses of multinationals—for example, the Swift bankruptcy of the early 1970s—and by the labor riots of 1969 and 1971 in the auto-manufacturing city of Córdoba. The bankruptcy of the meatpacking company Swift was exploited by nationalist politicians, labor unionists, and employers for partisan political gain. The beef trade—Argentina's "mother industry"—had long provided fertile soil for reactionary nationalism. As early as 1917, an

---

[4] CGT: *Órgano Oficial de la Confederación General del Trabajo* (hereafter CGT) 10 (1968): 1; *Revista CGT* (weekly publication of the dissident union CGT de los Argentinos), nos. 1, 6, 22, and 29 (1968); *Jornadas Económicas CGT* (1963), 9, 19; *Informes Laborales*, June 1971, 34; Godio 1991, 185–86, 191, 195, 215–16.

[5] Rogelio García Lupo (1971) pointed out in CGT during 1968 that nearly 200 officers in the army were appointed as top executives of as many domestic and foreign-owned firms.

[6] CGT 10 (1968): 1, 5; *Revista CGT*, nos. 1, 6, 22, and 29 (1968); *Jornadas Económicas CGT* (1963), 9, 19; *Informes Laborales*, June 1971, 34; Spalding 1988.

improbable alliance between ranchers and consumers, conservatives and socialists tried to "fight with energy against the [meat] trusts, those octopuses
which damage, arrest, and destroy commercial independence and free production" (Smith 1969, 76). Swift, an American company, had operated in
Argentina since 1907. In 1970 it ranked among the country's top 10 firms in
terms of revenue, when it came to the brink of bankruptcy due to competition
from rural packing houses, price-raising tactics on the side of cattle breeders
and fatteners, and increasing difficulties and restrictions in foreign markets,
including a disease-related international embargo of Argentine beef in 1967–
69 that was partially lifted only as late as 1997. Making matters worse, Swift
had just been acquired in 1968 by an unscrupulous conglomerate based in
the Bahamas (Deltec), which engaged in all sorts of dubious financial operations and scandalous transfer pricing arrangements so as to decapitalize its
new Argentine subsidiary. Swift's creditors filed suit in 1970, but legal proceedings dragged on until 1976, when a court ordered the liquidation of the company. In the meantime, many a politician surreptitiously tried to tilt the balance in favor of his preferred side, to the dismay of public opinion (Lewis
1992, 319–27; Rock 1987, 351; Smith 1969, 57–81).

The labor riots of Córdoba—the *Cordobazo*—had far-reaching consequences for the country as well as for foreign multinationals. A town of
800,000, Córdoba was Argentina's dominant automobile-manufacturing center until the mid-1960s. Echoing the classic dependency argument, local
unionists held the foreign auto companies Renault and FIAT responsible for
the decline of the industry, pointing out that they brought machinery "obsolete back home" and used components "made outside of the country." Moreover, labor feared that local auto components manufacturers would be taken
over by the multinationals "when they feel like it, under conditions of exploitation and sub-exploitation, the former owners being a very typical local bourgeoisie subservient to the monopolies." During 1969 small incidents in the
auto and transportation sectors escalated into a general strike after the most
radical of the Peronist national unions stepped in, seeing the crisis as an opportunity to advance their populist attacks on the government's austerity policies
and on the multinationals. The riot ended in 15 deaths. A second *Cordobazo*
took place in 1971 as a wave of factory occupations, looting, and rioting that
resulted in only one death but forced one general out of power and complicated the next general's task to the point of facilitating Perón's return from
exile in 1973. In their own view, the unionists were simply trying to break the
"Holy Alliance among imperialism, our oligarchy, and the armed forces." The
Cordobazos set Argentina into a spiral of acute sociopolitical turmoil (Calello
and Parcero 1984, 241; Brennan 1994; Flores 1994; Lewis 1992, 369–87; San
Martino de Dromi 1992, 311–14).

During most of the 1960s and into the 1970s, unions reacted to multinationals with hostility because of their populist mentality and the government's

unabated repression (McGuire 1997, 112–63). While the government promoted the presence of multinationals as necessary evils in its import-substitution effort (cell 1 in table 5.2), the unions saw the multinationals as villains (cell 2 in table 5.3). And during Peronism's second, though brief, spell in power between 1973 and 1976, union leaders supported the nationalization of foreign firms.[7]

The first military junta of 1976–81 reversed course once again with a radical and fast-paced opening of the economy to foreign investors and traders, and initiated a "dirty war" against labor and the Left that claimed over 9,000 lives (Munck 1988). Still, populist behaviors were not eradicated, with job absenteeism remaining at double-digit rates (Lewis 1992, 438, 474). The unionists complained that "the agents of the multinational companies infiltrated the government so as to push a program of denationalization and colonization."[8] A few years later, the national union leadership sent a defiant letter to the once powerful economy minister, José Martínez de Hoz: "The liquidation of our national industry . . . is your greatest victory. . . . For all of this we say to you, 'Mister Joe, mission accomplished: and we believe your friend Rockefeller and your friends from the international lending institutions (IMF and the Inter-American Development Bank) will recognize and reward you for it' " (Ranis 1992, 39). Subsequent juntas, as growth slumped, undid the liberal economic reforms in 1981–83, grotesquely mismanaged the economy, and sealed their fate in a desperate attempt to appease labor turmoil by invading the windswept Malvinas Islands—a sparsely populated British colony off Argentina's coast also known as the Falklands.

After the return to democracy, the unions did everything possible to undermine President Raúl Alfonsín's stabilization policies and to discourage foreign investment. Between 1983 and 1989 the CGT staged as many as 13 general strikes against the president. True to their populist mentality, the unions attacked economic austerity measures as well as plans for privatizing state companies, for they were "Argentine capital accumulated through the work of the people." The CGT turned its back on the facts that one in six employed Argentines was on the state's payroll at the time, government spending had reached 60 percent of GNP, and 40 percent of the budget was allocated to subsidizing the losses of the state enterprises (Abós 1984; San Martino de Dromi 1992, 440–76, 1996, 1153; Lewis 1992, 250, 488; McGuire 1997, 193–94).[9] Faced by the unions' formidable opposition, the president ultimately failed to bring inflation under control, stepping down short of completing his six-year term.

[7] *Realidad Económica* 17 (1974): 98–104, 18 (1974): 110–11, 22 (1975): 54–63.

[8] CGT Azopardo's Archive, press communiqués of February 1983 and 16 October 1984. See also 28 April 1982, 31 March 1983, 1 April 1986; and Godio 1991, 318, 354.

[9] Interview, Saúl Ubaldini, secretary-general of the CGT during the 1980s, Buenos Aires, 4 October 1996.

The desperate political, economic, and social situation of the late 1980s helped elect Peronist presidential candidate Carlos Menem on a campaign platform long on symbolism ("Follow Me, I Won't Disappoint You," was his slogan) and short on details about his future course of action. Once in power, Menem took advantage of the situation to push liberal economic reforms, in a remarkable show of Peronist pragmatism. Two key policy initiatives were the opening of the economy to foreign investment and an ambitious privatization program (Toulan and Guillén 1997). Of the 54 privatizations completed until February 1993, foreign multinationals participated in 37 of them (Kosacoff and Bezchinsky 1994, 135–39). Privatizations, currency stabilization, trade liberalization, and administrative reforms undermined the political and economic power of the unions. While some factions of the labor movement indicated their desire to move away from populism by increasing the size of the pie rather than fighting about its distribution, others remained uncompromisingly combative: "We the workers will never allow our homeland to be turned into a colony." The head of the state employees' unions claimed that "the only thing that is being privatized are the profits, while losses are being nationalized" (San Martino de Dromi 1992, 476–87, 1996, 1358–59, 1378–92; Etchemendy and Palermo 1998; Ranis 1992, 214–15). Many union leaders were proving to be out of touch not only with a reality of bankrupt state firms, but also with the rank and file. In plebiscites held at several state-owned companies, workers voted in favor of privatization (Ranis 1996, 1992, 133–36, 210). And surveys of the general population also confirm that a majority desired privatization and economic liberalization (McGuire 1997, 235).

While some unions supported the government's privatization and foreign investment policies, they did not do so out of true belief in the idea that multinationals were good for the country. Rather, it was a pragmatic reaction to the desperate economic situation of the 1980s and early 1990s, which had reduced the unions' power and influence. President Alfonsín himself briefly enjoyed the support of the more pragmatic unions during 1986–87 in exchange for populist wage hikes. These collaborative unions then played a key role in Menem's successful 1989 election. Multinationals are still largely seen by Argentine unions as necessary evils rather than partners, in a manner reminiscent of the situation created by Perón's retreat from economic nationalism in 1952–55 (McGuire 1997, 204, 234). The most open-minded unions have sought to rebuild their organizational autonomy and resources by establishing new social services for members, taking stakes in privatized firms, and creating firms to act as subcontractors to the privatized companies, but without switching ideological gears (Levitsky and Way 1998). Meanwhile, the dissident labor organizations have renewed their antiforeign attacks (McGuire 1997, 216–41; Murillo 1997). The unions' stance has had important implications. For example, multinationals operating in Argentina do not stand out for their worker-training efforts (Fuchs 1994), and the feelings of mutual distrust still run deep. As we shall see next, organized labor's ideologies toward foreign investors in Korea initially emphasized the same themes as in Argentina: multinationals plunder natural assets and exploit labor, legitimate authoritarian regimes, and threaten national sovereignty. Korean unions, though, tended over time to accept an arm's-length approach given their modernizing attitudes in the context of an export-led economic model.

South Korea: From Villains to Arm's-Length Collaborators

The roots of Korean labor's antiforeign attitudes lie deep in recent experiences of colonial rule and military intervention and have been kept alive by the country's dependence on foreign military and economic powers right up to the present. Not surprisingly, Korean labor adopted the villain image of foreign multinationals during the turbulent 1940s and 1950s. The rapid export-led growth strategy initiated in the early 1960s relied on the participation of foreign multinationals as arm's-length collaborators, only rarely as direct investors, and on the availability of a large pool of cheap and docile labor. Korean workers and unions did not challenge the export-led model per se, but reacted against the deplorable working conditions at the export-oriented plants, fighting the abuses of the multinationals from the 1960s to the 1980s under authoritarian regimes. Thus, opposition labor unions and grassroots organizations shaped the pattern of multinational activity in the country, rendering repressive labor regimes such as export-processing zones unfeasible, but eventually legitimating such other restrictive arm's-length schemes as export contracts and minority joint ventures in which Korean firms retained managerial control. Organized labor's hostility toward a direct, unrestricted presence of multinationals persists even after the transition to democracy due to continuing repression of union activities. As Koo (1993a, 4) has put it, "South Korea is by no means a docile and quiescent society happily engaged in the pursuit of economic prosperity led by a strong, mercantile state."

Even though organized labor's predicament in Korea during the 1950s was very different than in Argentina, it adopted a similar antiforeign ideology. No socialist party ever emerged in Korea, and, after two foreign occupations— Japan's and the United States'—the communist movement was essentially nationalistic rather than class-based. Nor was a *trades* unionism feasible because the handicrafts had declined during the Yi dynasty's long period of rule, 1392–1910 (Koo 1993b, 136; Amsden 1989, 192–95, 324–25). Japanese colonialism, U.S. occupation, and South Korean authoritarianism all succeeded at preventing the free unionization of labor through restrictive legislation and outright repression (Cumings 1997, 367–77).

Organized labor's reaction to foreign economic involvement in Korea had traditionally been mixed with the political aspiration of independence. The Korean independence movement emerging out of Japanese colonial rule—

supported by the National Council of Korean Labor Unions—called for the nationalization of Japanese and pro-Japanese Korean property, and of all basic heavy industries, natural resources, and means of communication and transportation (Hart-Landsberg 1993, 120–21). During the years immediately following World War II multinationals were clearly seen as villains by the labor unions. In response, the United States sought the collaboration of conservative, right-wing interests to destroy the Communist worker unions and to create the organization that would later become the long-lived Federation of Korean Trade Unions or FKTU (Hankuk noch'ong). The zenith of this period of reckless repression was reached during the Chungryangri railroad strike of 1947, which ended in hundreds of deaths and thousands of arrests (Koo 1993b, 134–35). During the 1950s the economic disorder induced by the Korean War and President Rhee's repressive practices only reinforced labor's hostility toward the multinationals.

In a sharp departure from previous policy, General Park Chung Hee (1961–79) pursued a political and economic program of economic independence and export-led growth on the basis of large, Korean-owned firms. Multinationals were only permitted to operate as arm's-length collaborators in export-processing zones or in minority joint ventures and export contracts with Korean firms (Amsden 1989). While export-processing activities tended to exclude Korean firms, joint ventures and export contracts allowed them to learn how to produce massive amounts of goods at low cost in collaboration with foreign multinationals (Amsden 1989; Lim 1985; Westphal, Rhee, and Pursell 1979).

Export-led growth required low wages and labor docility. General Park's 1961 Plan for the Reorganization of Labor Groups purged the FKTU leadership and turned it into the organizational vehicle to "work toward national security by eliminating all pro-communist and counter-revolutionary elements and establish a system of unified industrial unionism to overcome organizational disorder and to prevent undisciplined labor disputes" (Lee 1987; Sohn 1989). The Park regime achieved a true regimentation of labor with the authoritarian Yushin constitution of 1971, introduced to make sure that international economic turbulence would not undermine Korean competitiveness and that the ongoing push into heavy and chemical industries would succeed (Chu 1998; Lie 1998, 98–118).

The few foreign multinationals that ventured into Korea during the 1960s and 1970s made a bad reputation for themselves by exploiting a pool of cheap labor disciplined by a repressive regime. The first foreign investment project took place in 1962. Normalization of relations with Japan in 1965—which paved the way for increased foreign investment—was marked by acute protests (Kim 1971). The creation of duty-free export-processing zones attracted U.S. and, especially, Japanese assemblers, who used Korean labor until wages increased steeply in the late 1980s. Strikes over unionization and working conditions first erupted at these plants in the late 1960s (Signetics, Oak Electronics, Korea Pfizer), which mostly employed young women, inducing General Park to restrict labor organizing at foreign-invested plants (West 1987; Deyo 1989, 135; M. B. Lee 1993; H.-J. Kim 1993; Nam 1994, 1996). The official and dominant FKTU union then stated its support for the arm's-length collaborator image promoted by the government, that is, the "effort to attract multinational corporations," and offered to "defer the organization of a labor union for six to twelve months after the firm has arrived, limiting ourselves to setting up a vehicle for mutual understanding between labor and management" (Kei 1977, 74).

In spite of Park's efforts to control workers through the FKTU union, labor dissidence rose, especially at the export-processing zones, and began to organize itself into (illegal) unions. At the center of the problem was the lack of worker rights and the appalling working conditions that characterized the first two decades of rapid economic growth in Korea. The multinationals operating at export-processing plants were found to be particularly exploitative of labor. In addition, when faced by labor unrest or unionization drives, several American and Japanese multinationals allowed the police to discipline striking workers or simply decided to leave Korea without paying back wages and other debts. Tellingly, General Park's assassination in 1979 was triggered by a mounting wave of labor unrest over pay and working conditions initiated at foreign firms in the Masan export-processing zone.[10]

Park's successor, General Chun, asserted his authority after the Kwanju massacre of 1980, which showed the working class that foreign economic powers were willing to go along with repression and that the dominant union confederation (FKTU) was a puppet organization. An outburst of creative criticism followed as intellectuals and workers composed countless novels, poems, movies, plays, and visual art against Japanese and American economic imperialism. Worker-poets depicted how the government had turned Korea into "a paradise for U.S.-based multinationals." The United States was described as a "ruthless hegemon," a "careless colossus," and a "Coca-colonizer." Antimultinational cartoons were used by the clandestine labor unions in their organizing efforts. Foreign multinationals came under attack for their "imperialistic plunder" (J.-B. Lee 1994, 206–7, 217–18, 230–31, 253–69). Clearly, workers and their emerging union organizations were flatly opposed to the direct presence of foreign multinationals, especially in the export-processing zones.

These and other opposition movements coalesced in the *minjung* (common people) movement of the 1980s, which exploited the increasingly large gap between the workers and the official FKTU union. It was formed by 23

---

[10] See Asia Watch 1990, 87–92, 100–103; Hart-Landsberg 1993, 182–85; Ogle 1990, 104–5; Choi 1989; Nam 1994; Kei 1977; H.-J. Kim 1993; J.-B. Lee 1994, 176–78; Lim 1985, 109–19; Rodgers 1990; West 1987; Deyo 1989; Vogel and Lindauer 1997; Haggard 1990, 53–54.

organizations of workers, farmers, intellectuals, journalists, and church activists in reaction to increased income inequality, repression, and an emerging class-based polarization of society (Koo 1993b; Lie 1998; Shorrock 1986). Its ideology combined elements of nationalism and nativism and became virulently anti-American and anti-Japanese. In 1984, *minjung* leaders sent an "open letter" to President Reagan accusing his administration of maintaining " 'friendly ties' with the military dictatorship. . . . The U.S. multinational corporations already in Korea are collecting huge profits through unfair contracts and through the sheer size of their capital" (Shorrock 1986, 1209–10).

Criticism of multinationals remained intense through the late 1980s, especially because they allowed or sponsored violent crackdowns on union activists—hiring *kusadae* or strikebreaking thugs—and threatened to pull out of the country, as in the cases of Control Data, Motorola, Tandy, and Pico Products (Lee 1987; Liem and Kim 1992). The secretary of the Coordinating Council of Trade Unions at Foreign Invested Companies bitterly complained in 1989 that "the profits [of foreign firms] came from the efforts of Korean laborers—laborers who ate noodles and lived in small rooms." The general secretary of the International Metalworkers' Federation, Herman Rebhan, was often approached by Korean unionists asking for help. He explained in a written statement that "the use of kusadae is a throwback to Chicago-type violence of the 1930s. Motorola in Korea is behaving as if Koreans were second-class inhabitants of the world and Korea was an economic colony for multinational companies."[11] Reportedly, more than half of *minjung* drama performances in 1992–93 were labor-related, often criticizing the exploitative behavior of U.S. multinationals (J.-B. Lee 1994, 259).

The dissident labor unions organized at the industry and company levels successfully mounted a major strike wave in 1987–88. They benefited from the acute scarcity of skilled labor to staff the country's booming large-scale plants in such heavy industries as chemicals, shipbuilding, machinery, and automobiles. These strikes resulted in sharp wage increases. It would be wrong, however, to argue that Korean unions behaved in a populist way when attempting to extract wage concessions. The unions were certainly militant and occasionally violent, but they were opportunistic rather than populist (Song 1994, 173).[12] They knew a tight labor market with negligible unemployment afforded them great power. Repression had long kept wage increases

---

[11] *Los Angeles Times*, 10 April 1989, pt. 4, p. 1. See also Rodgers 1993, 441–505; *Financial Times*, 19 February 1989, 4; *Journal of Commerce*, 5 May 1989, 3A, and 31 October 1991, 1A.

[12] The assessment that Korean unions are far from populist in their mentality and policy was corroborated during telephone interviews with union leaders and labor scholars: Kim Yoo Sun, deputy director of the Korean Labor and Society Institute, former director of policy planning at the KCTU, and member of the Tripartite Commission, 31 May 1999; Lee Byoung-Hoon, formerly leader of the IBM Korea labor union, 4 June 1999; Son Ho Chul, professor, Seo-kang University, Seoul, 2 June 1999.

well below productivity gains. This was especially true between 1979 and 1986. Thus, after the relaxation of authoritarian rule in 1987, workers and unions used their market power to raise their share of the benefits from rapid economic growth (Soon 1994, 85–92; H.-J. Kim 1993, 149; Wilkinson 1994). Moreover, unions never condoned or encouraged absenteeism, which is extremely low in Korea. The wage hikes had the expected effect of making export-processing investments unprofitable. Thus, the most significant objection of the dissident unions toward the arm's-length collaborator image—the exploitation of labor at the foreign-controlled, export-processing plants—was to lose significance as Korea's wage advantage eroded. The dissident labor organizations were now ready to join the more moderate FKTU confederation in admitting multinationals as minority collaborators in joint ventures or as marketers of Korean-made products, with Korean-owned firms retaining managerial control.

The disputes at the Korean subsidiaries of IBM, Motorola, Tandy, and Citibank—all majority or wholly owned by their parent corporations—illustrate the reasoning behind the restrictive ideology of the labor unions toward the multinationals. Unions organized at the plant level showed little patience with the usual arguments to justify the unrestricted presence of multinationals. Labor leaders stated in 1990 that "multinationals do not enhance our technology nor give us job opportunities for free" (S. Y. Lee 1990). The leader of the IBM labor union in the late 1980s flatly rejected the image of multinationals as partners, referring to them as a "pernicious influence" (B. H. Lee 1990). International observers noted that unions at foreign-owned companies in Korea exhibited little concern for their jobs. They were simply opposed to working for foreign-owned and managed companies, preferring instead to have multinationals as arm's-length collaborators in the forms of minority joint ventures and export contracts (Byington 1990). Foreign bank employees involved in the 1989 strikes stated that they had to endure the "pain and humiliation of working at a foreign-owned company," a stigma that did not exist when working for a Korean firm holding the dominant stake in a joint venture with a multinational.[13] In one survey of opinion in the mid-1990s, over half of the population rejected foreign direct investment without Korean control, while 66 percent opposed lowering import tariffs to meet international standards and agreements.[14]

Even after democracy was reestablished in the early 1990s, labor unions clung to their negative image of the multinationals, whose presence in the country can only be tolerated as arm's-length collaborators in the pursuit of

---

[13] *Far Eastern Economic Review*, 4 May 1989, 68–69. Interview with Lee Byoung-Hoon, Philadelphia, 25 March 1998, and telephone interview, 4 June 1999.

[14] See *Computing*, 8 September 1994. On popular opposition to U.S. pressure during the Uruguay negotiation round of the GATT, see J.-B. Lee 1994, 289.

export-led growth. The reason for the lack of change in union ideology has to do with the government's unwillingness to take labor into account during the transition to democracy in the early 1990s, and to recognize and observe full labor rights (Chu 1998; Mo 1996). The freedoms of association and assembly and the right to collective bargaining are not fully recognized or guaranteed in Korea, a fact repeatedly denounced by the United Nations, International Labor Office, and OECD—organizations in which the country holds membership (Dicker 1996). For example, the more combative Korean Confederation of Trade Unions (KCTU, Minjoo noch'ong) was not legalized until early 1998 in spite of its rapid membership growth after 1987, especially in the crucial automobile, shipbuilding, and heavy industries. Even the most routine labor activities such as actions demanding improved work conditions frequently end in police charges and arrests. Accordingly, Korean unions—not only the dissident KCTU but also the more conciliatory FKTU—position themselves in cell 3 of table 5.3; that is, they defend modernizing ideas about export-led growth but combined with restrictions on the activities of foreign firms. As Mo (1999) notes, unions remain confrontational in their approach to most issues, including foreign investment, not because of ideological rigidity or populist mentality but because the government has changed its mind so frequently about the role that labor ought to play in Korea and the lack of clear procedural rules as to how industrial relations are to be conducted.

In early 1998—barely two months after Korea's financial collapse—then president-elect Kim Dae-jung "appealed to the people to shed nationalistic sentiment to attract foreign investment" so as to overcome the severe foreign debt crisis.[15] Unions, however, engaged in antigovernment demonstrations and strikes in response to layoffs and the possibility of foreign investors taking over Korean firms. For example, a union leader at Korea Telecom rhetorically asked himself, "Do foreign investors want our economy to survive? . . . Once they get profits, they will leave."[16] The few takeovers of bankrupt firms by foreign multinationals have produced a backlash of resentment and resistance against foreigners.[17] President Kim Dae-jung—although a longtime opposition leader who had spent many years in prison or under house arrest during the 1970s and 1980s—indulged in labor repression after assuming office. "Under a barrage of criticism from foreign and domestic capital for not using the 150,000 riot police at his disposal to break the Hyundai strike [in July 1998], President Kim promised to faithfully enforce the new labor laws [allowing layoffs] in future disputes." When the KCTU struck at Mando Ma-

---

[15] *Korea Times*, 19 January 1998, 4 November 1998, 20 November 1998; *Korea Herald*, 11 May 1998; *Korea Central Daily*, 21 January 1998, sec. 3, pp. 1, 3, sec. 2, p. 11, 22 January 1998, sec. 2, pp. 1, 4.
[16] *International Herald Tribune*, 13 July 1998.
[17] *Korea Times*, 20 November 1998, 13 January 1999, and 30 August 1999.

chinery—the largest auto parts company, in the process of being taken over by foreign investors after going bankrupt in late 1997—Kim sent 14,000 riot police and arrested 1,600 union members (Crotty and Dymski 1998, 19). Not surprisingly, Kim's attempts to bring peak business and labor organizations to a national tripartite commission together with government representatives have not been successful.[18]

The analysis of the crisis by the KCTU is most revealing of the continuing aversion to foreign intervention and investment coupled with a firm belief in the export-led model of growth. In a letter presented to U.S. Treasury secretary Robert Rubin, the KCTU criticized the IMF bailout for imposing a set of policies—high interest rates, fiscal austerity, credit restriction measures—that would undermine the "positive and dynamic elements of the Asian development model" (Crotty and Dymski 1998, 19). The unions are furious about the policies imposed by the IMF and about the behavior of foreign firms in the wake of the crisis. The National Financial Labor Union has stated that "foreign capitalists have been destroying the lives of Korean workers after the financial crisis of late 1997." They have even filed a suit against the IMF for the hardship caused by high interest rates, after gathering over 300,000 support signatures (*Korea Times*, 14 October 1999; *Hankuk Ilbo*, 12 October 1999). These statements and actions leave no doubt whatsoever that Korean labor unions feel excluded from the political and economic decision-making process.

Both the unions and the government understand that labor unrest tends to scare off the multinationals. The government attempted during 1998 to introduce labor reforms so as to make it easier to hire and fire. The fierce resistance of the unions has by and large prevented such changes from taking place. As both labor and business leaders recognize, political conditions are not yet ripe for the unions to adopt more favorable attitudes toward the multinationals. With unemployment rising as a result of the 1987 financial crisis, unions are wary, and their leaders insist on the need for the government to guarantee basic "stakeholder" rights in the enterprise before foreign multinationals are allowed to operate without restrictions, that is, to become partners, as opposed to arm's-length collaborators. Some union leaders observed in interviews that arm's-length arrangements such as joint ventures have the advantage of neither surrendering complete control to the foreigners nor letting the chaebol run the economy without facing competition.[19] Korea has thus far failed to accommodate the working class in a well-functioning industrial rela-

[18] Crotty and Dymski 1998. See also *Korea Times*, 28 August 1998, and 1, 15, 22, and 24 September 1998, 8 February 1999, 1 March 1999; *Korea Herald*, 12 and 18 May 1998; 10 September 1998; *Business Week*, 7 July 1998, 48.

[19] Telephone interviews, Choi Jung Ki, director of the Employment and Welfare Department at the Federation of Korean Industries, and member of the Tripartite Commission, 1 June 1999; Lee Byung-Hoon, 4 June 1999; and Kim Yoo Sun, 31 May 1999.

tions systems in a way conducive to greater worker commitment and higher value-added production (Frenkel and Peetz 1998). As we shall see next, it takes special political circumstances for organized labor to accept the presence of foreign multinationals as partners.

Spain: From Villains to Partners

Spanish leftist unions harbored antiforeign ideologies during the 1950s and 1960s under an authoritarian regime. Since the 1970s, however, they have come to adopt overly favorable attitudes toward foreign multinationals in a context of democracy and integration with Europe. Unions have heralded multinationals as political and economic partners, as the ideal agents to help create jobs, transfer technology, and assist in modernizing the country. Only the much diminished anarchist unions have refused to welcome foreign investment, given their rejection of collective bargaining and European integration. Democracy, liberal economic policies, and union friendliness have prompted a massive arrival of long-term foreign direct investment.

Spanish attitudes and ideologies toward foreign investment have always been greatly affected by political dynamics. Surprisingly, conservatives and other right-wingers have frequently sided with the detractors of the multinationals, while liberals and leftists have more often than not welcomed them with varying degrees of enthusiasm. This pattern was first established as far back as the anti-Napoleonic counterrevolution and the struggles between liberals and conservatives to impose their views throughout the nineteenth century. Liberal intellectuals saw in foreign investors not only a most welcome source of capital and entrepreneurship but also a way of counterbalancing the return to the old regime and of introducing liberalism or, at least, more tolerant political practices. For example, the usually irreverent and caustic writer and journalist Mariano José de Larra stated in 1833: "A foreign investor who rushes to an unknown country so as to risk his own money brings new capital into circulation, contributes to society, which benefits immensely from his talent and money. If he loses, he is a hero; if he wins, it is only fair that he receives the reward for his hard work, because he is giving us something we would otherwise not get" (De Larra 1993, 198–99).

Similarly, in one of his historical novels of the *National Episodes* series, Benito Pérez Galdós presented foreign investment as a way, however costly, to break with the country's geographical and cultural and political isolation: "Oh, Northern Railway Company, fortunate escape route to the European world, divine breach for civilization! Blessed be one thousand times the gold of the French Jews and Protestants that made your existence possible; lucky the ones who paved your way through the crust of the old Spain. . . . For a thousand reasons we praise you, Northern Railway Company, and even if you did *not* achieve organizational perfection . . . everything shall be pardoned for the immense benefits that you have conferred upon us" (Pérez Galdós 1986, 43–44). The railway celebrated by Pérez Galdós in 1907 connected Madrid to southern France and then Paris and was the usual escape route for Spanish political exiles. It was built with the financial assistance of the Peréire brothers.

After welcoming foreign investment in railways, utilities, and certain manufacturing industries, the dominant mood in the country turned decisively against foreign investors and traders toward the end of the nineteenth century. Antiforeign sentiment, coupled with import-substitution dreams, was to reach a climax in the aftermath of the Civil War of 1936–39, when the Franco dictatorship became dominated by nationalist policymakers. Foreign interests in railways, mining, and telecommunications were nationalized, and a series of tight financial controls made foreign investment virtually impossible (Campa and Guillén 1996). The limitations of the import-substitution model became apparent by the mid-1950s. Starting in 1959, liberal economic reforms substituted steep tariff barriers for nontariff barriers to trade and encouraged the arrival of multinationals in capital-intensive industries. During the 1960s Spain was among the fastest growing economies in the world, matching Japan's rates, in part thanks to foreign investment under the restrictive conditions of cell 3 in table 5.2.

The evolution of the ideological stand of the labor unions since the 1960s has been both remarkable and momentous for the unfolding of foreign investment in Spain, and it has generally been consistent with the liberal and leftist inclination to accept the multinationals, provided the right political conditions were in place. The Socialist (UGT), Communist (CCOO), Christian-Socialist (USO), and anarchist (CNT) unions opposed the Franco dictatorship—albeit following different strategies—and participated in the return to democracy during the late 1970s. These (clandestine) unions organized protests and strikes and lobbied foreign governments, unions, and international organizations in their attempts to undermine the compulsory corporatist system of joint, vertical representation of workers and employers prevalent since the 1940s (Fishman 1990; Guillén 1994, 175–85). Up until shortly after the dictator's death in 1975, union leaders, members, and sympathizers suffered unspeakable acts of repression, including torture and murder. Many were tried and jailed for military rebellion. The limited and tightly controlled mechanisms for collective bargaining introduced by Franco in the late 1950s so as to better sustain a capitalist, export-led model of growth and help the regime appear more liberal to the external world allowed clandestine unionists to challenge, among other things, the presence of the foreign multinationals.

As in Argentina and Korea, the Spanish unions took offense at the multinationals during the 1960s for being the agents of capitalist imperialism, providing support to the Franco dictatorship,[20] and failing to observe basic labor rights. "¡Ay España, quién te quiere y quién te USA!" [Poor Spain! Who loves you, and who USes you!], read a famous bumper sticker. Thus, the multinationals would sit back and watch how the Labor Ministry jailed strikers, only to sack them 48 hours later for not showing up for work. Given that strikes were illegal, workers were temporarily suspended or summarily fired by the labor authorities anyway. In response to such practices, the clandestine unions would contact their counterpart labor organizations in the home country of the multinational so as to expose its outrageously inconsistent behavior. In an example among many involving American or European multinationals, the United Auto Workers distributed in the United States a leaflet criticizing the Chrysler Corporation for being "more francoist than Franco himself" in its treatment of striking workers at its Madrid plant in January of 1969. As in Korea, this tactic proved successful more often than not.[21]

Given these behaviors and the widespread suspicions about the motives of multinationals doing business in a protected market and under a dictatorial regime, labor leaders proposed to monitor and curtail the activities of these companies in a variety of ways. Unlike in Argentina, though, they calibrated their criticisms and recommendations very carefully lest the multinationals' job-creation activities in Spain would be endangered. Thus, the Socialist union UGT's "Minimalist Program" of 1972 contained a rather mild and vague proposal to "rigorously control foreign capital invested in Spain."[22] This union's worker-training courses included a remarkable session on how to deal with foreign firms: "*Multinational enterprises are a consummated, irreversible fact. The time to quarrel over whether we should reject or accept their existence has passed. What we can discuss is the way in which the working class ought to deal with them.*"[23]

By the early 1980s, economic and political conditions were ripe for the unions' unmitigated acceptance of foreign multinationals. Spain adopted a

---

[20] *Boletín de la Unión General de Trabajadores de España en el Exilio*, January 1955, 6–7; February 1955, 7–8; December 1959, 4–5; and January–February 1960, 9.

[21] The leaflet was reproduced, translated into Spanish, in *Boletín de la Unión General de Trabajadores*, July 1970, 3. Other similar instances of repression took place at FIAT, Philips, Montefibre, Solvay, Authi, Lilly, Kodak, Sears, General Electric, Uniroyal, Olivetti, Firestone, Danone, and Atlas Copcco. See *UGT: Boletín de la Unión General de Trabajadores de España*, January 1972, 4; March 1973, 14; January 1974, 5; May 1974, 7; July–August 1974, 9; September 1974, 3, 6; November 1974, 4, 7–10; December 1974, 16; March 1975, 10–17; April 1975, 12–16; July–August 1975, 18; October 1975, 21–23; March 1976, 6; April 1976, 16; June 1976, 21; December 1976, I:2. See also *Unidad Obrera*, the official publication of CCOO de Madrid, 1st fortnight, June 1977, 12; 15–30 September 1977, 4; and *Acción: Periódico Obrero de Barcelona y Provincia*, 1971–74.

[22] *UGT*, July 1972, 9.

[23] *UGT*, September 1974, 8, 12; emphasis added.

democratic constitution in 1978 and was yearning to join the European Union, which it did in 1986. Unlike in Argentina and Korea, labor unions participated in the entire process of political transition, and their views were somewhat influential in shaping economic and social policymaking (Bermeo 1994a, 1994b; Fishman 1990). Thus, multinationals were no longer the collaborators of a dictatorial regime, nor could they easily take advantage of the working class, which was relatively well organized, protected by favorable labor legislation, and politically enfranchised in a democratic worker representation system. As the union leaders of the time expressed in interviews with the author, the transition to democracy and the empowerment of the labor organizations made it possible to abandon the "inordinate fears" about the multinationals.[24] The Communist CCOO would not wait much longer than its Socialist counterpart to openly express its acceptance of foreign investment, although with some strings attached: "Foreign investments are at first acceptable if informed by the following principles: prioritization of labor-intensive industries . . . avoidance of investments in technologies that are obsolete in the home country of the multinational . . . promotion of investments in industries in which Spain lacks technological know-how or suffers from underinvestment . . . absorption of the technology being transferred . . . reinvestment of profits . . . release of operational information to the government and the unions . . . respect for workers' rights in all the subsidiaries of the multinational worldwide."[25]

The unions' new favorable attitudes toward foreign investors were due not only to the transition to democracy—which guaranteed a respect for workers' rights and greater accountability, as demanded by CCOO in the above excerpt—but also to their own shift from a populist to a modernizing mentality. As Álvarez-Miranda (1996, 219–48) has documented, during the 1970s the Spanish Left abandoned its long-standing isolationist and anticapitalist proposals to embrace pro-European views *(europeísmo)*, a development that helped pave the way for the massive arrival of foreign investment since 1985. Spanish labor unions behaved as moderate and fairly constructive agents during the 1970s and 1980s, rejecting the extremes of populism, and accepting wage growth below inflation in the face of massive unemployment (Bermeo 1994a, 1994b, 116; Fishman 1990; Hamann 1998). The modernizing mentality of the unions came to dominate discussions of topics such as economic policymaking, industrial restructuring, and foreign investment. In a sharp de-

[24] Interviews, Nicolás Redondo, Madrid, 24 June 1998, and Marcelino Camacho, Madrid, 22 June 1998. Redondo was secretary-general of UGT from 1976 to 1994. Camacho was secretary-general of CCOO between 1976 and 1987. See also *Unidad Obrera*, 1st fortnight, October 1979, 10–11; UGT Metal 1980, 5, 15–21.

[25] *Gaceta Sindical*, April 1981, 17.

parture from the mentality of the 1960s, the Communist and Socialist unions began to argue in the late 1970s that the small size of the Spanish market required an integration with Europe, a greater export and competitiveness effort, and a rejection of the import-substitution model.[26] Thus, the unions had shifted their ideological position all the way from cell 2 to cell 4 in table 5.3 and had rejoined the liberals in the country against the isolationist and antiforeign position defended by the conservatives and right-wingers.

Spanish organized labor became utterly persuaded that foreign multinationals could bring to Spain jobs, technology, and even sociopolitical improvements. Thus, union leaders came not only to the conclusion that "few countries in the world, not even the richest ones, can afford to do without the experience, technology, and capital of the multinational enterprises," but also to accept the proposition that multinationals could make a key positive political and social contribution: A type of employer that was, or could be, much more sensible, progressive, and democratic than the average Spanish entrepreneur. Thus, foreign multinationals became a factor of "modernization of the weak and unequivocally reactionary domestic entrepreneurial community," or as the leader of the Communist CCOO put it in an interview with the author, "Spain needed the multinationals because of the lack of a viable domestic bourgeoisie. Without a dynamic bourgeoisie there is no chance of making the transition from preindustrial feudalism to industrial capitalism, and without capitalism there can be no transition to the socialist and communist society."[27] Tellingly, the Socialist and Communist unions have actively participated in efforts to court foreign investors, including General Motors, Volkswagen, and DuPont.[28] And the multinationals have responded like true partners by stepping up their investments in Spain and spending on training per worker three times as much as domestically owned firms (Mineco 1994, 269, 290–94).

Naturally, the emerging consensus among union leaders that multinationals could indeed become political and economic partners was not easy to sustain during economic downturns, when multinationals scaled back their

[26] See CCOO's publications: *Unidad Obrera*, 2d fortnight, November 1979, 10–11; *II Congreso de la Confederación Sindical de CCOO: Informe general y resoluciones aprobadas*, in *Cuadernos Gaceta Sindical* 1 (1981): 15; *III Congreso de la Confederación Sindical de CCOO*, special issue of *Gaceta Sindical* (1984): 37. Also, by UGT, *Resoluciones del XXXII Congreso* (Madrid, 1980), 111–12; and Redondo's interview in *Aragón/Express*, 3 November 1979, 13. Interviews with Carlos Martín Urriza, staff economist of CCOO, Madrid, 30 June 1998, and with Jesús Pérez, executive secretary of UGT, and Antonio González, director of the Technical Staff of UGT, Madrid, 1 July 1998, also confirmed the modernizing mentality of the unions.

[27] *Unión*, 4 September 1981, supplement, 3; *Gaceta Sindical*, May 1981, 49; *Unión Sindical*, May 1979, 12; interview, Marcelino Camacho. Camacho was a metalworker at Perkins Hispania, a subsidiary of International Harvester.

[28] See UGT Metal 1980; interview, Nicolás Redondo.

investment plans or even divested.[29] Jobs are, of course, the key issue for the unionists as well as for most of the population, given that unemployment has stubbornly stayed at over 15 percent of the active population since the early 1980s. Employment represents a goal that could even justify state subsidies and other emoluments to attract, or prevent from leaving, job-creating foreign investments. Thus, in 1993 the official journal of the Socialist union UGT argued that Spain ought to "subordinate institutional [i.e., state] support for the multinationals to the preservation of production inside Spain's borders, so that foreign subsidiaries do not degenerate into mere distributors of foreign products once they have captured market share."[30] In fact, the labor unions have often voiced their preference for greenfield investments, and their criticism of foreign acquisitions of Spanish companies and speculative investments in the stock market. "We are witnessing neither the unfolding of industrial activity nor investments in firms so as to create jobs, but rather the arrival of money to speculate in the stock market and to gain control of firms at low prices. . . . We *welcome the arrival of foreign money,* but aimed at founding new firms and creating jobs instead of at buying firms."[31]

The roles of democratic consolidation and of a modernizing mentality in prompting the Socialist and Communist unions to adopt a favorable ideological image of the multinational firm stands in sharp contrast with the unreconstructed mentalities and arguments of the anarchist union, the CNT, which has lost much of its past clout among Spanish workers (with the sole exception of schoolteachers). First of all, one should bear in mind that anarchist unions reject social productivity pacts and development policies seeking to accelerate economic growth, are weary of collective bargaining, and are deeply distrustful of the state, no matter how democratic. Accordingly, the CNT's image of the multinational enterprise remains anchored in the past. "Workers depend on the decisions made at the powerful foreign capitalist complex. Hundreds of thousands of workers labor, and more of them will in the future, under the authority of a foreign employer: paces of work, human relations policies, collective bargaining . . ."[32]

Second, Spanish anarchists reject the defense of foreign multinationals on the basis of their contributions to employment because in their view jobs

[29] *UGT,* June 1978, 30; *Gaceta Sindical,* January 1987, 47; *Unión,* 1 August 1981, 1, 4 September 1981, 4, 4 September 1981, supplement, 3, and 4 November 1981, 3. See also *Journal of Commerce,* 4 April 1994, 7A; *International Herald Tribune,* 2–3 April 1994; *época,* 5 June 1995, 24–28.

[30] *Unión,* September 1993, 22.

[31] *Gaceta Sindical,* September 1987, 5, 17–19; emphasis added. See also January 1991, 20; January 1992, 4; June 1997, 13; *Unidad Obrera,* 1st fortnight, December 1979, 8–9, and September 1992, 6–13.

[32] CNT: *Órgano de la Confederación Nacional del Trabajo,* October 1978, 6–7. See also February 1990, 18, 205; July 1996, 4, 217–18; January 1997.

created by multinationals also help increase the power of the government and the police, and they happen to be highly polluting.[33] Third, they have repeatedly exposed the hasty efforts by the various dictatorial and democratic governments in Spain to offer favorable investment terms, including subsidies and lax regulations, and have more persistently rung the alarm over foreign acquisitions of Spanish firms as a by-product of EU membership.[34] Fourth, the anarchists have been much more critical of the manipulative potential of the new managerial and organizational techniques brought to Spain by the multinationals, especially Japanese ones: "Today, directly from Japan, the world's *second* largest exporter of stupidities, comes a new managerial activity called 'quality circles.' In simple terms, workers must know. . . . Thus, besides those of us who favor the abolition of the ownership of the means of production are those who not only work for somebody else's profit but also must 'brainstorm' in order to propose to the management 'brilliant' ideas that make the firm even stronger."[35]

It is important to underline in closing that the anarchists cannot be blamed for ideological inconsistency. They have denounced the economic and political development of the Soviet Union, China, and Cuba as much as they have criticized the capitalist countries. This "Neither Trilateralist Capitalism nor Bureaucratic Socialism" attitude has prompted some noted anarchist political economists like Abraham Guillén (no relation to the author) to apply the same logic of criticism normally levied against the multinationals headquartered in the capitalist countries to the generally neglected phenomenon of Soviet industrial and service foreign investment. In his remarkable 1987 article, "Soviet Capitalism: The Last Stage of Imperialism," Guillén published a list of 72 Soviet multinational corporations with foreign investment holdings in 22 capitalist countries.[36] Unlike their Socialist and Communist counterparts, the anarchist unions have not altered their views and strategies after the return to democracy and have dismissed modernizing attitudes and policies as oppressive and inherently undesirable. In short, the famous anarchist motto, "No god, no king, no owner, no religion, no state," might be appended with the phrase, "no multinationals."

With the sole exception of the rather marginal anarchist union, Spanish organized labor has come to accept and celebrate foreign investment as part of its modernizing mentality. The anarchists have not joined in precisely be-

[33] *CNT*, February 1990, 18.

[34] *CNT*, March 1979, 6; January 1981, 5; April 1985, 12.

[35] *CNT* 78 (1985): 7; emphasis added. This piece comments on the introduction of quality circles at Nissan Motor Ibérica. See also another article, January 1994, 6–7, criticizing Toyota's lean production.

[36] *CNT*, April 1987, 8–9. Abraham Guillén (1913–1993) went into exile in Buenos Aires after having been a political commissary in an anarchist militia during the Spanish Civil War of 1936–39.

cause they have clung to populist economic ideas. The overall Spanish population is also friendly to foreign investment, but believes that multinationals possess too much power in Spanish society, an opinion less prevalent among the unionized working class than among the young, the unemployed, and the middle and upper social strata (CIRES 1995, 884–85). As the multinationals' collaboration with the Franco dictatorship and their abusive industrial relations practices receded into the past, the unions began to welcome foreign investors as job creators and technology providers. Democracy and the abandonment of populist attitudes in favor of modernizing ones by the unions paved the way for the full acceptance of foreign multinationals as partners.

Conclusion

Domestic actors such as labor unions do not respond to foreign multinationals in similar ways across countries, nor do their views converge as their countries develop and become more integrated in the global economy. Rather, labor unions adopt attitudes, ideologies, and policies that reflect their economic mentalities and their interpretation of the political situation in their country. Argentine, Korean, and Spanish labor unions initially coincided in their assessment of multinationals as foreign imperialists taking advantage of poor workers or cheap natural resources, providing authoritarian governments with international support, and even threatening national sovereignty. Union ideologies shifted in divergent ways over time and across countries. This finding casts doubt on the thesis that industrialization or integration in the global economy produces convergence in industrial relations.

Argentine unions have supported import-substitution efforts since the 1940s, regarding multinationals as villains. The unions' populist mentality in a country thought to be geopolitically isolated but endowed with vast natural wealth lies at the heart of the negative image of the multinationals. Unions opposed policies favoring foreign investment except during times of economic emergency, when they accepted multinationals as necessary evils, provided the government did not engage in labor repression. Korea's colonial past and continued dependence on foreign powers have made direct foreign ownership ideologically difficult to justify. Unions—though modernizing in their approach—fought direct foreign involvement in export-processing zones, preferring instead that multinationals enter into arm's-length export contracts or minority joint ventures with locally owned firms.

While in both Argentina and South Korea unions have been largely excluded from the political and policymaking process, in Spain labor unions played a crucial role in the transition to democracy and in the inception of the new system of industrial relations. Moreover, their views were taken into account when it came to the design of the country's modernizing economic strategy of increasing economic openness and integration with Europe. In this context, the unions came to see the foreign multinationals as partners in development, as job creators, and as a modernizing element in a country thought to be disadvantaged by a scarcity of entrepreneurial initiatives. Thus, unions in these countries diverged in their assessment of foreign multinationals. They initially adopted the villain image to later abandon it in favor of either the necessary-evil (Argentina), collaborator (Korea), or partner image (Spain), depending on the political regime and the dominant economic mentality.

Labor union ideologies toward foreign investment continue to diverge. Even the least combative Argentine unions have only reluctantly accepted the liberal economic reforms of the 1990s. They have rebuilt their resource and power base by pursuing entrepreneurial activities and providing their members with social services without committing themselves ideologically to a liberal policy toward multinationals, thus keeping their options open for the future. The Korean situation is also open-ended, albeit in a different sense. It is unclear how the various unions will ultimately respond to the probable increase in direct foreign economic activity in Korea as the result of the IMF-led bailout. Labor leaders are instinctively using a nationalist rhetoric to protect jobs and incomes. If this is an indication of future strategy, there could be a reawakening of explicitly hostile attitudes toward the multinationals, especially those allowed to acquire and restructure bankrupt Korean companies. In Spain, by contrast, the main unions have thrown their weight behind policies tending toward full economic integration with Europe and the global economy, including the presence of multinationals.

The Spanish experience provides an important reference point for the debate over the relationship between economic and political development. Spain illustrates that organized labor may be an important and influential actor in the process of economic growth, and that it has to be taken into account when it comes to deciding the quantity and quality of participation by foreign multinationals. In Korea and Argentina labor was temporarily relegated to the political background through repression. Organized labor's ideologies of foreign investment are far from epiphenomenal; they can and do shape political and economic change. Thus, Argentine unions long acted as a constraint on attempts to open the economy to foreign investment, while Korean workers and unions have contributed to the national consensus about doing business with the multinationals only at arm's length. In Spain, by contrast, the unions' friendly attitude facilitated the arrival of vast amounts of foreign investment during the 1980s and 1990s. Multinationals based in Spain continue to upgrade their facilities and to improve the skills of their workforce, unlike in Argentina and Korea.

The case of Spain also illustrates an important point about the sequence between economic and political development. Organized labor can be encouraged and empowered to become the organizational vehicle to articulate the aspirations and fears of different groups of workers and employees early on in the process of economic development or reform. In so doing, a solution that is not only acceptable to most groups but also better suited to the strengths and weaknesses of each country might be easier to devise and implement.

The favorable attitude of the Spanish unions toward the multinationals, however, is *not* to be taken as the only practical or possible response by organized labor under democratic conditions. For historical or geopolitical reasons, labor unions may choose to oppose massive foreign equity investment. What the evidence and analysis in this chapter demonstrate is that unions can only be expected to be a constructive social and political force if democratic transition precedes, or at least goes hand in hand with, economic reform. Thus, even the most appropriate and competent market-based reforms, including permissive policies toward foreign investment, are bound to produce less than ideal outcomes under authoritarian government with incomplete labor rights. In the next two chapters I explore how, among other factors, the presence of foreign multinationals shapes efforts to develop two key industries, automobiles and banking. I shall also emphasize the importance of ideologies, for the efforts undertaken by the Argentine, South Korean, and Spanish states to develop automobile manufacturing and banking have been profoundly affected by a host of assumptions and interpretations.

PART TWO

ORGANIZATIONAL CHANGE AND

PERFORMANCE

SIX

DEVELOPING INDUSTRY: AUTOMOBILE AND

COMPONENT MANUFACTURING

A roaring racing car . . . is more beautiful than the winged
Victory of Samothrace.
(F. T. Marinetti, The Futurist Manifesto, in Banham 1980, 103)

MORE OFTEN than not, policymakers have paid token attention to the institutions underlying successful development, as discussed in chapter 1. In the next two chapters I illustrate how institutions shape development outcomes by looking at two crucial industries: automobiles and banking. In this chapter I note the unique features of the most modernist and symbolic industry in the economy—automobile manufacturing—and compare the rise of final assembly and component manufacturing in South Korea, Spain, and Argentina. State policies not consistent with underlying patterns of organization are found to flounder, eventually giving way to others that use the strengths of the society as leverage in the global economy. In the next chapter I apply a similar logic of analysis to banking, observing that most developing countries have used banks as instruments for industrial policy, as opposed to viewing banking as yet another industry with great growth potential.

The Automobile Industry and Development

The automobile industry plays a unique role in the economy. It is large and linked to many other upstream and downstream activities, ranging from steel, glass, plastics, and rubber to electronics, machine tools, financial services, and insurance. It is also a highly regulated industry because of safety and environmental concerns. The industry has a major effect on the balance of payments, technological development, and national defense. Moreover, it is a highly visible industry and thus regarded by most governments as a key sector that symbolizes development success. It is the quintessentially *modernist* industry of the twentieth century (Banham 1980; Guillén 1997), by far the most intensively studied manufacturing sector of the economy, and a constant source of new ideas about management and organization (see Drucker 1972; Sloan 1972; Womack, Jones, and Roos 1991). Moreover, theories of development have paid a considerable amount of attention to automobiles and recommended very different policies, ranging from laissez-faire (modernization, neoclassical) to protection (dependency) and subsidization (late-industrialization) of domestic producers.

In a recent paper, Nicole Biggart and I have argued that what makes the automobile industry so interesting to comparative students of development is that it includes both a large-scale, capital-intensive activity (final assembly), and a myriad of relatively knowledge-intensive, flexible activities related to component manufacturing (Biggart and Guillén 1999).[1] Although many auto components are certainly mass-produced (tires, screws, simple electronic parts, etc.), most companies need to adapt in flexible ways to the requirements of mass-volume final assembly. As a result, the organizational and social underpinnings of auto assembly and component manufacturing tend to be very different, making it difficult for countries to excel at both activities by themselves. Thus, a comparative analysis of automobile components and assembly helps assess the successes and failures of various development policies as they interact with underlying patterns of organization.

Globalization has changed the industry in recent decades. In order to thrive, auto assemblers need to have a presence in at least two of the three major markets—Europe, NAFTA, and East Asia. Component manufacturers have been forced to serve assemblers not just in their home country but worldwide, co-locating their plants so as to supply parts just in time (Guillén 1994, 291–93; McKinsey 1996; Womack, Jones, and Roos 1991). Increasingly, components manufacturers directly supplying the assemblers—the so-called first-tier suppliers—are collaborating on product design and development with their customers. The trend toward close relationships between assemblers and suppliers that cut across national boundaries or are replicated in many different locations throughout the world supports the view of globalization outlined in chapter 1: globality enhances the importance of the ability to network.

Among the three countries considered in this book only Spain has been able to excel at both automobile assembly and components. This dual success has been made possible by the active, direct, and wholesale participation of foreign multinationals. With only a few exceptions, however, Spanish-owned firms have failed to make a dent in technological development and international competition. Figure 6.1 shows the evolution between 1970 and 1995 of each country's exports of assembled passenger cars and of auto components, expressed as a percentage of GDP. Since the early 1980s, Spain has increased

---

[1] This chapter builds on the arguments and evidence presented in Biggart and Guillén 1999. I am grateful to Nicole Biggart for allowing me to elaborate on the contents of this paper. The new evidence presented in this chapter draws on some 25 interviews and plant visits conducted in Spain, Argentina, and South Korea between 1993 and 1998, as well as on multiple statistical and secondary sources.

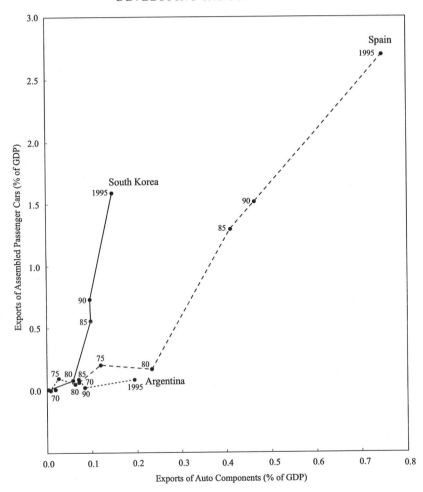

Figure 6.1. Exports of Assembled Passenger Cars and of Auto Components, 1970–1995. (*International Trade Statistics Yearbook*, several years; Feenstra, Lipsay, and Bowen 1997).

very rapidly its exports of both cars and components, while Korea has achieved growth only in exports of cars. Argentina has never attained high levels of exports of automotive products, although exports of components increased in the early 1990s mostly as a result of the implementation of bilateral balanced-trade arrangements with neighboring Brazil. And among firms in the three countries, only one Korean assembler—Hyundai—and a handful of Spanish component manufacturers have managed to develop a proprietary technology base and a strong reputation. Thus, neither the Korean nor the Spanish experience has yielded ideal outcomes.

South Korea: Automobiles and Megalomania

Nowhere is the infatuation of the Korean state and business elites with large industrial undertakings more manifest than in the automobile industry. Beginning in the late 1960s, the state and big business combined forces to make sure that the country would eventually become a player in the world auto industry. Their attention, however, focused on assembly to the virtual neglect of components manufacturing. The domestic market was literally sealed off from the rest of the world, providing a steadily growing source of sales with which to subsidize export attempts. When the largest chaebol realized the importance of the automobile for economic growth, they all tried to enter the industry, frequently via acquisition of existing manufacturers. By the late 1980s three chaebol—Hyundai, KIA, and Daewoo—dominated automobile assembly and components manufacturing. A few years later Korea became the world's fifth largest assembler of cars with over two million units produced annually. With the entry of Samsung and the Asian crisis of 1997, however, excess installed capacity and technological backwardness became painfully apparent. KIA went bankrupt in late 1997 and Daewoo in mid-1999, while Hyundai's capacity utilization dropped to less than 60 percent, and Samsung was forced to reconsider its expensive adventure.

As in other heavy industries—for example, chemicals and steel—state policies toward automobile manufacturing were first geared toward import-substitution, turning export-oriented during the late 1970s. The late-industrialization model to be applied was simple: a few chosen entrepreneurs were enticed to enter the industry through cheap loans. They established technology and marketing ties with Japanese and U.S. manufacturers, learning how to assemble massive numbers of low-quality cars with a large proportion of imported components. The first export-oriented efforts were undertaken in the form of original equipment manufacturing (OEM) contracts, especially with U.S. firms. Later, Korean companies tried to establish their own dealership networks and even foreign production facilities in the United States, Europe, and South and central Asia. Such expansion, however, rested on shaky foundations: borrowed technology and money, and a weak components industry tightly linked to the fortunes of the assemblers, with no export potential of its own.

The key question about the development of the automobile industry in Korea is why the country succeeded at becoming a major producer and exporter of assembled cars, but failed miserably at component manufacturing. As Biggart and Guillén (1999, 730) point out, "small auto repair shops, engine rebuilders, and components manufacturers actually pre-date the establishment of the country's assemblers" during the 1960s. The single most important factor is the Korean pattern of social organization—patrimonialism—

which privileges large business actors, therefore making it easier for firms to undertake large-scale activities for which vast amounts of (cheap) capital and (subservient) labor are required (Biggart 1990; Fields 1995, 38–44; Krugman 1994; Lee et al. 1996). Automobile assembly—not component manufacturing—is one such activity.

Government Policy and the Development of the Industry

Automobile-related activities started on Korean soil during the Japanese occupation, although they mostly had to do with repairing and remodeling. In the mid-1950s the Cheval Auto Company assembled the first passenger cars out of military discard parts. At roughly the same time another auto assembler emerged, Ha Dong-Hwan Automobile Production. These early assembly activities, however, were low-volume undertakings, with no two cars or minibuses produced being alike (Lee 1996, 169)

As Clifford (1994, 254) has aptly described it, the (modernist) feeling in the military government during the early 1960s was that "any self-respecting country should make its own cars." One year after the 1961 coup, the Automobile Industry Protection Law introduced a complete ban on imports of assembled cars, which lasted until the late 1980s. Saenara ("New Nation") Motors was the first firm to take advantage of protectionism. It established a plant assembling knocked-down kits (KDKs) from Nissan. Saenara was controlled by collaborators of the founder of the infamous Korean Central Intelligence Agency. The assembly line was mired in organizational and technical problems, completing fewer than 3,000 vehicles before it was shut down in 1963 because of the shoddy quality of the cars and its involvement in a foreign-made auto smuggling scheme (Clifford 1994, 254; Lee 1996, 169–70). A second experiment sprung up in 1963 when KIA Industries (formerly Kyungsung Precision) allied itself with Mazda of Japan to assemble three-wheeled vehicles.

In a move typical of Korean nationalist-modernizing policymaking, the government forced all existing assemblers in 1964 to merge into Shinjin Motor Industries. Contravening the logic of components manufacturing as a flexible and decentralized activity, 75 major suppliers were also grouped together. Shinjin had been assembling microbuses since 1962 and a failed small car since 1963, of which only 322 units were produced (Lee 1996, 170). Shinjin was able to secure a technology deal with Toyota in 1966. The government's desire to concentrate all production in one firm, though, proved elusive. "From the start, the auto industry was both a symbol of national pride and a victim of factional infighting among groups trying to control a business through which large amounts of cash flowed" (Clifford 1994, 255). Other entrepreneurial initiatives took place during the 1960s. Asia Automobile Industries was founded in 1965, and Hyundai entered the industry in 1967.

"Despite this flurry of activity, the Korean industry produced only 3,430 units in 1966, which increased to a still minimal 28,819 by 1971" (Lee 1996, 171).

Lacking a proprietary technology base, local producers lured foreign auto companies into partnerships by promising them a slice of the growing and profitable domestic market. When Toyota broke its ties to Shinjin in the early 1970s, General Motors rushed in to create a 50–50 joint venture, GM Korea, which failed to introduce models that would succeed in the market. Nationalized by the government, the company muddled through as Saehan ("New Korea") Motors until it was sold to Daewoo in 1978. Meanwhile, Asia Automobile developed ties to FIAT of Italy, and KIA strengthened its relationship with Mazda. Because of its frustrating experience assembling Ford knocked-down kits, Hyundai decided to go it alone in 1970 and develop its own car, the Pony, which was first assembled in 1976 after having reverse-engineered the Ford Marina. The government forced Asia and KIA to merge in 1976, and Daewoo acquired Saehan in 1978. The Korean auto industry had come to be dominated by the "Big Three"—Hyundai, KIA, and Daewoo (Lee 1996, 172; Clifford 1994, 253–61). These three firms would spearhead Korea's aggressive international expansion during the late 1980s and 1990s.

The Rise of Exports and Foreign Investment

As in other industries, the Korean government shifted its import-substitution incentives toward export-oriented ones through pricing and lending policies. Auto companies first sold important amounts of cars in foreign markets via original equipment manufacturing (OEM) exports—Daewoo made the Pontiac LeMans for GM during the mid-1980s, and KIA assembled the Ford Festiva after the government allowed it to reenter the passenger car market in 1986. These experiences, however, proved limited in success and prevented the Korean companies from building in-house product development and marketing skills. Of the Big Three, Hyundai would prove the most visionary and successful in exports, although Daewoo would eventually install more assembly capacity offshore.

In 1976 Hyundai exported the first six Pony cars, to Ecuador, in exchange for bananas (Green 1992, 414). Exports to developing Latin American and South Asian countries during the late 1970s, however, never exceeded 20,000 annual units. In 1984 Hyundai Motor targeted the Canadian market. The Pony became the largest foreign import within months. Quality problems, however, tarnished its reputation so badly that sales dropped after 1986, the year it started to sell the Excel in the U.S. market. With the Excel, Hyundai stunned the industry by grabbing a 7.1 market share of the American subcompact segment within a year (260,000 units), aided by a strong yen. Sales stagnated in 1988, however, dropping to levels below 110,000 annual units by the early 1990s as widespread quality problems turned customers away from

Hyundai dealerships. Better-equipped models like the Accent, Sonata, Elantra, and Scoupe fared better in customer ratings, but failed to allow Hyundai to gain more than 1.5 percent of total auto sales in the U.S. market during the 1990s. Daewoo (with the Pontiac LeMans) and KIA (Ford Festiva) faced a similar fate, the former peaking at 64,000 units in 1988 and the latter at 69,000 in 1989. Subsequently, KIA has enjoyed moderate success with its Sportage sport utility vehicle. Quality ratings continue to haunt the Korean makes. Fortunately for Hyundai, KIA has recently replaced it at the bottom of the quality rankings. Still, in 1995 J. D. Power & Associates found in a survey of new car owners that all four Korean export models ranked at the bottom with an average of 193 problems per 100 cars, versus the industry average of 110 (Kraar 1995, 152; Clifford 1991, 42).

The Koreans' frustrated dreams for the North American market—and European protectionism—led them to pursue opportunities in South and central Asia, eastern Europe, and Latin America. While in the 1980s fewer than 1,000 Korean-made automobiles were sold in South Asia, by 1993 the Big Three exported over 100,000 units to the region. In the late 1990s, Korean auto firms' export ratios reached 50 percent of total production, of which half was destined to developed markets in North America and Europe, and the other half to developing markets in Asia, Latin America, the Middle East, and eastern Europe.

The Korean auto export boom, however, has come at a cost. Export sales have been less profitable than domestic sales—and in some cases not profitable at all. As has been widely documented (Amsden and Kang 1995, 16; Green 1992, 419), the government allowed automakers to set domestic prices above world prices, effectively subsidizing export efforts with inflated domestic prices.

The Koreans have made greater inroads into emerging markets via foreign direct investment than through exports, frequently extracting favorable financial terms from local banks and joint venture partners. On the eve of the 1997 Asian crisis, Hyundai Motor had established assembly plants with various degrees of ownership in five different Latin American, eastern European, and South Asian emerging economies, with further expansion plans into six additional countries. KIA had a manufacturing presence in seven emerging countries, with expansion planned for five others. Finally, Daewoo had joint ventures in nine countries and plans for two others (*Korea Economic Weekly*, 26 May 1997, 21). All of these investments must be understood in the context of the Koreans' limited success in the most advanced markets because of poor product quality and rising protectionism. Korean auto firms could not approach emerging markets as exporters given the trebling of labor costs in Korea during the late 1980s. As of the mid-1990s, the auto operations of the Big Three were not making reasonable returns on their by now long-standing investments, and only Hyundai had succeeded at developing a proprietary technology base (Amsden and Kang 1995; L. Kim 1998).

Samsung's Entry and the Collapse of 1997

The status quo of the Big Three was first challenged in 1976 by Samsung, one of the three largest chaebol, when it considered bidding for Asia Automobile—later acquired by KIA. Samsung tried again in the mid-1980s, unsuccessfully pursuing a series of joint venture agreements with Chrysler, Nissan, Honda, Toyota, and Volkswagen. In spite of the difficulties faced by the Big Three in international markets, the Samsung chaebol insisted for a third time on entering the industry during the early 1990s. By 1992 it had secured the permission to enter the commercial vehicle business using Nissan technology, but with the explicit prohibition of even considering the passenger car market. Yet, Samsung knew very well that in the Korean context of "institutionalized patrimonialism" (Biggart 1990), no self-respecting chaebol could neglect such an important industry as automobiles. As early as 1993, Samsung initiated conversations with Toyota, Nissan, BMW, and Volkswagen to secure technology for a passenger car. When these negotiations failed, Samsung mounted an unprecedented hostile takeover attempt over KIA, which also failed (Lee 1996, 180–84).

By the end of 1994, Samsung's relentless efforts had secured a technological agreement with Nissan and the government's reluctant approval to initiate passenger car production, to the dismay of the Big Three. The timing looked good: exports were recovering again, the economy was booming, and Samsung was enjoying windfall profits from semiconductor exports that could be used to pay for its automobile investment. Samsung Motors was founded in March 1995, with planned capacity of a quarter million units by 1998, against the resistance of the Big Three (Lee 1996, 185–87; Lew 1999, 158–65). Production began in 1996, with most of the units being sold to Samsung chaebol employees. As predictions of excess installed capacity in the auto industry became true and semiconductor prices plunged worldwide, Samsung found itself unable to cross-subsidize auto production with chip profits or to find markets for the output. During the early months of 1997, Samsung spread rumors that KIA was nearly bankrupt and hinted that it would gladly take over. Subsequent events, however, would change the situation in momentous ways.

The Asian economic crisis of 1997 assessed a major blow to the Korean auto industry. Not only did domestic sales plummet by over 50 percent, hitting profits hard, but the Koreans' most important international markets, those in emerging economies, stagnated or collapsed as well. During the first months of the crisis Korean exports dipped 4 percent in unit terms, and nearly 21 percent in dollar terms. The weakness of the yen further added to the troubles.

The crisis has made excess capacity painfully apparent. I visited Hyundai Motor six months before the beginning of the crisis in December 1997. The company had already run out of storage space for its finished, yet unsold, vehicles inside its sprawling Ulsan complex, the largest single auto assembly facility in the world (1.5 million cars). By late 1998 the Korean auto industry was operating at 40 percent capacity, down from 68 percent during 1997 (KAMA 1998; *Korea Herald*, 18 September 1998).

Tellingly, the devaluation of the won has not helped Korean automobile makers. Price cuts in foreign markets translate into meager sales increases because Korean cars are already positioned at the low end of the market. In addition, a devalued currency has meant higher equipment, component, and debt-servicing outlays. Within weeks of the devaluation, the KIA chaebol went bankrupt, but was allowed to continue operating after the government nationalized its debt. As of December 1996, KIA had accumulated liabilities amounting to more than six times its equity (see table 7.1 in chap. 7). In the midst of a deep recession and rising unemployment and labor unrest, however, the government could not possibly shut down the largely worthless company. The government organized a competitive bidding for KIA in mid-1998. Hyundai, Daewoo, Samsung, General Motors, and Ford each presented bids. Much to the dismay of state officials, however, they offered low prices and asked for a forgiveness of KIA's debt. The bidding process was canceled in September 1998, and Ford and GM announced that they would not bid if a second round were organized (*Korea Times*, 21 and 30 August 1998, 13 September 1998). The second round was also canceled for a similar reason as the first. In the fall of 1998 Samsung was still far away from its stated goal of making a quarter million cars, and the United States was putting pressure on Korea to lower tariffs on imported autos (just 11,200 foreign cars were sold in Korea during 1997), and to simplify administrative procedures (*Korea Herald*, 18 September 1998). After a couple of years as the world's fifth largest automaker, Korea had fallen back to seventh place. Capacity utilization rates dropped to below 70 percent even with the increase in export sales as the result of the weakened won (*Korea Times*, 17 May 1999, 4 October 1999).

As in such other heavy industries as petrochemicals and shipbuilding, the key problem with the Korean automobile industry is excess capacity. Consolidation and downsizing could provide a painful solution to the situation. Events have demonstrated, however, that consolidation is hard, and downsizing unthinkable. Daewoo took over Ssangyong's tiny four-wheel drive vehicle operation (100,000 capacity) in January 1998. In late 1998 Hyundai was announced the winner in the bid for KIA and Asia, while Samsung agreed to transfer its automobile venture to Daewoo in exchange for the latter's electronics unit. The Samsung-Daewoo deal, however, was met by considerable opposition from labor unions and suppliers, and by skepticism from industry analysts. It fell apart rather quickly. Then, in the summer of 1999 the Daewoo chaebol went bankrupt, triggering a new wave of negotiations among the companies, the government, and foreign multinationals, especially General Motors (*Korea Times*, 13 and 19 October 1999; *Hankuk Ilbo*, 13 October 1999). Consolidation without restructuring, however, does not fix the problem of excess capacity. But if the prospects for the Korean assembly industry are bleak, the predicament of the country's component suppliers is even worse.

The Plight of Korean Component Manufacturers

In addition to the traditional dominance by big business, the Korean state's policies toward the auto industry undermined the components sector, which in many other countries tends to include myriad small and medium enterprises. While the Automobile Industry Protection Law of 1962 and the Automobile Industry Basic Promotion Plan of 1969 prohibited imports of assembled cars, tariff-free imports of components were allowed. Naturally, assemblers prospered while local parts manufacturers suffered. It was not until the late 1970s that content requirements were raised from 20 to 90 percent for a car assembled in Korea to qualify as "Korean" (Green 1992). When local content requirements were belatedly increased, the large assemblers had no choice but to integrate vertically or to rely on chaebol-affiliated firms for parts because the independent suppliers had been driven out of business by imports. And even then, the assemblers relied on Korean suppliers only for "nonlethal" components, especially if cars were destined to foreign markets (EIU 1996b; Green 1992, 412).

A case in point is Korea's most advanced auto company. Fourteen different firms belonging to the Hyundai chaebol supply Hyundai Motor Company with everything from steel and aluminum to paint, glass, electronic components, and mechanical parts. In addition, Hyundai Motor sources machinery from four other Hyundai firms, software from two, and a variety of financial services from five. Hyundai-made container ships carry the autos to export markets, and the chaebol's general trading company handles the administrative, wholesaling, and insurance activities (Amsden 1989, 175–88; Amsden and Kang 1995, 12). Not even Henry Ford in his heyday achieved a comparable degree and scope of vertical integration. The chaebol's fixation with control even led to forbidding component manufacturers from selling not only to a competing chaebol but also to maintenance shops or car owners directly. This ban is currently being reexamined by the major assemblers (*Korea Times*, 5 October 1999). The assemblers' obsession with controlling their suppliers became such a problem that even the World Bank noted it in a 1980 report: "in Korea every firm tries to make everything on its own rather than to purchase some components from the outside" (quoted in Lew 1999, 138).

In spite of the efforts to emulate the Japanese, Korea has actually failed to create a "tiered," vibrant sector of competitive component firms that collaborate with each other and with the assembler in product design, cost cutting, and quality enhancement (Dyer, Cho, and Chu 1998; EIU 1996b; Lee 1996, 138–39; McKinsey 1996, 109–12). "Progress . . . is very slow, as assemblers find it hard to give up control over any part of design, however trivial" (McKinsey and Co. 1996, 116). Of some 170 major Korean suppliers surveyed by MIT's International Motor Vehicle Program, over half depended on one of the top three assemblers for 50 percent or more of their total sales, and roughly 40 percent of the suppliers depended on them for 80 percent or more (Lee 1996, 61). Few Korean suppliers have ever attempted to export to foreign assemblers (EIU 1996b). Moreover, worker-manager and union-firm relations in the auto industry are perhaps the most adversarial in the country, in both the assembly and the components sector (Y. S. Lee 1993).

The dependence of component suppliers on the big assemblers proved fatal in the aftermath of the 1997–98 crisis. When the KIA chaebol folded, a dozen of its most important suppliers followed suit, the only difference being that the Korean government would bail out only the assembler and not the smaller firms (*Korea Times*, 30 August 1997). During the first year of the crisis nearly 200 suppliers shut down as sales of automobiles in the domestic market and abroad plummeted (*Korea Times*, 18 September 1998). Without viable export opportunities of their own, Korean components firms are up for a major overhaul in the next few years.

As documented in figure 6.1, Korea has failed to become a major exporter of auto components but is a force to be reckoned with in assembled cars. In particular, Hyundai Motor has accumulated valuable capabilities, managed to develop somewhat of a proprietary technology base (its R&D over sales already was 3.5 percent in 1975, reaching 4.4 percent by 1994), and is a well-known brand throughout the world (Amsden 1989; Amsden and Kang 1995; L. Kim 1998). Both the underlying pattern of social organization—institutionalized patrimonialism—and government policies of the nationalist-modernizing variety favored large-scale undertakings requiring huge amounts of labor and capital at the expense of the more flexible and knowledge-intensive component-related activities. Clearly, Korea could not possibly excel in auto parts. Neighboring Taiwan—socially endowed with the opposite set of resources—has indeed developed an export prowess in components without exporting a single assembled vehicle (Biggart and Guillén 1999). Although at first sharing with Korea an obsession with economies of scale, Spain departed from this pattern by allowing foreign multinationals to set up assembly plants and, later, take over local component manufacturers, resulting in high exports of both kinds of products. As in Korea, modernist policymaking inflicted harm on the industry at several points in time.

Spain: Success through Internationalization

Spain is best known around the world for its tourist attractions and agricultural products. Most people are stunned to learn that the automobile industry is the country's largest both in terms of production and exports. Spain runs head to head with South Korea as the world's fifth largest auto assembler, behind the United States, Japan, Germany, and France. Moreover, since three-fourths of output are exports, Spain ranks as the fourth largest exporter of motor vehicles, surpassed only by Japan, Germany, and France, and well ahead of the United States and Korea. The auto assembly and components industry accounts for 6 percent of GDP and 24 percent of merchandise exports. The components sector comprises over 1,100 firms with 215,000 employees, and exports about half of its production as nonassembled components for the original and replacement markets (García 1998; MIE 1996, 133–43). Moreover, Spanish auto parts plants are among the most efficient in the world (Andersen Consulting 1994), and several Spanish-owned component firms have become multinationals in their own right, with production plants on four continents.

Spain's secret is called foreign direct investment. The country's silent rise to prominence in the world automobile industry has to do with the fact that all assembly lines and over three-fourths of component manufacturing are accounted for by foreign-owned companies, which see their Spanish operations in the context of the European marketplace. Multinationals located in Spain must compete among themselves not only for domestic and export sales, but also for skilled workers and supplies. After decades of inconsistent, counterproductive, and largely ineffective import-substitution policies in assembly and components, the state embraced a policy of liberalism and internationalism toward the industry during the late 1970s and 1980s, precisely when the effort at economic integration with Europe was gaining speed. As a result, multinationals took over existing facilities and created new ones, turning the country into an export hub for subcompact cars and certain components. Although no domestic make survived as an independent firm, and many components firms came under foreign control, a few domestically owned parts manufacturers emerged strengthened from this process, becoming world market leaders in their respective product lines. The switch from nationalist to pragmatic policymaking, however, brought about not only growth but also the destruction of some indigenous capabilities.

Government Policies: From Import-Substitution to Liberalization

The history of the Spanish automobile industry has been shaped by the direct involvement of two key actors: the state and foreign multinationals. As in Taiwan and Korea, a lack of indigenous technology, and the confusion of military with purely economic goals, marked the origin of modern auto assembly. The first high-volume passenger car assembly line became operational in the mid-1950s as a joint venture (SEAT) among the state's enterprise holding (INI), the Italian manufacturer FIAT, and six domestic banks.[2] Students of economic development would identify the Spanish state during the late 1940s and 1950s as "relatively autonomous." Moreover, navy officer and engineer Juan Antonio Suanzes, a personal friend of ruling dictator General Franco, enjoyed a considerable degree of autonomy as both founding president of the INI holding (1941–63) and minister of industry (1938–39 and 1945–51). Privileged freedom of action within the regime allowed Suanzes a direct say in how the emerging auto industry would be organized (Guillén 1994, 178; San Román 1995; Martín Aceña and Comín 1991, 228–29).

The founding of a state-owned company with the participation of local banks and foreign technology partners, however, was not the only viable option—there were private domestic entrepreneurs with experience in both assembly and components, and willing to develop a domestic auto industry. As in Korea, though, policymakers ignored the incipient assembly operations of small workshops and several private initiatives. Between 1939 and 1946 the INI opposed and defeated one attempt by General Motors (in association with the March banking family), another by Ford (both of which had been present in Spain since the 1920s), and two attempts by the Urquijo banking group and Italy's FIAT to set up auto companies with mass-production capabilities. The Urquijo-FIAT joint ventures also had the participation of a small-scale, though prestigious, domestic auto manufacturer, Hispano-Suiza. Another small firm, Eucort, attempted in 1945 to obtain credit and permissions from the state to turn itself into a large-scale assembler, based on its relatively modest operations employing 900 workers who assembled an average of two automobiles per day. The INI, though, insisted on playing a direct role in the industry with its own truck and auto companies (ENASA and SEAT). The government later allowed two French companies—Renault and Citroën—to set up assembly operations, with SEAT being guaranteed the lion's share of the domestic market (Carreras and Estapé Triay 1998; San Román 1995, 104–24).

Following standard import-substitution practice, the state protected the domestic market through tariffs and quotas. A stringent local content requirement of 90 percent and the favorable financing terms awarded to the state company SEAT and the multinationals during the 1950s and 1960s combined

[2] The Ford Motor Company started assembling knocked-down kits in Spain (KDKs) during the early 1920s. On the eve of the Spanish Civil War of 1936–39 its Spanish subsidiary employed some 750 workers and had plans to establish a new factory. The Franco government was resentful of Ford's resistance to supplying vehicles on credit, and preferred to take the development of the auto industry in its own hands. The Spanish subsidiary of Ford languished until the state took it over in 1954. Its facilities were acquired by Massey Ferguson in 1967 (Estapé Triay 1997).

to choke the development of private domestic initiatives. The small assembly workshops that had developed from the 1920s to the 1940s went under. The myriad repair workshops and auto components manufacturers that flourished in the shadow of the domestic assembly operations and the once burgeoning import business languished during the 1950s and 1960s as the three large-scale assemblers pursued vertically integrated strategies or persuaded some of their foreign suppliers to co-locate in Spain. In addition, Citroën and Renault were forced to set up their lines in relatively backward and sparsely populated areas, far away from the traditional enclaves of automobile-related activity: Renault in and around Valladolid (1955), in central Castille, and Citroën in Vigo (1959), in remote and impoverished Galicia, Franco's home region in Spain's northwest.

Given the incentives provided by the state, both the assemblers and the components producers focused on the domestic market, with exports never exceeding 10 percent of total production until the mid-1970s. The presence of three automakers inside a protected though relatively narrow market meant that plants were not of minimum efficient scale and model production runs were relatively short, resulting in inflated prices. Protectionism bred complacency, with profitability being the highest in Spanish industry (Banco Urquijo 1970). The status quo created during the 1950s was not upset by the entries of Authi, Talbot, and Chrysler during the late 1960s, all of which failed after the first oil crisis. The heavy involvement of an autonomous state had resulted in the destruction of the flourishing, albeit small-scale, auto assembly and components workshops, and the creation of a backward assembly industry protected by steep barriers (Bolsa de Madrid 1981; Hawkesworth 1981; Auto-Revista 1987).

Although output continued to rise through the first oil crisis of 1973–76, thanks to subsidized export growth, the second shock of 1979 hit the industry very hard after years of lagging investment, sluggish productivity growth, and technological backwardness. The last Franco governments in the early to mid-1970s and the first democratic ones in the late 1970s reversed three decades of automobile policy by introducing far-reaching liberalization measures. Old and new assemblers would be allowed to expand capacity or set up new plants, wholly own their operations, source components from abroad almost freely, and specialize in the European marketplace. In compensation, foreign assemblers were required to invest heavily, create jobs, and raise exports to at least two-thirds of output. Attracted by such emoluments, new foreign entries took place. Ford's first automobile rolled off its Almussafes, Valencia, assembly line in 1976, General Motors completed its Figueruelas, Saragossa, facility in 1982, and Volkswagen acquired a controlling stake in SEAT and took over its Navarre factory in 1986. The new entrants specialized in small passenger vehicles for export (e.g., Ford's Fiesta, GM-Opel's Corsa, and VW's Polo), while the older plants of Renault and Citroën were expanded and retooled

(Bolsa de Madrid 1981). By the late 1980s, Spain had become the fifth largest automobile assembler in the world, and the fourth in terms of exports, with all assembly operations under foreign control after Volkswagen took over the state-owned SEAT factories. During 1998 and 1999 the assemblers were competing with each other for airtime when it came to announce their new investments in facilities to cope with strong growth in domestic and export sales (*El País*, 21 May 1999; *Actualidad Económica*, 28 June–4 July 1999, 66–79).

A Vibrant Components Sector

The liberal policies initiated in the 1970s and deepened during the 1980s as Spain prepared for European Union membership had the assembly sector in mind, not components. The shift from import-substitution policies à la dependency theory to liberal local content requirements took the components sector by storm. More than 20 percent of jobs in auto components were lost during the years of crisis and restructuring. Although diametrically opposed, the liberal policies of the 1980s achieved a result similar to the one produced by the protectionist policies initiated in the late 1940s: a debacle among existing component manufacturers. While in the 1940s and 1950s a relatively autonomous state strangled private initiatives in auto assembly and stymied the growth of components manufacturers, the liberalization reforms of the 1970s and 1980s had the unintended effect of throwing hundreds of auto components firms out of business and placing the industry under heavy foreign control. In 1979, the government approved the first major foreign acquisition, Robert Bosch's takeover of Femsa, the largest domestic components manufacturer at the time. Between 1979 and 1994—when Exide Corporation of the United States acquired the battery maker Tudor, one of the world's largest—dozens of Spanish component firms were bought by foreigners. Overall, the proportion of foreign-controlled auto parts companies, weighted by sales, grew from 37 percent in 1973 to 56 percent in 1983, and to a staggering 71 percent in 1990 (Bolsa de Madrid 1986; Auto-Revista 1986, 83, 130, 166–72, 179, 219; MICT 1991; EIU 1996a).

As a member of the European Union since 1986, Spain has become a world center for subcompact automobile and parts manufacturing (Andersen Consulting 1994; Bolsa de Madrid 1986; EIU 1996a). The components industry has attained world standards of competitiveness, unlike Korea's. According to the OECD, auto parts and other transportation equipment is one of Spain's comparative areas of technological strength, as measured by the number and specialization of patents (Archibugi and Pianta 1992, 76–77). An Andersen Consulting (1994) study—conducted in conjunction with researchers at Cambridge University and the University of Wales—ranked Spanish labor productivity in auto components manufacturing the highest in the world, topping even Japan ("Gain in Spain" 1994; EIU 1996a; Sernauto 1996, 37, 45).

It is clear, however, that these favorable aspects of the auto components industry in Spain are not only the result of local entrepreneurial initiatives, but also the outcome of the heavy involvement of foreign capital and technology.

Unlike in Korea, the Spanish components sector has produced world-class, domestically owned companies thanks to, and not in spite of, the arrival of foreign multinationals. Reviewing the four most telling cases throws additional light on the strengths and weaknesses of the Spanish approach to developing an automobile industry. The four companies are among the top 30 automotive suppliers in the world, and command leading global market shares in their respective product lines (García 1998).

Tudor is the leading automotive battery manufacturer in Spain and the third largest in Europe with a market share of around 15 percent. The Sociedad Española del Acumulador Tudor SA was founded in 1897 in Madrid. The firm manufactures automotive, industrial, and submarine batteries, and a variety of auto parts. For decades, Tudor was the largest Spanish multinational company, with manufacturing operations on four continents. In the 1920s it established battery production facilities in Portugal. Battery manufacturing in Angola and Mozambique started in the 1960s. During the 1970s exports soared to 45 percent of total production, and new foreign investments in production were undertaken in Venezuela and Morocco. Meanwhile, expenses in R&D grew steadily, including research on battery weight reduction, electric-powered cars, and battery recycling, with laboratories being located in Spain and Germany. Tudor's internationalization proceeded at an accelerated pace during the 1980s, with foreign sales reaching 75 percent of the total. By the early 1990s the firm had production plants in nine European countries, organized under four area groups (Spanish, Portuguese, German, and Scandinavian), and in such distant locations as Venezuela, Angola, Mozambique, Central African Republic, Macau, and India. As of 1995 almost half of Tudor's auto batteries and around 70 percent of its industrial batteries were manufactured outside Spain. The firm also opened over 20 sales and marketing subsidiaries abroad, and acquired Elbak Maschinenbau GmbH of Austria, Hagen Batterie AG of Germany, and Neste Battery of Finland.

The growth and international expansion of Tudor had much to do with the stimulating effect of foreign investment in auto assembly and parts in Spain. Tudor invested in technology and marketing at home and abroad and became a leading supplier to multinational companies as well as a major player in the battery replacement market. The company, though, started to decline under intense competition from European firms after Spain became a member in 1986, and because of its own managerial mistakes. By 1993 Tudor had 1,400 employees, revenues of $179 million, and losses amounting to 15 percent of sales. Both employees and sales have declined ever since. The triggering event took place in late 1993, when its longtime institutional owner, the Banesto bank, was intervened by the central bank after its management engaged in dubious financial operations that affected its solvency. Banesto's new owner, Banco Santander, decided to focus on banking and divest from industrial companies (see chap. 7). Tudor was then sold to Exide Corporation of the United States in the face of the government's and the labor unions' opposition. Tudor's operations in Europe are being consolidated with others owned by Exide, and Tudor has divested from plants in Scandinavia, the Netherlands, Austria, and Germany, while expanding some of its Spanish operations and shutting down others (*Expansión*, 27 August 1996, 5; *Financial Times*, 26 September 1995, 1; *New York Times*, 26 September 1995, C4).

While the Tudor case is not one of ultimate success, there are three other components firms whose future looks solid and bright. Grupo Antolín-Irausa (over 2,100 employees and $201 million in sales) is the world's largest manufacturer of ceiling panels for autos (over 7 million units annually), and a leading maker of seats, door locks, and electric devices for windows. Its first Spanish factories were set up near Renault's assembly lines in central Castille during the 1960s. In the 1970s it opened facilities nearby Ford's new plant on the Mediterranean, and Land Rover Santana's assembly operations in southern Spain. After demonstrating its high quality and reliability, the company was asked by foreign assemblers to set up shop abroad. Presently, the firm is present in more than 10 countries: wholly owned operations in Portugal, France, Germany, the United Kingdom, and the Czech Republic; and joint ventures in Turkey, the United States, South Africa, India, Brazil, and Mexico. R&D centers are located in Spain and Italy. The company remains under family control.

Another successful family-owned components company is Barcelona-based Ficosa International (nearly 2,500 employees, $229 million in sales, and $102 million in exports). It makes electric wiring and systems, mirrors, door locks, and windshield wipers for Opel (GM), Ford, Volkswagen-SEAT, Nissan, Renault, Matra, PSA (Peugeot and Citroën), BMW, and Mercedes-Benz. Almost half of its production in Spain is accounted for by exports. The firm's first operations date back to the early 1950s. Internationalization occurred in the late 1980s and 1990s, when Ficosa set up production facilities in France, Portugal, the United Kingdom, Mexico, Argentina, Brazil, and India. Design centers are located in Spain, the United Kingdom, Germany, France, and Detroit, Michigan (Durán and Úbeda 1996; *Financial Times*, 19 January 1998, 19; *Actualidad Económica*, 1 July 1996, 10–14). Like Grupo Antolín, Ficosa remains under the control of the founding family.

The fourth case of an internationally successful Spanish auto components company is part of the Mondragón group of worker-owned cooperatives, located in the Basque Country (see chap. 3). Fagor Ederlan presently employs 1,300 workers and sells $155 million worth of cast-iron and aluminum diecast components, and other auto parts. Its exports amount to $107 million. Fagor has demonstrated that cooperatives need not limit themselves to their surrounding region or even to their country of origin. It has established foreign production plants in the United Kingdom, the United States, and Mexico, and acquired the auto parts subsidiaries of Ford and Volkswagen in Argentina and Brazil. Fagor Ederlan supplies engine blocks to the European operations of Opel, Renault, Rover, and Volkswagen; safety parts to BMW; knuckles, manifolds, and brake drum discs to Honda; various auto parts to Daimler-Benz, FIAT, Jaguar, and Audi; and is developing the Puma diesel engine jointly with Ford. It is undoubtedly the most successful and sophisticated auto components worker-owned cooperative in the world.

The cases of Tudor, Grupo Antolín-Irausa, Ficosa, and Fagor Ederlan illustrate the importance of patterns of corporate control. Tudor became controlled by a bank that offered it patient capital for several decades, although the latter's adventures during the 1990s ultimately proved a curse. Grupo Antolín and Ficosa as family firms, and Fagor as a worker cooperative, have enjoyed more stable and lasting ownership arrangements that have allowed them to grow organically without taking on much debt or falling into the hands of international investors. Although the arrival of foreign capital to the Spanish components sector could have been regulated in such a way that more domestic companies survived, its generally beneficial effects should not be neglected. Foreign auto parts firms revolutionized production methods and helped raise quality standards. Spain can boast high exports of both assembled cars and components thanks to its ability to attract and nurture foreign investment. Multinationals have contributed to an upgrading of technological and organizational skills, indirectly benefiting the domestically owned sector. The Argentine case, however, will demonstrate that foreign capital and management are not always a panacea, and that their effects depend on the institutional conditions in the host country.

Argentina: The Curse of Populism

After decades of backwardness, the Argentine auto industry is now starting to change as a result of economic liberalization and trade integration with Brazil. Presently, the assembly sector includes Volkswagen, CIADEA (Renault), Sevel (Peugeot), Ford, General Motors, FIAT, and Toyota. Total output of passenger cars reached a record high of just over 300,000 autos in 1994, declining to 225,000 in 1995 as a consequence of the recession induced by the Mexican crisis, and recovering to 270,000 in 1996 and a record 445,000 in 1997, to decline again in 1998 and 1999 as a result of the fallout from the Asian crisis and Brazil's devaluation. Exports reached about half of total output in 1997, although mostly destined to Brazil and subject to sharp fluctuations from year to year (Auto-Revista 1997; Case and Mandel-Campbell 1998; Nofal 1989).

The Failures of Government Policy

As in Korea and Spain, the first high-volume assembly operations were established some 35 years ago after the state erected high protection walls and introduced import-substitution incentives for both assembled autos and parts. Although assembly based on knocked-down kits started in 1916 by Ford—and the state itself entered the industry in 1951 with Industrias Aeronáuticas y Mecánicas del Estado—large-scale assembly was not a reality until Industrias Kaiser Argentina (IKA), a subsidiary of the ailing U.S. firm, set up a factory in 1955, in part to dispose of its antiquated equipment. Uneasiness with President Perón's motives and policies discouraged other foreign multinationals from considering an entry into the Argentine market (Jenkins 1984; MacDonald 1988; Nofal 1989).

The new government emerging out of the 1958 presidential election was eager to promote the auto industry and to attract foreign capital so as to substitute imports for local production. Over the next decade as many as 21 different assemblers were allowed to operate, frequently as joint ventures between large local business groups and a foreign automotive company. They basically assembled foreign-made components, given that the government initially asked them to add on location a minimum of only one-third of the value of each car. Because of the fragmentation of the industry, the production costs of the Argentine assemblers averaged four times higher than in the United States or Europe, and output per worker stood at a mere *three* vehicles a year. The main 13 assemblers made as many as 68 different models during the 1960s, sharing a total market size never exceeding 200,000 units (Nofal 1989). In spite of high costs and meager market shares, they were nonetheless able to make profits by charging inflated prices in a protected market (Jenkins 1984). By some estimates, General Motors' internal rate of return in Argentina exceeded 50 percent during 1963–65 (Nofal 1989, 41; Sourrouille 1980).

The import-substitution policies of the 1960s succeeded at creating an auto assembly industry, however inefficient and inward-looking, but made a critical mistake that proved devastating to the auto components sector. Over a mere five years (1964–68) local content requirements were raised from 55 percent to 90–95 percent. This regulation neglected that Argentina—unlike Spain—lacked a vibrant sector of small and medium-sized firms prepared to supply auto components (Biggart and Guillén 1999). In response to the government's impatience, the assemblers had no choice but to integrate vertically, even into such areas as forging, castings, axles, transmissions, and suspensions, either by creating new suppliers or acquiring local firms. Like in Korea, components manufacturers never took foreign markets seriously. Unlike in that country, however, the assembly plants located in Argentina were solely geared toward the domestic market. Thus, components firms faced no incentives to improve quality or cut costs (Jenkins 1984; Nofal 1989).

The government realized in the late 1960s and early 1970s that new incentives were needed to further encourage auto components production and exports. Policies, however, tended to benefit the vertically integrated assemblers and not the small and medium-sized firms (Nofal 1989, 167–97). By 1972, over half of auto parts production was controlled by foreign capital, and 85 percent of exports of components were accounted for by the largest firms (Montero 1996, 34; Bisang, Burachik, and Katz 1995, 248; Dorfman 1983, 200–201; Sourrouille 1980, 158–67; Nofal 1989).

The Argentine auto industry suffered from the zigzags in policymaking and the country's extreme degree of political and economic instability. After peaking in 1973 at 293,000 units, auto assembly declined until the early 1990s to annual volumes as low as 100,000, not far from the prewar record of 76,000 units back in 1929 (Jenkins 1984). This downward trend was exacerbated between 1979 and 1982 when the military junta experimented with a set of mutually inconsistent neoliberal policies. At the industry level, the military government lowered both local content requirements and tariffs on assembled cars (the outright prohibition of imports had been lifted in 1976). At the macroeconomic level, the junta pursued tight monetary policies that increased the value of the currency. Predictably, the combination of freer trade and an overvalued currency made it very hard for domestic producers to compete. Moreover, the attempt to stabilize the economy by curbing domestic demand devastated the inward-looking auto industry (Nofal 1989, 216–17). Disillusioned by stagnant demand and political turmoil, GM left in 1978, and Citroën and Chrysler quit the following year. The state-owned firm abandoned auto production in 1980. The brutal neoliberal policies implemented by the juntas had achieved dismal results: automotive-related employment and output fell by 25 percent, while the trade deficit in automobiles skyrocketed as imports were liberalized and the incipient exports of components or finished autos dwindled (Montero 1996; Nofal 1989). As Biggart and Guillén (1999, 739) noted, both "the import-substitution policy of the 1960s and the neoliberal program of the late 1970s contained the same error: ignoring the strengths and weaknesses in the underlying industrial structure."

The 1990s have witnessed a rapid transformation of the Argentine auto industry. Trade liberalization in the context of the Mercosur customs union with Brazil has produced more cross-border specialization and integration, a trend foreshadowed in 1988 by the Argentina-Brazil Automotive Free Trade Agreement. Foreign multinationals no longer think of Brazil and Argentina as separate, compartmentalized markets. Rather, they have been setting up a total of six new, efficient-scale plants and engaging in trade. Still, three-fourths of Argentine automotive exports go to Brazil and are covered under the balanced-trade arrangements for the automobile industry built into the Mercosur treaty: in order to avoid duties, firms must balance their imports of components and assembled vehicles across the Argentine-Brazilian border with imports of an equal value (Bisang, Burachik, and Katz 1995; CEPAL 1999; Chudnovsky, López, and Porta 1997). The treaty also provides for steep barriers against imports from third countries and for minimum local content requirements. This situation is rather precarious for two reasons. First, Brazil's economy and auto market are five times greater than Argentina's, and production costs tend to be lower there, thus encouraging multinationals to emphasize investments in Brazil to the detriment of Argentina in preparation for fully liberalized trade between the two countries. Second, Brazil's economic situation is far more delicate than Argentina's. During the fall of 1998 assembly plants in Córdoba, Argentina, had to send workers home on 75 percent pay for several days a week because of plunging sales in Brazil. The devaluation of the Brazilian currency in early 1999 harmed Argentine exporters, given the country's sacred policy of keeping the value of the peso pegged to the U.S. dollar so as to keep inflation under control (Case and Mandel-Campbell 1998; *La Nación*, September 17, 1998). During the first eight months of 1999 Argentine automobile production plummeted by 46 percent relative to the same period of 1998, sales dropped by 26 percent, and exports by 68 percent (*Argentina Monthly*, September 1999).

Brasil-dependencia—export-dependency on Brazil—will be hard to change in the short run (*La Nación*, 22 November 1998). Costs in the Argentine auto industry are much higher than in Europe and Japan. As a spokesman for Ford Argentina complains, "we have tried to sell in Chile, but it is more profitable for the company's Chilean sales subsidiary to import the Ford Escort from Spain than from Argentina" (Hudson 1998). The special automotive regime in the Mercosur was supposed to expire by 2000 (nothing endures like the provisional). Argentina, though, has lobbied hard to extend certain privileges until 2004: a monitoring system to make sure trade between Argentina and Brazil does not become too unbalanced in the latter's favor, a common external tariff on assembled cars of 35 percent (up from 18.6 percent), and a local content requirement of 60 percent, with imports of certain sophisticated components not available within Mercosur taxed at 14 percent (CEPAL 1999, 28–37; *La Nación*, 19 December 1998, 19 September 1999, 13 October 1999). In automobiles, as in other manufactured products, Mercosur represents an extension of import-substitution policies rather than their abandonment (see chap. 2).

The Predicament of Component Manufacturers

Presently, the Argentine auto components sector is very fragmented given the relatively small size of the industry: 400 firms, 35,700 employees, and value added representing a mere 0.45 percent of total GDP, or 3.50 percent of manufacturing GDP. Exports are 16 percent of the industry's output, representing only 4.4 percent of total Argentine exports. Trade with Brazil in auto components has increased quickly since the creation of Mercosur. However, it is the seven existing assemblers who dominate it, because they are required to balance their imports of components with exports if they want to avoid tariffs. Small and medium companies are not active exporters (Auto-Revista 1997). Moreover, Brazilian components manufacturers are reaping most of the benefits. Only one in five cars assembled in Argentina has an Argentine-made engine, and Argentina is running a deficit with Brazil (*AméricaEconomía*, 12 August 1999, 20–24). Even after a decade of economic growth and selective liberalization, the Argentine components sector is still unprepared to meet the challenges of the global economy. Part of the blame, though, rests with the government, which has made a mistake similar to the one of the 1960s and the 1970s. Although it has set up myriad programs to help small and medium firms be more competitive (CEPAL 1999, 89–105), trade policies are favoring the wrong type of components firms: those owned by or tied to the large assemblers at the expense of independent small and medium enterprises.

The renegotiation and extension of the special trade arrangement with Brazil beyond 2000 is likely to hurt component manufacturers and benefit the assemblers. While the assemblers would like free trade inside Mercosur combined with a steep external tariff—they have specialized facilities in Argentina and Brazil—Argentine component manufacturers prefer more protection from Brazilian and third-party companies alike. Components firms, however, are not as politically influential as the assemblers (Case and Mandel-Campbell 1998; *Financial Times*, 27 July 1998, Survey, 5; *La Nación*, 4 November 1997).

In spite of the successes of the liberal economic program of the 1990s, the Argentine economy in general and the automobile industry in particular are still suffering from a scarcity of export-capable firms (Chudnovsky, López, and Porta 1997; Toulan and Guillén 1997; Guillén and Toulan 1997). The populist policies of many of Argentina's 45 economy ministers over the last 50 years helped to reinforce the fundamentally inward-looking character of the country's manufacturing community. In addition, the distrust of foreign multinationals has run so deep that a Spanish solution to the exhaustion of the import-substitution model has not come easy in Argentina (chap. 5). Foreign automobile multinationals came to Argentina halfheartedly, with a short-term attitude, teaming up with local partners so as to reduce risks, and hardly competing against each other. Government incentives led them to integrate vertically, a move that choked the small and medium-sized firms. More recently, balanced-trade arrangements with Brazil have only offered a temporary respite for the industry, which is following an import-substitution model of growth with the Mercosur as the target market.

On Developing Industry

The rise of the auto industry in South Korea, Spain, and Argentina illustrates the importance of historically developed institutional factors in shaping economic growth. At various points, the three states experimented with import-substitution and export-oriented policies. These policies interacted with existing categories of actors—small versus large and domestic versus foreign firms—in unexpected ways, producing a variety of unintended outcomes. Ultimately, only Spain has succeeded at becoming a leading exporter of both passenger cars and auto parts, and only Korea has been able to develop a domestically owned assembly industry with growing proprietary R&D and design capabilities. Moreover, while the interests of assemblers and component manufacturers are reasonably aligned with each other in Spain, in Argentina and Korea they find themselves at odds on most issues.

In Korea and Spain the emphasis shifted from import-substitution to exports by the late 1970s, but without allowing for a domestically owned auto components sector to fully develop. By privileging new actors at the expense of preexisting ones, possibilities for innovation and growth were thwarted. Thus, state policies benefited large business groups at the expense of small and medium enterprises in Korea, and state-owned or foreign firms to the detriment of local entrepreneurs in Spain. The Big Three passenger car assemblers in Korea integrated vertically on the basis of state protection, subsidized credit, and duty-free imports of certain components, a policy mix that made it virtually impossible for an independent components sector to develop. When government incentives shifted toward exports, the only viable component supply strategy for the chaebol was to continue building vertical and exclusive relationships with tightly controlled firms. The continued strength of the chaebol—a characteristic of nationalist-modernizing development paths—has hampered the components sector up to the present.

As Biggart and Guillén (1999, 740) have noted for the Spanish case, "an autonomous state twice assumed that domestic entrepreneurs were unprepared, unsuitable, or hopeless prospects, first in the 1950s and then in the 1980s." Following in a long tradition of contempt for the entrepreneurial and financial communities, state technocrats thought that the traditionalism of local management and capital rendered them incapable of succeeding in the automobile industry. After the limitations of direct intervention in such a global industry as automobiles became apparent, the government decided instead to attract massive export-oriented foreign investment. The new pragmatic-modernizing policy, however, had a key side effect. Liberalization of trade and freedom of establishment during the industrial crises of the 1970s forced many local auto suppliers into bankruptcy, paving the way for foreign multinationals both in assembly and components to turn the country into an export platform for subcompact cars. Unlike in Argentina, however, the arrival of foreign multinationals was tied to export incentives and competitive relationships between parts suppliers and assemblers in the context of a European market undergoing integration.

In Argentina the state presided over the proliferation of small-scale auto assemblers protected by steep tariffs without encouraging export-oriented growth. The rushed implementation of incentives for assemblers to purchase components locally produced an inefficient pattern of backward vertical integration. More recently, balanced-trade arrangements with Brazil have further delayed the adaptation of Argentine components manufacturers to the global economy.

The three countries' experiences illustrate that states have a very hard time trying to impose new patterns of behavior on preexisting structures of actors and relationships among them. The organizational dynamics of development paths acquire a momentum of their own. While other manufacturing industries differ from automobiles in important ways, this chapter has shown that countries are not organizationally prepared to succeed in every single activity. Auto assembly and component manufacturing differ in important ways, making it hard for any one country to succeed at both. Countries in which big business dominates may excel in assembly, but are bound to have a hard time in components. As we shall see in the next chapter, states have also misread the social and organizational strengths and weaknesses underlying the service-sector activities of their countries, and failed to recognize that services are not merely support activities of manufacturing but can also play a role in their own right.

SEVEN

DEVELOPING SERVICES: BANKING AS AN INDUSTRY IN ITS OWN RIGHT

We always try to get free money.
(President of a top-four Korean chaebol, June 1997)

En la Argentina, todo lo que se mueve se promueve
[In Argentina everything in motion is by promotion].
(An old jibe about economic populism in Argentina)

There are only two kinds of bankers: conservative bankers
and bad bankers.
(Emilio Botín, chairman of Spain's Banco Santander)

BANKING is as prominent and symbolic an industry as automobile manufacturing. Banks tend to play a critical role in developing countries wishing to industrialize quickly because manufacturing growth requires the transfer of massive amounts of resources from backward to dynamic economic sectors, and from foreign lenders to targeted domestic recipients. Beginning with Gerschenkron (1962), the literature has studied banks mainly from the point of view of their contribution to the development of manufacturing industry, placing a strong emphasis on state-bank and bank-industry relations. In spite of decades of research, there is no agreement in the literature as to whether the banking sector—and financial markets in general—should be organized according to market- or state-centered principles in order to accelerate growth. While modernization and neoclassical theories recommend a market-based financial system, dependency and late-industrialization generally take sides with the state-centered view (Loriaux 1991, 1997; Amsden 1989; Fry 1995; Zysman 1983). Regardless how this controversy is finally, if ever, resolved, previous research has established that the degree of state interventionism in banking has varied greatly across developing countries and over time (Fields 1995; Haggard and Lee 1993; Haggard and Maxfield 1993; Loriaux 1997; Maxfield 1997; Pérez 1997; Woo 1991; Zysman 1983).

Rather than presenting yet another comparative study of the role of banks in promoting manufacturing, this chapter answers an even more intriguing and far-reaching question: under what conditions do countries develop a banking sector that becomes not only an effective contributor to manufacturing growth but also an internationally competitive industry in its own right?

South Korea and Argentina have historically failed—albeit in different ways— at developing reasonably stable and well-functioning banking sectors. Spanish banks became prominent actors in the economy at the turn of the century. Until recently, they grew at the expense of manufacturing firms, creating industrial groups around them. They have long ranked among the most profitable and better run in the world and have recently catapulted themselves internationally as major foreign investors.

Previous scholarship on economic development—with its strong modernist bias—has largely focused on the determinants of *industrial* growth, under the assumption that services are merely "support" activities contributing to industrialization. A vibrant banking sector, however, can potentially offer many other benefits in addition to effective and efficient resource mobilization and allocation to industrial investors. First, it can help increase savings rates by developing new products, distribution channels, and services. Second, it creates large numbers of jobs, ranging from low-skilled bank tellers to highly educated financial analysts and managers. Third, like the automobile industry, it generates multiple linkages to other activities, such as insurance, tourism, education, information services, software, and telecommunications. And fourth, if banks become internationally competitive and start expanding abroad, they may create new market opportunities for other domestic firms, manufacturing or otherwise.

A comparison of banks in South Korea, Argentina, and Spain offers exciting insights into the development of banking services. For a variety of political and ideological reasons, each country designed different roles for its banks to play. South Korea nationalized the banks and used them to support rapid growth in heavy industry under its export-oriented, nationalist-modernizing strategy. By contrast, Argentine banks succumbed during the 1980s after years of import-substitution policies and excessive government borrowing, and became increasingly dominated by foreigners during the 1990s. Finally, Spain gave its private banks a considerable degree of freedom of action, although it also flirted with state-owned development banks and introduced legislation encouraging nonprofit savings banks to mushroom. Korean banks did fulfill their role as lenders to export-oriented industry, but only at the cost of their own demise when investments in heavy manufacturing proved out of touch with a reality of worldwide excess capacity during the late 1990s. Spanish banks managed to weather domestic banking crises, financial liberalization, and foreign competition during the 1980s to establish themselves as the leading foreign investors throughout Latin America and as key European players during the 1990s. Comparative statistics for the banking systems of developed and developing countries appear in table 7.1, showing that market and profit opportunities are greater in the latter than in the former.[1]

---

[1] The analysis in this chapter is based on over 30 semistructured interviews with bankers, bank regulators, and government officials in South Korea, Argentina, and Spain. Some of the inter-

TABLE 7.1
Banking in Selected Developed and Newly Industrialized Countries, circa 1995

	Bank Share in Financial Intermediation[a]	State-Owned Banks (% total assets)[b]	Foreign Banks (% total assets)	Noninterest Operating Costs[c]	Net interest Margins[d]
Argentina	98	36	22	8.5	9.2
Brazil	97	48	9	6.0	6.8
Chile	62	14	21	3.0	6.1
Colombia	86	23	4	7.3	8.3
Mexico	87	28	1	3.9	5.1
Venezuela	92	30	1	5.7	8.1
Hong Kong	—	0	78[e]	1.5	2.2
Singapore	71	0	80	1.4	1.6
Indonesia	91	48	4	2.4	3.3
India	80	87	7	2.6	2.9
Malaysia	64	8	16	1.6	3.0
South Korea	38	13	5	1.7	2.1
Taiwan	80	57	5	1.3	2.0
Thailand	75	7	7	1.9	3.7
Spain	—	—	2[f]	3.0[f]	—
Germany	77	50[e]	4	1.1	1.4
Japan	79	0	2	0.8	1.1
United States	23	0	22	3.7	3.7

Source: Goldstein and Turner 1996; Maudos, Pastor, and Quesada 1997.
[a] Assets as a percentage of the assets of banks and nonbank financial institutions in 1994.
[b] 1994.
[c] As a percentage of total assets, averaged over the 1990–94 period.
[d] As a percentage of total assets, averaged over the 1990–94 period.
[e] Not directly comparable to percentages for other countries.
[f] Estimated.

The rise of the Spanish banks as major foreign investors is especially striking given the paucity of "multinational" retail banks in the world (Tschoegl 1987). Unlike other manufacturing and service industries, it is not easy for banks to benefit from cross-border economies of scale or to monopolize knowledge about banking. In the sections below I examine the subordinate—yet critical—role played by the banks in South Korean industrialization. Next, I examine Argentina's experiment with foreign-owned banks in the 1990s after de-

---

views in Argentina and Spain were conducted in collaboration with my Wharton colleague Adrian E. Tschoegl (Guillén and Tschoegl 1999). I have also made extensive use of the existing literature on banking and development, local newspapers and magazines, and a variety of statistical sources.

cades of banking nationalism. The South Korean and Argentine experiences serve as background to understanding the Spanish banks' paradoxical history of strangling manufacturing firms and their more recent international success. Lastly, I reflect on the different ways in which newly industrialized countries may approach the development of such a critical service sector as banking.

Industrialization and Banking in South Korea

If all developing countries had followed South Korea's nationalist-modernizing route to development, then the state-centered literature on the role of banking in late industrialization would be right on the mark. For it is hard to find another country in which banks have been more subordinated to the desires of a developmental state bureaucracy seeking to accelerate growth in heavy industry. Reviewing the South Korean case is instructive because it illustrates how governments may become obsessed with manufacturing to the complete neglect of services as job-creating and wealth-generating economic activities.

Banks as Policy Instruments

The importance of banks as instruments of the South Korean state in its policy of rapid manufacturing growth was a direct consequence of a key ideological decision: to keep foreign investors at bay. As analyzed in chapter 5, South Korea's traditional dependence on foreign powers led General Park Chung Hee to implement extremely restrictive policies toward foreign investors. South Korea, however, could not possibly develop without foreign money. During the 1950s international aid—mostly from the United States—poured into the country, while reparation payments from Japan and foreign capital in the forms of loans and investments in export-processing zones arrived during the 1960s. Later, Korean companies started to set up joint ventures with foreign multinationals in industries such as automobiles, chemicals, and electronics but continued their reliance on foreign loans. What the Koreans liked about international aid, reparations payments, foreign loans, and export-processing zones was that these arrangements did not entail a complete "surrender" to foreign capital; that is, management and ownership of the key production assets in the country could remain in Korean hands. The risk of miscalculation, of course, would also be owned by Koreans.

International aid, reparation payments, and foreign loans had to be allocated to entrepreneurs. In order to coordinate this process tightly and expeditiously, General Park expropriated banks owned by corrupt chaebols in 1961, shortly after becoming president. Ever since, Korean banks have been puppets in the hands of a state bureaucracy willing and able to orchestrate manufacturing growth, especially in heavy industry. Foreigners have been utterly prevented from playing a major role in banking (see table 7.1).

Although many Korean entrepreneurs were ready to take the money made available by the government, few would consider investing it in the relatively less profitable export-oriented activities or in heavy industry, two priorities of General Park's.[2] Therefore, the government introduced the so-called policy loans, that is, subsidized export, machinery acquisition, and heavy industry loan programs. The extent of subsidization that this scheme achieved is unprecedented in the history of economic development, save for Japan. During the 1970s policy loans accounted for 40 percent of all domestic lending. As Fields (1995, 104) and Woo (1991, 163–68) document, between the early 1970s and the early 1980s the government's favorite entrepreneurs received policy loans at *negative* real (i.e., inflation-adjusted) interest rates, sometimes as low as minus 20 percent (see fig. 7.1). As the scale and scope of policy loan programs were reduced during the 1980s and 1990s, the chaebol acquired stakes in the privatized domestic banks and borrowed directly from foreign moneylenders (see below). Even in the late 1990s, on the eve of the Asian crisis, the president of one of the top four chaebol would admit in an interview with the author that his group always tried to obtain "free money."[3]

Not surprisingly, the chaebol diversified into a bewildering array of industries, assuming mountains of debt. In fact, Korean companies are on average the most leveraged in the developing world. The debt-to-equity ratios plotted in figure 7.2 for Korea, Taiwan, Spain, Japan, Germany, and the United States reveal the extent to which the Koreans tried to emulate the Japanese in heavy industrial development. While average debt-to-equity ratios have fluctuated mostly between 60 and 200 percent in Taiwan, Spain, Germany, and the United States throughout the post–World War II period (in Argentina they average about 70 percent for publicly traded firms), Japanese and Korean companies have reached levels as high as 500 percent, with some individual companies or business groups exceeding 5,000 percent. Such extraordinarily high debt-to-equity ratios could be taken as indication that banks played an exceedingly important role in Japanese and Korean industrialization. The truth is, however, that the banks have merely been instruments of the nationalist-modernizing state (Johnson 1982; Amsden 1989). There is an important difference, though, between Japanese and Korean banks. While in Japan many banks are associated with a keiretsu, Korean banks have been under the

---

[2] See Woo 1991, 169, regarding the lower rates of returns obtained in export sales when compared to domestic sales. Several managers of electronics firms admitted in interviews conducted in October 1995 and June 1997 that it was usual for Korean companies to subsidize export losses with profits from domestic sales inside a protected market.

[3] Interview, Seoul, 3 June 1997.

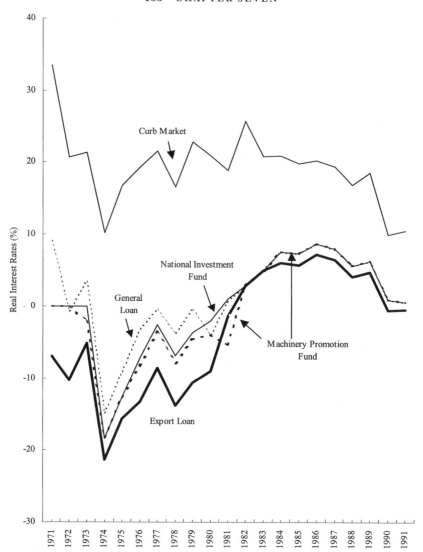

Figure 7.1. Free Money for Korean Industry, 1971–1991. Real (i.e., inflation-adjusted) interest rates were calculated by subtracting the GNP deflator rate from a nominal loan rate. The curb market rate is the informal rate at which small savers lend money to commercial and business borrowers. (Fields 1995, 104; Woo 1991, 164, 198).

Figure 7.2. Debt-Equity Ratios for Nonfinancial Firms. (OECD, *Financial State-ments of Nonfinancial Enterprises* [several years]; Republic of Korea, *Financial Statistics Yearbook* [several years]; Leipziger 1998).

ownership and/or control of the state. Thus, the Korean state has had more of a free hand to allocate funds, and also to make mistakes.

The difficulties associated with highly leveraged firms in an international context of rising oil prices, interest rates, and protectionism forced President Park to bail out the highly leveraged chaebol in the early 1970s at the expense of small firms and savers. A similar combination of adverse factors forced President Chun to initiate a reorganization and consolidation of producers, a of macroeconomic adjustments, and a mild liberalization of financial services during the early 1980s in the face of a widening trade gap and mounting inflation (Amsden 1989, 96–99, 104–5; Haggard and Kaufman 1995, 83–91; Woo 1991, 148–59, 177–79). As part of Chun's reform packet, the banks were formally privatized, although the government continued to appoint its top personnel and to set interest rates (Fields 1995, 53–58, 98–99). While some of the worst excesses in subsidizing loans were eliminated, the process of capital accumulation by the largest chaebol continued unabated during the 1980s and into the 1990s as more favorable international conditions—falling oil prices, interest rates, and value of the U.S. dollar—allowed Korean authorities to relax the tight-credit policies of the early 1980s (Fields 1995, 98; Moon 1994).

When President Chun formally privatized the banks in 1981, the largest chaebol took stakes in them, although rarely exceeding the legal limit of 8 percent (Fields 1995, 111–14; Lee 1997, 74–77). By 1997, Samsung had stakes in 15 different banks, and its rivals Hyundai, Daewoo, LG, Ssangyong, KIA, Hyosung, and Hanwha in at least six each (*Korea Times*, 3 October 1997). Moreover, the chaebol controlled a majority of the investment and finance companies and insurance firms created after Chun's reforms, and took advantage of the liberalization of international borrowing. After decades of funneling subsidized loans to the chaebol, the state realized that they had become too large to be allowed to fail. Unless they misbehaved politically—like Kukje in 1985—the chaebol could count on the continued financial backing of the state (Bedeski 1994, 88; Eckert 1993, 107; Fields 1995, 111, 127–31; E. M. Kim 1997, 181–203). "My business risk is Korea's sovereign risk," commented one chaebol manager in an interview with the author. Or as an executive at the Banque Nationale de Paris once remarked, making a loan to a Korean firm was "tantamount to making a loan to the government. . . . It was a Korea Inc. loan" (quoted in Cumings 1998, 55; see also Mo and Moon 1999, 183). Naturally, the chaebol borrowed huge amounts of money from foreign lenders in order to fund their ambitious expansion plans, which were no longer as tightly overseen by the state as in the past. As Woo (1991, 13) puts it, Korea came to be in a "state of permanent receivership."

The Crisis of 1997

The wholesale and indiscriminate use of the banks as an instrument of heavy industrialization—a policy aptly described by Woo (1991) as "a race to the swift"—certainly lies at the root of Korea's moment of reckoning in 1997. The enormous pain that the crisis inflicted on the country's small and medium enterprises, banks, and chaebol, perhaps in that order, was not merely the result of "misguided" development policies and daring business expansion plans. It was exacerbated, some even say triggered, by international conditions and impositions. Not surprisingly, the Koreans refer to 3 December 1997 as the beginning of the "IMF era," and workers carry banners with the phrase, "I'MFired." But first, the facts.

On the eve of the crisis many of the largest Korean chaebol had debt-to-equity ratios in excess of 400 percent, and in some cases 1,000 percent (see table 7.2). They had borrowed heavily from domestic and international banks, especially since 1995. The lifting of capital controls and the breakdown of the government's monitoring of financial matters during the 1990s further contributed to the Korean firms' borrowing extravaganza. In 1996 the Korean economy slowed down as a result of an overvalued won and a worldwide

TABLE 7.2
Financial Characteristics of the Top 30 South Korean Chaebol, 1996

Chaebol	Total Assets (billions of won)	Total Sales (billions of won)	Net Income (billions of won)	Net Worth- Total Assets Ratio (%)	Debt- Equity Ratio (%)	Guarantee- Equity Ratio (%)
Hyundai	52,821	67,991	179	19	437	29.7
Samsung	50,711	60,113	129	27	267	16.9
LG	37,068	46,674	360	22	347	18.3
Daewoo	34,240	38,253	328	23	339	—
Sunkyong	22,743	26,641	292	21	384	7.3
Ssangyong	15,802	19,446	−98	20	409	—
Hanjin	13,910	8,708	−191	15	556	—
KIA	14,206	12,144	−129	16	519	—
Hanwha	10,592	9,658	−185	12	751	—
Lotte	7,754	7,193	53	34	192	19.9
Kumho	7,390	4,447	−6	17	482	—
Halla	6,627	5,294	23	5	2,065	—
Dong Ah	6,289	3,886	37	22	355	—
Doosan	6,369	4,043	−108	13	688	—
Daelim	5,849	4,832	12	19	423	—
Hansol	4,214	2,513	−7	26	292	—
Hyosung	4,131	5,478	35	21	370	17.8
Dong Kuk	3,698	3,075	92	31	218	—
Jinro	3,937	1,481	−155	3	3,081	—
Kolon	3,840	4,134	23	24	318	—
Kohap	3,653	2,522	30	14	590	—
Dongbu	3,417	3,153	−15	28	251	—
Tong Yang	2,631	1,847	3	25	308	—
Haitai	3,398	2,716	36	13	658	—
New Core	2,797	2,279	23	8	1,224	409.7
Anam	2,638	1,985	12	17	478	—
Hanil	2,599	1,277	−122	15	578	—
Keo Pyong	2,296	1,059	−6	22	347	—
Miwon	2,233	2,114	−31	19	417	—
Shinho	2,139	1,209	−6	17	489	319.4

Source: Federal Trade Commission, Republic of Korea; Korea Herald, 1 September 1998.

slump in the demand for steel, ships, and semiconductors, all key export industries for Korean firms. Moreover, nearly 60 percent of the country's foreign debt was short term (Mo and Moon 1999).

Predictably, some of the most highly leveraged chaebol started to go bust. The chain of corporate bankruptcies, however, started well before the official beginning of the Asian crisis in July 1997. In January 1997 the large construction and steel chaebol Hanbo collapsed, prompting the Bank of Korea to report its concern to the government (*Korea Times*, 29 January 1999). Competitor Sammi followed suit in March. During the spring several other chaebol folded: food-to-construction group Haitai, beverages-to-construction conglomerate Jinro, and retailing giant Dainong. Interviews conducted by the author during the month of June revealed that chaebol owners were already expecting widespread bankruptcies among the largest chaebol due to falling sales and rampant capacity underutilization. A new wave of bankruptcies took place after Thailand's debacle, including automobile maker KIA (later auctioned off to the Hyundai group), and machinery giant Halla (now controlled by the Ford Motor Co.). In October 1997 foreign banks began to call in their loans and to suspend automatic rollovers (Mo and Moon 1999). In addition, other chaebol were forced to sell major subsidiaries (e.g., Ssangyong), to obtain bankruptcy avoidance loans (New Core, Jindo, Shinho, Hanwha, Tong-Il, Kohap, and Woobank Construction), or merge their various companies (Kohap, Hyosung, Shinwon). On 21 November 1997, the government made a request for IMF standby loans, and on 3 December the IMF bailout was announced after foreign reserves had been depleted in an effort to defend the won. In 1998 another top-15 chaebol collapsed, Dong-Ah. In the summer of 1999, Daewoo, the fourth-ranked chaebol and one of the world's largest multinationals, went technically bankrupt, with foreign creditors seizing some of the company's overseas assets and inventory. The *Financial Times* (5 November 1999, 18) labeled it the "world's biggest corporate bankruptcy" ever, with total debt reaching $73 billion (see also *Korea Times*, 12 September 1999). In all, 10 of the top 30 chaebol listed in table 7.2 were severely affected by the crisis, with five of them going bankrupt. Rumors were circulating in the fall of 1999 about financial difficulties at the country's largest chaebol, Hyundai (*Korea Times*, 5 October 1999). In 1998 the economy posted a 5.8 percent fall in output, with unemployment trebling to 6.8 percent.

The Asian crisis begs the question of how could the East Asian and Korean "miracles" turn into disasters within a few weeks. Robert Wade has posed the question aptly. "Was the Asian Slump caused by the build up of vulnerabilities in the real economy, with panicky investor pullout as merely the trigger or messenger of a necessary market correction? Or was it caused largely by the normal workings of underregulated national and international financial markets, the panicky pullout itself being a prime cause?" His own reply is equally accurate. "The short answer is some of both" (Wade 1998d, 693). Thus, the collapse of the South Korean economy and financial sector in 1997 is neither proof of the ills of globalization nor the definitive indictment of the South Korean model of development. Rather, it represents a sober reminder of the importance of being different in the global economy. Let us examine the real and the financial aspects of the Asian and Korean crisis in turn.

The real, underlying problem in East Asia is that countries in the region have been competing against each other for a share of the global market using the same template: low-cost mass production of goods designed and marketed, though not always manufactured, by foreign multinationals (see Krugman 1994). Asian countries that steered away from this strategy—most notably Taiwan with its dynamic and responsive small and medium enterprises (Fields 1995; Orrù, Biggart, and Hamilton 1997)—have escaped the turmoil largely unscathed. South Korean firms' effort to invest in proprietary technology, distribution, and marketing is another, still incomplete attempt to become different (see chap. 8). At the root of the Asian crisis lies the commitment of vast amounts of resources—labor and borrowed money—to megalomaniac industrial and construction projects: shipbuilding, automobiles, petrochemicals, electronics, and office space (Krugman 1994; Wade 1998, 1539; Wade and Veneroso 1998c, 31). This mobilization of resources was fueled by the cultural and elite competition behaviors that Biggart (1998) has called "deep finance" in the case of South Korea. The unrealistic assumptions about economic and export growth underlying such large-scale investments in new production capacity had to become apparent sooner or later. And they did so at the worst possible moment, that is, when the Japanese economy, financial system, and currency were unusually weak.

As Wade notes, however, the turmoil in Asia also demonstrates that what I call modernist approaches to economic development and adjustment cause more harm than good in a global world by preventing countries and firms from being different. The severity of the crisis by country has been proportional not only to the underlying overcapacity problem but also to the degrees to which local financial institutions were in trouble and cross-border capital flows liberalized. During the 1980s and 1990s the leading Western powers and the international lending agencies persuaded and pressured Asian governments, including the South Korean, to adopt a set of liberal rules concerning capital mobility. Meanwhile, companies continued to borrow, and banks— both local and foreign—continued to lend. When confidence in the region began to erode after the Thai debacle, capital moved out and currencies plunged. Governments once able to control capital flows could only sit and watch. And when the IMF moved in to provide bailout loans, it misread the problem in proposing high interest rates to stabilize currencies, ignoring or downplaying their harmful effects on the highly indebted companies throughout the region. As Wade (1998d, 700) has put it, the IMF misdiagnosed the situation "as a macroeconomic balance-of-payments problem . . . rather than as a microeconomic debt deflation problem, and as a crisis of excess consumption rather than excess investment." Translation into the language of the comparative institutional approach: the underlying social organization of the production side of the economy was not taken into account.

Free capital mobility and tight monetary policies are part of the one-size-fits-all policy toolkit that the IMF uses in its rescue operations. It represents a modernist approach to economic and financial adjustment that may work for some countries and in some situations—perhaps Mexico and Argentina in 1995. It is a recipe, however, that is institutionally incompatible with high national savings and a leveraged business sector, as a chorus of highly respected neoclassical and political economists affiliated with some of the world's finest universities has indicated (Bhagwati 1998; Feldstein 1998; Krugman 1998; Rodrik 1998; Sachs 1998; Wade 1998; Wade and Veneroso 1998a, 1998b, 1998c, 1998d).

Many throughout the region and in the West now applaud Malaysia's heretic decision not to conform with IMF recommendations by imposing controls on short-term capital flows (New York Times, 4 September 1999, B1–B2), a policy that even free-market fanatic Chile kept in the books until 1999. In Korea's case, even capital controls could well have been unnecessary. According to Martin Feldstein (1998, 24–26), a Harvard economist of impeccable neoclassical credentials, some "coordinated action by creditor banks to restructure its short-term debts" could have been enough to cope with the situation of "temporary illiquidity rather than fundamental insolvency." In this context, the IMF's role would have been restricted to providing some bridge loans, but never a massive $57 billion financial package tied to structural reforms whose effects not even the IMF fully understands. Korea did not need the IMF's harsh medicine: the economy was growing at 8 percent, and the current account deficit was on the decline when the crisis struck. Restrained consumption and vigorous investment, that is, household frugality and financial leverage, were precisely what allowed Korean firms to grow fast over the last four decades. The IMF's dual imposition of tight monetary and fiscal policies and of wholesale organizational restructuring of its business and financial sectors aggravated the effects of the crisis, ostensibly in terms of economic growth and unemployment, and less apparently in terms of organizational capabilities. As Feldstein (1998, 28) has warned, "imposing detailed economic prescriptions on legitimate governments would remain questionable even if economists were unanimous about the best way to reform the countries' economic policies." Moreover, "the current structure of the Korean economy may now be well suited to Korea's stage of economic and political development and to Korean cultural values." The IMF's policies, if implemented fully, may prevent South Korean businesses from following their instincts and desires to be different in the global economy, even at the cost of making mistakes, which they have indeed. More important, many of the capabilities developed by the chaebol over the last three decades may be lost as a result of their sudden decline, dismemberment, or collapse. For example, most chaebol have been forced to downsize or dismantle the group-level planning office as a result of the crisis (*Korea Times*, 23 November 1998; see also chap. 3).

In agreement with Feldstein, the Korean Confederation of Trade Unions, known neither for its moderation nor for its taste for neoclassical economics, issued a balanced and accurate assessment of the situation. In a letter presented to U.S. Treasury secretary Robert Rubin in July 1998, it argued that the "blanket disavowal of the Asian economy" made the IMF incapable of appreciating the "positive and dynamic elements of the Asian development model which made 'miraculous' growth over such a short period possible" (Crotty and Dymski 1998, 19). This is precisely what a comparative institutional critique of international intervention in the Asian crisis would argue: diversity was not respected, with yet unknown consequences for the preservation of the manufacturing and organizational capabilities accumulated over the previous 40 years.

International monetary institutions, however, cannot to be blamed for the surreal investments made by some of the chaebol on the basis of overly optimistic growth projections, or for the structural weakness of Korean banks in the institutional context of nationalist-modernizing development. Moreover, the chaebol's behavior continues to have harmful consequences for other sectors of the economy. While the five largest chaebol have found it relatively easy to raise money in the stock and bond markets—swallowing two-thirds of new stock and bond issuance by Korean companies, up from 28 percent in 1997—the second-tier chaebol and the smaller firms are finding it much harder to obtain funds (*Korea Times*, 21 December 1998; *Economist*, 5 December 1998, 90). As of June 1998, only a few firms affiliated to the largest chaebol had managed to reduce their debt-to-equity ratios below 200 percent, as requested by the government (Liebermann and Mako 1998, 7; *Korea Herald*, 1 September 1998). Moreover, chaebol ownership has become more cohesive, with the proportion of listed subsidiaries controlled by either the owner or another chaebol subsidiary growing from 23 to 32 percent during the crisis (*Korea Times*, 13 September 1999). Chaebol owners promised they would change their old ways, but they have so far failed to do so. Even President Kim Dae-jung, the country's first president from the southwestern region traditionally disadvantaged by the government and the conglomerates (Cholla), has admitted that "never have I dreamt that chaebol restructuring would be as difficult. This is the toughest task in my entire life" (*Korea Times*, 7 September 1999).

Banks and banking have also suffered immensely from the crisis. Most of the country's leading banks have become technically bankrupt, given that large proportions of their loan portfolios were worthless. But unlike in Japan, that was not the only damage inflicted on the banking sector. Korea's national-ist-modernizing strategy prevented the banks from operating as banks. They have merely been puppets in the hands of a developmental state determined to accelerate manufacturing growth by lending free money to a highly selective group of reckless chaebol owners. In fact, bank profitability declined over the years as industrial companies became more and more dependent on bank loans (Chang 1992, 49). The top managers of the banks have always been appointed following political criteria, with little concern for professional competence. As a result, the banks focused on their (captive) corporate customers and neglected the development of retail mortgage and consumer loan markets. They also failed to acquire capabilities in project evaluation, credit risk assessment, internal auditing, and new product development and marketing. "Backward Korean banking practices have been a source of much ridicule; some have dismissed them as little more than 'pawnshops' " (*Wall Street Journal*, 9 December 1997, as cited by Mo and Moon 1999, 183; see also Chung 1994; *Economist*, 1 December 1996, 101–2).

Proposed solutions to the financial aspects of the Korean crisis are still shy of dealing with the underlying weaknesses of the banking sector—poor capitalization and lack of managerial capabilities. In late 1998, the government, following a suggestion made by the Federation of Korean Industries, welcomed the suggestion to let the largest 50 chaebol jointly create a megabank by first acquiring either Korea First Bank or Seoul Bank, and then capitalizing it. The chairman of the Federation of Korean Industries and founder of Daewoo, Kim Woo-choong, presented his vision of the role of the banks and of the roots of the country's economic collapse about a year before his own conglomerate went into bankruptcy: "The underdeveloped financial sector is the biggest cause behind Korea's economic crisis. Thus, the nation is in need of a leading super bank capable of providing high-quality financial services to industrial firms" (*Korea Herald*, 16 September 1998; see also 3 November 1998). In this account, the chaebol have not made any mistakes in investing the huge amounts of money that the government lent them at subsidized rates through the banking system.

The government is not willing to sell banks to foreigners in order to "avoid excessively low bidding," preferring instead to bless the ongoing wave of bank mergers, which will likely benefit the chaebol once again at the expense of small firms, savers, and bank customers (*Korea Times*, 17 December 1998; *Korea Herald*, 18 December 1998). In 1999, the government reluctantly agreed to sell one of the largest banks, Korea First (nationalized earlier in the crisis), to Newbridge Capital of the United States. Meanwhile, negotiations with Hongkong Shanghai Banking Corporation over the sale of Seoulbank, also nationalized during the crisis, foundered over issues about classification and treatment of nonperforming debt (*Korea Times*, 19 September 1999).

The problem with Korean reform efforts—recapitalization of the banks, reduction of cross-subsidization and mutual loan guarantees, specialization of the chaebol in core areas of competence—is that they have historically been attempted during times of crisis, and usually under pressure from foreign countries or the IMF (Fields 1995, 53–62). Neither the government nor the chaebol, however, are genuinely interested in reform. The former wishes to retain control over key aspects of the economy, and the latter yearn to continue operating as in the past. As a result, the government engages in complex negotiations with the chaebol owners that result in dilatory tactics on both sides with the hope that conditions will improve. Foreign investors and creditors are invited to join committees that end up breaking up; grandiose "Big Deals" to restructure industries by swapping assets among chaebol are launched only to flounder as a result of disagreements over managerial control and valuations, or because of the collapse of one of the chaebol involved; and plans to sell stakes in companies or assets to foreign investors are abandoned in favor of a "Korean" solution (*Korea Times*, 8 April, 7 May, and 13 October 1999; *Korea Herald*, 8 October 1998; see also chaps. 4 and 6). As the Korean economy began to show signs of improvement in 1999, the deepest structural reforms were deemed no longer necessary (*Korea Times*, 2 June 1999).

A comparative institutional perspective on development indicates that there are good reasons for this pattern of behavior to occur. For nearly three decades South Korea has been able to grow fast on the basis of a heavily subsidized and leveraged business sector, and to export itself out of financial trouble, as in the early 1970s and early 1980s. Two years after the onset of the 1997 crisis, it seems clear that the South Korean government and chaebol have been buying time, hoping that sustained economic expansion in the United States would enable a turnaround of the domestic economy without implementing the far-reaching reforms recommended (imposed?) by the IMF. In fact, preliminary figures for the second half of 1999 indicated that the South Korean economy was once again enjoying growth at 7–8 percent annual rates, and in November 1999 the government announced that it would not use up the entire IMF bailout loan initially negotiated in 1997 (*Korea Times*, 30 November 1999). Thus, the direst predictions about an economic collapse and the IMF's argument that recovery would not be possible without wholesale institutional reform following the American model now seem to be exaggerated. South Korea is coming out of the crisis, once again, by being different.

The difficulties of overcoming the 1997 crisis, however, should not be underestimated, for two reasons. First, Korean companies are not the only ones trying to increase exports to weather financial difficulties. Thai, Indonesian, Malaysian, and Chinese as well as Latin American firms are also trying to sell increasingly large amounts of cheap, undifferentiated products in world markets. Second, the liberal financial reforms of the 1980s and 1990s—for which external pressure and Korea's own eagerness to join the OECD quickly are to blame—have now rendered the shaky balance sheets of Korean companies vulnerable to the vagaries of international financial flows. When confidence in emerging economies began to erode after Thailand's collapse in July 1997, international money managers started to wonder about the high debt-equity ratios and massive short-term debt of Korean companies. Subsidies and financial leverage eventually proved to be incompatible with liberalized financial flows across borders. Korea's daring industrialization drive, fueled by high debt-equity ratios, required an orchestration of capital flows and the tight coordination of the chaebol by the state (Krugman 1998; Sachs 1998; Wade 1998; Wade and Veneroso 1998a, 1998b, 1998c). Unfortunately, the Korean state's response to the crisis was hampered by the absence of an economic planning board, which had been dismantled by President Kim Young Sam in the early 1990s to "polish Korea's application" for membership in the OECD (Cumings 1998, 54–55). The government was also hand-tied by commitments to lift capital controls and by the always difficult process of negotiation among interest groups (see chap. 5). "The Korean banks were not ready to compete under the newly deregulated environment. In the name of globalization and democratization . . . the government failed to supervise and monitor their activities to the point of negligence" (Mo and Moon 1999, 184).

Korea can boast a dozen manufacturing companies on the Fortune Global 500 list of the largest corporations in the world. Not a single Korean bank has enough international stature to make it onto the list. The argument in this section has been that the rise of Korean manufacturers came at the expense of the service sector in general, and banking in particular. The government's blind nationalist-modernizing policies regarding finance have prevented Korea from developing its banking services industry, not only as a support activity that is surely essential to any process of economic development, but also as a vibrant service sector that can generate jobs and wealth in its own right.

Banking under Argentina's Erratic Populism

The Argentine banking sector has had to endure the ups and downs of a country mired in the chronic instability of erratic populism. Federal, provincial, and municipal banks—many of which still exist—have traditionally dominated Argentine banking. After decades of subordination to the desires of economic policymakers wishing to develop manufacturing industry, the reforms of the 1990s have favored an approach to banking centered on creating the conditions for a solid consumer-oriented sector, with a high degree of foreign ownership.

The Role of Banks under Erratic Populism

Argentina's import-substitution effort from the 1940s to the 1970s placed enormous stress on the financial system. A strong state-owned sector developed while private banks fell in the hands of business groups also trying to enter manufacturing industries lured by the protectionist incentives created by the state (Dorfman 1983, 358–75; Lewis 65–67; table 7.1). In 1946 the Peronists nationalized the private banks out of ideological fervor, placing them under the close supervision of the central bank, which was given the prerogative of approving every loan or investment. In 1973 the banks were nationalized for a second time after Perón's return to power (Lewis 1992, 159). Local, provincial, and national banks also mushroomed under erratic populism. Their financial performance was historically dismal compared to the private banking sector (Clarke and Cull 1999). The neoliberal financial reforms implemented by the first military junta after 1976 were draconian and momentous. Deregulation and interest rate hikes resulted in a most complicated banking crisis in early 1980, just a couple of years before the Latin American debt crisis wreaked havoc in financial markets across the region (Lewis 1992, 465–69; Rozenwurcel and Bleger 1997).

In spite of President Alfonsín's (1983–89) good intentions, the failure of his repeated attempts at macroeconomic and financial stabilization produced unprecedented capital flight and credit rationing, especially as hyperinflation set in during the late 1980s. After decades of neglect and politicization, the Argentine banking sector was among the developing world's most backward (Molano 1997). Opinion surveys indicate that in Argentina, as in the rest of Latin America, the population does not "trust" the banks as providers of financial services (Clancy 1998). As in the past, bank depositors generally paid the price for the government's use of the banks as fiscal and industrial policy instruments (Mas 1995). As in Korea, banks failed to develop capabilities in the most basic aspects of their business: risk assessment, information systems, marketing, and so on. Unlike in Korea, though, the Argentine government committed itself to a radically different course of action in the 1990s that allowed the banking industry to start moving away from being a mere support activity of manufacturing. This change was fundamentally made possible by a changing attitude toward foreign investors.

Stabilization, Liberalization, and Foreign Ownership

The monetary, economic, and financial reforms of the 1990s have turned the Argentine financial system into a most attractive activity, especially for foreign investors (Rozenwurcel and Bleger 1997; Toulan and Guillén 1997). The foreign banks' presence in Argentina dates back to the golden era of frontier natural resource and agricultural development at the turn of the century, when the country was deeply involved in international trade under laissez-faire policies. Citibank arrived in 1914 and Bank of Boston in 1917. Since the 1980s, the number of foreign-owned private banks has fluctuated around a slight growth trend, helped by the government's removal in 1994 of operating and ownership restrictions. There were 27 foreign banks in 1980, 32 in 1985, and 34 in 1997.

Most foreign banks traditionally participated in the wholesale and corporate market, with Citibank and Bank of Boston being the only two important foreign banks active in the retail market, although they focused on attracting upper-income customers (*AméricaEconomía*, 12 August 1999, 37–40). In the 1990s the government and the owners of the private banks—mostly business groups—saw foreign acquisitions as a solution to the perennial problems of inefficiency and backwardness of banking activities in Argentina. Thus, Canada's Bank of Nova Scotia acquired stakes in Banco Quilmes (1995 and 1997), closely associated with the Quilmes enterprise group; Chilean-Spanish OHCH bought Banco Tornquist (1996) from Crédit Lyonnais; Spanish BBV acquired Banco Francés del Río de la Plata (1996) and Banco de Crédito Argentino (1997); Spanish Banco Santander acquired Banco Río de la Plata (1997) from the Pérez Companc group; and Hongkong and Shanghai Banking Corporation acquired Banco Roberts (1997), previously associated with the Roberts and Alpargatas groups. As a result, between March and May 1997 the foreign banks' share of assets in Argentine banking jumped from about 22 to 37 percent, their share of loans from 19 to 44 percent, and of deposits from 19 to 41 percent. Foreign banks now control some 500 retail branches, mostly in the greater Buenos Aires area, where 41 percent of the country's population lives. Interviews at the Banco Central de la República Argentina confirm that regulators welcomed the entry of the foreign banks for their financial solidity, managerial capabilities, and desire to compete for market share among themselves. In fact, the foreign-owned banks are growing organically, expanding services, and introducing new products, while the government banks have stagnated.

The Argentine banking system, though, is still exposed to the typical vicissitudes of an open emerging economy. Financial-sector turbulence has been aggravated by the freeing of cross-border capital movements to support the peso's convertibility or peg to the dollar—the centerpiece of the government's inflation-busting policy (Calcagno 1997; Molano 1997; Rozenwurcel and Bleger 1997). In addition to the impossibility of engaging in countercyclical policy, convertibility has placed enormous stress on the banking system during times of crisis. The "tequila" shock of December 1994 resulted in a 20 percent fall in deposits as account holders withdrew the better part of their balances and sent money abroad. By March 1995, roughly one in three Argentine banks was technically bankrupt. When regulators raised capital adequacy ratios and increased required reserve levels, banks responded by merging or by selling themselves to better-capitalized foreigners. The number of commercial banks continued to fall during the following years. As of late 1998 there were 138 financial institutions, down from 469 in 1980 and 220 in 1990. Both state-owned and private banks saw their numbers dwindle. Other parts of the financial system also came under increasing foreign control, including private pension funds, mutual funds, and insurance companies. The Brazilian "flu" of 1999 accelerated the trends toward concentration and foreign ownership.

Argentina, however, remains an attractive banking market, with high net interest margins and operating costs, thus offering tremendous opportunities for well-prepared banks (table 7.1). Moreover, there is plenty of room for growth. Brazil, Mexico, and Chile have ratios of deposits and credit relative to GDP that are twice and even three times greater than Argentina's 15 and 18 percent, respectively (Molano 1997, 2). As Guillén and Tschoegl (1999, 11) note, "nowhere is this situation more evident than along Calle Reconquista in downtown Buenos Aires. Convoys of armored trucks block traffic as they deliver or load cash at the Central Bank or at the headquarters of the leading banks." In an attempt to reassert control over cash movements, the government ordered in 1991 that wages be paid through a bank. Argentines pay for cars and homes in cash. Roughly one-third of the Argentine adult population lacks a bank account, and only one in six has a credit card, a proportion lower than in less developed Chile or Mexico. The endurance of habits acquired to cope with hyperinflation perhaps accounts for the wariness with which Argentines continue to see the banking sector.

Although the Argentine retail banking system is far from being a model to imitate, it does compare favorably to the Korean. Foreign ownership may not be a panacea, but it is helping restore confidence and improve service standards. Argentine erratic populism destroyed the banking system. The economic opening of the 1990s at least provided a viable banking model, if still subject to the jitters so characteristic of emerging economies. As I shall describe next, the Spanish financial system offers an alternative to both Korea's subordination of the banks as instruments of nationalist-modernizing policymaking and Argentina's sell-off to foreign banks.

Spanish Banks Go International

The Korean banking sector is a case of utter collapse after decades of subservience to the state's nationalist-modernizing goals, while the Argentine system has barely survived under erratic populism until liberalization landed much of it into foreign hands. By contrast, the Spanish banks have challenged conventional wisdom in both international management and development studies after demonstrating that retail banking is a service industry with enormous potential in its own right and not merely a support activity of manufacturing. Their historical record, however, also contains a long history of strangling local firms with high interest rates and fees.

Spanish Banks Come of Age

The world of retail banking has been turned upside down by two Spanish banks—Banco Santander Central Hispano (BSCH) and Banco Bilbao Vizcaya Argentaria (BBVA). In less than a decade they simultaneously became the largest foreign commercial banks in Latin America and placed themselves among the largest and most active in the new single European market for financial services through alliances and minority equity stakes. Until the 1990s, however, they had little international experience and stature. Since 1994 the Spanish banks have "conquered" significant assets and market shares throughout Latin America, acquiring nearly 50 leading domestic institutions, compared to merely 13 by all other foreign banks combined, including Citibank, Deutsche Bank, Banque Nationale de Paris, Banque Nationale Agricole, Bank of Nova Scotia, Bank of Montréal, and Hongkong Shanghai Banking Corporation (see Guillén and Tschoegl 1999 for a complete list of acquisitions). In the so-called euro zone, BSCH and BBVA are among the four largest in terms of market capitalization (*Actualidad Económica*, 28 June–4 July 1999, 90–91).

It is important to place the Spanish banks' Latin American adventure in the context of the deregulation of oligopolistic industries in Spain and Europe. It is *large* Spanish firms that have "rediscovered" Latin America during the 1980s and 1990s. Small and medium manufacturing firms had been investing there since the 1960s. Starting in the mid-1990s Spanish firms in telecommunications, air transportation, insurance, power and water utilities, construction, gas, and oil as well as banking have taken over Latin America, literally. Deregulation, liberalization, and falling profit margins in Spain and Europe forced large firms in these sectors, long used to cozy oligopolistic relationships among them, to look for new markets. After decades of mutual neglect, Spain and Latin America are now forging strong foreign investment ties, albeit primarily in one direction. Spain already is the largest foreign investor in Argentina, and one of the largest in Chile and Peru. Trade flows, however, remain unimportant (Arregui Giménez 1994; Campa and Guillén 1996a, 1996b; Durán 1999).

The Spanish banks' adventure in Latin America is not only breathtaking but also pathbreaking because rarely have banks sought to dominate mass-market retail banking in so many foreign countries (Tschoegl 1987). How come Spanish and not British, French, Dutch, German, American, or Japanese banks have shown the world how to create a multinational network of retail financial services? While there are some obvious answers to this question (e.g., cultural and linguistic affinities), more complex factors and circumstances must be invoked in order to account for the superiority of Spanish banks relative to local institutions as well as other foreign entrants in Latin America (Guillén and Tschoegl 2000). Perhaps even more puzzling, such influential newspapers and magazines as the *Financial Times, Banker,* and *Euromoney* have fallen over themselves to praise the top Spanish banks after ranking them among the best capitalized, most profitable, and best run in the world (*Financial Times,* "Spain: Banking, Finance & Investment," 19 October 1999; *Banker,* July 1998, 20). How could this be possible in a country that a mere generation ago had 42 percent of its population working on the land, only a meager industrial base, no service sector of international stature, and that was classified by the World Bank as a developing country?

Banks and Economic Development in Spain

In Spain banking is a matter of secrecy and intrigue. Popular wisdom traditionally refers to the church, the military, and the banks as the *poderes fácticos*— the powers that be (Muñoz 1969). Banks are both feared and resented because they have long "banked on privilege," to paraphrase political scientist Sofía Pérez (1997). Their connections to the state bureaucracy and to the various political regimes guaranteed that foreign competition would be kept at bay. Local firms and consumers long suffered from high interest rates and fees. Until the 1980s, it was unheard of for a major bank not to report a profit and to pay out dividends. Regulation, however, was not always favorable to them. Banking laws, like the one enacted by the Franco regime in 1940, made it almost impossible for banks to grow domestically other than by acquisition. After launching an export-led development strategy during the late 1950s and early 1960s, the government passed a new banking law in 1962 that allowed commercial banks to expand into related financial services as well as take stakes in industrial companies. This universal banking model eventually led the biggest banks to organize business groups around them (see chap. 3). In addition to regulation, private banks have had to take into account the presence of savings banks, credit cooperatives, and official credit institutions. The savings banks (*cajas de ahorro*), more privileged but also more regulated than the banks, are semipublic institutions with strong regional roots. The credit cooperatives are also tremendously well established in a country with a long and strong tradition of worker involvement in the creation and management of self-owned enterprises, of which the Mondragón group of cooperatives is just one example among many (see chap. 3). During the 1960s the state also created the nemesis of the private banks—official credit institutions—as policy instruments to promote industrial and agricultural activities, although it never used them as aggressively as the Korean government did. In the midst of such "regulated privilege," how did the banks become formidable international competitors?

Moreover, the banks have had to deal with a capable, cautious, and increasingly powerful central bank. Initially created in 1782, the Banco de España became a real central bank with the Banking Act of 1921. It was nationalized in 1946. Over the next 40 years the central bank grew in influence and clout with economic policymakers—many of whom were trained at its prestigious Research Department—and won ever greater supervisory powers (Pérez 1997). From the 1960s to the 1980s central bankers tried to reform financial markets and the government's deficit-financing practices so that inflation could be curbed, a goal that proved elusive until the mid-1980s. The 1994 Law of Autonomy gave the central bank the tools and the independence necessary to focus on monetary stability, unlike in Korea, where it is still dependent on the Ministry of Finance, or Argentina, where a currency board is responsible for maintaining a one-to-one parity with the U.S. dollar. The central bank still is the supervisor of the banking sector.

Tight regulation and protection from foreign competition led since the 1950s to a situation in which both banking costs and profits were high (Pérez 1997). The chairmen of the so-called Big Seven—Banco de Bilbao, Banco Central, Banco Español de Crédito (Banesto), Banco Hispano-Americano, Banco Popular, Banco Santander, and Banco de Vizcaya—began to meet once a month for lunch so as to exchange information, fix prices, and lobby the government. Their political position within the authoritarian regime of General Franco was quite different from that of the Korean banks under the equally authoritarian Park regime. While the Korean banks were expropriated from their corrupt owners in 1961, the Spanish banks were given a great degree of autonomy and privilege, becoming one of the pillars of support for the Franco regime (De Miguel 1975; Tortella 1961, 331–48; Pérez 1997, 59–60).

Over the years, the Big Seven managed time and again to find a mutual accommodation with the government and the central bank, at the expense of bank customers. In the first third of the century the banks had already played a key role in expanding the infrastructure for development: electricity generation and distribution, railways, oil refining and distribution, construction, and so on. Later, several of the largest banks participated in the export-led growth strategy of the 1960s by building extensive holdings of industrial companies (Torrero 1991). Not surprisingly, banks have always been found to be at the core of the Spanish network of intercorporate relations (Tamames 1977; Muñoz 1969; Aguilera 1998; Torrero 1991). The consequences of the high profile of the banks in the Spanish economy were quite harmful. As mentioned in chapter 2, between the late 1970s and the early 1990s the financial costs of Spanish nonfinancial firms were on average greater than their return on investment (Maroto Acín 1990). Spanish banks behaved as moneylenders and commercial partners of industrial firms. As a result, nonfinancial firms "with a bank among their top three shareholders are less profitable and more leveraged" (Cuervo-Cazurra 1995, 7).

The Shakeup of the Late 1980s and the 1990s

The pragmatic-modernizing governments of the 1980s and 1990s pursued ambivalent policies vis-à-vis foreign banks. On the one hand, they wished to put competitive pressure on the banking cartel so as to reduce interest rates and fees, and to improve service standards. On the other, the government was lobbied by the banking cartel, several of its key economic ministers had banking backgrounds, and it warmed up to the idea of promoting large "banking champions" that could match the prowess of their European counterparts. In addition, the 1977–85 banking crises, which affected 58 institutions, added to the government's desire to err on the regulatory and conservative side (Cuervo 1989). The banks succeeded at influencing key reform efforts introduced by the pragmatic-modernizing democratic governments—restructuring of deficit financing in the early 1980s, membership in the European Union in 1986, and liberalization of the stock market in 1988—in ways that safeguarded their interests (Pérez 1997). In particular, a seven-year protection period was negotiated as part of Spain's European Union (EU) accession treaty of 1986. Even after 1992, foreign banks have not been able to gain much by way of market share, given the barriers to entry established by the incumbents, that is, high retail branch density, heavy advertising, and dense alliance networks. It seems clear that government officials were willing to let foreign multinationals take over manufacturing; the financial sector, however, was an entirely different matter.

The relatively cozy banking sector has gone through a period of upheaval since the mid-1980s. The regulatory environment in the Spanish banking market changed, mostly to the benefit of nonfinancial firms and individual customers. "Branch expansion was deregulated for private commercial banks in 1985; interest rate ceilings disappeared in 1987; investment coefficients that had frozen a very significant share of total assets in regulated loans and public debt were gradually eliminated; the ban on branch expansion for savings banks beyond their regional markets was lifted in 1989; the limitation that prevented savings banks from performing specialized financial activities disappeared in the late 1980s; and the coefficient on demand deposits was dramatically reduced in 1990" (Maudos, Pastor, and Quesada 1997, 214). In response to these reforms, the intensity and pattern of competition changed. Santander was the first to make the unprecedented competitive move of offering interest on current accounts (*supercuentas*). It also revolutionized the mortgage loan market by substituting cash-flow techniques of loan approval for the collateral method. From then on, the Spanish banking market would become much more competitive both in terms of price, product differentiation, and service. Banks invested in information technology and employee training. Their operating costs dropped, especially for savings banks and smaller banks (Maudos, Pastor, and Quesada 1997, 243). Given the new competitive environment, the chairmen of the largest banks were forced to discontinue their monthly luncheons in 1990.

Perhaps the most noticeable consequence of deregulation was the flurry of merger activity among the Big Seven. After several unsuccessful attempts at hostile takeovers, some of them encouraged by the government in its drive to create champions, the Big Seven became the Big Four. In 1988 Bilbao and Vizcaya merged into BBV, with Bilbao executives soon taking control at the helm. (Bilbao's chairman, José Ángel Sánchez Asiaín, was fond of saying that the merger combined not two *culturas* but one *cultura* and one *incultura*.) Banco Central and the much weakened Hispano-Americano merged in 1991 to form Banco Central Hispano (BCH). Lastly, in 1994 Santander easily (some say excessively) outbid BBV and BCH to acquire 48 percent of Banesto in an auction that the Banco de España organized after having rescued the bank from technical bankruptcy. The disgruntled Vizcaya executives who lost control at BBV after the merger were then recruited by Santander to run Banesto. In early 1998 Santander made a tender offer for the remaining shares of Banesto and now controls 97 percent of the bank.

Meanwhile, the government reorganized its banks to create Argentaria in 1991, which it then gradually privatized, keeping a "golden share" in it. The government also allowed the savings banks—hitherto restricted to their provinces of origin—to expand nationally and encouraged mergers among them. In fact, they have gained in market share at the expense of the banks. Both the private banks and the savings banks have become active participants in newly deregulated service industries such as telecommunications, utilities, mass retailing, government procurement, and broadcasting.

In early 1999 Santander and BCH took the country by storm with their surprise merger into Banco Santander Central Hispano (BSCH). Before the turn of the century, six of the Big Seven banks had become the Big Two, BBV and BSCH, dwarfing Banco Popular. As of June 1999, BSCH was the largest bank of the euro zone in terms of market capitalization (37 billion euros), followed by Deutsche Bank (32 billion), ABN Amro (30 billion), and BBV (29 billion). BSCH was the fourth largest if United Kingdom banks were included (*Actualidad Económica*, 28 June–4 July 1999, 90–91). BSCH has cross share-holdings with Royal Bank of Scotland, Commerzbank, and Grupo Champalimaud (Portugal) and holds stakes in Société Génerale, San Paolo IMI, and Banque Commerciale du Maroc. BBV, for its part, is also a key player in Europe, with its stakes in Crédit Lyonnais and Banca Nationale del Lavoro (*El País Negocios*, 13 June 1999). Never in Spanish history have banks had such a powerful presence in Europe. The century's last merger was announced in October 1999 when BBV took over Argentaria, a bank with limited foreign retail operations (except for the branches of the official export-import bank) but a large domestic market share.

Three Banks, Three Styles, Three Experiences in Internationalization

The most intriguing aspect of recent events in Spanish banking is the widely different styles of the three top banks that played the leading roles in international expansion during the 1990s: Santander, BBV, and BCH (Guillén and Tschoegl 1999, 2000). Banco Santander was founded in 1857 as an issuing and a commercial bank specializing in the Spanish-American trade flowing through the northern port city of Santander. Given the postwar regulatory restrictions, Santander grew during the 1940s and 1950s via acquisition, consolidating a national network of branches only as late as the 1970s. It was a midsized institution with a good reputation among competitors and customers for being well organized and managed. When during the mid-1980s its bigger rivals became entangled in internal power struggles or in difficult mergers, Santander waited for the right moment to break with the cartel and start competing. At long last, between 1989 and 1992 Santander revolutionized Spain's retail banking by introducing high-yield checking and savings accounts, mutual funds, and low-interest mortgages. In 1993 Santander created the first telephone banking service in Spain, and a joint venture with British Telecom on value-added services in voice, data, and image transmission. Competitive responses and the already high density of bank branches, however, prevented Santander from increasing its market share by more than a few percentage points. The only fast way to grow was to merge or acquire. The acquisition of Banesto's assets, including its extensive branch network in rural Spain, catapulted the Banco Santander Group to the very top of the ranking of domestic banks. It also entailed, however, an arduous process of untangling the complicated web of industrial holdings that Banesto had woven over the years.

Santander stands out for its international expansion, which started in the late 1980s with several small acquisitions (notably Portugal's Banco de Comércio e Indústria in 1990) and alliances (Royal Bank of Scotland). Santander's only incursion into the U.S. commercial banking market took place in 1991 when it acquired 13.3 percent of First Fidelity Bancorporation for $650 million. This pirouette paid off when First Fidelity merged with First Union in 1995, making Santander the largest single shareholder in the seventh largest U.S. bank. Santander sold its stake in June 1997 for $2.2 billion, which it used to amortize the goodwill of its Latin American acquisitions.

It is important to understand the personalities behind Santander's rise to prominence. The chairman during its latest period of growth was Emilio Botín

(b. 1934), who in 1986 succeeded his father. The latter had turned the bank from a sleepy provincial institution into one of Spain's Big Seven. The family has controlled the bank since the 1950s, as the Botíns own about 3 percent of the bank's voting shares and occupy several key senior slots and directorships. Initially, Santander's Latin American expansion was implemented by Ana Patricia Botín, the chairman's eldest child and heir apparent until the merger with BCH in 1998. After getting a B.A. from Harvard, she worked for J. P. Morgan in Madrid and New York. She joined Santander in 1988 to manage its emerging markets and investment-banking operations, and then serve as CEO of Santander Investment, the investment-banking arm. Santander had pulled out of much of Latin America shortly after the start of the Latin American "lost decade" with the 1982 debt crisis. Botín's ambitious goal was to build Santander Investment into the "Goldman, Sachs of Latin America." However, she fell well short of that goal before the merger with BCH in 1999 caused her to resign (*AméricaEconomía*, 17 June 1999, 34–42).

Although the initial impetus for Santander's Latin American acquisitions came from the investment-banking arm, the more recent expansion was undertaken by the main commercial unit. Santander has turned itself into a truly multinational retail-banking corporation. It generally bought majority stakes and put its brand name on them. It has also tended to impose its own management, especially in the areas of marketing, credit risk, audits, and systems. Like the other Spanish banks, Santander has introduced throughout Latin America some of the products first designed for the home market, for example, high-yield accounts, low-cost mortgages, and the lottery-linked checking accounts. In 1997 Santander's Latin American operations accounted for almost 50 percent of foreign assets and for 48 percent of net attributable profits.

Banco Central Hispano (BCH) — now merged with Santander — arrived in Latin America relatively late. It relied on joint ventures with local partners because of the weaker capitalization of Banco Hispano-Americano, the problems in its holdings of industrial companies, and its scarcity of managerial personnel. In southern Latin America BCH allied itself with the Lúksic group, one of the largest family-controlled industrial and service conglomerates in Chile. In Colombia it joined forces with the Gilinski group. The turmoil in emerging markets since 1998, however, has lent more credence to its more cautious and gradual approach to Latin American market entry. With the creation of BSCH in 1999, many of BCH's holdings in the region were reorganized or sold. In particular, the holding company jointly owned with the Lúksic group was in the process of being dismantled in mid-1999.

BBV is a very different bank, although equally successful. It is the result of the 1988 merger of Banco de Bilbao and Banco de Vizcaya. Banco de Bilbao started in 1856 as an issuing and commercial bank serving the banking needs of businessmen and traders in the northern industrial and port city after which it is named. In the decades following its founding the bank became a key actor in the industrial development of the steelmaking Basque Country. It remained focused on the domestic market until very recently, acquiring many other smaller local and provincial banks along the way. Banco de Vizcaya started in 1901, also in Bilbao. It too acquired other local banks. Both Bilbao and Vizcaya became full-fledged industrial as well as commercial banks during the 1960s as Spain developed a manufacturing economy (Tamames 1977; Torrero 1991). Further acquisitions of bankrupt institutions took place during the early 1980s (Cuervo 1989).

Bilbao and Vizcaya traditionally recruited many of their managers among the graduates of the prestigious, Jesuit-run Universidad de Deusto (Guillén 1989, 201–2). They have always been among Spain's most professional and best-managed organizations. An element of tradition persists, however. One can still identify among the bank's top executives some of the most distinguished names of the so-called Neguri bourgeoisie, a tight group of families that played a key role in Basque and Spanish industrialization at the turn of the century. BBV has always been shrewd enough to maintain friendly relations with both the Spanish and Basque governments. While BBV's operating headquarters are based in Madrid, its annual shareholders' meeting takes place in Bilbao at the bank's address of incorporation.

The chairman and CEO of the merged BBV rely on team decision making to a much greater extent than Santander. Accordingly, BBV has not engaged in such daring operations as Santander's partial acquisition of First Fidelity in the United States. In Latin America BBV was also more cautious than Santander. It originally tended to buy minority stakes, providing the project was large enough and BBV had management control. As the bank accumulated operating experience, it has adopted majority ownership and started using its own brand (*AméricaEconomía*, 4 June 1998, 45.) Now BBV has appointed a manager in Madrid to be responsible for BBV América, which includes all its Latin American operations and which accounted for 23 percent of consolidated assets and 17 percent of net attributable profits in 1997.

Why Did the Spanish Banks Expand throughout Latin America?

My research with Adrian Tschoegl (Guillén and Tschoegl 1999, 2000) clearly indicates that the rise to prominence of the Spanish banks in Latin America is primarily a response to an increasingly competitive environment in Spain and Europe. The Spanish banks had accumulated experience in retail banking services during the late 1980s and early 1990s just before Latin American countries opened their markets to foreign competition. Growth and profit opportunities in Latin America were much greater than in Spain or Europe. Noninterest costs and intermediation margins in Latin America are the highest among the emerging economies (table 7.1). Analysts at Morgan Stanley stated in 1997 that "the rationale behind this dramatic build-up [of the Spanish banks in Latin America] appears to be a desire to achieve a wider geographic spread of earnings and thus to reduce the relative dependence on income generation from the domestic market, where concerns remain about the possible impact of the implementation of EMU on peseta spreads and foreign exchange income and increasing competitive pressures from the *Cajas* [savings banks] network" (Broughton and Ripert 1997). Moreover, banks from other countries were either in financial trouble (e.g., Japan, France, Italy) or undertaking expansion elsewhere (Germany). Only Hongkong and Shanghai Banking Corporation and several Canadian banks joined the Spaniards in their pursuit of several of the Latin American markets.

The Spanish banks shifted their rivalry from a saturated domestic market to international ones, following the pattern observed by international management scholars for oligopolistic competition (Hymer 1976; Knickerbocker 1973). Several of the bankers we interviewed at BBV, Santander, and BCH confirmed that they are constantly watching each other, and that their most important competitors in the world are those based in the home country, even though nearly half of their sales and profits are presently coming from their overseas operations (Guillén and Tschoegl 2000). Moreover, it is not uncommon for executives to move from one of the big banks to another, sometimes in droves (as when Vizcaya executives "deserted" to Banesto). The current head of BSCH's Latin American operations was once the chairman and CEO of Argentaria (now part of BBVA), and the CEO of BSCH used to work for BBV.

The instability caused by the Asian crisis reverberated throughout Latin America during the summer of 1998. As a result, the shares of the foreign banks with investments in the region lost as much as half of their value between July and October. Banks with less of a direct exposure (e.g., BCH or Hongkong Shanghai Banking Corp.) suffered less than those with an extensive and direct presence (Santander, BBV). Thus, it is not yet clear which entry strategy was the best (*El País*, 5 October 1998). It seems safe to argue, however, that the pragmatic-modernizing development path on which Spain embarked during the 1980s was the prelude to the banks' increasingly important role as providers of services not only to industry but also to retail consumers domestically and internationally. The banks thus transformed themselves from being a burden on the economy to playing a role as major wealth generators.

On Developing Services

The comparison of the banking industries of Korea, Argentina, and Spain helps correct some modernist misconceptions about the role of banks in the process of economic development. The conventional literature and policy prescriptions on financial development—whether inspired by market-driven or state-centered conceptions—have been biased toward a view of banking as a support activity in the effort to promote growth in manufacturing. Not surprisingly, few developing countries have attempted to create the conditions for the banking industry to emerge as a job creator and wealth generator in its own right. The most noteworthy exceptions are of course the entrepôt economies of Singapore, Hong Kong, and Panama (Choi, Park, and Tschoegl 1996; Haggard 1990, 100–125). In most other cases, the banking sector has been sacrificed in the name of higher development goals.

The literature, however, has overlooked perhaps the most striking and instructive case: Spain. This relatively large country with a long history of troubled industrialization efforts and a manufacturing industry dominated by foreign multinationals has emerged as the world's most important source of foreign direct investment in commercial banking. The rise of the Spanish banks to prominence illustrates the usefulness of a comparative institutional theory of development. From the 1950s to the 1970s the Spanish state created development banks in an effort to accelerate industrial growth but without choking private initiatives in banking, which had been important since the turn of the century. After the state-led industrial promotion program faltered in the 1970s and a banking crisis eliminated the most reckless and unsuccessful private banks, pragmatic-modernizing policies tending toward integration in the European Union—including a wide-ranging reform of financial markets—created the conditions for the strongest private banks to emerge as major international competitors as well as innovative service providers in the Spanish market. The government's realization of the existence of well-prepared actors in the banking sector, and its grudging willingness to respect their long-standing relationships to other parts of the economy, prepared the stage for the rise of an internationally competitive service industry. Interestingly, a century after Spain lost the remnants of its empire, a new breed of conquistadors have made banking history and turned Madrid—not Seville!—into a leading financial center.

Interviews with regulators, policymakers, and bankers throughout Latin America reveal that the arrival of the foreign banks—especially the Spaniards—has brought a wave of fresh air to the region's commercial banking (Guillén and Tschoegl 2000). Not only have foreign banks brought much-needed capital with them but also managerial skills, new products, and marketing techniques. Arguably, the Spanish banks have been at the forefront of this change because they had developed strong competitive capabilities in the home market. The historical balance sheet for the Spanish banks, however, contains liabilities in addition to assets. For a long period of time, the cartel of the Big Seven banks strangled manufacturing firms, especially small and medium-sized ones, with high interest rates and fees. This pattern of behavior, however, seems today a thing of the distant past.

The Argentine and Korean banking sectors are a far cry from the Spanish. Argentina has made important changes in its traditional approach to the banking sector. Foreign investment has improved the functioning of this most critical service industry for both corporate and individual customers. Korea, by contrast, is still enmeshed in a major clash between the intransigent nationalists and those proposing a pragmatic opening to foreign trade and investment. The sorry state of the Korean financial system should be hard enough evidence to warrant a drastic change of policy. Unfortunately, many in the country and the state bureaucracy still see the banks as symbols of national independence and instruments of industrial policy. If Argentina, however belatedly, has been able to realize the intrinsic institutional weaknesses in its economy and to shift policy, why can't Korea? The answer is that social organizational patterns change only with difficulty. A comparative institutional perspective on development requires abandoning all dogmas—whether market-driven or state-centered—so as to focus on how each country can develop its own approach to organizing firms, markets, and industries, including financial services.

EIGHT

ON GLOBALIZATION, CONVERGENCE,
AND DIVERSITY

Difference must be recognized . . . [and] seen *not* as the negation
of similarity, its opposite, its contrary, and its contradiction. It must
be seen as comprising it: locating it, concretizing it, giving it form.
(Geertz 1998, 96)

I N PREVIOUS chapters I have compared organizational change in three
newly industrialized countries during the 1950–99 period. I have presented evidence on a bewildering array of diversity in economic action
and organizational form at the firm and industry levels of analysis. My narra-
tive has made systematic comparisons among Argentina's love-hate affair with
globality, Korea's single-minded, nationalist drive to increase exports and outward foreign investment, and Spain's pragmatic engagement with the global
economy (chaps. 2–5). At the organizational level, I have documented the
awesome might of the diversified Korean chaebol, the adaptability of the Argentine *grupos*, and the vibrancy of Spain's worker-owned cooperatives and
small and medium enterprises. I have analyzed how each of these types of
firms has engaged the global economy by networking across borders. I have
also provided evidence on Korean and Argentine organized labor's reserva-
tions about the presence of foreign multinationals, and Spanish labor's partnership with them. Spanish labor unions engaged the global economy and
enjoy recognition and influence. In Argentina, by contrast, they are rather
powerless, even though they do not have to face the repressive practices of
the Korean government.

Table 8.1 lays out in schematic form the argument linking development
paths to organizational change. Organizational change under pragmatic-modernizing development conditions, as illustrated by the case of Spain, results
in an economy dominated by foreign multinationals (especially in manufacturing), small and medium enterprises, and large firms in such oligopolistic
industries as banking, utilities, telecommunications, oil, and gas. Spain also
illustrates that this path to development, and the pattern of organizational
change induced by it, is facilitated by labor union ideologies and policies that
are pro-globalization and see multinationals as partners. Pragmatic-populist
conditions, as exemplified by Argentina, privilege the proliferation of business
groups as well as foreign multinationals. This outcome is compatible with

TABLE 8.1
Development Paths and Organizational Change in Argentina, South Korea, and Spain

Level of Inward Flows	Level of Outward Flows	
	High (Modernizing)	Low (Populist)
High (pragmatic)	Spain Pragmatic-Modernizing: HIGH: Allow Imports and Inward investment HIGH: Export-led growth and Outward investment Organizational forms: Foreign MNEs; SMEs; Large oligopolistic firms Organized labor's ideologies: Pro-globalization, MNEs = partners <div align="right">4</div>	Argentina Pragmatic-Populist: HIGH: Allow Imports and Inward investment LOW: Import substitution and Local investment Organizational forms: Foreign MNEs; Business Groups; some SMEs Organized labor's ideologies: Anti-globalization, MNEs = necessary evils 1
Low (nationalist)	3 South Korea Nationalist-Modernizing: LOW: Protectionism and Local ownership HIGH: Export-led growth and Outward investment Organizational forms: Business groups; State-owned enterprises Organized labor's ideologies: Pro-globalization, MNEs = arm's-length collaborators	2 Initial Conditions, CIRCA 1950 Nationalist-Populist: LOW: Protectionism and Local ownership LOW: Import substitution and Local investment Organizational forms: State-owned enterprises; Large oligopolistic firms Organized labor's ideologies: Anti-globalization, MNEs = villains

Note: MNEs stands for multinational enterprises, SMEs for small and medium enterprises.

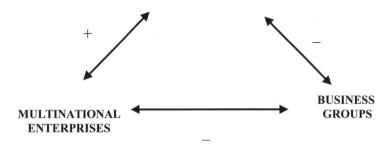

Figure 8.1. The Ecology of Organizational Forms under Conditions of Globalization.

reluctant attitudes toward globalization and foreign investment on the part of labor unions. Finally, South Korea's nationalist-modernizing path results in the dominance of the economy by large business groups (and the occasional state-owned firm in certain industries) at the expense of foreign multinationals and small and medium-sized firms.

The effects of development paths on organizational change are self-reinforcing and tend to acquire a momentum of their own. In some cases countries have "switched" development paths, as in South Korea from nationalist-populist to nationalist-modernizing during the early 1960s, or in Spain from nationalist-populist to nationalist-modernizing during the 1960s and to pragmatic-modernizing during the 1980s. These changes resulted in important organizational transformations. In other moments, however, the organizational logic of development paths has proved too powerful for either the government or financial crises to derail it. For example, several South Korean presidents have unsuccessfully attempted to curb the power of the chaebol since the 1970s. Either way, the organizational consequences of development paths were felt throughout the economy.

Thus, chapters 2–5 identified the dynamics of change among the three main types of organizational forms that one finds across newly industrialized countries—small and medium enterprises, large business groups, and multinational enterprises. As reflected in figure 8.1, small and medium enterprises and large business groups are often at odds with each other. If the latter can take advantage of asymmetric foreign trade and investment conditions, smaller firms suffer and find it difficult to innovate and export, as the Korean situation exemplifies. If, on the other hand, foreign multinationals are allowed to invest under relatively free conditions, small and medium enterprises eventually thrive as they become suppliers to the multinationals or emulate their patterns of behavior, as in the Spanish context. Large business groups, however, see their importance reduced by the arrival of foreign multinationals under relatively free conditions. The Argentine situation lies somewhere in between the vibrancy of Spanish smaller enterprises and the might of the Korean business groups, with state-owned enterprises playing an important role until the early 1990s.

After assessing the effects of development paths on organizational change, chapters 6 and 7 evaluated each pattern of organizational change at the industry level from the point of view of its strengths and weaknesses in the global economy. Spain's success in automobile assembly and component manufacturing thanks to foreign investment contrasts with Korea's prowess in automobile assembly but beleaguered component manufacturers and with Argentina's unrewarding attempts to develop a viable industry. People who do not object to foreign ownership might find the Spanish experience appealing, while those concerned with indigenous technological development might opt for Korea's route. In the financial services industry the comparison is among Korea's use of the banks as instruments of industrial policy, Argentina's relatively stable financial system, and Spain's world-class banks. Again, those concerned about foreign ownership might like the Spanish solution better than the Argentine one, while those worried about the power of the banks over industry might prefer the Korean approach. The automobile and banking case studies clearly establish that there is no objectively best way. It all depends on one's political and ideological preferences.

Contrary to the dire predictions of virtually every previous development theory, small and medium enterprises were found to play a vibrant role as exporters and foreign investors as long as political-economic conditions do not favor business groups. Moreover, family-owned, even managed, firms can be every bit as dynamic and competitive as "modern" enterprises with fully bureaucratic managerial and control structures (chaps. 3 and 4). Therefore, there appears to be no good reason why "traditional" social structures cannot contribute to economic development. In fact, they frequently become a key resource for development, as proposed by the comparative-institutional approach.

Each empirical chapter presented evidence on variation and diversity within countries as well as across countries. Some business groups performed better than others (e.g., Techint better than Pérez Companc, chap. 3), and the same was found to be true of small and medium enterprises (chap. 4), subsidiaries of foreign multinationals (chap. 5), large oligopolistic firms (chaps. 6 and 7), and worker-owned cooperative groups (chap. 3). The corollary is that organizations approach development and globalization in different ways within the constraints of their country's development path. They yearn to be different as a way of making a dent in the global economy. And they excel and fail at different things.

In this concluding chapter I first recapitulate the evidence presented in the book to demonstrate that the various paths taken by newly industrialized countries and their firms have resulted in combinations of strengths and weaknesses, of achievements and failures. Then I discuss three cardinal questions of our global era: whether there is a development glass ceiling separating the poor countries from the rich; whether globalization leads to homogeneity or diversity; and whether the economic must take precedence over the political for countries and firms to succeed in the global economy or vice versa.

Assessing Development Paths

Modernist policymakers and social scientists would like us to believe that there has to be a one best way, a perfect or most efficient organizational form or mode of integration in the global economy that eventually predominates. A comparative institutional perspective on development and globalization, by contrast, not only celebrates the diversity of the world, but also argues that there is *no room for the one best way* in the global economy. There is simply no arrangement or course of action that can deliver everything at once, either at the country, industry, or organizational level of analysis. The evidence presented in this book suggests that neither Argentina nor South Korea nor Spain can be proposed as a perfect model of economic and sociopolitical development. Each path to development brings with it not only strengths and achievements but also weaknesses and failures.

At first sight, it might be obvious for some people to argue that maybe Spain and South Korea could be proposed as models of two different successful development paths, while Argentina exemplifies a wrongheaded approach to development. For one thing, the growth in per capita GDP over the last half-century has been much faster in Spain and South Korea than in Argentina (see fig. 8.2).

Aggregate macroeconomic figures, however, are only part of the story. Tables 8.2 and 8.3 present a more nuanced, multidimensional assessment of each country's strengths and weaknesses, successes and failures. Argentina can boast monetary stability and openness to the global economy as considerable achievements in a region of the world mired in inflation and antiforeign attitudes. Multinationals are unambiguously betting on a country considered to be a basket case just a decade ago. Its economic weaknesses and failures, however, are equally noteworthy. The country has one of the best-educated populations in the world, but is utterly dependent on foreign technology and know-how. Most importantly, Argentina has thus far been unable to reverse decades of inward-looking development. Exports are still low relative to the size and potential of the economy (a mere 9 percent of GDP compared to 38 for Korea and 26 for Spain; see table 8.3), and the country's close integration

Figure 8.2. GDP per Capita for Selected Countries, 1870–1994.
(Madison 1995, 194–205).

with Brazil has retarded restructuring in key industries such as automobiles, chemicals, petrochemicals, and steel. It is only a mild exaggeration to conclude that most Argentine firms have not yet abandoned the import-substitution frame of mind.

By contrast to Argentina, South Korea has demonstrated it can export everything from chips to ships, to paraphrase the motto of one of the country's leading chaebol. Moreover, Korea is easily the newly industrialized country with the stronger proprietary technology base, especially in electronics, even though it is still heavily dependent in other fields. These are no minor achievements for a country that was among Asia's poorest just a generation ago. Korea's economic weaknesses and outright failures, however, make it difficult to propose as a model to emulate, contrary to late-industrialization proponents. The country's financial system is in disarray, and the small and medium enterprise sector has been so disadvantaged that it cannot contribute its fair share in terms of innovation, exports, and foreign investment.

Like Korea, Spain represents in many ways a story of success. After decades of wrongheaded policies and subservience to interest group pressures, the country has been able to put its house in order and pursue full economic and monetary integration with Europe. This is, again, no minor achievement for a country that was among the most isolated on the continent just a generation ago. Integration with Europe has resulted in a massive presence of foreign multinationals, which has contributed to the decline of large Spanish-owned manufacturing firms but the rise of a vibrant sector of small and medium

TABLE 8.2

Achievements and Strengths, Failures and Weaknesses of the Economic
and Sociopolitical Development of Argentina, South Korea, and Spain

	Argentina		South Korea		Spain	
	Achievements, Strengths	Failures, Weaknesses	Achievements, Strengths	Failures, Weaknesses	Achievements, Strengths	Failures, Weaknesses
conomic	Monetary stability, economic opening	Meager exports, technological dependency	Export prowess, increasing technological development	Small and medium enterprises, financial system	Integration in Europe, world-class banks	Unemployment, technological dependency
ocio-olitical	Democracy, reconciliation	Corruption, income inequality	Improved standard of living, democracy	Difficult consensus building, lack of labor rights	Democracy, consensus building	Remains of corporatist privileges

enterprises. A second unique achievement is the stability and competitiveness of its banking sector, which is making history in terms of international expansion. There is, however, no shortage of weaknesses and failures in the Spanish development experience. First and foremost, unemployment remains the highest among the industrialized countries, reaching almost 50 percent among the youngest age group until the early 1990s. Simply put, half of the baby-boom generation has been wasted or underemployed. The human drama is truly breathtaking: unrealized dreams of personal independence and a shattered sense of dignity among the young. The other weakness of the Spanish economy is its limited ability to generate technological innovations, a situation that is reducing the country's potential in the global economy.

Argentina, South Korea, and Spain also have mixed records when it comes to sociopolitical development (see table 8.2). The three countries have made a transition to democracy after decades of authoritarian or semiauthoritarian rule. In addition, Argentina achieved national reconciliation during the 1980s after years of bitterness, turmoil, and near civil war. Meanwhile, Korea has been able to improve the standard of living of its population as a whole, without generating inequality. And Spain has forged a strong consensus behind most of the key social, political, and economic issues affecting the country—with the notable exception of how to accommodate the aspirations of centrifugal nationalist movements. Sociopolitical weaknesses and failures are also apparent in each country. Argentina suffers from degrees of corruption and income inequality that Korea and Spain seem to have avoided. (The income ratio for the top 20 percent of households relative to the bottom 20 percent is 11 in Argentina but only 6 in Korea and 4 in Spain. In vast Argentina the

TABLE 8.3
Argentina, South Korea, and Spain, 1997: An Overview

	Argentina	South Korea	Spain
A. General features			
Population (million)	35.7	46.0	39.3
GDP per capita (international $)	10,300	13,590	15,930
Annual GDP growth rate, 1990–95 (%)	5.7	7.2	1.1
Unemployment (%)	17.2	6.0	20.4
Consumer price index inflation (annual %)	0.5	4.4	2.0
Consumer price index inflation (average annual % 1990–96)	15.8	5.8	5.0
B. Social and political features			
Annual population growth (%)	1.29	0.97	0.17
Population in largest metropolitan area (% of total)	41.2	25.9	10.4
Life expectancy at birth, females (years)	76.8	76.0	81.5
Illiteracy (% population aged 15 or more)	3.5	2.8	2.8
Newspaper circulation (per 1,000)	144	412	104
Telephones (per 1,000 population)	191	444	403
Female labor force (% of total)	30.7	40.0	36.2
Income inequality (ratio of top 20% to bottom 20%)	10.8	5.7	4.4
Form of state	Presidential republic	Presidential republic	Parliamentary monarchy
Territorial organization	Federal states	Regions	Autonomous regions
C. Money and finance			
National currency	Peso	Won	Peseta
Exchange rate regime	Currency board	Floating	EU Monetary Union
Gross domestic savings (% of GDP), 1996	18.1	34.5	21.4
Stock market capitalization (% of GNP), 1996	15.1	28.7	43.1

TABLE 8.3
Argentina, South Korea, and Spain, 1997: An Overview *(continued)*

	Argentina	South Korea	Spain
D. Foreign trade, investment, and debt			
Exports of goods and services (% GDP)	9.0	38.1	25.5
Imports of goods and services (% GDP)	10.7	38.8	24.6
Most important export	Foodstuffs	Electronics	Automotive goods
Main trading partners	Mercosur, U.S.	U.S., Asia, EU	European Union, U.S.
Inward foreign direct investment stock (% of GDP)	12.3	3.5	19.0
Outward foreign direct investment stock (% of GDP)	2.4	3.8	9.0
Total debt service (% of GNP)	6.3	3.3	—
Fortune global 500 firms, 1998	0	14	5
Membership in trade blocs	Mercosur, 1991	None	EU, 1986
Membership in the IMF since	1956	1955	1958
Membership in the OECD since	—	1996	1961
Membership in the International Labour Office since	1919	1991	1956[a]
E. Technology and know-how			
Royalty payments (% of GDP)	0.074	0.545	0.294
Royalty receipts (% of GDP)	0.002	0.057	0.040
R&D expenditure (% of GDP)	0.2	2.6	0.9
Number of patents obtained in the U.S. up to 1991	473	1,213	1,979
Number of patents obtained in the U.S., 1992–1996	166	5,634	1,217
Number of ISO 9000 certificates, 1998	807	7,729	6,412

Source: Economist Intelligence Unit; *Fortune*; International Finance Corporation; United Nations; U.S. Patent Office; World Bank.
Note: Figures are for 1997 unless otherwise indicated.
[a] Spain was a member of ILO between 1919 and 1941.

capital city's metropolitan area is home to a staggering 41 percent of the population compared to 26 in Korea and just 10 in Spain.) Korea has yet to learn how to build consensus in a country in which regional, rural-urban, and class divides loom large, and it also needs to recognize and enforce full labor rights. Spain, for its part, needs to eradicate the remaining corporatist interests that are still privileging certain business and professional groups.

Three Key Debates of the Global Era

As I anticipated in chapter 1, the comparative institutional approach and the empirical evidence presented in this book help answer three key questions about the global era. Is there a development glass ceiling? Does globalization produce homogeneity or diversity in the world? Should economic growth take precedence over political reform or vice versa? Consistent with the view of globalization advanced in this book, I shall argue that globalization does not necessarily create a glass ceiling between poor and rich countries, that it produces diversity in economic action and organizational form, and that it is better to engage it with a high degree of social consensus based on fully legitimate political institutions than under authoritarian government.

A Development "Glass Ceiling"?

The most influential works in the sociology of development have long argued that (some of) the newly industrialized countries may have been successful at raising incomes, but that economic growth has not rendered them any less dependent on the core of advanced economies, and that, in many cases, "dependent development" has forced them to rely to a greater extent on capital, technology, and other resources from abroad (Cardoso and Faletto [1973] 1979; Evans 1979; Furtado 1970; Frank 1967; Prebisch 1950).[1] Thus, another way of assessing the strengths and weaknesses of the different development paths followed by Argentina, South Korea, and Spain is to examine whether they have reduced their traditional dependence on core countries, that is, to see whether they have broken through the glass ceiling of development and are poised to join the elite club of the world's most advanced countries or not.

In spite of rapid growth since the 1960s, neither South Korea nor Spain seems to have reduced the huge gap separating it from advanced countries like Germany, Japan, or the United States, whose per capita incomes are twice as high (see fig. 8.2; Pritchett 1997). Besides, membership in the club of the world's most advanced countries only obtains to nation-states that are home

---

[1] The felicitous term *dependent development* was made famous by Evans (1979), although it was used earlier by Cardoso and Faletto ([1973] 1979, 174, 213) and by Furtado (1970, 137).

to major multinational corporations, develop their own technology, at least in some fields, invest in the quality of the workforce, and sell their products in world markets with a recognizable brand on them. The issue of whether a glass ceiling separates the already rich from those aspiring to be rich is also important because, among theories of development, only dependency and world-system theories argue that a ceiling in fact exists. The modernization, late-industrialization, neoclassical, and comparative-institutional perspectives are more optimistic about development possibilities.

Table 8.3 presents data on foreign trade, investment and debt (panel D) as well as on technology (panel E) that help answer this vexing question. On the one hand, the three countries remain "dependent" on the most advanced core economies, albeit in different ways. Argentina appears to depend on foreign direct investment and foreign debt, but its technological dependency is limited, given that its meager exports are mostly of raw or semiprocessed foodstuffs and other natural resources. South Korea, by contrast, seems to be heavily reliant on foreign loans and technology in support of its phenomenal export effort but not on foreign direct investment. Spain differs from South Korea in its apparently massive dependence on foreign direct investment, but foreign loans are unimportant. Naturally, these differences are due to the development path taken by each country. On the other hand, however, the data in panels D and E of table 8.3 indicate that Spain is not only a large recipient of foreign direct investment but also an important foreign investor abroad— the stock of outward FDI is nearly half the stock of inward FDI, and it is growing much more rapidly—while South Korea is a heavy borrower of foreign technology but is spending a relatively high proportion of its GDP on research and development, and its numbers of U.S. patents and ISO 9000 quality certificates are soaring. Let's examine each country's success at breaking through the glass ceiling.

South Korea has developed thanks to massive borrowings of foreign money, technology, and marketing know-how. The literature on South Korean industrialization agrees that this country's phenomenal economic growth was based on technological learning rather than innovation (Amsden 1989; Bernard and Ravenhill 1995; L. Kim 1993, 1997). As explained in chapters 5 and 7, foreign loans have played a key role in a country that preferred to curtail the activities of foreign multinationals. Highly leveraged chaebol applying foreign technology to a diversity of export-oriented industrial endeavors have been the engines of Korean economic growth.

Until the 1990s, three decades after adopting an export-led strategy, Korea neglected technology development, unlike its neighbor and role model— Japan (Bernard and Ravenhill 1995; Smith 1997). Royalty payments for foreign technology grew very rapidly to represent more than 0.5 percent of GDP annually. Since the early 1990s, however, Korea and Taiwan have surged ahead as the two most technologically successful newly industrialized countries (Amsden and Mourshed 1997). For example, South Korean R&D expenditure (2.6 percent of GDP) and patents in the United States have increased more than fourfold since 1991 (see table 8.3). In 1997 alone one Korean company, Samsung Electronics, obtained some 1,300 patents in the United States, ranking sixth in the world after such powerhouses as IBM, Canon, NEC, Motorola, and Sony (Gomes-Casseres and Lee 1988; L. Kim 1997; Lall 1990; STEPI 1995; *Korea Herald*, 13 January 1999). Not surprisingly, about 80 percent of Korean patents in the United States are accounted for by the six largest business groups and by the state-owned steel firm (POSCO). Half of the patents have to do with one single field, electronics. As Smith (1997, 748–49) has documented, however, "the great majority of South Korean R&D in 1992 is still 'reverse engineering.' . . . The engineer directing Samsung's Consumer Electronics R&D Center grudgingly admitted [in a 1992 interview] that . . . 'so far our R&D activity has been limited to developing parts by using things like reverse engineering.' "

Innovation in marketing has also lagged behind manufacturing growth. Until the early 1990s, more than 80 percent of Korea's exports were accounted for by original equipment manufacturing (OEM) contracts, that is, an arrangement by which a Korean company would manufacture a product for sale abroad under a foreign company's brand, which would handle all the marketing and distribution activities (Bernard and Ravenhill 1995). Nowadays roughly half of Korean exports are branded (Park 1994). Whether branded or not, Korean products tend to target the low end of international markets. Korea firms make relatively cheap products with little or no differentiation, following a strategy of beating their rivals in global markets on the basis of price. More often than not, the Korean trade deficit has risen as the country increases its exports. The reason is simple. Korean companies frequently sell their products in foreign markets at prices below cost. Their profits are greater for domestic than export sales. In many cases, exports are not profitable at all, as a variety of scholars and my own field interviews suggest (Amsden 1989, 69–70; Bernard and Ravenhill 1995; Fields 1995, 195; Lim 1985, 95–96; Westphal, Rhee, and Pursell 1979; Woo 1991, 169). Korean firms can sustain such dumping in international markets because they make windfall profits in the protected domestic market. But any export increase requires imports of technology, machinery, and key components whose prices cannot be manipulated downward. The combination of low selling prices for exports and high cost of critical imported components and machinery results in low or zero profitability of export sales.

South Korea is certainly poised at the threshold of the advanced world. Its rapid technological development and strong export orientation will pay huge dividends in the future. In addition, the country is home to capable firms with a growing reputation in world markets. The financial crisis and bailout of 1997 — in addition to inflicting havoc upon the country's industrial structure—has also reminded Koreans that the highly leveraged strategy may permanently keep the country dependent on volatile foreign sources of capital. A more balanced mix of foreign debt and direct investment may actually provide South Korea with more degrees of freedom in the global economy, as its current president is fond of arguing. Despite the uncertainties surrounding the resolution of the crisis, South Korea seems to be on its way to shattering the glass ceiling: its chaebol are increasingly investing in technology, brand reputation, and foreign manufacturing and distribution facilities. If only small and medium-sized firms could also join the trend, South Korea would approach its goal of becoming an advanced country much faster.

Spain presents a paradox. This most dynamic country has made great inroads in terms of catching up with its rich European neighbors. However, it appeared until very recently that pragmatic-modernizing development would swallow local entrepreneurial activities and the country would irresistibly fall into the hands of foreign multinationals—"dependent development" at its best. As in Korea with nationalist-modernizing development, the 1990s have proved that the glass ceiling can be eventually shattered with a pragmatic-modernizing strategy: small and medium enterprises, worker-owned cooperative groups, and a few large domestically owned firms in oligopolistic industries have prospered at the same time that foreign multinationals have taken over large segments of the Spanish economy. A sharp division of labor among organizational forms has emerged. Foreign multinationals dominate large-scale manufacturing, especially the assembly and capital goods industries. Small and medium enterprises are thriving either as suppliers to larger firms (including many multinationals) or as niche marketers. Large, domestically owned firms have become major international competitors in such previously regulated industries as banking, utilities, telecommunications, oil, and gas. Spanish firms—both large and small—have established a brand reputation for themselves and invested abroad in pursuit of production and market opportunities; some have even invested in technology.

Like South Korea, however, Spain has a way to go, albeit a different one. The country still suffers from the self-defeating "let-them-invent" attitude that Miguel de Unamuno unwittingly helped legitimize at the turn of the century (Robles 1987, 42). Spain pays dearly for foreign technology (0.3 percent of GDP every year). Domestic R&D expenditures grew rapidly during the 1980s, but they stagnated during the 1990s and still amount to a tiny 0.9 percent of GDP, the lowest rate in the OECD except for the other newly industrialized member countries (Greece, Portugal, Turkey, and Mexico), and considerably lower than Korea's 2.6 percent. Moreover, the government's share of total R&D expenditure has been sliding.

Few Spanish firms have managed to develop pockets of comparative technological strength, perhaps only in fabricated metals, industrial machinery, and transportation, primarily auto parts and railway equipment, as found by an OECD study (Archibugi and Pianta 1992, 69, 76–77). These firms tend to be small in size (see chaps. 4 and 6). Neither funding from the government nor from abroad has contributed significantly to developing these distinctive technological capabilities (INE 1994, 64). Firms with majority foreign control have increased their R&D expenditures only slightly faster than domestically controlled firms. Regardless of ownership, the more export oriented the firm, the greater the expenditure on R&D. As a result of these pusillanimous R&D efforts, patents filed and obtained by Spanish firms in the United States are not increasing as rapidly as those by Korean firms, even though Spain has traditionally been more innovative (table 8.3). Most patents filed by Spanish businesses in the United States are the result of the efforts of small and medium enterprises in fields such as machinery, electromechanical goods, metals, and, to a lesser extent, pharmaceuticals.

A similar picture emerges from an analysis of worker-training efforts. Leaving aside the well-documented disarray of the public technical and vocational training system, firms have traditionally spent scant resources on the upgrading of worker skills (Cobo Suero 1994, 1124–25, 1193–1203). Most worker training has to do with the absorption of foreign technology; apprenticeships in firms are still quite rare. In 1993, firms with 200 or more workers spent just $592 per employee on training-related activities, 10 percent down from 1992. This amounts to merely 0.86 percent of total wage and salary expenditures and 0.40 percent of gross value added. Slightly over half of all workers underwent some kind of training in 1993, totaling an average of 42 hours per worker, or 2.5 percent of total on-the-job hours. Overall, the worst performers are firms in the state-owned sector, those that do not export, or those controlled by domestic capital. Their workers receive on average 25 percent fewer hours of training, and the training expenditure per worker is about half. The firms most highly committed to worker training are by far those controlled by foreign capital. When compared to domestically controlled private firms, they devote twice as many hours and three times as much money to training per worker. Aside from foreign firms, medium-sized firms employing 300–499 workers spend about 50 percent more on training than either smaller or larger firms (Mineco 1994, 269, 290–94).

A bright spot on the horizon is the increasingly important role of Spanish firms as foreign investors in manufacturing and marketing. Small and medium-sized firms led the way, starting with a few pioneers in the 1960s and then massively during the 1980s and 1990s. Dozens of medium-sized manufacturers of branded food products, beverages, textiles, clothing, furniture, books, fabricated metals, domestic appliances, pharmaceuticals, machinery, automobile parts, and luxury goods are now established across the world. Medium-sized providers of such services as transportation, security, fast food, printed information, and software have also expanded abroad (Campa and Guillén 1996a; Durán 1996, 1997). During the 1990s large firms in banking, construction, utilities, telecommunications, specialty steels, oil, and gas joined their smaller counterparts (Durán 1999; see also chap. 7). This flurry of foreign activity has resulted in ever greater proportions of Spanish firms establishing their own foreign distribution channels (Campa and Guillén 1999), and in net foreign direct investment *outflows* as of the late 1990s, for the first time in recent history. The better part of the Spanish economy remains dependent on foreign technology (as should be expected in the case of a medium-sized country). In terms of foreign direct investment, by contrast, Spain has become *inter*dependent with—not merely dependent on—the global economy.

Unlike South Korea and Spain, Argentina seems far from the advanced countries. Its annual royalty payments are relatively low (0.07 percent of GDP) not because it relies on its own technology and know-how (R&D expenditures run a tiny 0.2 percent of GDP, and few Argentine firms hold patents) but because the country's exports are small, except for technology-light goods such as unprocessed foodstuffs, minerals, and crude oil. The country's technology policy is in disarray, especially after the 1995 and 1998 downturns, and neither foreign nor domestic firms invest much on R&D (Bisang 1994b; Chudnovsky, López, and Porta 1997; Katz and Bercovich 1993). Job-training efforts are extremely limited, with multinationals spending only enough money to make it possible for workers to operate the machinery and equipment (Fuchs 1994; Wiñar 1988). Few Argentine brands are known internationally, and these mostly in Brazil.

Argentina's erratic populism has perhaps lasted too long. Dependence on volatile international commodity markets was once replaced by dependence on a protected domestic market, and, more recently, by dependence on the Mercosur. Few firms have escaped from the harmful long-term effects of Argentina's pattern of trade. Unlike in Korea, both foreign direct investment and foreign debt are high. In particular, debt servicing consumes a staggering 6.3 percent of GDP every year. In spite of its accomplishments (see table 8.2) and the many benefits that foreign multinationals may have brought to the country, Argentina's path does not seem to lead through the glass ceiling.

It is very important to note that the two most successful countries at reducing their degrees of dependency—South Korea and Spain—have implemented neoclassical economic policies to a much *lesser* extent than the least successful, Argentina. During the 1990s the Argentine economy underwent one of the swiftest and most far-reaching economic liberalization programs in the world. Meanwhile, South Korea and Spain adopted economic reforms not only more gradually and reluctantly, but also in conjunction with heavy doses of active industrial dirigisme (Korea) or of compensating social welfare policies (Spain). Thus, it is not at all clear that the mere adherence to liberal economic principles lies at the heart of success in the global economy. On the contrary, the evidence presented in this book represents a sober reminder that blind economic liberalization is no magic bullet. Moreover, the experiences of South Korea and Spain illustrate that there are at least two different ways of shattering the glass ceiling.

Homogeneity versus Diversity

The previous section has cast doubt on the notion that globalization produces a dual structure of countries in the world, as argued by dependency and world-system theories. The comparative-institutional approach also takes issue with the tenet of modernization, late-industrialization, and neoclassical theories that globalization causes convergence in patterns and (eventually) outcomes of change. Rather, globalization is seen as encouraging diversity. If globalization is a process by which actors in the world become more aware of each other, then it multiplies the chances of linkage and the possibilities for exchange. As actors become less bound by location, they will find it easier to develop their own identity. In the modern world cross-border brokers such as the state and other powerful organizations played a key role in the adoption and diffusion of new possibilities for economic action and organizational form. The enhanced possibilities for networking in a global world make it easier for individuals, communities, firms, and labor unions to bypass brokers, to look around by themselves, to adopt the patterns of economic action and organizational form that they find most appealing. Thus, a comparative-institutional approach argues that globalization encourages diversity rather than homogeneity. In so doing, it takes sides with an expanding group of social scientists critical of the conventional wisdom that globalization generates convergence.[2]

The evidence presented in this book supports the view that globalization encourages diversity. The empirical chapters document the growing interconnections among actors and the resulting diversity in economic action and organizational form. Governments, firms, and labor unions in Argentina, South Korea, and Spain not only did not converge in their approach to development and globalization; they actively sought to be different. For example, the Korean chaebol have succeeded at mobilizing vast amounts of labor and capital, while Argentine groups have demonstrated their ability to reinvent themselves under changing circumstances, and worker-owned cooperative groups and small and medium enterprises in Spain have thrived under the conditions created by full economic integration with Europe. In so doing, each of these organizational forms engaged globalization by establishing ties within and across borders that enabled them to be different. In sum, development and integration with the global economy have taken place along differ-

---

[2] Albrow 1997, 86, 144, 149, 189; Cox 1996, 28, 30 n. 1; Friedman 1994, 210–11; Giddens 1990, 64, 175, 1991, 21–22; Mazlish 1993, 4; McMichael 1996, 177, 190–97, 234–35; Robertson 1992, 27, 145, 1995, 34–35; Zelizer 1999; see also Guillén 2001.

ent paths, producing different patterns of organizational change, and resulting in different combinations of strengths and weaknesses.

The evidence for diversity in Argentina, South Korea, and Spain resonates with the findings of other scholars of the global economy. At the firm level, Doremus et al. (1998) write that national systems of innovation, trade, and investment remain firmly in place and affect the structure and behavior of multinationals as they leave their home countries and expand throughout the world. Stopford and Strange (1991, 1–2) argue that the increasingly complex interaction between multinationals and states has produced a divergence in outcomes. Orrù, Biggart, and Hamilton (1997) draw a number of systematic comparisons among East Asian and western European countries demonstrating that unique national patterns of organization not only persist over time but also contribute to the international competitiveness of each country's firms. Studies of cross-national corporate governance practices have found little, if any, convergence in terms of stockholding, the presence of institutional investors, executive compensation, hostile takeovers, and reliance on debt finance, in spite of the globalization of financial markets and foreign direct investment (Guillén 2000b; La Porta, Lopez-de-Silanes, and Shleifer 1999, 512–13). Furthermore, La Porta et al. (1998) report that cross-national differences in corporate governance are not systematically associated with faster rates of economic growth; that is, there are several economically sound ways of governing the firm.

At the industry level, political scientists working within the "varieties of capitalism" tradition have documented that French, German, Japanese, and American firms compete in world markets following different templates that build on their countries' institutional strengths (Dore [1973] 1990; Hollingsworth, Schmitter, and Streeck 1994; Murmann 1998; Soskice 1998; Streeck 1991, 1995; Storper and Salais 1997, 131–48; Ziegler 1995, 1997). And at the country level, Garrett (1998, 1–4, 10–11, 34–37, 51, 74; 1999) echoes the same theme by rejecting simplistic views about convergence. He demonstrates that in the context of a global economy at least two paths are possible for national economic and social policymakers: adherence to neoclassical economics or to social democratic corporatism. He finds no convergence in government taxation and expenditure as a result of globalization. Finally, Pritchett (1997) has found "divergence, big time" in income levels across countries over the last century in spite of massive development efforts and increasing globalization.

Among social scientists, only "world society" researchers have consistently found convergence as a result of the worldwide expansion of rationalized state structures and markets. Their measure of convergence, however, focuses at a relatively high level of abstraction and analysis, namely, "matters such as citizen and human rights, the natural world and its scientific investigation, socioeconomic development, and education" (Meyer et al. 1997, 145, 148, 152–

54, 161). And even at that high level, they find that "the world as a whole shows increasing structural *similarities of form* among societies without, however, showing increasing *equalities of outcomes* among societies" (Meyer and Hannan 1979, 3, 13–15). As the empirical evidence in this book shows, wide differences in organizational form also exist across and within countries if measurements are made at the industry or firm levels of analysis.

Taken together, the empirical evidence provided by sociologists and political scientists supports well the case for diversity, or at least resilience, in cross-national patterns. Globalization is not homogenous in its effects, nor does it invite or force countries and firms to converge on a universally superior pattern of organization and economic behavior. The empirical evidence presented in this book corroborates the importance of diversity in the global economy, and the futility of thinking in terms of "best practices" and convergence.

The Sequence of Economic and Political Change

The thesis that political reform can—or even should—wait for economic development or adjustment became popular during the 1980s and 1990s as globalization enthusiasts proclaimed the triumph of economics over politics. Its proponents point to countries such as Singapore, South Korea, Taiwan, Malaysia, China, and Chile as proof of the effectiveness of authoritarian (or even totalitarian) regimes when it comes to raising countries up economically or rescuing them from economic trouble. In particular, military or single-party authoritarian regimes are said to be more adept at making painful macroeconomic adjustments to global economic forces, promoting investment, or tempering pressures for immediate consumption, as in the cases of South Korea, Indonesia, Thailand, Chile, Mexico, and Taiwan during the 1980s. As Przeworski and Limongi (1993) point out, however, there is little theoretical or empirical support in the literature to make the argument that regime type affects economic outcomes.

There are at least four empirical problems with the argument that newly industrialized countries with a dictatorial regime do better in terms of economic growth, especially in an era of globalization. First, new democracies frequently have a poor record in terms of economic performance compared to authoritarian regimes precisely because it is during times of crisis that most dictatorships collapse or give way to a democratic transition under pressure from a disgruntled business community and labor unrest. New democracies in Argentina, Bolivia, Brazil, Peru, the Philippines, and Uruguay, among other countries, inherited acute economic problems from economically incompetent dictatorships, a circumstance that made it hard for them to deliver good economic results in the short run (Haggard and Kaufman 1995). In other cases, dictators happened to pass away in the midst of a world economic crisis, as in Spain (1975).

Second, the relatively few authoritarian regimes that manage to make effective macroeconomic adjustments before the transition to democracy begins are generally able to do so at the cost of engaging in wholesale repression, as the cases of Chile and South Korea during the 1980s illustrate. And repression does not nearly always work: Many authoritarian regimes force disastrous economic reforms upon business and labor, as in Argentina during the late 1970s. Third, authoritarian regimes are not the only ones that have succeeded at introducing economic reforms. There are cases of new democracies that inherit an economy in crisis from a preceding dictatorship and manage to make a "dual" or simultaneous economic and political transition, namely, Spain and Portugal during the late 1970s and 1980s (Bermeo 1994a, 1994b; see also Centeno 1994 and chap. 5).

The fourth and most compelling reason why it makes sense not to subordinate political reform to economic adjustment has to do with the nature of globalization itself. Authoritarian regimes have a very hard time dealing with globalization. Cross-border flows of information, people, goods, and money just make it more difficult to control populations and economic actors, and to get away with repression. For example, during the 1960s and early 1970s Spanish unions benefited from the presence of foreign multinationals, which could not mistreat their Spanish workers without arousing international criticism (see chap. 5). The South Korean government could not deal with labor unrest in 1987 as harshly as it used to in the past because of the international publicity surrounding the upcoming Seoul Olympic Games of 1988, another manifestation of globalization (Stephens 1988). More recently, the Zapatista rebels in Mexico were able to turn global awareness of repression and hardship in the Chiapas region into political advantage in their ongoing clash with the Mexican government.

China, it might seem, provides the counterexample to South Korea and Mexico in that a totalitarian regime can successfully navigate the waters of the global economy without loosening its repressive grip on the society and the polity. The case of China is also important to sort out because of the infamous comparison with Russia and its failed reform efforts. China, however, has not succeeded (so far at least) because it is a dictatorship. A brief comparison of the transitional economies of eastern Europe illuminates this question because they all made the transition to democracy during the early 1990s but have exhibited different degrees of economic success. As Spicer, McDermott, and Kogut (2000) and Stark and Bruszt (1998) argue, the secret for success in eastern Europe has had to do with adopting "gradualist" policies as opposed to "shock therapy." Piecemeal privatization and transition to the market enables actors—businesses, financiers, labor unions, consumers—to reposition themselves in the economy and to overhaul their networks of relationships in ways that are consistent with a market setting. By contrast, mass privatization and other "big bang" policies lead to distress, disassembly, chaos, and corruption. Poland and Hungary have done much better than Russia and the Czech Republic because they have implemented reforms in a gradual way, much to the dismay of "shock therapy" enthusiasts (Sachs 1993). Moreover, democracy and active labor participation in politics and economic policymaking in Poland have helped—not hindered—a successful transition to the market economy (Spicer, McDermott, and Kogut 2000; Stark and Bruszt 1998). The eastern European cases help to understand that China has not succeeded because it is a totalitarian regime focused on a swift transition to the market but because it has adopted gradualist policies—unlike Russia (for the dissenting view, see Sachs and Woo 1997). Gradualism preserves actors and enables them to reconstruct their networks of relationships, while shock therapy tends to destroy whatever strengths and resources exist in a country's social organization.

Beyond the historical contingencies of each individual country case, there is a cardinal reason in favor of democracy and democratic control in the global era. Globalization and development invite more democratic political control over the economy, not less. The world is made of a variety of different strands of capitalism that must coexist if the global economy is to work smoothly (Rodrik 1998). The myth of a global economy free from political interference is just that, a wrongheaded and impracticable ideal entertained by most libertarians and free-market fundamentalists, some visionary dictators, and a not negligible number of technocrats of various political persuasions. Political dialogue, negotiation, and compromise are not only legitimate in a global economy but necessary. Citizens must be able to exert democratic control over markets, firms, and multilateral organizations, to voice their concerns, and to elect officials whom they deem well prepared to formulate and implement policies.

. . . . .

Globalization raises the likelihood of actors being aware of each other, potentially offering endless opportunities for them to relate to one another. It compels us to abandon modernist dogmas as to what is the best policy for development, the optimal way to organize markets and industries, the right organizational form, the best managerial practice. It asks us instead to look for the differences across and within countries, regions, communities, industries, and organizations; to look for what makes each of them unique and valuable. Globalization is neither to be opposed as a menace nor to be celebrated as a panacea; it is to be engaged: comprised, located, given form. To be sure, a global world is more unpredictable and ambiguous than the modern world of the recent past. But it allows individuals and organizations to grow out of the straightjackets of location and the modern nation-state, to express themselves in a more boundless way, to pursue their identities without having to conform to a dominant model or paradigm. The task of a comparative institutional theory of development is precisely to provide an understanding of how difference empowers and enriches without denying the unity and mutual awareness that globalization entails.

APPENDIX
DATA AND SOURCES

This appendix lists the large-sample surveys of firms and the interviews conducted for this book, and the libraries, archives, and manufacturing plants visited.

LARGE-SAMPLE SURVEYS OF FIRMS

1. Survey of 120 firms of the 20 largest firms each of 10 manufacturing industries in Spain using a closed-item questionnaire. Conducted during 1993 in collaboration with Professor José Manuel Campa of New York University with funding from the Carnegie Bosch Institute for Applied Studies in International Management.

2. Survey of 1,150 exporting firms in Spain with 25 or more employees using a closed-item questionnaire. Conducted by the Spanish Institute for International Trade (ICEX) in 1992.

3. Survey of 1,200 respondents representative of the adult population in Spain. Conducted in collaboration with Professor Juan Díez Nicolás, director of the CIRES survey research institute. Questions on attitudes toward foreign investment included in a larger survey of economic and political attitudes in 1995.

4. Survey of 163 manufacturing firms in the Province of Mendoza, Argentina, using a closed-item questionnaire during 1995. Conducted in collaboration with Professor Omar N. Toulan of McGill University under the auspices of the MIT–Province of Mendoza Collaborative Project.

5. Census of 3,971 foreign direct investments by Korean companies undertaken between 1960 and 1995. Compiled by the Bank of Korea.

INTERVIEWS

A. Argentina

Raúl Arenas, Director of Public Relations, Peñaflor, Maipú, Mendoza, 31 October 1995

Roberto Arizu, General Manager, Bodegas Leoncio Arizu, Luján de Cuyo, Mendoza, 31 October 1995

Juan Miguel Arranz, Vice President, Santander Investment, Buenos Aires, 7 May 1998

Eduardo Arrotea Molina, General Manager, Telefónica de Argentina, Buenos Aires, 24 March 1995

Sebastián Bagó, President, Laboratorios Bagó, Buenos Aires, 4 October 1996

Daniel Blas Sánchez, President, Federación de Cooperativas Vitivinícolas Argentinas (Fecovita), Maipú, Mendoza, 30 October 1995

Rubén A. Ciani, Director for Agricultural and Agroindustrial Markets, Ministry of Agriculture, Buenos Aires, 9 October 1996

Rodolfo A. Corvi, Assistant General Manager, BBV Banco Francés, Buenos Aires, 7 May 1998

Carlos M. Fedrigotti, President, Citibank Argentina, Buenos Aires, 8 May 1998

Fernando Fragueiro, Dean, Instituto de Altos Estudios Empresariales, Buenos Aires, 4 October 1998

Rodolfo Gabrielli, Former Governor, Province of Mendoza, Boston, 20 February 1996

Ricardo Augusto Gallo, Vice President, Banco de Boston, Buenos Aires, 22 March 1995

Julio J. Gómez, President, Asociación de Bancos de la República Argentina, Buenos Aires, 8 May 1998

Héctor Helman, Director of Training and Development, Sociedad Comercial Macri, Buenos Aires, 24 October 1995

Alejandro Henke, Deputy Director, Superintendency of Financial Institutions, Banco Central de la República Argentina, 7 May 1998

Néstor Huici, freelance consultant, Buenos Aires, 3 October 1996

Bernardo Kosacoff, Coordinator of Industrial Studies, Comisión Económica para América Latina (CEPAL), 24 October 1998

Roberto Luis Lamm, CEO, Industrias Alimenticias Mendocinas (ALCO), Tupungato, Mendoza, 30 October 1995

Roberto Maiorana, Product Director, Industrias Metalúrgicas Pescarmona (IMPSA), Godoy Cruz, Mendoza, 1 November 1995

Enrique L. Mallea, General Manager, YPF Gas, Buenos Aires, 6 October 1996

Leonidas Montaña, President, National Institute of Industrial Technology, Buenos Aires, 3 October 1996

Jorge Montoya, CEO Latin America, Procter and Gamble, Buenos Aires, 24 March 1995

Enrique Pourteau, Vice President, YPF, Buenos Aires, 26 October 1995

Daniel E. Rennis, Director of Corporate Financial Planning and Investor Relations, Pérez-Companc Group, Buenos Aires, 4 October 1996

Enrique Ruete, CEO of Banco Roberts, Buenos Aires, 22 March 1995

Adriano Senetiner, President, Nieto y Cía., San José, Mendoza, 30 October 1995

Jorge Sinardi, Vice President for Human Resources, Pérez-Companc Group, Cambridge, Mass., 1 April 1996, and Buenos Aires, 4 October 1996

Gloria Sorensen, Staff Economist, BBV Banco Francés, Buenos Aires, 7 May 1998

Javier Tizado, CEO, Siderar, Buenos Aires, 23 March 1995

Carlos D. Tramutola, Executive Director, STRAT, Buenos Aires, 25 October 1998

Saúl Ubaldini, Secretary-General of the CGT during the 1980s, Buenos Aires, 4 October 1996

B. South Korea

Chang Byung-ju, President, Daewoo Group, Seoul, 2 June 1997

Choi Jung Ki, Director of the Employment and Welfare Department at the Federation of Korean Industries, and member of the Tripartite Commission, telephone interview, 1 June 1999

Lee Byoung-Hoon, formerly leader of the IBM Korea labor union, Philadelphia, 25 March 1998, and telephone interview, 4 June 1999

Ji Dong-Hyun, Staff Economist, Korea Institute of Finance, Seoul, 30 May 1997

Kang In-Ku, Executive Vice President, GoldStar Co., Seoul, 17 March 1994

Hwang Byeong Joon, Manager, Bohae Brewery (phone interview), 10 November 1998

Hwang K. S., Managing Director, Planning Division, Anam Industrial Co., Seoul, 3 June 1997

Kim Hyung-Kee, Head, Research and Survey Department, Korea Productivity Center, Seoul, 29 May 1997

Kim Yong-Geun, Director, International Business Division, Ministry of Trade, Industry and Energy, Seoul, 29 May 1997

Kim Yoo Sun, Deputy Director of the Korean Labor and Society Institute, former Director of Policy Planning at the KCTU, and member of the Tripartite Commission, telephone interview, Monday, 31 May 1999

Kwon Yong-Won, Deputy Director, Industrial Technology Planning Division, Ministry of Trade, Industry, and Energy, Seoul, 29 May 1997

Lee Byung-Ju, Director, Enterprise Group Division, Fair Trade Commission, Republic of Korea, Seoul, 30 May 1997

Lee Sehoon, President and CEO, HanGlas Group, Seoul, 4 June 1997

Min Joon-Hong, Managing Director, Coated Film Business, SKC, Suwon, Kyonggi-Do, 15 November 1995

Min K. S., Executive Vice President, Hyundai Heavy Industries, Ulsan, 17 March 1994

Min Kwan-Hong, Editor, *Korea Money*, Seoul, 3 June 1997

Noh Gun-Sik, President, Electronics Group, Samsung Europe, Philadelphia, 24 September 1998

Paik Man-Gi, Director General for Technology Policy, Ministry of Trade, Industry, and Energy, Seoul, 29 May 1997

Shin Jung-Hee, President, Dongwha Duty Free Shop, Seoul, 3 June 1997

Son Ho Chul, Professor, Seo-kang University, Seoul, telephone interview, 2 June 1999

Yang Ho-Seung, Managing Director, Corporate Planning, Sunkyong Industries, Seoul, 17 November 1995

Yang Young Mo, Managing Director, Administration and Industrial Relations, Yukong Limited, Ulsan, 18 March 1994

Yun Jong Yong, CEO and President, Samsung Display Devices, Seoul, 19 March 1994

C. Spain

Interviews marked by an asterisk (*) were conducted by research assistant Laura Chaqués, Ignacio Madrid, or Carlos Pereira.

Miguel A. Aleixandre, Export Manager, Sáez Merino, Valencia, 1 December 1994*

Luis Amor, Marketing Director, Pascual Hermanos, Valencia, 30 September 1994*

Evaristo Arias, International Manager, Campofrío, Madrid, 12 June 1994*

Víctor Barallat, Director of Strategy and Investor Relations, Banco Santander, Madrid, 25 June 1998

Francisco Barberá, Export Director, Géneros de Punto Ferrys, Canals, Valencia, 30 September 1994*

Antonio Bernardo Sirgo, CEO, Duro-Felguera, La Felguera, Asturias, 29 December 1993

Josep Lluís Bonet, General Manager, Freixenet, Sant Sadurní d'Anoia, Barcelona, 8 November 1994*

Marcelino Camacho, Secretary-General of Comisiones Obreras, CCOO (1978–87), Madrid, 22 June 1998

Jesús Centenera, International Manager, Indas, Pozuelo de Alcorcón, Madrid, 10 November 1994*

Ángel Corcóstegui, CEO and Vice President, Banco Central Hispano, Madrid, 17 June 1998

Álvaro Cuervo, Professor at the University of Madrid, Madrid, 18 June 1998

Antonio Ferrero, International Manager, Nutrexpa, Barcelona, 2 November 1994*

Jaime Ferry, CEO, Fábricas Asociadas de Muñecas Onil (FAMOSA), Onil, Alicante, 10 January 1995*

William Floistad, Export Manager, Osborne, Cádiz, 28 November 1994*

Fernando Florenzano, CEO, Cobra, Madrid, 8 June 1994

Mikel Gabilondo, Export Manager, Comercial Ufesa, Vitoria, 20 September 1994*

Joaquim Garcia, Planning Director, La Seda de Barcelona, Barcelona, 14 November 1994*

Manuel García Aranda, Director of Training and Publications, Spanish Institute for Foreign Trade (ICEX), Madrid, 17 June 1994

Richard Gardner, U.S. Ambassador to Spain, Cambridge, Mass., 18 October 1994

Antonio González, Director of the Technical Staff of UGT, Madrid, 1 July 1998

J. Guiridi, Manager, Azkoyen, Peralta, Navarra, 28 December 1994*

John Hardiman, formerly CEO of Ford Europe, Cambridge, Mass., 13 October 1994, 8 March and 5 May 1995, and 1 May 1996

Diego Hidalgo, entrepreneur, Cambridge, Mass., 27 October 1994

Sixto Jiménez, CEO, Viscofán, Pamplona, 19 December 1996*

Jorge Llorens, General Manager, Isolux-Wat, 13 June 1994

Antonio López García, President, Amper, Madrid, 9 June 1994

José María Maravall, Minister of Education (1982–88), Cambridge, Mass., 27 October 1993, and Madrid, 9 June 1994

Francisco Martín, General Director, Banco Santander, Cambridge, Mass, 27 April 1994

Carlos Martín Urriza, Staff Economist of CCOO, Madrid, 30 June 1998

Ricardo Martínez Rico, Director of the Undersecretary's Staff, Ministry of Trade and Tourism, Madrid, 15 June 1994

Francisco Novela, CEO, Comelta, Madrid, 6 September 1994*

Melchor Ordóñez, CEO, La Casera, Madrid, 9 June 1994

A. Pajares, Manager, Bodegas Miguel Torres, Barcelona, 4 January 1995*

Tomás Pascual Gómez-Cuétara, Adjunct to the Presidency, Leche Pascual, Madrid, 1 June 1994

Eladio Pérez, CEO, Agemac Tecnoseveco, Vilanova del Camí, Barcelona, 7 November 1994*

Jesús Pérez, Executive Secretary of Unión General de Trabajadores, Madrid, 1 July 1998

José María Planells, CEO, Anecoop, 29 November 1994

Francisco Pons López, CFO, Indo, Hospitalet d'Llobregat, Barcelona, 27 October 1994*

Juan Carlos Rebollo, CFO, Grupo Antolín-Irausa, Burgos, 15 November 1994*

Nicolás Redondo, Secretary-General of Unión General de Trabajadores (1976–1994), Madrid, 24 June 1998

Luis Reig, General Manager, Ficosa International, Barcelona, 11 November 1994*

Jaime Requeijo, Vice President, Banco Zaragozano, 14 June 1995

José Luis Rhodes de Diego, CEO, Patentes Talgo, Madrid, 6 June 1994

Luis Javier Rodríguez García, Director of the Inspection Bureau for Credit and Savings Institutions, Banco de España, Madrid, 17 June 1998

Juan Rodríguez Inciarte, General Director, Banco Santander, Cambridge, Mass., 27 April 1994

José Luis Rodríguez del Saz, Director of Communications and Public Relations, BBV, Madrid, 22 June 1998

Eduardo Sánchez Junco, CEO of Hola SA, Madrid, 21 June 1995

Ignacio Santillana, former CEO of Telefónica Internacional, Philadelphia, 21 February 1997

Jesús Sarasa, CEO, Agropecuaria Navarra Sociedad Cooperativa, Pamplona, 20 December 1994*

Félix Solís, President, Bodegas Félix Solís, Valdepeñas, Valladolid, 26 October 1994*

Ramón Talamás, CEO, Cirsa, Barcelona, 17 November 1994*

Ramón Tamames, Professor, formerly Member of Parliament, Madrid, 21 June 1995

José Antonio Ugarte, President, Ulma Sociedad Cooperativa, Oñati, Guipúzcoa, 13 December 1994*

José María Vázquez Quintana, President, Telefónica Investigación y Desarrollo, Cambridge, Mass., 15 March 1994

Ángel Velasco, CEO, Ansa-Lemforder, Burgos, 14 October 1994*

Carlos Yarza, Manager, Fagor Electrodomésticos Sociedad Cooperativa, Mondragón, Guipúzcoa, 23 October 1994*

José Miguel Zaldo, CEO, Grupo Tavex (Algodonera San Antonio), Madrid, 24 September 1994*

José Antonio Zamora Rodríguez, General Technical Secretary, Ministry of Commerce and Tourism, Madrid, 15 June 1994

Mario Zubía, CEO, Urssa Sociedad Cooperativa, Vitoria, 1 November 1994*

PLANT VISITS

A. *Argentina*

Agroindustrias Inca (fruit canning), Mendoza, 3 November 1995

Alpargatas (clothing factory), Buenos Aires, 24 March 1995

Bodegas Leoncio Arizu (winery), Luján de Cuyo, Mendoza, 31 October 1995

Bodega Nieto y Cía. (winery), San José, Mendoza, 31 October 1995

Federación de Cooperativas Vitivinícolas Argentinas (winery), Maipú, Mendoza, 30 October 1995

Industrias Alimenticias Mendocinas, ALCO (food processing), Tupungato, Mendoza, 30 October 1995

Industrias Metalúrgicas Pescarmona, IMPSA (turbines and other heavy machinery), Godoy Cruz, Mendoza, 1 November 1995

Peñaflor (winery), Maipú, Mendoza, 31 October 1995

B. South Korea

Anam Industrial Co. (semiconductors), Seoul, 2 June 1997
Daewoo Heavy Industries (shipbuilding), Okpo, 3 June 1997
HanGlas (automotive glass), Seoul, 4 June 1997
Hyundai Heavy Industries (shipbuilding), Ulsan, 19 March 1994
Hyundai Motor Company (automobiles), Ulsan, 19 March 1994 and 3 June 1997
GoldStar Co. (videocassette recorders), Seoul, 17 March 1994
POSCO (integrated steelmaker), Po'hang, 18 March 1994
SKC (videotapes and compact discs), Suwon, Kyonggi-Do, 15 November 1995
Yukong Limited (oil refinery), 18 March 1994

ARCHIVES AND LIBRARIES

Asociación del Congreso Panamericano de Ferrocarriles, Buenos Aires
Asociación Española de Fábricas de Equipos y Componentes para Automoción
   (Sernauto), Library, Madrid
Asociación Española de Normalización y Certificación (AENOR), Madrid
Asociación de Fábricas Argentinas de Componentes (AFAC), Buenos Aires
Baker Library, Harvard Business School, Boston
Banco de España, Library, Madrid
Bank of Korea, Foreign Investment Department, Seoul
Biblioteca Nacional, Madrid
Biblioteca Nacional de la República Argentina, Buenos Aires
Cámara de Curtidores, Buenos Aires
Cámara de Industriales Ferroviarios, Buenos Aires
Centro de Estudios e Investigaciones Laborales (CEIL), Buenos Aires
CGT Azopardo Archives, Buenos Aires
Comisión Económica para América Latina (CEPAL), Buenos Aires
Comisión Nacional del Mercado de Valores, Library, Madrid
Consejo Económico y Social, Library, Madrid
Fundación Fondo para la Investigación Económica y Social, Library, Madrid
Fundación Invertir Argentina, Buenos Aires
Fundación Pablo Iglesias, Library, Madrid
Fundación Primero de Mayo, Library, Madrid
Harvard-Yentching Library, Cambridge, Mass.
Instituto Argentino de Ferrocarriles, Buenos Aires
Instituto Nacional de Comercio Exterior (ICEX), Library, and Database, Madrid
Instituto Nacional de Estadística, Madrid
Instituto Nacional de Estadística y Censos, Buenos Aires
Instituto Nacional de Industria, Library and Archives, Madrid
Instituto Nacional de Vitivinicultura, Buenos Aires and Mendoza
International Motor Vehicle Program, Cambridge, Mass.
Korea Alcohol and Liquor Industry Association, Seoul
Korea Automobile Manufacturers Association (KAMA), Seoul
Korea External Trade Association (KOTRA), Seoul and New York
Korea Federation of Banks, Seoul
Korea Federation of Small Business, Seoul

Korea Productivity Center, Seoul
Korean Industrial Advancement Administration, Seoul
Korean National Institute of Technology and Quality, Seoul
Ministerio de Economía, Biblioteca, Buenos Aires
Ministerio de Economía y Hacienda, Biblioteca, Madrid
Ministry of Finance and Industry, Seoul
National Assembly Library, Seoul
New York Public Library, New York
Unión Industrial Argentina, Library, Buenos Aires
Seoul National University Library, Seoul
Sociedad Rural Argentina, Library, Buenos Aires
Younsei University Library, Seoul

REFERENCES

Abós, Álvaro. 1984. *Las organizaciones sindicales y el poder militar, 1976–1983*. Buenos Aires: Centro Editor de América Latina.

Acevedo, Manuel, Eduardo M. Basualdo, and Miguel Khavisse. 1990. *¿Quién es quién? Los dueños del poder económico, Argentina, 1973–1987*. Buenos Aires: Editora/12.

Adams/Jobson's Wine Handbook, 1996. 1996. New York: Adams/Jobson.

Adelman, Jeremy. 1994. "Post-Populist Argentina." *New Left Review* 203 (January–February): 65–91.

Aguilera, Ruth V. 1998. "Directorship Interlocks in Comparative Perspective: The Case of Spain." *European Sociological Review* 14 (4) (December): 319–42.

Albrow, Martin. 1997. *The Global Age*. Stanford, Calif.: Stanford University Press.

Almirón, Fernando. 1995. "Cómo es la crisis del poder sindical." *La Prensa*, 26 March, 6–7.

Alonso, José Antonio, and Vicente Donoso. 1994. *Competitividad de la empresa exportadora española*. Madrid: ICEX.

———. 1995. "La internacionalización de la empresa y el apoyo público." *Economistas* 64:194–203.

Álvarez-Miranda, Berta. 1996. *El sur de Europa y la adhesión a la Comunidad: Los debates políticos*. Madrid: CIS and Siglo XXI.

Amsden, Alice H. 1985. "The State and Taiwan's Economic Development." Pp. 78–106 in *Bringing the State Back In*, ed. Peter B. Evans, Dietrich Rueschemeyer, and Theda Skocpol. Cambridge: Cambridge University Press.

———. 1989. *Asia's Next Giant: South Korea and Late Industrialization*. New York: Oxford University Press.

———. 1990. "Third World Industrialization: 'Global Fordism' or a New Model?" *New Left Review* 182 (July–August): 5–31.

———. 1994. "Why Isn't the Whole World Experimenting with the East Asian Model to Develop? Review of *The East Asian Miracle*." *World Development* 22 (4): 627–33.

Amsden, Alice H., and Jong-Yeol Kang. 1995. "Learning to Be Lean in an Emerging Economy: The Case of South Korea." International Motor Vehicle Program Sponsors Meeting, Toronto.

Amsden, Alice H., and Mona Mourshed. 1997. "Scientific Publications, Patents, and Technological Capabilities in Late-Industrializing Countries." *Technology Analysis and Strategic Management* 9 (3): 343–59.

Amsden, Alice H., and Takashi Hikino. 1994. "Project Execution Capability, Organizational Know-How, and Conglomerate Corporate Growth in Late Industrialization." *Industrial and Corporate Change* 3 (1): 111–47.

Andersen Consulting. 1994. *Worldwide Manufacturing Competitiveness Study: The Second Lean Enterprise Report*. London: Andersen Consulting.

Aoyagi, Takahiro, et al. 1994. "The Internationalization of Samsung's VCR Production." Term paper, International Management. Cambridge: MIT Sloan School of Management.

Apter, David. 1965. *The Politics of Modernization*. Chicago: University of Chicago Press.

Archibugi, Daniele, and Mario Pianta. 1992. *The Technological Specialization of Advanced Countries*. London: Kluwer Academic Publishers.

Arias, María Eugenia, and Mauro F. Guillén. 1998. "The Transfer of Organizational Management Techniques Across Borders." Pp. 110–37 in *The Diffusion and Consumption of Business Knowledge*, ed. José Luis Alvarez. London: Macmillan.

Arregui Giménez, Andrés. 1994. "Internacionalización de las empresas de servicios públicos." *Información Comercial Española* 735 (November): 131–39.

Asia Watch. 1990. *Retreat from Reform: Labor Rights and Freedom of Expression in South Korea*. New York: Asia Watch.

Asia-Pacific Infoserv, Inc. 1991–97. *Korea Company Handbook*. Several semiannual issues. Seoul: Asia-Pacific Infoserv, Inc.

———. 1995–97. *Korea Company Yearbook*. Several annual issues. Seoul: Asia-Pacific Infoserv, Inc.

Auto-Revista. 1986. "25 años de automoción en España." *Auto-Revista* 1455 (28 December–4 January): 19–401.

———. 1987. "Asociación Española de Fabricantes de Equipos y Componentes para Automoción 1967–1987." *Auto-Revista* (October): 1–147.

———. 1997. "Mercosur: La mayor fuerza emergente." *Auto-Revista* 1976 (3–9 June): 33–55.

Azpiazu, Daniel. 1997. "élite empresaria en la Argentina: Terciarización, centralización del capital, privatización y beneficios extraordinarios." Working paper No. 2. Buenos Aires: Facultad Latinoamericana de Ciencias Sociales (FLACSO).

Baily, Samuel L. 1967. *Labor, Nationalism, and Politics in Argentina*. New Brunswick, N.J.: Rutgers University Press.

Balassa, Bela, Gerardo M. Bueno, Pedro-Pablo Kuczynsky, and Mario Henrique Simonsen. 1986. *Toward Renewed Economic Growth in Latin America*. Washington, D.C.: Institute for International Economics.

Balvé, Beatriz S. 1990. "Los nucleamientos político-ideológicos de la clase obrera. Composición interna y alineamientos sindicales en relación a gobiernos y partidos. Argentina, 1955–1974." Working Paper No. 51. Buenos Aires: Centro de Investigaciones en Ciencias Sociales.

Banco Urquijo. 1970. *Evolución a largo plazo de la industria del automóvil en España*. Madrid: Banco Urquijo.

Banham, Reyner. 1980. *Theory and Design in the First Machine Age*. Cambridge: MIT Press.

Bank of Korea. 1995. *Overseas Direct Investment Statistics Yearbook, 1995*. Seoul: Bank of Korea.

Baranson, Jack. 1971. *La industria automovilística en los países en desarrollo*. Madrid: Tecnos.

Bark, Taeho. 1991. "Government Policies and Direct Foreign Investment in Korea." Pp. 232–50 in *Direct Foreign Investment*, ed. Banamex. Mexico City: Banamex.

Barley, Stephen R., and Pamela S. Tolbert. 1997. "Institutionalization and Structuration: Studying the Links between Action and Institution." *Organization Studies* 18 (1): 93–117.

Barney, Jay. 1986. "Strategic Factor Markets: Expectations, Luck, and Business Strategy." *Management Science* 32 (10): 1231–41.

Beckerman, Paul. 1995. "Central-Bank 'Distress' and Hyperinflation in Argentina, 1989–1990." *Journal of Latin American Studies* 27 (3) (October): 663–82.

Bedeski, Robert E. 1994. *The Transformation of South Korea: Reform and Reconstitution in the Sixth Republic under Roh Tae Woo, 1987–1992.* New York: Routledge.

Bekinschtein, José Alberto. 1995. "Apertura externa y patrón de comercio: El comercio exterior argentino y su consistencia con el escenario global." Pp. 95–132 in *Hacia una nueva estrategia exportadora: La experiencia argentina, el marco regional y las reglas multilaterales,* ed. Bernardo Kosacoff. Buenos Aires: Universidad Nacional de Quilmes.

Bell, Clive. 1987. "Development Economics." Pp. 818–26 in *The New Palgrave: A Dictionary of Economics,* ed. John Eatwell, Murray Milgate, and Peter Newman. New York: Stockton Press.

Beltrán, Miguel. 1977. *La élite burocrática española.* Madrid: Tecnos.

Bendix, Reinhard. [1956] 1974. *Work and Authority in Industry.* Berkeley and Los Angeles: University of California Press.

Ben-Porath, Yoram. 1980. "The F-Connection: Families, Friends, and Firms and the Organization of Exchange." *Population and Development Review* 6 (1) (March): 1–30.

Berger, Suzanne. 1996. Introduction to *National Diversity and Global Capitalism,* ed. S. Berger and Ronald Dore. Ithaca, N.Y.: Cornell University Press.

Bermeo, Nancy. 1994a. "Sacrifice, Sequence, and Strength in Successful Dual Transitions: Lessons from Spain." *Journal of Politics* 56 (3) (August): 601–27.

———. 1994b. "Spain: Dual Transition Implemented by Two Parties." Pp. 89–127 in *Voting for Reform,* ed. Stephan Haggard and Steven B. Webb. Washington, D.C.: World Bank.

Bernard, Mitchell, and John Ravenhill. 1995. "Beyond Product Cycles and Flying Geese: Regionalization, Hierarchy, and the Industrialization of East Asia." *World Politics* 47 (2) (January): 171–209.

Best, Michael. 1990. *The New Competition: Institutions of Industrial Restructuring.* Cambridge: Harvard University Press.

Bethell, Leslie, ed. 1993. *Argentina since Independence.* New York: Cambridge University Press.

Bhagwati, Jagdish. 1998. "The Capital Myth: The Difference between Trade in Widgets and Dollars." *Foreign Affairs* 77 (3) (May–June): 7–12.

Biggart, Nicole Woolsey. 1990. "Institutionalized Patrimonialism in Korean Business." *Comparative Social Research* 12:113–33.

———. 1998. "Deep Finance: The Organizational Bases of South Korea's Financial Collapse." *Journal of Management Inquiry* 7 (4) (December): 311–20.

Biggart, Nicole Woolsey, and Mauro F. Guillén. 1999. "Developing Difference: Social Organization and the Rise of the Auto Industries of South Korea, Taiwan, Spain, and Argentina." *American Sociological Review* 64 (5) (October): 722–47.

Biggart, Nicole Woolsey, and Marco Orrù. 1997. "Societal Strategic Advantage: Institutional Structure and Path Dependence in the Automotive and Electronics Industries of East Asia." Pp. 201–39 in *State, Market, and Organizational Form,* ed. Ayse Bugra and Behlul Usdiken. Berlin: Walter de Gruyter.

Bisang, Roberto 1994a. "Perfil tecno-productivo de los grupos económicos en la industria argentina." Working Paper No. 94-12-1671. Santiago: CEPAL.

———. 1994b. "Industrialización e incorporación del progreso técnico en la argentina." Working Paper No. 54. Buenos Aires: CEPAL.

Bisang, Roberto, Gustavo Burachik, and Jorge Katz. 1995. "La reestructuración del aparato productivo en la industria automotriz." Pp. 243–68 in Hacia un nuevo modelo de organización industrial: El sector manufacturero argentino en los años 90, ed. R. Bisang, G. Burachik, and J. Katz. Buenos Aires: Alianza Editorial.

Bisang, Roberto, Mariana Fuchs, and Bernardo Kosacoff. 1995. "Internacionalización de empresas industriales argentinas." Pp. 175–229 in Hacia una nueva estrategia exportadora: La experiencia argentina, el marco regional y las reglas multilaterales, ed. B. Kosacoff. Buenos Aires: Universidad Nacional de Quilmes.

Bisang, Roberto, and Bernardo Kosacoff. 1995. "Tres etapas de la búsqueda de una industrialización sustentable: Exportaciones industriales argentinas, 1974–1993." Pp. 23–93 in Hacia una nueva estrategia exportadora: La experiencia argentina, el marco regional y las reglas multilaterales, ed. B. Kosacoff. Buenos Aires: Universidad Nacional de Quilmes.

Block, Fred. 1994. "The Roles of the State in the Economy." Pp. 691–710 in Handbook of Economic Sociology, ed. Neil J. Smelser and Richard Swedberg. Princeton, N.J.: Princeton University Press.

Bloom, Martin. 1992. Technological Change in the Korean Electronics Industry. Paris: Organization for Economic Cooperation and Development.

Blumberg, Paul. [1968] 1973. Industrial Democracy: The Sociology of Participation. New York: Schocken.

Boix, Carles. 1998. Political Parties, Growth, and Equality: Conservative and Social Democratic Economic Strategies in the World Economy. New York: Cambridge University Press.

Bolsa de Madrid. 1981. La industria del automóvil en España. Madrid: Bolsa de Madrid.

———. 1986. La industria de equipos y componentes para automoción en España. Madrid: Bolsa de Madrid.

Bonet, José Luis. 1993. "La competitividad del cava: El caso Freixenet." Papeles de Economía Española 56:399–401.

Borello, José Antonio. [1993] 1994. "From Craft to Flexibility: Linkages and Industrial Governance Systems in the Development of a Capital Goods Industry in Medoza, Argentina, 1895–1990." Working Paper No. 12. Buenos Aires: Centro de Estudios Urbanos y Regionales.

Boyer, Robert. 1996. "The Convergence Hypothesis Revisited: Globalization but Still the Century of Nations?" Pp. 29–59 in National Diversity and Global Capitalism, ed. Suzanne Berger and Ronald Dore. Ithaca, N.Y.: Cornell University Press.

Braudel, Ferdinand. [1979] 1992. The Perspective of the World. Vol. 3 of Civilization and Capitalism, Fifteenth–Eighteenth Century. Berkeley and Los Angeles: University of California Press.

Brennan, James P. 1994. The Labor Wars in Córdoba, 1955–1976. Cambridge: Harvard University Press.

Bresser Pereira, L. C. 1993. "Economic Reforms and Economic Growth: Efficiency and Politics in Latin America." Pp. 15–76 in *Economic Reforms in New Democracies*, ed. L. C. Bresser Pereira et al. Cambridge: Cambridge University Press.

Brooke, James. 1995. "South Korea Strives for a Market in Latin America." *New York Times*, 6 April, D8.

Broughton, Alan, and Arnaud Ripert. 1997. *European Banking: Spain, the Spanish Banking System*. New York: Morgan Stanley.

Bruton, Henry J. 1998. "A Reconsideration of Import Substitution." *Journal of Economic Literature* 36 (June): 903–36.

Bueno Campos, Eduardo. 1987. *Dirección estratégica de la empresa*. Madrid: Pirámide.

Bunel, Jean. [1991] 1992. *Pactos y agresiones: El sindicalismo argentino ante el desafío neoliberal*. Mexico City: Fondo de Cultura Económica.

Burawoy, Michael. 1985. *The Politics of Production: Factory Regimes under Capitalism and Socialism*. London: Verso.

Burt, Ronald S. 1992. *Structural Holes: The Social Structure of Competition*. Cambridge: Harvard University Press.

Bustamante, Jorge E. 1989. *La república corporativa*. Buenos Aires: Emecé.

Byington, Lisa M. 1990. "The Effects of the Korean Labor Movement on the Economy of the Republic of Korea and on U.S. Investment in the Republic of Korea." *George Washington Journal of International Law and Economics* 24 (1): 149–93.

Calcalgno, Alfredo F. 1997. "Convertibility and the Banking System in Argentina." *CEPAL Review* 61 (April 1997): 63–90.

Calello, Osvaldo, and Daniel Parcero. 1984. *De Vandor a Ubaldini*. Buenos Aires: Centro Editor de América Latina.

Campa, José Manuel, and Mauro F. Guillén. 1996a. "Spain: A Boom from Economic Integration." Pp. 207–39 in *Foreign Direct Investment and Governments*, ed. John H. Dunning and Rajneesh Narula. New York: Routledge.

_____. 1996b. "Evolución y determinantes de la inversión directa en el extranjero por empresas españolas." *Papeles de Economía Española* 66: 235–47.

_____. 1999. "The Internalization of Exports: Firm and Location-Specific Factors in a Middle-Income Country." *Management Science* 45 (11) (November): 1463–78.

Campbell, John L. 1998. "Institutional Analysis and the Role of Ideas in Political Economy." *Theory and Society* 27:377–409.

Campbell, John, and Leon Lindberg. 1990. "Property Rights and the Organization of Economic Activity by the State." *American Sociological Review* 55 (5) (October): 3–14.

Campillo, Manuel. 1963. *Las inversiones extranjeras en España, 1850–1950*. Madrid: Manfer.

Cantwell, John. 1989. *Technological Innovation and the Modern Corporation*. Oxford: Basil Blackwell.

Cardoso, Fernando Henrique, and Enzo Faletto. [1973] 1979. *Dependency and Development in Latin America*. Berkeley and Los Angeles: University of California Press.

Cardozo, Javier. 1989. "The Argentine Automotive Industry: Some Unavoidable Issues for a Re-Entry Strategy." IMVP International Policy Forum Paper. Cambridge: MIT.

Carreras, Albert, and Salvador Estapé Triay. 1998. "Entrepreneurship, Organization, and Economic Performance among Spanish Firms, 1930–1975: The Case of the Motor Industry." Working paper, Universitat Pompeu Fabra, Barcelona.

Carreras, Albert, and Xavier Tafunell. 1993. "La gran empresa en España, 1917–1974: Una primera aproximación." Revista de Historia Industrial 3:127–75.

Carruthers, Bruce G. 1994. "When Is the State Autonomous? Culture, Organization Theory, and the Political Sociology of the State." Sociological Theory 12 (1) (March): 19–44.

Casado, Montserrat. 1995. "La capacidad tecnológica de la economía española: Un balance de la transferencia internacional de tecnología." Información Comercial Española 740 (April): 153–70.

Case, Brendan M., and Andrea Mandel-Campbell. 1998. "Auto Fever." Latin Trade, May, 40–46.

Castells, Manuel. 1996. The Rise of the Network Society. Cambridge, Mass.: Blackwell.

Castells, Manuel, and Alejandro Portes. 1989. "World Underneath: The Origins, Dynamics, and Effects of the Informal Economy." Pp. 11–37 in The Informal Economy: Studies in Advanced and Less Developed Countries, ed. A. Portes, M. Castells, and Lauren A. Benton. Baltimore: Johns Hopkins University Press.

Caves, Richard E. 1989. "International Differences in Industrial Organization." Pp. 1127–1250 in Handbook of Industrial Organization, ed. R. Schmalensee and R. D. Willig. Amsterdam: North Holland.

Centeno, Miguel A. 1994. "Between Rocky Democracies and Hard Markets: Dilemmas of the Double Transition." Annual Review of Sociology 20:125–47.

———. 1997. "Blood and Debt: War and Taxation in Nineteenth-Century Latin America." American Journal of Sociology 102 (6) (May): 1565–1605.

CEPAL. 1999. Hacia un mejor entorno competitivo de la producción automotriz en Argentina. Final report. Buenos Aires: Comisión Económica para América Latina.

Chandler, Alfred D., Jr. 1977. The Visible Hand. Cambridge: Harvard University Press.

———. 1990. Scale and Scope. Cambridge: Harvard University Press.

Chang, Chan Sup, and Nahn Joo Chang. 1994. The Korean Management System. Westport, Conn.: Quorum.

Chang, Lawrence. 1992. "Financial Mobilization and Allocation: The South Korean Case." Studies in Comparative International Development 27 (4): 41–53.

Chang, Sea Jin. 1995. "International Expansion Strategy of Japanese Firms: Capability Building through Sequential Entry." Academy of Management Journal 38 (2) (April): 383–407.

Chen, Che-Hung. 1986. "Taiwan's Foreign Direct Investment." Journal of World Trade Law 20 (6) (November–December): 639–64.

Cho, Dong-Sung. 1987. The General Trading Company: Concept and Strategy. Lexington, Mass.: Lexington Books.

Cho, Dong-Sung, and Jeong-Do Heo. 1989. "Anatomy of Korean General Trading Company." Pp. 21–55 in Management behind Industrialization: Readings in Korean Business, ed. Dong-Ki Kim and Linsu Kim. Seoul: Korea University Press.

Choi, Jang Jip. 1989. Labor and the Authoritarian State: Labor Unions in South Korean Manufacturing Industries, 1961–1980. Seoul: Korea University Press.

———. 1993. "Political Cleavages in South Korea." Pp. 13–50 in State and Society in Contemporary Korea, ed. Hagen Koo. Ithaca, N.Y.: Cornell University Press.

Choi, Sang Rim, Daekeun Park, and Adrian E. Tschoegl. 1996. "Banks and the World's Major Banking Centers, 1990." *Weltwirtschaftliches Archiv* 132 (4): 774–93.

Chu, Yin-Wah. 1998. "Labor and Democratization in South Korea and Taiwan." *Journal of Contemporary Asia* 28 (2): 185–202.

Chudnovsky, Daniel, and Andrés López. 1995. "Política tecnológica en la Argentina: ¿Hay algo más que *laissez faire*?" Working Paper No. 20. Buenos Aires: Centro de Investigaciones para la Transformación (Cenit).

Chudnovsky, Daniel, Andrés López, and Fernando Porta. 1997. "Market or Policy Driven? The Foreign Direct Investment Boom in Argentina." *Oxford Development Studies* 25 (2): 173–87.

Chul, Y. S. 1994. "South Korea's Top Bureaucratic Elites, 1948–1993." *Korea Journal* 34 (3): 5–19.

Chung, Un Chan. 1994. "Is Financial Deregulation a Panacea?" Pp. 105–22 in *The Korean Economy at a Crossroad*, ed. Sung Yeung Kwack. Westport, Conn.: Praeger.

Church, Roy. 1993. "The Family Firm in Industrial Capitalism: International Perspectives on Hypotheses and History." *Business History* 35 (4) (October): 17–43.

CIRES. 1995. *La realidad social en España, 1993–1994*. Madrid: CIRES.

Clancy, Rockwell. 1998. "Consumidores y banca en Latinoamérica: La grieta de la confianza." *Mercado*, September, 177–82.

Clarke, George R. G., and Robert Cull. 1999. "Why Privatize? The Case of Argentina's Public Provincial Banks." *World Development* 27 (5): 865–86.

Clegg, Stewart, and Cynthia Hardy. 1996. "Organizations, Organization, and Organizing." Pp. 1–28 in *Handbook of Organization Studies*, ed. S. Clegg, C. Hardy, and Walter W. Nord. London: Sage.

Clifford, Mark. 1991. "Model of Paradox." *Far Eastern Economic Review*, 31 January, 40–42.

———. 1994. *Troubled Tiger: Businessmen, Bureaucrats, and Generals in South Korea*. New York: M. E. Sharpe.

Cobo Suero, Juan Manuel. 1994. "Educación." Pp. 1107–1276 in *V Informe sociológico sobre la situación social de España*, ed. Miguel Juárez. Madrid: Fundación FOESSA.

Collins, Randall. 1997. "An Asian Route to Capitalism: Religious Economy and the Origins of Self-Transforming Growth in Japan." *American Sociological Review* 62 (6) (December): 843–65.

Cook, Maria Lorena. 1998. "Toward Flexible Industrial Relations? Neo-Liberalism, Democracy, and Labor Reform in Latin America." *Industrial Relations* 37 (3): 311–36.

Cooke, William N. 1997. "The Influence of Industrial Relations Factors on U.S. Foreign Direct Investment Abroad." *Industrial and Labor Relations Review* 51 (1): 3–17.

Cooke, William N., and Deborah S. Noble. 1998. "Industrial Relations Systems and U.S. Foreign Direct Investment Abroad." *British Journal of Industrial Relations* 36 (4) (December): 581–609.

Cox, Robert W. 1996. "A Perspective on Globalization." Pp. 21–30 in *Globalization: Critical Reflections*, ed. James H. Mittelman. Boulder, Colo.: Lynne Rienner Publishers.

Crotty, James, and Gary Dymski. 1998. "Can the Korean Labor Movement Defeat the IMF?" *Dollars and Sense* (November–December): 16–20.

Cuartas, Javier. 1992. *Biografía de El Corte Inglés*. Barcelona: Libros Límite.

Cuervo, Álvaro. 1989. *La crisis bancaria en España, 1977–1985*. Barcelona: Ariel.

Cuervo-Cazurra, Álvaro. 1995. "Conflict of Interest When Banks Are Shareholders and Debtholders of Firms: The Case of Spain." Term paper. MIT Sloan School of Management.

———. 1996. "Does Ownership Matter? The Relationship between Corporate Governance and Strategy." Working paper, MIT Sloan School of Management.

Cumings, Bruce. 1987. "The Origins and Development of the Northeast Asian Political Economy." Pp. 44–83 in *The Political Economy of the New Asian Industrialism*, ed. Frederic Deyo. Ithaca, N.Y.: Cornell University Press.

———. 1989. "The Abortive Abertura: South Korea in the Light of Latin American Experience." *New Left Review* 173 (January–February): 5–32.

———. 1997. *Korea's Place in the Sun: A Modern History*. New York: Norton.

———. 1998. "The Korean Crisis and the End of 'Late' Development." *New Left Review* 231 (September–October): 43–72.

Cusumano, Michael A. 1985. *The Japanese Automobile Industry: Technology and Management at Nissan and Toyota*. Cambridge: Council on East Asian Studies and Harvard University Press.

De la Balze, Felipe A. 1995. *Remaking the Argentine Economy*. New York: Council on Foreign Relations.

De la Sierra, Fermín, Juan José Caballero, and Juan Pedro Pérez Escanilla. 1981. *Los directores de grandes empresas españolas ante el cambio social*. Madrid: Centro de Investigaciones Sociológicas.

De Larra, Mariano José. 1993. *Artículos*. Madrid: Cátedra.

De Miguel, Amando. 1974. *Sociología del Franquismo: Análisis ideológico de los ministros del régimen*. Madrid: Euramérica.

De Miguel, Amando, and Juan J. Linz. 1963. "El Mercado Común, el capital extranjero y el empresario español." *Productividad* 26 (January–March): 18–41, and 27 (April–June): 37–62.

Delgobbo, Alberto, and Hugo Kantis. 1991. "Competitividad e Internacionalizacion de las PyMES Metalmecanicas. Estudios de Casos en la Provincia de Santa Fe." CEPAL Working Paper No. 27. Buenos Aires: CEPAL.

Deyo, Frederic C. 1989. *Beneath the Miracle: Labor Subordination in the New Asian Industrialism*. Berkeley and Los Angeles: University of California Press.

———. 1990. "Economic Policy and the Popular Sector." Pp. 179–204 in *Manufacturing Miracles*, ed. Gary Gereffi and Donald L. Wyman. Princeton, N.J.: Princeton University Press.

Diaz-Alejandro, Carlos F. 1965. "On the Import Intensity of Import Substitution." *Kyklos* 18 (3): 495–511.

Dicker, Richard. 1996. "South Korea Labor Rights Violations under Democratic Rule." *UCLA Pacific Basin Law Journal* 14:196–242.

Dietz, James L. 1986. *Economic History of Puerto Rico*. Princeton, N.J.: Princeton University Press.

DiMaggio, Paul J., and Walter W. Powell. 1983. "The Iron Cage Revisited: Institutional Isomorphism and Collective Rationality in Organizational Fields." *American Sociological Review* 48 (2) (April): 147–60.

Djelic, Marie-Laure. 1998. *Exporting the American Model.* New York: Oxford University Press.

Dobbin, Frank. 1994. *Forging Industrial Policy: The United States, Britain, and France in the Railway Age.* New York: Cambridge University Press.

Dore, Ronald. [1973] 1990. *British Factory, Japanese Factory: The Origins of National Diversity in Industrial Relations.* Berkeley and Los Angeles: University of California Press.

Doremus, Paul N., William W. Keller, Louis W. Pauly, and Simon Reich. 1998. *The Myth of the Global Corporation.* Princeton, N.J.: Princeton University Press.

Dorfman, Adolfo 1983. *Ciencuenta años de industrialización en la Argentina 1930–1980.* Buenos Aires: Ediciones Solar.

Dornbusch, Rudiger, and Sebastian Edwards. 1991. "The Macroeconomics of Populism." Pp. 7–13 in *The Macroeconomics of Populism in Latin America,* ed. R. Dornbusch and S. Edwards. Chicago: University of Chicago Press.

Douglas, Mary. 1986. *How Institutions Think.* Syracuse, N.Y.: Syracuse University Press.

Dunning, John H., and Rajneesh Narula. 1994. *Transpacific Foreign Direct Investment and the Investment Development Path: The Record Assessed.* South Carolina Essays in International Business No. 10. Columbia: Center for International Business Education and Research, University of South Carolina.

———, eds. 1995. *Catalyst for Change: Foreign Direct Investment, Economic Structure, and Governments.* New York: Routledge.

Durán Herrera, Juan José. 1992. "Cross-Direct Investment and Technological Capability of Spanish Domestic Firms." Pp. 214–55 in *Multinational Investment in Modern Europe,* ed. John Cantwell. Aldershot, England: Edward Elgar.

———, ed. 1996. *Multinacionales españolas I.* Madrid: Pirámide.

———, ed. 1997. *Multinacionales españolas II.* Madrid: Pirámide.

———, ed. 1999. *Multinacionales españolas en Iberoamérica.* Madrid: Pirámide.

Durán Herrera, Juan José, and Fernando Úbeda. 1996. "El círculo virtuoso tecnológico en el sector de componentes del automóvil español: El caso de Ficosa." Pp. 129–66 in *Multinacionales Españolas I,* ed. J. J. Durán Herrera. Madrid: Pirámide.

Dyas, G. P., and H. T. Thanheiser. 1976. *The Emerging European Enterprise.* Boulder, Colo.: Westview.

Dyer, Jeffrey H., Dong Sung Cho, and Wujin Chu. 1998. "Strategic Supplier Segmentation: The Next 'Best Practice' in Supply Chain Management." *California Management Review* 40 (2) (winter): 57–77.

Eckert, Carter J. 1993. "The South Korean Bourgeoisie." Pp. 95–130 in *State and Society in Contemporary Korea,* ed. Hagen Koo. Ithaca, N.Y.: Cornell University Press.

Eckert, Carter J., et al. 1990. *Korea Old and New: A History.* Seoul: Ilchokak.

EIU. 1989. *The Automotive Industry in the Developing Countries.* London: Economist Intelligence Unit.

EIU. 1996a. "The Automotive Components Industry in Spain: Foreign Companies Drive Sector Growth." *Europe's Automotive Components Business*, 1st quarter, 71–86.

———. 1996b. "The Automotive Supply Base of South Korea: Achievements and Challenges." *Motor Business Asia-Pacific*, 3d quarter, 104–24.

Encarnation, Dennis J. 1989. *Dislodging Multinationals: India's Strategy in Comparative Perspective*. Ithaca, N.Y.: Cornell University Press.

Enderwick, Peter. 1985. *Multinational Business and Labour*. New York: St. Martin's Press.

Epstein, Edward C. 1992. "Democracy in Argentina." Pp. 3–19 in *The Argentine Democracy*, ed. E. C. Epstein. Westport, Conn.: Praeger.

Esping-Andersen, Gosta. 1985. *Politics against Markets: The Social Democratic Road to Power*. Princeton, N.J.: Princeton University Press.

Espitia, Manuel. 1984. "Rentabilidad y coste del capital de la empresa española no financiera, 1962–1984." *Situación* 4:62–83.

Estapé Triay, Salvador. 1997. "Del fordismo and toyotismo: Una aproximación al caseo de Motor Ibérica: Perspectiva Histórica, 1920–1995." *Economía Industrial* 315:185–95.

Etchemendy, Sebastián, and Vicente Palermo. 1998. "Conflicto y Concertación: Gobierno, Congreso, y Organizaciones de Interés en la Reforma Laboral del Primer Gobierno Menem, 1989–1995." *Desarrollo Económico* 37 (148) (January–March): 559–90.

Ettlinger, N. 1997. "An Assessment of the Small-Firm Debate in the United States." *Environment and Planning* 29:419–42.

Euh, Yoon-Dae, and Sang H. Min. 1989. "Foreign Direct Investment from Developing Countries: The Case of Korean Firms." Pp. 56–109 in *Management behind Industrialization: Readings in Korean Business*, ed. Dong-Ki Kim and Linsu Kim. Seoul: Korea University Press.

Evans, Peter B. 1979. *Dependent Development*. Princeton, N.J.: Princeton University Press.

———. 1995. *Embedded Autonomy: States and Industrial Transformation*. Princeton, N.J.: Princeton University Press.

———. 1997a. "The Eclipse of the State? Reflections on Stateness in an Era of Globalization." *World Politics* 50 (October): 62–87.

———, ed. 1997b. *State-Society Synergy: Government and Social Capital in Development*. Berkeley: University of California at Berkeley International and Area Studies, no. 94.

Evans, Peter B., and Gary Gereffi. 1979. "Foreign Investment and Dependent Development: Comparing Brazil and Mexico." Pp. 111–68 in *Brazil and Mexico: Patterns of Dependent Development*, ed. Sylvia Ann Hewlett and Richard S. Weinert. Philadelphia: Institute for the Study of Human Issues.

Evans, Peter B., Dietrich Rueschemeyer, and Theda Skocpol. 1985. "On the Road towards a More Adequate Understanding of the State." Pp. 347–66 in *Bringing the State Back In*, ed. P. B. Evans, D. Rueschemeyer, and T. Skocpol. Cambridge: Cambridge University Press.

Evans, Peter B., and John D. Stephens. 1988. "Studying Development since the Sixties: The Emergence of a New Comparative Political Economy." *Theory and Society* 17 (5): 713–45.

Feenstra, Robert C., Robert E. Lipsey, and Harry P. Bowen. 1997. "World Trade Flows, 1970–1992, with Production and Tariff Data." NBER Working Paper No. 5910. Cambridge, Mass.: National Bureau of Economic Research.

Feenstra, Robert C., Tzu-Han Yang, and Gary G. Hamilton. 1999. "Business Groups and Product Variety in Trade: Evidence from South Korea, Taiwan, and Japan." *Journal of International Economics* 48:71–100.

Feldstein, Martin. 1998. "Refocusing the IMF." *Foreign Affairs* 77 (2) (March–April): 20–33.

FIEL (Fundación de Investigaciones Económicas Latinoamericanas). 1995. *Indicadores de Coyuntura: Número Especial*, No. 350.

Fields, Karl J. 1995. *Enterprise and the State in Korea and Taiwan.* Ithaca, N.Y.: Cornell University Press.

Fienberg, Stephen 1980. *The Analysis of Cross-Classified Categorical Data.* Cambridge: MIT Press.

Fishman, Robert M. 1990. *Working-Class Organization and the Return to Democracy in Spain.* Ithaca, N.Y.: Cornell University Press.

Fligstein, N. 1990. *The Transformation of Corporate Control.* Cambridge: Harvard University Press.

——. 1996. "Markets as Politics: A Political-Cultural Approach to Market Institutions." *American Sociological Review* 61 (4) (August): 656–73.

Flores, Gregorio. 1994. *SITRAC-SITRAM: Del Cordobazo al Clasismo.* Buenos Aires: Ediciones Magenta W.

Fomento de la Producción. 1976. *Las 1500 mayores empresas españolas.* Barcelona: Fomento de la Producción.

——. 1994. *Las 2500 mayores empresas españolas.* Barcelona: Fomento de la Producción.

——. 1996. *Los campeones de la exportación española.* Barcelona: Fomento de la Producción.

——. 1997. *Las 2500 mayores empresas españolas.* Barcelona: Fomento de la Producción.

Frank, André G. 1967. *Capitalism and Underdevelopment in Latin America.* New York: Monthly Review Press.

Frenkel, Stephen J., and Jeffrey A. Harrod. 1995. *Industrialization and Labor Relations: Contemporary Research in Seven Countries.* Ithaca, N.Y.: ILR Press.

Frenkel, Stephen J., and David Peetz. 1998. "Globalization and Industrial Relations in East Asia: A Three-Country Comparison." *Industrial Relations* 37 (3) (July): 282–310.

Friedman, Jonathan. 1994. *Cultural Identity and Global Process.* London: Sage.

Fry, Maxwell J. 1995. *Money, Interest, and Banking in Economic Development.* Baltimore: Johns Hopkins University Press.

Fuchs, Mariana. 1994. "Calificación de los recursos humanos e industrialización: El desafío argentino de los años noventa." Working Paper No. 57. Buenos Aires: CEPAL.

Fujita, Masataka. 1996. "Small and Medium-Sized Enterprises in Foreign Direct Investment." Pp. 9–70 in *International Technology Transfer by Small and Medium-Sized Enterprises*, ed. Peter J. Buckley, Jaime Campos, Hafiz Mirza, and Eduardo White. London: Macmillan.

Fundación Invertir Argentina. 1995. *Foreign Direct Investment in Argentina, 1994–1995*. Buenos Aires: Fundación Invertir Argentina.

Furtado, Celso. 1970. *Obstacles to Development in Latin America*. Garden City, N.Y.: Doubleday.

"The Gain in Spain Falls Mainly in Parts." 1994. *Economist*, 5 November, 67.

Galve Górriz, Carmen, and Vicente Salas Fumás. 1992. "Estructura de propiedad de la empresa española." *Información Comercial Española* 701:79–90.

García, Florentino. 1998. "La industria auxiliar de la automoación se acelera." *El País Negocios*, 3 May, 12.

García Lupo, Rogelio. 1971. *Contra la ocupación extranjera*. Buenos Aires: Editorial Centro.

Garrett, Geoffrey. 1998. *Partisan Politics in the Global Economy*. New York: Cambridge University Press.

———. 1999. "Trade, Capital Mobility, and Government Spending around the World." Working paper, Department of Political Science, Yale University.

Gatto, Francisco. 1995. "Las exportaciones industriales de pequenas y medianas empresas." Pp. 133–73 in *Hacia una nueva estrategia exportadora: La experiencia argentina, el marco regional y las reglas multilaterales*, ed. Bernardo Kosacoff. Buenos Aires: Universidad Nacional de Quilmes.

Geertz, Clifford. 1963. *Peddlers and Princes: Social Development and Economic Change in Two Indonesian Towns*. Chicago: University of Chicago Press.

———. 1973. *The Interpretation of Cultures: Selected Essays*. New York: Basic Books.

———. 1995. *After the Fact: Two Countries, Four Decades, One Anthropologist*. Cambridge: Harvard University Press.

———. 1998. "The World in Pieces: Culture and Politics at the End of the Century." *Focaal: Tijdschrift voor Antropologie* 32:91–117.

Geiger, Theodor. 1932. *Die soziale Schichtung des deutschen Volkes: Soziographischer Versuch auf Statistischer Grundlage*. Stuttgart: Ferdinand Enke.

Gereffi, G. 1989. "Rethinking Development Theory: Insights from East Asia and Latin America." *Sociological Forum* 4 (4): 505–33.

———. 1990a. "Paths of Industrialization: An Overview." Pp. 3–31 in *Manufacturing Miracles*, ed. G. Gereffi and Donald L. Wyman. Princeton, N.J.: Princeton University Press.

———. 1990b. "Big Business and the State." Pp. 90–109 in *Manufacturing Miracles*, ed. G. Gereffi and Donald L. Wyman. Princeton, N.J.: Princeton University Press.

———. 1994a. "The Organization of Buyer-Driven Global Commodity Chains." Pp. 95–122 in *Commodity Chains and Global Capitalism*, ed. G. Gereffi and M. Korzeniewicz. Westport, Conn.: Greenwood.

———. 1994b. "The International Economy and Economic Development." Pp. 206–33 in *Handbook of Economic Sociology*, ed. Neil J. Smelser and Richard Swedberg. Princeton, N.J.: Princeton University Press.

Gereffi, Gary, and Donald L. Wyman, eds. 1990. *Manufacturing Miracles: Paths of Industrialization in Latin America and East Asia.* Princeton, N.J.: Princeton University Press.

Gerlach, Michael L. 1992. *Alliance Capitalism: The Social Organization of Japanese Business.* Berkeley and Los Angeles: University of California Press.

Gerschenkron, Alexander. 1962. *Economic Backwardness in Historical Perspective.* Cambridge: Harvard University Press.

Giddens, Anthony. 1984. *The Constitution of Society.* Berkeley and Los Angeles: University of California Press.

_____. 1990. *The Consequences of Modernity.* Stanford, Calif.: Stanford University Press.

_____. 1991. *Modernity and Self-Identity.* Cambridge, Mass.: Polity Press.

Gilpin, Robert 1987. *The Political Economy of International Relations.* Princeton, N.J.: Princeton University Press.

Godio, Julio. 1991. *El movimiento obrero argentino, 1955–1990.* Buenos Aires: Legasa.

Goldstein, M., and P. Turner. 1996. "Banking Crises in Emerging Economies: Origins and Policy Options." BIS Economic Papers No. 46.

Gomes-Casseres, Benjamin, and Seung-Joo Lee. 1988. "Korea's Technology Strategy." HBS Case 9-388-137 Rev. 1/89. Boston: Publishing Division, Harvard Business School.

González Cerdeira, Xulia. 1996. "La empresa industrial en la década de los noventa: Actividad tecnológica." Working Paper No. 9609. Madrid: Fundación Empresa Pública.

Granovetter, Mark. 1983. "Small Is Bountiful: Labor Markets and Establishment Size." *American Sociological Review* 49 (3) (June): 323–34.

_____. 1985. "Economic Action and Social Structure: The Problem of Embeddedness." *American Journal of Sociology* 91 (3) (November): 481–510.

_____. 1995. "Coase Revisited: Business Groups in the Modern Economy." *Industrial and Corporate Change* 4 (1): 93–130.

Green, Andrew E. 1992. "South Korea's Automobile Industry." *Asian Survey* 32 (5): 411–28.

Guillén, Mauro F. 1987. "Antiamericanism in Europe: The Case of Spain." *International Forum at Yale* 7 (3): 14–16.

_____. 1989. *La profesión de economista: El auge de economistas, ejecutivos y empresarios en España.* Barcelona: Ariel.

_____. 1994. *Models of Management: Work, Authority, and Organization in a Comparative Perspective.* Chicago: University of Chicago Press.

_____. 1997a. "Scientific Management's Lost Aesthetic: Architecture, Organization, and the Taylorized Beauty of the Mechanical." *Administrative Science Quarterly* 42 (4) (December): 682–715.

_____. 1997b. "Business Groups in Economic Development." Pp. 170–74 in *Best Paper Proceedings,* Academy of Management Annual Meeting, Boston.

_____. 1998a. "International Management and the Circulation of Ideas." *Trends in Organizational Behavior* 5: 47–63.

_____. 1998b. Review of *The Collapse of the American Management Mystique,* by Richard R. Locke. *Business History Review* 72 (2) (summer): 364–66.

Guillén, Mauro F. 1999. "Institutional Structures, Organizational Learning, and Sequential Foreign Expansion: South Korean Firms and Business Groups in China, 1987–1995." *East Asian Economic Perspectives* 10 (March): 14–37.

——. 2000a. "Business Groups in Emerging Economies: A Resource-Based View." *Academy of Management Journal* 43 (3) (June): 362–80.

——. 2000b. "Corporate Governance and Globalization: Is There Convergence across Countries?" *Advances in International Comparative Management* 13: 177–206.

——. 2000c. "Organized Labor's Images of Multinational Enterprise: Divergent Ideologies of Foreign Investment in Argentina, South Korea, and Spain." *Industrial and Labor Relations Review* 53 (3) (April): 419–42.

——. 2001. "Is Globalization Civilizing, Destructive, or Feeble? A Critique of Five Key Debates in the Social-Science Literature." *Annual Review of Sociology* 27, 235–60.

Guillén, Mauro F., and Omar N. Toulan. 1997. "New Organizational Forms of Internationalization in Latin America: The Experience of Argentine Firms." *Organization* 4 (4): 552–63.

Guillén, Mauro F., and Adrian E. Tschoegl. 1999. "The New Conquistadors: Spanish Banks and the Liberalization of Latin American Financial Markets." Teaching case study, Wharton School, University of Pennsylvania.

——. 2000. "The Internationalization of Retail Banking: The Case of the Spanish Banks in Latin America." *Transnational Corporations* 9 (3) (December): 63–97.

Gurr, T. R. 1990. *Polity III: Political Structures and Regime Change, 1800–1995*. Computer database. Ann Arbor, Mich.: Inter-University Consortium for Political and Social Research.

Gutman, Graciela. 1993. "Cambios y reestructuración recientes en el sistema agroalimentario en la Argentina." Pp. 337–78 in *El desafío de la competitividad*, ed. Bernardo Kosacoff et al. Buenos Aires: Alianza.

Habermas, Jürgen. 1983. "Modernity—an Incomplete Project." Pp. 3–15 in *The Anti-Aesthetic: Essays on Postmodern Culture*, ed. Hal Foster. Port Townsend, Wash.: Bay Press.

Haggard, Stephan. 1990. *Pathways from the Periphery: The Politics of Growth in the Newly Industrializing Countries*. Ithaca, N.Y.: Cornell University Press.

Haggard, Stephan, and Tun-jen Cheng. 1987. "State and Foreign Capital in the East Asian NICs." Pp. 84–135 in *The Political Economy of the New Asian Industrialism*, ed. Frederic Deyo. Ithaca, N.Y.: Cornell University Press.

Haggard, Stephan, and Robert R. Kaufman. 1995. *The Political Economy of Democratic Transitions*. Princeton, N.J.: Princeton University Press.

Haggard, Stephan, and Chung H. Lee. 1993. "The Political Dimension of Finance in Economic Develoment." Pp. 3–20 in *The Politics of Finance in Developing Countries*, ed. S. Haggard et al. Ithaca, N.Y.: Cornell University Press.

Haggard, Stephan, and Sylvia Maxfield. 1993. "Political Explanations of Financial Policy in Developing Countries." Pp. 293–325 in *The Politics of Finance in Developing Countries*, ed. S. Haggard et al. Ithaca, N.Y.: Cornell University Press.

Haggard, Stephan, and Chung-in Moon. 1993. "The State, Politics, and Economic Development in Postwar South Korea." Pp. 51–93 in *State and Society in Contemporary Korea*, ed. Hagen Koo. Ithaca, N.Y.: Cornell University Press.

Hamann, Kerstin. 1998. "Spanish Unions: Institutional Legacy and Responsiveness to Economic and Industrial Change." *Industrial and Labor Relations Review* 51 (3) (April): 424–44.

Hamilton, Gary G., and Nicole W. Biggart. 1988. "Market, Culture, and Authority: A Comparative Analysis of Management and Organization in the Far East." *American Journal of Sociology* 94 (supplement): S52–S94.

Hamilton, Gary G., and Robert C. Feenstra. 1995. "Varieties of Hierarchies and Markets: An Introduction." *Industrial and Corporate Change* 4:51–91.

Harrison, Bennett. 1994. *Lean and Mean: The Changing Landscape of Corporate Power in the Age of Flexibility*. New York: Basic Books.

Harvey, David. 1989. *The Condition of Postmodernity*. Oxford: Blackwell.

Hawkesworth, Richard E. 1981. "The Rise of Spain's Automobile Industry." *National Westminster Bank Quarterly Review*, February, 37–48.

Hayek, Friedrich A. von. 1944. *The Road to Serfdom*. Chicago: University of Chicago Press.

Henderson, Gregory. 1968. *Korea: The Politics of the Vortex*. Cambridge: Harvard University Press.

Henisz, W. 1998. "The Institutional Environment for International Investment." Ph.D. diss., Haas School of Business, University of California, Berkeley.

Hikino, Takashi, and Alice H. Amsden. 1994. "Staying Behind, Stumbling Back, Sneaking Up, Soaring Ahead: Late Industrialization in Historical Perspective." Pp. 285–315 in *Convergence of Productivity: Cross-National Studies and Historical Evidence*, ed. William J. Baumol et al. New York: Oxford University Press.

Hill, C. W. L., and Robert E. Hoskisson. 1987. "Strategy and Structure in the Multiproduct Firm." *Academy of Management Review* 12 (2): 331–41.

Hirschman, Albert O. 1958. *The Strategy of Economic Development*. New Haven, Conn.: Yale University Press.

———. 1968. "The Political Economy of Import-Substituting Industrialization in Latin America." *Quarterly Journal of Economics* 82:2–32.

———. 1982. "Rival Interpretations of Market Society: Civilizing, Destructive, or Feeble?" *Journal of Economic Literature* 20 (December): 1463–84.

Hirst, Paul, and Grahame Thompson. 1996. *Globalization in Question*. London: Polity.

Hofstede, Geert. 1980. *Culture's Consequences: International Differences in Work-Related Values*. Newbury Park, Calif.: Sage.

———. 1991. *Cultures and Organizations*. New York: McGraw-Hill.

Hollingsworth, J. Rogers, Philippe C. Schmitter, and Wolfgang Streeck. 1994. "Capitalism, Sectors, Institutions, and Performance." Pp. 3–16 in *Governing Capitalist Economies: Performance and Control of Economic Sectors*, ed. J. Hollingsworth, P. C. Schmitter, and W. Streeck. New York: Oxford University Press.

Hong, Sunghoon, and Sidney J. Gray. 1995. "FDI Motivations and Location Patterns: Major Korean Electronics Companies and the European Union." Paper presented at the Academy of International Business Annual Meeting, Seoul.

Hoskisson, Robert E. 1987. "Multidivisional Structure and Performance: The Contingency of Diversification Strategy." *Academy of Management Journal* 30 (4) (December): 625–44.

Hoskisson, Robert E., and Michael A. Hitt. 1990. "Antecedents and Performance Outcomes of Diversification: A Review and Critique of Theoretical Perspectives." *Journal of Management* 16 (2): 461–509.

Hudson, Peter. 1998. "Ford Argentina, atrapada por el Mercosur." *AméricaEconomía*, 9 April, 24.

Huff, W. G. 1994. *The Economic Growth of Singapore*. New York: Cambridge University Press.

Hymer, Stephen. 1976. *The International Operations of National Firms: A Study of Direct Foreign Investment*. Cambridge: MIT Press.

IDEA. 1995. *Productividad: Eje del bienestar general*. Thirtieth Annual Colloquium. Buenos Aires: Instituto para el Desarrollo Empresarial de la Argentina.

IEF. 1993. *Las empresas españolas en las fuentes tributarias*. Madrid: Instituto de Estudios Fiscales, Ministerio de Economía y Hacienda.

IEPB. 1995. *Trends in Foreign Investment*. Seoul: International Economic Policy Bureau, Ministry of Finance and Economy, Republic of Korea.

IFC. 1998. *Emerging Stock Markets Factbook*. Washington, D.C.: International Finance Corporation.

INDEC (Instituto Nacional de Estadistica y Censos). 1994. *Comercio Exterior Argentina*.

INE. 1994. *Estadística sobre las actividades en investigación científica y desarrollo tecnológico (I+D) 1991*. Madrid: Instituto Nacional de Estadística.

Jacobs, Norman. 1985. *The Korean Road to Modernization and Development*. Urbana: University of Illinois Press.

James, Daniel. 1981. "Rationalisation and Working Class Response: The Context and Limits of Factory Floor Activity in Argentina." *Journal of Latin American Studies* 13 (2) (November): 375–402.

Janelli, Roger L. 1993. *Making Capitalism: The Social and Cultural Construction of a South Korean Conglomerate*. Stanford, Calif.: Stanford University Press.

Jenkins, Rhys. 1984. "The Rise and Fall of the Argentine Motor Vehicle Industry." Pp. 41–73 in *The Political Economy of the Latin American Motor Vehicle Industry*, ed. Rich Kronish and Kenneth S. Mericle. Cambridge: MIT Press.

JETRO. 1997. "APEC Auto Industry SMEs Rev Their Engines." <www.jetro.go.jp>.

Johnson, Chalmers. 1982. *MITI and the Japanese Miracle*. Stanford, Calif.: Stanford University Press.

Jones, Geoffrey, and Mary B. Rose. 1993. "Family Capitalism." *Business History* 35 (4) (October): 1–16.

Jones, Leroy P., and Il Sakong. 1980. *Government, Business, and Entrepreneurship in Economic Development: The Korean Case*. Cambridge: Council on East Asian Studies, Harvard University.

Juri, María E., and Raúl Mercau. 1990. "Privatización en la Argentina: El caso de Bodegas y Viñedos Giol." *Estudios de la Fundación Mediterráneo* 13 (53) (January–March): 3–19.

KAMA. 1998. *Korean Automobile Industry, 1998*. Seoul: Korea Automobile Manufacturers Association.

Kang, M.-H. 1996a. *Chaebo-kwa Han Kook Kyung Je.* Expanded ed. Seoul: Na-Nam Chool-Pan.

Kang, M.-H. 1996b. *The Korean Business Conglomerate.* Berkeley: Institute of East Asian Studies, University of California.

Kanter, Rosabeth Moss. 1995. *World Class: Thriving Locally in the Global Economy.* New York: Simon and Schuster.

Katz, Harry C. 1993. "The Decentralization of Collective Bargaining." *Industrial and Labor Relations Review* 47 (1) (October): 3–22.

Katz, Jorge M., and Nestor A. Bercovich. 1993. "National Systems of Innovation Supporting Technical Advance in Industry: The Case of Argentina." Pp. 451–75 in *National Innovation Systems,* ed. Richard Nelson. New York: Oxford University Press.

Katz, Jorge M., and Bernardo Kosacoff. 1983. "Multinationals from Argentina." Pp. 137–219 in *The New Multinationals,* ed. Sanjaya Lall. New York: Wiley.

Katzenstein, Peter J. 1985. *Small States in World Markets: Industrial Policy in Europe.* Ithaca, N.Y.: Cornell University Press.

Kaufman, Robert R., and Barbara Stallings. 1991. "The Political Economy of Latin American Populism." Pp. 15–43 in *The Macroeconomics of Populism in Latin America,* ed. Rudiger Dornbusch and Sebastian Edwards. Chicago: University of Chicago Press.

Kei, Matsuo. 1977. "The Working Class in the Masan Free Export Zone." AMPO: *Japan-Asia Quarterly Review* (special issue): 67–78.

Kennedy, Paul. 1993. *Preparing for the Twenty-First Century.* New York: Random House.

Kenney, Martin, and Richard Florida. 1993. *Beyond Mass Production: The Japanese System and Its Transfer to the U.S.* Oxford: Oxford University Press.

Kerr, Clark, John T. Dunlop, Frederick Harbison, and Charles A. Myers. [1960] 1964. *Industrialism and Industrial Man.* New York: Oxford University Press.

Khanna, Tarun, and Krishna Palepu. 1997. "Why Focused Strategies May Be Wrong for Emerging Markets." *Harvard Business Review* 75 (4) (July–August): 41–50.

———. 1999. "Policy Shocks, Market Intermediaries, and Corporate Strategy: The Evolution of Business Groups in Chile and India." *Journal of Economics and Management Strategy* 8 (2) (summer): 271–310.

Kim, Eun Mee. 1997. *Big Business, Strong State.* Albany: State University of New York Press.

Kim, Hwang-Joe. 1993. "The Korean Union Movement in Transition." Pp. 133–61 in *Organized Labor in the Asia-Pacific Region,* ed. Stephen Frenkel. Ithaca, N.Y.: ILR Press.

Kim, Kwan Bong. 1971. *The Korea-Japan Treaty Crisis and the Instability of the Korean Political System.* New York: Praeger.

Kim, Linsu. 1993. "National System of Industrial Innovation: Dynamics of Capability Building in Korea." Pp. 357–83 in *National Innovation Systems,* ed. Richard Nelson. New York: Oxford University Press.

———. 1997. *Imitation to Innovation: The Dynamics of Korea's Technological Learning.* Boston: Harvard Business School Press.

———. 1998. "Crisis Construction and Organizational Learning: Capability Building in Catching-up at Hyundai Motor." *Organization Science* 9 (4) (July–August): 506–21.

Kim, Wook. 1994. "The Political Economy of Growth: *Chaebols* and Korean Economic Growth." *Korea Observer* 25 (1) (spring): 65–104.

Kirk, Donald. 1994. *Korean Dynasty: Hyundai and Chung Ju Yung.* Armonk, N.Y.: M. E. Sharpe.

Knickerbocker, F. T. 1973. *Oligopolistic Reaction and Multinational Enterprise.* Boston: Division of Research, Graduate School of Business Administration, Harvard University.

Kobrin, Stephen J. 1997. "The Architecture of Globalization: State Sovereignty in a Networked Global Economy." Pp. 146–71 in *Governments, Globalization, and International Business*, ed. John H. Dunning. New York: Oxford University Press.

———. 1998. "Development after Industrialization: Poor Countries in an Electronically Integrated Global Economy." Paper presented at the workshop "Globalization of Multinational Enterprise Activity and Economic Development," University of Strathclyde.

Kogut, Bruce. 1985. "Designing Global Strategies: Comparative and Competitive Value-Added Chains." *Sloan Management Review* 26 (4) (summer): 15–28.

———. 1991. "Country Capabilities and the Permeability of Borders." *Strategic Management Journal* 12 (special issue): 33–47.

Kohli, Atul. 1994. "Where Do High Growth Political Economies Come From? The Japanese Lineage of Korea's 'Developmental State.'" *World Development* 22 (9): 1269–93.

Koo, Bohn Young. 1985. "The Role of Direct Foreign Investment in Korea's Economic Growth." Pp. 176–216 in *Foreign Trade and Investment: Economic Development in the Newly Industrializing Asian Countries*, ed. Walter Galenson. Madison: University of Wisconsin Press.

Koo, Hagen. 1993a. "Introduction." Pp. 1–11 in *State and Society in contemporary Korea*, ed. H. Koo. Ithaca, N.Y.: Cornell University Press.

———. 1993b. "The State, *Minjung*, and the Working Class in South Korea." Pp. 131–62 in *State and Society in Contemporary Korea*, ed. H. Koo. Ithaca, N.Y.: Cornell University Press.

Koo, Suk Mo. 1994. "Korea's Big Business Groups and International Competitiveness." Pp. 151–66 in *The Korean Economy at a Crossroad*, ed. Sung Yeung Kwack. Westport, Conn.: Praeger.

Korea Statistical Yearbook. 1997. Seoul: National Statistics Office.

Kosacoff, Bernardo. 1999. "El caso argentino." Pp. 65–164 in *Las multinacionales latinoamericanas: Sus estrategias en un mundo globalizado*, ed. Daniel Chudnovsky, Bernardo Kosacoff, and Andrés López. Mexico City: Fondo de Cultura Económica.

———, ed. 1995. *Hacia una nueva estrategia exportadora: La experiencia argentina, el marco regional y las reglas multilaterales.* Buenos Aires: Universidad Nacional de Quilmes.

Kosacoff, Bernardo, and Gabriel Bezchinsky. 1994. "New Strategies of Transnational Corporations in Argentina." *CEPAL Review* 52 (April): 129–53.

Kraar, Louis. 1995. "Korea's Automakers Take On the World." *Fortune*, 6 March, 152–58.

Krugman, Paul. 1994. "The Myth of Asia's Miracle." *Foreign Affairs* 73 (6) (November–December): 62–78.

———. 1998. "Saving Asia: It's Time to Get Radical." *Fortune*, 7 September, 75–80.

Kumar, Krishna, and Kee Young Kim. 1984. "The Korean Manufacturing Multinationals." *Journal of International Business Studies* 15 (1) (spring–summer): 45–61.

Kuruvilla, Sarosh, and C. S. Venkataratnam. 1996. "Economic Development and Industrial Relations: The Case of South and South East Asia." *Industrial Relations Journal* 27 (1) (March): 9–23.

Kuruvilla, Sarosh. 1996a. "Linkages between Industrialization Strategies and Industrial Relations/Human Resource Policies: Singapore, Malaysia, The Philippines, and India." *Industrial and Labor Relations Review* 49 (4) (July): 635–57.

———. 1996b. "National Industrialization Strategies and Their Influence on Patterns of HR Practices." *Human Resource Management Journal* 6 (3): 22–41.

La Porta, Rafael, Florencio Lopez-de-Silanes, and Andrei Shleifer. 1999. "Corporate Ownership around the World." *Journal of Finance* 54 (2) (April): 471–517.

La Porta, Rafael, Florencio Lopez-de-Silanes, Andrei Shleifer, and Robert W. Vishny. 1998. "Law and Finance." *Journal of Political Economy* 106 (6): 1113–55.

Lazonick, William, and Mary O'Sullivan. 1996. "Organization, Finance, and International Competition." *Industrial and Corporate Change* 5 (1): 1–49.

Lee, Boong-Kyu. 1994. "Stimulating the Will to Innovate in Private and Public Enterprises: Korean Technology Policy." Working paper, MIT Sloan School of Management.

———. 1996. "Weak-Node Networks: International Competitive Implications of Organizational Dynamics in the Korean Automobile Industry and Its Supplier Management." Ph.D. diss., MIT Sloan School of Management.

Lee, Byung Hoon. 1990. "Labor Movement of Foreign-Invested Companies and the Problem of Nationalism." Pp. 239–58 in *Retrospection of Twenty Years of Democratic Labor Movement in Korea*. Sponsored by the Memorial Foundation of Jun Tae-Il. Seoul: Segye (in Korean).

Lee, Chung H. 1992. "The Government, Financial System, and Large Private Enterprises in the Economic Development of South Korea." *World Development* 20 (2): 187–97.

Lee, Dong-Ok, Keunchul Lee, Jae-Jin Kim, and Gill-Chin Lim. 1996. "The Korean Automobile Industry—Challenges and Strategies in the Global Market." *Journal of International Marketing* 4 (4): 85–96.

Lee, Jae-Bong. 1994. "Cultural Representation of Anti-Americanism: The Negative Images of the United States in South Korean Literature and Arts, 1945–1994." Ph.D. diss., University of Hawaii.

Lee, Jeong Taik. 1987. "Economic Development and Industrial Order in South Korea." Ph.D. diss., University of Hawaii.

Lee, Michael Byungnam. 1993. "Korea." Pp. 245–69 in *Industrial Relations around the World*, ed. Miriam Rothman. Berlin: Walter de Gruyter.

Lee, Sang Young. 1990. "Present Conditions and Future of the Labor Movement at Foreign-Invested Companies in Korea." Pp. 101–62 in *Multinational Companies and the Korean Labor Movement*. Seoul: Paeksan Suhdang (in Korean).

Lee, Yeon-ho. 1997. *The State, Society, and Big Business in South Korea*. New York: Routledge.

Lee, Yong Sook. 1993. "Industrial Subcontracting and Labor Movement: The Korean Automotive Industry." *Journal of Contemporary Asia* 23 (1): 24–40.

Leff, Nathaniel. 1978. "Industrial Organization and Entrepreneurship in Developing Countries: The Economic Groups." *Economic Development and Cultural Change* 26:661–75.

———. 1979. "Entrepreneurship and Economic Development." *Journal of Economic Literature* 17:46–64.

Leipziger, Danny M. 1988. "Industrial Restructuring in Korea." *World Development* 16 (January): 121–35.

Levitsky, Steven, and Lucan A. Way. 1998. "Between a Shock and a Hard Place: The Dynamics of Labor-Backed Adjustment in Poland and Argentina." *Comparative Politics* 30 (2) (January): 171–92.

Levitt, Theodore. 1983. "The Globalization of Markets." *Harvard Business Review* 61 (3) (May–June): 92–102.

Levy, B. 1991. "Transaction Costs, the Size of Firms, and Industrial Policy: Lessons from a Comparative Case Study of the Footwear Industry in Korea and Taiwan." *Journal of Development Economics* 34:151–78.

Lew, Seok-Jin. 1999. "Democratization and Government Intervention in the Economy: Insights on the Decision-Making Process from the Automobile Industrial Policies." Pp. 135–70 in *Democracy and the Korean Economy*, ed. Jongryn Mo and Chung-in Moon. Stanford, Calif.: Hoover Institution Press.

Lewis, P. H. 1992. *The Crisis of Argentine Capitalism*. Chapel Hill: University of North Carolina Press.

Lie, John. 1998. *Han Unbound: The Political Economy of South Korea*. Stanford, Calif.: Stanford University Press.

Liebermann, Ira W., and William Mako. 1998. "Korea's Corporate Crisis." Private Sector Development Department, World Bank.

Liem, Ramsay, and Jinsoo Kim. 1992. "The Pico Korea Workers' Struggle, Korean Americans, and the Lessons of Solidarity." *Amerasia Journal* 18 (1): 49–68.

Lim, Hyun-Chin. 1985. *Dependent Development in Korea, 1963–1979*. Seoul: Seoul National University Press.

Lincoln, James R., Michael L. Gerlach, and Christina L. Ahmadjian. 1996. "*Keiretsu* Networks and Corporate Performance in Japan." *American Sociological Review* 61 (1) (February): 67–88.

Lindberg, Leon N., John L. Campbell, and J. Rogers Hollingsworth. 1991. "Economic Governance and the Analysis of Structural Change in the American Economy." Pp. 3–34 in *Governance of the American Economy*, ed. J. L. Campbell, J. R. Hollingsworth, and L. N. Lindberg. New York: Cambridge University Press.

Linz, Juan J. 1964. "An Authoritarian Regime: Spain." Pp. 291–341 in *Cleavages, Ideologies, and Party Systems: Contributions to Comparative Political Sociology*, ed. Erik Allardt and Yrjö Littunen. Helsinki: Academic Bookstore.

———. 1970. "From Falange to Movimiento-Organización: The Spanish Single Party and the Franco Regime." Pp. 128–203 in *Authoritarian Politics in Modern Society: The Dynamics of Established One-Party Systems*, ed. Samuel Huntington and Clement Moore. New York: Basic Books.

———. 1981. "A Century of Politics and Interests in Spain." Pp. 365–415 in *Organizing Interests in Western Europe*, ed. Suzanne Berger. New York: Cambridge University Press.

Linz, Juan J., and Amando de Miguel. 1966. *Los empresarios ante el poder público.* Madrid: Instituto de Estudios Políticos.

Lipset, Seymour Martin. 1981. *Political Man: The Social Bases of Politics.* Baltimore: Johns Hopkins University Press.

———. 1996. *American Exceptionalism: A Double-Edged Sword.* New York: Norton.

Litvak, Lily. 1975. *A Dream of Arcadia: Anti-industrialism in Spanish Literature, 1895–1905.* Austin: University of Texas Press.

Locke, Richard M. 1995. *Remaking the Italian Economy.* Ithaca, N.Y.: Cornell University Press.

Locke, Richard M., and Kathleen Thelen. 1995. "Apples and Oranges Revisited: Contextualized Comparisons and the Study of Comparative Labor Politics." *Politics and Society* 23 (3): 337–67.

López, Andrés, and Fernando Porta. 1995. "Nuevas Modalidades de Inserción Internacional." Pp. 231–77 in *Hacia una nueva estrategia exportadora: La experiencia argentina, el marco regional y las reglas multilaterales,* ed. Bernardo Kosacoff. Buenos Aires: Universidad Nacional de Quilmes.

Loriaux, Michael. 1991. *France after Hegemony: International Change and Financial Reform.* Ithaca, N.Y.: Cornell University Press.

———. 1997. "The End of Credit Activism in Interventionist States." Pp. 1–16 in *Capital Ungoverned: Liberalizing Finance in Interventionist States,* ed. M. Loriaux et al. Ithaca, N.Y.: Cornell University Press.

Louch, Hugh, Eszter Hargittai, and Miguel Angel Centeno. 1998. "Who Calls Whom? Networks and Globalization." Paper presented at the Annual Meetings of the American Sociological Association, San Francisco.

MacDonald, Norbert. 1988. "Henry J. Kaiser and the Establishment of an Automobile Industry in Argentina." *Business History* 30 (3) (July): 329–45.

MacIntyre, Andrew, ed. 1994. *Business and Government in Industrialising Asia.* Ithaca, N.Y.: Cornell University Press.

Maddison, Angus. 1989. *The World Economy in the Twentieth Century.* Paris: Organization for Economic Cooperation and Development.

———. 1995. *Monitoring the World Economy, 1820–1992.* Paris: Organization for Economic Cooperation and Development.

Magaziner, Ira C., and Mark Patinkin. 1989. "Fast Heat: How Korea Won the Microwave War." *Harvard Business Review* 89 (1) (January–February): 83–92.

Mander, Jerry, and Edward Goldsmith, eds. 1996. *The Case against the Global Economy.* San Francisco: Sierra Club Books.

Mann, Michael. 1988. *States, War, and Capitalism.* Cambridge, Mass.: Blackwell.

Maravall, José María. 1970. *El desarrollo económico y la clase obrera: Un estudio sociológico de los conflictos obreros en España.* Barcelona: Ariel.

———. 1978. *Dictatorship and Political Dissent: Workers and Students in Franco's Spain.* London: Tavistock.

———. 1993. "Politics and Policy: Economic Reforms in Southern Europe." Pp. 77–131 in *Economic Reforms in New Democracies,* ed. L. C. Bresser Pereira et al. Cambridge: Cambridge University Press.

Mardon, Russell. 1990. "The State and Effective Control of Foreign Capital: The Case of South Korea." *World Politics* 43 (October): 111–38.

Markides, Constantinos C., and Peter J. Williamson. 1996. "Corporate Diversification and Organizational Structure: A Resource-Based View." *Academy of Management Journal* 39 (2) (April): 340–67.

Maroto Acín, Juan Antonio. 1990. "La situación empresarial en España, 1982–1989." *Cuadernos de Información Económica* 44–45:1–23.

Marshall, Alfred. 1919. *Industry and Trade*. London: Macmillan.

Martín Aceña, Pablo, and Francisco Comín. 1991. *INI: 50 años de industrialización en España*. Madrid: Espasa-Calpe.

Martinez, Robert E. 1993. *Business Elites in Democratic Spain*. Westport, Conn.: Praeger.

Marx, Karl. [1867, 1885, 1894] 1967. *Capital*. 3 vols. New York: International Publishers.

Mas, Ignacio. 1995. "Policy-Induced Disincentives to Financial Sector Development: Selected Examples from Latin America in the 1980s." *Journal of Latin American Studies* 27: 683–706.

Mason, Edward S., et al. 1980. *The Economic and Social Modernization of the Republic of Korea*. Cambridge: Council on East Asian Studies, Harvard University.

Maudos, Joaquín, José Manuel Pastor, and Javier Quesada. 1997. "Technical Progress in Spanish Banking, 1985–1994." Pp. 214–45 in *The Recent Evolution of Financial Systems*, ed. Jack Revell. London: Macmillan.

Maza Arroyo, Sofía de la. 1994. "Internacionalización de la banca española." *Información Comercial Española* 735 (November): 104–18.

Mazlish, Bruce. 1993. "An Introduction to Global History." Pp. 1–24 in *Conceptualizing Global History*, ed. B. Mazlish and Ralph Buultjens. Boulder, Colo.: Westview Press.

McGuire, James W. 1994. "Development Policy and Its Determinants in East Asia and Latin America." *Journal of Public Policy* 14 (2): 205–42.

———. 1997. *Peronism without Perón: Unions, Parties, and Democracy in Argentina*. Stanford, Calif.: Stanford University Press.

McKinsey and Co. 1994. *Latin American Productivity*. Washington, D.C.: McKinsey Global Institute.

———. 1996. "The Automotive Supply Base of South Korea: Achievements and Challenges." Pp. 104–24 in *Motor Business Asia-Pacific* (3d quarter). London: Economic Intelligence Unit.

McMichael, Philip. 1996. *Development and Social Change: A Global Perspective*. Thousand Oaks, Calif.: Pine Forge Press.

Mead, George H. 1934. *Mind, Self, and Society*. Chicago: University of Chicago Press.

Mercado. 1991. "Ranking de las 500 Empresas Lideres." *Mercado*, August, 41–64.

———. 1992. "Las 250 Empresas Que Más Exportan." *Mercado*, May, 51–58.

———. 1995a. "Las Empresas Que Más Exportan." *Mercado*, April, 100–121.

———. 1995b. "Las 1000 Que Más Venden." *Mercado*, June, 119–79.

Merton, Robert K. 1968. "Patterns of Influence: Local and Cosmopolitan Influentials." Pp. 441–74 in *Social Theory and Social Structure*. New York: Free Press.

Meyer, John W., John Boli, George M. Thomas, and Francisco O. Ramirez. 1997. "World Society and the Nation-State." *American Journal of Sociology* 103 (1) (July): 144–81.

Meyer, John W., and Michael T. Hannan. 1979. "National Development in a Changing World System: An Overview." Pp. 3–16 in *National Development and the World System: Educational, Economic, and Political Change, 1950–1970*, ed. J. W. Meyer and M. T. Hannan. Chicago: University of Chicago Press.

MICT. 1991. *Análisis de la situación y perspectivas competitivas del subsector de componentes de automoción*. 4 vols. Madrid: Ministerio de Industria, Comercio y Turismo.

MICYT. 1992. *Un panorama de la industria española*. Madrid: Ministerio de Industria, Comercio y Turismo.

———. 1993. *La industria aeroespacial española*. Madrid: Ministerio de Industria, Comercio y Turismo.

MIE. 1996. *Informe sobre la industria española*. Vol. 2. Madrid: Ministerio de Industria y Energía.

Mineco. 1994. *La negociación colectiva en las grandes empresas en 1993*. Madrid: Ministerio de Economía y Hacienda.

Mínguez Sanz, Santiago. 1994. "El cava: Su producción y comercialización." *El Campo* 130 (January): 111–21.

Mittelman, James H. 1996. "The Dynamics of Globalization." Pp. 1–19 in *Globalization: Critical Reflections*, ed. J. H. Mittelman. Boulder, Colo.: Lynne Rienner Publishers.

———. 1999. *The Globalization Syndrome*. Princeton, N.J.: Princeton University Press.

Mo, Jongryn. 1996. "Political Learning and Democratic Consolidation: Korean Industrial Relations, 1987–1992." *Comparative Political Studies* 29 (3): 290–311.

———. 1999. "Democratization, Labor Policy, and Economic Performance." Pp. 97–134 in *Democracy and the Korean Economy*, ed. J. Mo and Chung-in Moon. Stanford, Calif.: Hoover Institution Press.

Mo, Jongryn, and Chung-in Moon. 1999. "Epilogue: Democracy and the Origins of the 1997 Korean Economic Crisis." Pp. 171–98 in *Democracy and the Korean Economy*, ed. J. Mo and C. Moon. Stanford, Calif.: Hoover Institution Press.

Molano, Walter Thomas. 1997. "Financial Reverberations: Latin America's Private Banking System during the Mid-1990s." Working paper, SBC Warburg, New York.

Moon, C.-I. 1994. "Changing Patterns of Business-Government Relations in South Korea." Pp. 142–66 in *Business and Government in Industrializing Asia*, ed. Andrew MacIntyre. Ithaca, N.Y.: Cornell University Press.

Moore, Jonathan. 1990. "Traffic Jam." *Far Eastern Economic Review*, 21 June, 76–77.

Moori-Koenig, Virgina, Gabriel Yoguel, and Francisco Gatto. 1993. "Reflexiones Sobre la Competitividad de las Empresas PyMES en el nuevo Escenario de Apertura e Integracion. La Situacion de Firmas Metalmechanicas." Ministerio de Economía Working Paper No. IE/03. Buenos Aires: Ministerio de Economía.

Moreno, Lourdes, and Diego Rodríguez. 1996. "La empresa industrial en la década de los noventa: Actividad Exterior." Working Paper No. 9608. Madrid: Fundación Empresa Pública.

Motor Mundial. 1949. 2 (November): 1–68.

Mouzelis, Nicos. 1988. "On the Concept of Populism." *Politics and Society* 14 (3): 329–48.

Munck, Ronaldo. 1988. "Capital Restructuring and Labour Recomposition under a Military Regime: Argentina, 1976–83." Pp. 121–43 in *Trade Unions and the New Industrialization of the Third World*, ed. Roger Southhall. London: Zed Books.

Muñoz, Juan. 1969. *El poder de la banca en España*. Madrid: ZYX.

Muñoz, Juan, Santiago Roldán, and Angel Serrano. 1978. *La internacionalización del capital en España, 1959–1977*. Madrid: Edicusa.

Murillo, M. Victoria. 1997. "Union Politics, Market-Oriented Reforms, and the Reshaping of Argentine Corporatism." Pp. 72–94 in *The New Politics of Inequality in Latin America*, ed. Douglas A. Chalmers et al. Oxford: Oxford University Press.

Murmann, Johann Peter. 1998. "Knowledge and Competitive Advantage in the Synthetic Dye Industry, 1850–1914: The Coevolution of Firms, Technology, and National Institutions in Great Britain, Germany, and the United States." Kellogg Graduate School of Management, Northwestern University. Typescript.

Murtha, Tom P., and Stephanie Ann Lenway. 1994. "Country Capabilities and the Strategic State: How National Political Institutions Affect Multinational Corporations' Strategies." *Strategic Management Journal* 15 (summer): 113–29.

Nadal, Jordi. 1975. *El fracaso de la revolución industrial en España, 1814–1913*. Barcelona: Ariel.

Naisbitt, John. 1994. *Global Paradox: The Bigger the World Economy, the More Powerful Its Smaller Players*. New York: Morrow.

Naisbitt, John, and Patricia Aburdene. 1990. *Megatrends 2000*. New York: Morrow.

Nam, Jeong-Lim. 1994. "Women's Role in Export Dependence and State Control of Labor Unions in South Korea." *Women's Studies International Forum* 17 (1): 57–67.

———. 1996. "Labor Control of the State and Women's Resistance in the Export Sector of South Korea." *Social Problems* 43 (3): 327–38.

Nelson, Richard R. 1995. "Recent Evolutionary Theorizing about Economic Change." *Journal of Economic Literature* 33:48–90.

Nelson, Richard R., and Sidney G. Winter. 1982. *An Evolutionary Theory of Economic Change*. Cambridge: Belknap Press of Harvard University Press.

Nofal, María Beatriz. 1989. *Absentee Entrepreneurship and the Dynamics of the Motor Vehicle Industry in Argentina*. New York: Praeger.

North, Douglass C. 1990. *Institutions, Institutional Change, and Economic Performance*. New York: Cambridge University Press.

———. 1997. "Understanding Economic Change." Pp. 13–18 in *Transforming Post-Communist Political Economies*, ed. Joan M. Nelson, Charles Tilly, and Lee Walker. Washington, D.C.: National Academy Press.

O'Donnell, Guillermo A. 1979. *Modernization and Bureaucratic-Authoritarianism: Studies in South American Politics*. Berkeley: Institute of International Studies, University of California.

OECD. 1997. *Globalisation and Small and Medium Enterprises*. 2 vols. Paris: Organization for Economic Cooperation and Development.

Ogle, George E. 1990. *South Korea: Dissent within the Economic Miracle*. London: Zed Books.

Ohmae, Kenichi. 1990. *The Borderless World: Power and Strategy in the Interlinked Economy*. New York: Harper Business.

Oliver, Nick, Rick Delbridge, and James Lowe. 1996. "Lean Production Practices: International Comparisons in the Auto Components Industry." *British Journal of Management* 7: S29–S44.

Oneal, John R. 1992. "The Affinity of Foreign Investors for Authoritarian Regimes." *Political Research Quarterly* 47 (3): 565–88.

Önis, Ziya. 1991. "The Logic of the Developmental State." *Comparative Politics* 24 (1) (October): 109–26.

Orrù, M., N. W. Biggart, and G. G. Hamilton. 1991. "Institutional Isomorphism in East Asia." Pp. 361–89 in *The New Institutionalism in Organizational Analysis*, ed. Walter W. Powell and Paul J. DiMaggio. Chicago: University of Chicago Press.

———. 1997. *The Economic Organization of East Asian Capitalism*. Thousand Oaks, Calif.: Sage.

Ortega y Gasset, José. 1986. *La rebelión de las masas*. Madrid: Espasa-Calpe. English trans. *The Revolt of the Masses*. New York: Norton, 1932.

Park, Chung Hee. 1962. *Our Nation's Path: Ideology for Social Reconstruction*. Seoul: Dong-A.

Park, J. C. 1994. "Korean Exports: Their Development." *Ki-Eop Kyung-Young* (Journal of management) 435 (July): 36–39 (in Korean).

Peralta Ramos, Mónica. 1992. "Economic Policy and Distributional Conflict among Business Groups in Argentina: From Alfonsín to Menem, 1983–1990." Pp. 97–123 in *The Argentine Democracy*, ed. Edward C. Epstein. Westport, Conn.: Praeger.

Peres Núñez, Wilson. 1993. "The Internationalization of Latin American Industrial Firms." *Cepal Review* 49 (April): 55–74.

Pérez, Sofía. 1997. *Banking on Privilege: The Politics of Spanish Financial Reform*. Ithaca, N.Y.: Cornell University Press.

Pérez Díaz, Víctor. 1993. *The Return of Civil Society: The Emergence of Democratic Spain*. Cambridge: Harvard University Press.

Pérez Galdós, Benito. 1986. *La de los tristes destinos*. National Episodes Series No. 40. Madrid: Alianza.

Perrow, Charles. 1992. "Small Firm Networks." Pp. 445–70 in *Networks and Organizations*, ed. Nitin Nohria and Robert G. Eccles. Boston: Harvard Business School Press.

Peteraf, Margaret A. 1993. "The Cornerstones of Competitive Advantage: A Resource-Based View." *Strategic Management Journal* 14 (3) (March): 179–91.

Pieterse, Jan Nederveen. 1996. "The Development of Development Theory: Towards Critical Globalism." *Review of International Political Economy* 3 (4) (winter): 541–64.

Piore, Michael J., and Charles F. Sabel. 1984. *The Second Industrial Divide: Possibilities for Prosperity*. New York: Basic Books.

Polanyi, Karl. [1944] 1957. *The Great Transformation*. Boston: Beacon Press.

Porter, Michael E. 1990. *The Competitive Advantage of Nations*. New York: Free Press.

———. 1998. "Clusters and the New Economics of Competition." *Harvard Business Review* 76 (6) (November–December): 77–90.

Portes, Alejandro. 1997. "Neoliberalism and the Sociology of Development: Emerging Trends and Unanticipated Facts." *Population and Development Review* 23 (2) (June): 229–59.

Portes, Alejandro, and A. Douglas Kincaid. 1989. "Sociology and Development in the 1990s: Critical Challenges and Empirical Trends." *Sociological Forum* 4:479–503.

Powell, Walter W. 1990. "Neither Market Nor Hierarchy: Network Forms of Organization." *Research in Organizational Behavior* 12:295–336.

Prebisch, Raúl. 1950. *The Economic Development of Latin America and Its Principal Problems*. New York: United Nations.

Prensa Económica. 1975. "Las más grandes empresas de la Argentina." *Prensa Económica* 1: 7–94.

———. 1994. "El poder de los grupos económicas en la Argentina." *Prensa Económica* (June): 35–66.

———. 1995. "Ranking de exportadores." *Prensa Económica* 210 (June): 38–79.

———. 1998. "El mapa del poder." *Prensa Económica* 229 (August): 38–67.

Prial, Frank J. 1996. "Getting a Kick from Champagne." *New York Times*, 15 September, sec. 5, 15, 22.

Pritchett, Lant. 1997. "Divergence, Big Time." *Journal of Economic Perspectives* 11 (3): 3–17.

Przeworski, Adam, and Fernando Limongi. 1993. "Political Regimes and Economic Growth." *Journal of Economic Perspectives* 7 (3) (summer): 51–69.

Putnam, Robert D. 1993. *Making Democracy Work: Civic Traditions in Modern Italy*. Princeton, N.J.: Princeton University Press.

Ragin, Charles, and Daniel Chirot. 1984. "The World System of Immanuel Wallerstein: Sociology and Politics and History." Pp. 276–312 in *Vision and Method in Historical Sociology*, ed. Theda Skocpol. New York: Cambridge University Press.

Ramanujam, V., and P. Varadarajan. 1989. "Research on Corporate Diversification: A Synthesis." *Strategic Management Journal* 10 (6) (November–December): 523–51.

Ranis, Peter. 1992. *Argentine Workers*. Pittsburgh: University of Pittsburgh Press.

———. 1995. *Class, Democracy, and Labor in Contemporary Argentina*. New Brunswick, N.J.: Transaction.

Reich, Robert B. 1991. *The Work of Nations*. New York: Alfred A. Knopf.

Reinoso, Roberto, ed. 1987. *El periódico CGT, 1932–1937*. Buenos Aires: Centro Editor de América Latina.

Robertson, Roland. 1992. *Globalization: Social Theory and Global Culture*. London: Sage.

———. 1995. "Glocalization: Time-Space and Homogeneity-Heterogeneity." Pp. 25–44 in *Global Modernities*, ed. Mike Featherstone, Scott Lash, and R. Robertson. London: Sage.

Robles, Laureano, ed. 1987. *Epistolario completo Ortega-Unamuno*. Madrid: El Arquero.

Rock, David. 1987. *Argentina, 1516–1987: From Spanish Colonization to Alfonsín*. Berkeley and Los Angeles: University of California Press.

———. 1993. *Authoritarian Argentina*. Berkeley and Los Angeles: University of California Press.

Rodgers, Ronald A. 1990. "An Exclusionary Labor Regime under Pressure: The Changes in Labor Relations in the Republic of Korea since Mid-1987." *Pacific Basin Law Journal* 8 (1): 91–162.

_____. 1993. "Industrial Relations Policies and Practices in the Republic of Korea in a Time of Rapid Change: The Influence of American-Invested and Japanese-Invested Transnational Corporations." Ph.D. diss., University of Wisconsin.

Rodrik, Dani. 1997. *Has Globalization Gone Too Far?* Washington, D.C.: Institute for International Economics.

_____. 1998. "The Global Fix." *New Republic*, 2 November.

Roe, Mark J. 1993. "Some Differences in Corporate Structure in Germany, Japan, and the United States," *Yale Law Journal* 102 (8) (June): 1927–2003.

Rostow, Walt W. 1960. *The Stages of Economic Growth: A Non-Communist Manifesto.* Cambridge: Cambridge University Press.

Rozenwurcel, Guillermo, and Leonardo Bleger. 1997. "El sistema bancario argentino en los noventa: De la profundización financiera a la crisis sistémica." *Desarrollo Económico* 37 (146): 163–93.

Rueschemeyer, Dietrich, Evelyne Huber Stephens, and John D. Stephens. 1992. *Capitalist Development and Democracy.* Cambridge, Mass.: Polity Press.

Sabel, Charles F. 1982. *Work and Politics: The Division of Labor in Industry.* Cambridge: Cambridge University Press.

Sabel, Charles F., and Jonathan Zeitlin. 1985. "Historical Alternatives to Mass Production." *Past and Present* 108 (August): 133–67.

Sachs, Jeffrey. 1993. *Poland's Jump to the Market Economy.* Cambridge: MIT Press.

_____. 1998. "The IMF and the Asian Flu." *American Prospect*, March–April, 16–21.

Sachs, Jeffrey, and Wing Thye Woo. 1997. "Understanding China's Economic Performance." Working Paper No. 5935. Cambridge, Mass.: National Bureau of Economic Research.

Sakong, Il. 1984. "La economía coreana: Su desempeño en el pasado y sus perspectivas para el futuro." Pp. 277–95 in *Transnacionalización y periferia semiindustrializada*, ed. Isaac Minian. Mexico City: CIDE.

_____. 1993. *Korea in the World Economy.* Washington, D.C.: Institute of International Economics.

"Samsung Drives On towards Globalisation." 1994. *Financial Times*, 25 October.

San Martino de Dromi, María Laura. 1992. *Los sindicalistas: 150 años de protagonismo.* Buenos Aires: Ediciones Ciudad Argentina.

_____. 1996. *Argentina contemporánea: De Perón a Menem.* Buenos Aires: Ediciones Ciudad Argentina.

San Román López, Elena. 1995. *La industria del automóvil en España: El nacimiento de la SEAT.* Economic History Program Working Paper No. 9503. Madrid: Fundación Empresa Pública.

Sassen, Saskia. 1996. *Losing Control? Sovereignty in an Age of Globalization.* New York: Columbia University Press.

Schive, Chi. 1990. "The Next Stage of Industrialization in Taiwan and South Korea." Pp. 267–91 in *Manufacturing Miracles*, ed. Gary Gereffi and Donald L. Wyman. Princeton, N.J.: Princeton University Press.

Schmitter, Philippe C. 1974. "Still the Century of Corporatism?" Pp. 85–131 in *The New Corporatism: Social-Political Structures in the Iberian World*, ed. Frederick B. Pike and Thomas Stritch. Notre Dame, Ind.: University of Notre Dame Press.

Schumacher, Ernst F. 1975. *Small Is Beautiful: Economics As If People Mattered.* New York: Harper and Row.

Schumpeter, J. A. 1934. *The Theory of Economic Development*. Cambridge: Harvard University Press.

Scott, W. Richard. [1981] 1992. *Organizations: Rational, Natural, and Open Systems*. Englewood Cliffs, N.J.: Prentice-Hall.

———. 1995. *Institutions and Organizations*. Thousand Oaks, Calif.: Sage.

Sernauto. 1996. *La industria española de equipos y componentes para automoción en 1995*. Madrid: Sernauto.

Sguiglia, Eduardo. 1991. *El club de los poderosos: Historia pública y secreta de los grandes holdings empresariales argentinos*. Buenos Aires: Planeta.

Shin, Eui Hang, and Seung Kwon Chin. 1989. "Social Affinity among Top Managerial Executives of Large Corporations in Korea." *Sociological Forum* 4 (1): 3–26.

Shirlow, Peter, ed. 1995. *Development Ireland*. London: Pluto.

Shorrock, Tim. 1986. "The Struggle for Democracy in South Korea in the 1980s and the Rise of Anti-Americanism." *Third World Quarterly* 8 (4) (October): 1195–1218.

Silberman, Bernard S. 1993. *Cages of Reason: The Rise of the Rational State in France, Japan, the United States, and Great Britain*. Chicago: University of Chicago Press.

Simon, Hermann. 1992. "Lessons from Germany's Midsize Giants." *Harvard Business Review* 70 (2) (March–April 1992): 115–23.

———. 1996. *Hidden Champions: Lessons from 500 of the World's Best Unknown Companies*. Boston: Harvard Business School Press.

Sklair, Leslie. 1991. *Sociology of the Global System*. New York: Harvester Wheatsheaf.

Skocpol, Theda. 1984. "Emerging Agendas and Recurrent Strategies in Historical Sociology." Pp. 356–91 in *Vision and Method in Historical Sociology*, ed. T. Skocpol. New York: Cambridge University Press.

———. 1985. "Bringing the State Back In: Strategies of Analysis in Current Research." Pp. 3–37 in *Bringing the State Back In*, ed. Peter B. Evans, Dietrich Rueschemeyer, and T. Skocpol. Cambridge: Cambridge University Press.

Sloan, Alfred P., Jr. 1972. *My Years with General Motors*. Garden City, N.Y.: Anchor.

Smelser, Neil J. 1976. *The Sociology of Economic Life*. Englewood Cliffs, N.J.: Prentice-Hall.

Smelser, Neil J., and Richard Swedberg. 1994. "The Sociological Perspective on the Economy." Pp. 5–26 in *Handbook of Economic Sociology*, ed. N. J. Smelser and R. Swedberg. Princeton, N.J.: Princeton University Press.

Smith, Adam. [1776] 1976. *An Inquiry into the Nature and Causes of the Wealth of Nations*. Oxford: Clarendon Press.

Smith, David A. 1997. "Technology, Commodity Chains, and Global Inequality: South Korea in the 1990s." *Review of International Political Economy* 4 (4) (winter): 734–62.

Smith, Peter H. 1969. *Politics and Beef in Argentina*. New York: Columbia University Press.

Smith, W. Rand. 1998. *The Left's Dirty Job: The Politics of Industrial Restructuring in France and Spain*. Pittsburgh: University of Pittsburgh Press.

Snodgrass, Donald R., and Tyler Biggs. 1996. *Industrialization and the Small Firm*. San Francisco: International Center for Economic Growth.

Sohn, Hak-Kyu. 1989. *Authoritarianism and Opposition in South Korea*. New York: Routledge.

Solberg, Carl E. 1979. *Oil and Nationalism in Argentina.* Stanford, Calif.: Stanford University Press.

Song, Byung-Nak. 1990. *The Rise of the Korean Economy.* New York: Oxford University Press.

Song, Ho-Keun. 1994. "Working-Class Politics in Reform Democracy in South Korea." *Korea Journal of Population and Development* 23 (2) (December): 157–77.

Soon, Cho. 1994. *The Dynamics of Korean Economic Development.* Washington, D.C.: Institute for International Economics.

Soskice, David. 1999. "Divergent Production Regimes: Coordinated and Uncoordinated Market Economies in the 1980s and 1990s." Pp. 101–34 in *Continuity and Change in Contemporary Capitalism,* ed. Herbert Kitschett et al. New York: Cambridge University Press.

Sourrouille, Juan V. 1980. *Transnacionales en América Latina: El complejo automotor en Argentina.* Mexico City: Editorial Nueva Imagen.

Spalding, Hobart A. 1988. "U.S. Labour Intervention in Latin America: The Case of the American Institute for Free Labor Development." Pp. 259–86 in *Trade Unions and the New Industrialization of the Third World,* ed. Roger Southhall. London: Zed Books.

Spicer, Andrew, Gerald McDermott, and Bruce Kogut. 2000. "Entrepreneurship and Privatization in Central Europe." *Academy of Management Review* 25 (3) (July): 630–49.

Stallings, B. 1990. "The Role of Foreign Capital in Economic Development." Pp. 55–89 in *Manufacturing Miracles,* ed. Gary Gereffi, and Donald L. Wyman. Princeton, N.J.: Princeton University Press.

Stark, David, and László Bruszt. 1998. *Postsocialist Pathways: Transforming Politics and Property in East Central Europe.* New York: Cambridge University Press.

Steers, Richard M., Yoo Keum Shin, and Gerardo R. Ungson. 1989. *The Chaebol: Korea's New Industrial Might.* New York: Harper and Row.

Steinherr, A., and Ch. Huveneers. 1994. "On the Performance of Differently Regulated Financial Institutions: Some Empirical Evidence." *Journal of Banking and Finance* 18:271–306.

Stephens, Bernard. 1988. "Labor Resurgence in South Korea." *Nation,* 19 September, 193–96.

STEPI. 1995. *Review of Science and Technology Policy for Industrial Competitiveness in Korea.* Seoul: Science and Technology Policy Institute.

Stinchcombe, Arthur L. 1983. *Economic Sociology.* New York: Academic Press.

Stopford, John M., and Susan Strage. 1991. *Rival States, Rival Firms: Competition for World Market Shares.* New York: Cambridge University Press.

Storper, Michael, and Robert Salais. 1997. *Worlds of Production: The Action Frameworks of the Economy.* Cambridge: Harvard University Press.

Streeck, Wolfgang. 1991. "On the Institutional Conditions of Diversified Quality Production." Pp. 21–61 in *Beyond Keynesianism: The Socio-Economics of Production and Full Employment,* ed. E. Matzner and W. Streeck. Hants, England: Edward Elgar.

_____. 1995. "German Capitalism: Does It Exist? Can it Survive?" Discussion Paper 95/5. Cologne: Max-Planck Institut für Gesellschaftsforschung.

Strohl, Mitchell P. 1993. *Europe's High Speed Trains: A Study in Geo-Economics.* Westport, Conn.: Praeger.

Suárez, Sandra L. 1998. "A Tale of Three Islands: Tax Breaks and the Political Economy of Growth in Ireland, Puerto Rico, and Singapore." Book prospectus, Department of Political Science, Temple University.

Swidler, Ann. 1986. "Culture in Action." *American Sociological Review* 51 (2) (April): 273–86.

Tamames, Ramón. 1977. *La oligarquía financiera en España.* Barcelona: Planeta.

Tcha, MoonJoong. 1998. "Labor Disputes and Direct Foreign Investment: The Experience of Korea in Transition." *Economic Development and Cultural Change* 46 (2): 305–27.

Tilly, Charles. 1984. *Big Structures, Large Processes, Huge Comparisons.* New York: Russell Sage Publications Foundation.

———. 1990. *Coercion, Capital, and European States,* A.D. 990–1990. Oxford: Basil Blackwell.

Tizio, Carlos. 1995. "The Argentina Wine Industry." Mendoza, Argentina: Bodegas Norton SA. Photocopy.

Toharia Cortés, Luis. 1994. "Empleo y paro." Pp. 1277–1410 in *V Informe sociológico sobre la situación social de España,* ed. Miguel Juárez. Madrid: Fundación FOESSA.

Torrero, Antonio, ed. 1991. *Relaciones banca-industria: La experiencia española.* Madrid: Espasa-Calpe.

Tortella, Gabriel. 1994. *El desarrollo de la España contemporánea: Historia económica de los siglos XIX y XX.* Madrid: Alianza.

Toulan, Omar N. 1997. "Internationalization Reconsidered: The Case of Siderar." Working Paper No. 3938. Cambridge: MIT Sloan School of Management.

Toulan, Omar N., and Mauro F. Guillén. 1997. "Beneath the Surface: The Impact of Radical Economic Reforms on the Outward Orientation of Argentine and Mendozan Firms, 1989–1995." *Journal of Latin American Studies* 29 (May): 395–418.

Tschoegl, Adrian E. 1987. "International Retail Banking as a Strategy: An Assessment." *Journal of International Business Studies* 19 (2): 67–88.

Tschoegl, Adrian E., and Mauro F. Guillén. 1998. "The New Conquistadors: Spanish Banks and the Liberalization of Latin American Financial Markets." Case study, Wharton School, University of Pennsylvania.

U.S. Patent and Trademark Office. 1992. *Industrial Patent Activity in the United States. Part 1: Time Series Profile by Company and Country of Origin, 1969–1991.* Washington, D.C.: U.S. Patent and Trademark Office.

UGT Metal. 1980. *Simposio General Motors en España.* Madrid: UGT Metal.

UNCTD (United Nations Conference on Trade and Development). 1994a. *Small and Medium-Sized Transnational Corporations.* New York: United Nations.

———. 1994b. *World Investment Report, 1994: Transnational Corporations, Employment, and the Workplace.* New York: United Nations.

———. 1997. *World Investment Report, 1997.* New York: United Nations.

———. 1999. *World Investment Report 1999.* New York: United Nations.

Ungson, Gerardo, Richard M. Steers, and Seung-Ho Park. 1997. *Korean Enterprise: The Quest for Globalization.* Boston: Harvard Business School Press.

Van Hoesel, Roger. 1999. *New Multinational Enterprises from Korea and Taiwan*. New York: Routledge.

Vogel, Ezra F., and David L. Lindauer. 1997. "Toward a Social Compact for South Korean Labor." Pp. 93–121 in *The Strains of Economic Growth: Labor Unrest and Social Dissatisfaction in Korea*, ed. D. L. Lindauer et al. Cambridge: Harvard Institute for International Development and Korea Development Institute.

Wade, Robert. 1990. *Governing the Market: Economic Theory and the Role of Government in East Asian Industrialization*. Princeton, N.J.: Princeton University Press.

———. 1992. "East Asia's Economic Success: Conflicting Perspectives, Partial Insights, Shaky Evidence." *World Politics* 44 (2) (January): 270–320.

———. 1996. "Globalization and Its Limits: Reports of the Death of the National Economy Are Greatly Exaggerated." Pp. 60–88 in *National Diversity and Global Capitalism*, ed. Suzanne Berger and Ronald Dore. Ithaca, N.Y.: Cornell University Press.

———. 1998. "The Asian Debt-and-Development Crisis of 1997–? Causes and Consequences." *World Development* 26 (8): 1535–53.

Wade, Robert, and Frank Veneroso. 1998a. "The Asian Crisis: The High Debt Model versus the Wall Street-Treasury-IMF Complex." *New Left Review* 228 (March–April): 3–22.

———. 1998b. "Two Views on Asia: The Resources Lie Within." *Economist*, 7 November, 19–21.

———. 1998c. "The Gathering World Slump and the Battle over Capital Controls." *New Left Review* 231 (September–October): 13–41.

———. 1998d. "From 'Miracle' to 'Cronyism': Explaining the Great Asian Slump." *Cambridge Journal of Economics* 22:693–706.

Waisman, Carlos H. 1987. *Reversal of Development in Argentina: Postwar Counterrevolutionary Policies and Their Structural Consequences*. Princeton, N.J.: Princeton University Press.

Wallerstein, Immanuel. 1974. *The Modern World-System: Capitalist Agriculture and the Origins of the European World-Economy in the Sixteenth Century*. New York: Academic Press.

Waters, Malcolm. 1995. *Globalization*. New York: Routledge.

Weber, Max. [1922] 1978. *Economy and Society: An Outline of Interpretive Sociology*. 2 vols. Ed. Guenther Roth and Claus Wittich. Berkeley and Los Angeles: University of California Press.

West, James M. 1987. "South Korea's Entry into the International Labor Organization." *Stanford Journal of International Law* 23:477–546.

Westney, D. Eleanor. 1987. *Imitation and Innovation: The Transfer of Western Organizational Patterns to Meiji Japan*. Cambridge: Harvard University Press.

Westphal, Larry E., Yung W. Rhee, and Garry Pursell. 1979. "Foreign Influences on Korean Industrial Development." *Oxford Bulletin of Economics and Statistics* 41 (4) (November): 359–88.

Whitley, Richard. 1992. *Business Systems in East Asia: Firms, Markets, and Societies*. London: Sage.

Whyte, William Foote, and Kathleen King Whyte. [1988] 1991. *Making Mondragón: The Growth and Dynamics of the Worker Cooperative Complex*. Ithaca, N.Y.: ILR Press.

Wilkinson, Barry. 1994. "The Korea Labour 'Problem.'" *British Journal of Industrial Relations* 32 (3) (September): 339–58.

Wiñar, David. 1988. *La formación profesional en Argentina*. Montevideo: International Labour Office.

Womack, James P., Daniel T. Jones, and Daniel Roos. 1991. *The Machine That Changed the World: The Story of Lean Production*. New York: Harper Perennial.

Woo, Jung-En. 1991. *Race to the Swift: State and Finance in Korean Industrialization*. New York: Columbia University Press.

World Bank. 1994. *World Development Report, 1994*. New York: Oxford University Press for the World Bank.

——. 1996. *World Development Report, 1996*. New York: Oxford University Press.

——. 1999. *World Development Indicators, 1999*. CD-ROM. Washington, D.C.: World Bank.

Yeats, A. J. 1998. "Does Mercosur's Trade Performance Raise Concerns about the Effects of Regional Trade Arrangements?" *World Bank Economic Review* 12 (1) (January): 1–28.

Zelizer, Viviana A. 1999. "Multiple Markets: Multiple Cultures." Pp. 193–212 in *Diversity and Its Discontents: Cultural Conflict and Common Ground in Contemporary American Society*, ed. Neil J. Smelser and Jeffrey Alexander. Princeton, N.J.: Princeton University Press.

Ziegler, J. Nicholas. 1995. "Institutions, Elites, and Technological Change in France and Germany." *World Politics* 47 (3) (April): 341–72.

——. 1997. *Governing Ideas: Strategies for Innovation in France and Germany*. Ithaca, N.Y.: Cornell University Press.

Zysman, John. 1983. *Governments, Markets, and Growth: Financial Systems and the Politics of Industrial Change*. Ithaca, N.Y.: Cornell University Press.

INDEX